STATE, SOCIETY, AND UNIVERSITY IN GERMANY
1700–1914

State, society, and university in Germany
1700–1914

CHARLES E. MCCLELLAND

University of New Mexico

CAMBRIDGE UNIVERSITY PRESS

CAMBRIDGE

LONDON   NEW YORK   NEW ROCHELLE

MELBOURNE   SYDNEY

Published by the Press Syndicate of the University of Cambridge
The Pitt Building, Trumpington Street, Cambridge CB2 1RP
32 East 57th Street, New York, NY 10022, USA
296 Beaconsfield Parade, Middle Park, Melbourne 3206, Australia

First published 1980

Printed in the United States of America

Library of Congress Cataloging in Publication Data
McClelland, Charles E
State, society, and university in Germany, 1700–1914.
Bibliography: p.
1. Universities and colleges – Germany – History.
   2.   Germany – Intellectual life – History.
3.   Germany – History – 18th century.   I Title.
       LA727.M32   378.43   79–13575
           ISBN 0 521 22742 9

CONTENTS

PREFACE

This book examines one of the most durable of institutions of medieval origin – the university – in the context of a society that has always been ambivalent about change, but has often had it imposed by political authority. The German university has had, in the minds of many, a semimythical quality. Its name has been invoked so many times that arguments about higher education from Harvard to Hong Kong still include ritual references to it. In a world in which universities and the values for which they have stood appear to be facing an uncertain future, the glories of the bygone German university may appear as a part of a golden age. Yet they, too, emerged in tempestuous confrontation or smooth cooperation with larger social and political forces.

The book is for scholars – historians, sociologists, political scientists, educational theorists, and many more. But it is also meant for that growing legion of people who must make hard decisions about educational policy; they may appreciate the historical dimension to problems that sometimes seem insoluble by the competing nostrums of our day. Finally, this book is for all people who care about the past and future of universities. For them especially, I have sought to write in a manner accessible to the general reader.

For all these readers, I hope to offer a step back, a chance to contemplate the fate of a variant of the institution "university" not in its mythical dimension, but as a living, growing force. For this is a critical history of the German university system. It may seem at times to minimize unduly the spectacular achievements of German scholarship and science or the idealism of students, professors, or government officials. The reason for this is that my analysis is realistic rather than idealistic. Idealizations of the German university system abound. Even the radical German students who pressed flyers into my hands a decade ago, when I began this study, appeared to accept the idealizations of their environment by calling for the alteration of circumstances that existed only in their minds. Very few works have examined the more mundane causes of university conditions, however.

This book has been written from the premise that no social institution, including universities, can in fact attain the level of autonomy and independence that many university professors hold up as their ideal. Tensions between the "republic of letters" and the broader society are at worst necessary and at best fruitful. Both "town" and "gown" understand their need for each other, even though that symbiosis is traditionally clouded by resentment. I have here explored the ways in which the German university of the period before 1914 was better able than most to establish an immunity to the "town" – the broader society – but at the expense of reliance on another authority, the state.

The future of the university as an institution depends not only on its inner forces of resilience, which have been enormous, but on its treatment by much more powerful forces outside it. I hope that this study will show how the German university system was affected by its growing interaction with state and society. In 1933, German academics themselves realized all too late how awesome the disproportionate power of these outside forces can become. As for the future, this book will have achieved its purpose if it stimulates thought about the increasingly disproportionate confrontation among state, society, and the institution called "university" in all modern societies.

It is a pleasure to acknowledge and thank the many friends, colleagues, and organizations without whose aid and encouragement this book would never have been possible. Wilhelm Bleek, William Brickman, Konrad Jarausch, Vernon Lidtke, Peter Lundgreen, Wolfgang Mommsen, Thomas Nipperdey, and Lawrence Stone have all served as stimulators and critics of my thinking. Felix Gilbert, James Leith, Steven Kramer, R. R. Palmer, and Peter Paret have also kindly read and helped improve parts of the manuscript.

Many librarians and archivists on two continents have also helped me in thousands of ways. My special thanks are due to the Niedersächsische Staats- und Universitätsbibliothek (Göttingen), the Württemberg Hauptstaatsarchiv (Stuttgart), the Baden Generallandesarchiv (Karlsruhe), the Hessisches Staatsarchiv (Marburg), the Deutsches Zentralarchiv II (Merseburg), and the Deutsche Staatsbibliothek (East Berlin), all of which kindly opened their files to me. Furthermore, the libraries and archives of the following universities made printed and unprinted sources available to me: Berlin (Free University), Bonn, Giessen, Halle, Heidelberg, Jena, Leipzig, Marburg, Munich, Tübingen, and Vienna. The libraries of the University of Pennsylvania and the British Museum were also invaluable to my research.

This work owes a debt of thanks to organizations that have sponsored research trips – the Spencer Foundation, the American Philosophical Society, and the Research Allocations Committee of the University of New Mexico. A fellowship grant from the National Endowment for the Humanities enabled me to devote the year 1973–4 to research and writing.

C.E.McC.

Albuquerque, New Mexico

1

Introduction

Universities all over the world have become the object of unprecedented curiosity and study in recent decades. Spectacular growth in some cases, student agitation in others, and an alarming sense of rapid change in all cases have focused attention on the universities. Even before these events, the universities were quietly participating in a process termed by some authors an "academic" or "educational" revolution. Like the industrial revolution and the broader series of political revolutions begun in 1789, the educational revolution must be seen as a long process rather than an explosive event. Increasingly, the universities of the world have emerged, in the words of an important recent study, as "the current culmination of the educational revolution." The university has become "the lead component of an extensive process of change permeating modern society at many levels."[1] This sense of involvement in social change is not a mere reflection of the turbulent 1960s and 1970s, for as Abraham Flexner wrote in the 1920s: "The restraints which for centuries slowed down or limited adjustments have largely been removed. Societies have to act—intelligently, if possible—if not, then unintelligently, blindly, selfishly, impulsively. The weight and prestige of the university must be thrown on the side of intelligence. If the university does not accept this challenge, what other institution can or will?"[2]

Historians have come to realize more than ever the importance of education in the evolution of modern societies, just as they have more generally come to appreciate the importance of social evolution as a part of historical explanation. The history of higher education, and particularly of universities, has consequently become a matter of some importance for understanding the development of the modern world.

Of all the universities in Western society, those of Germany have probably had the greatest significance in modern times. They were the first to fuse teaching with research functions and thereby to create the very model of the modern university. They were the fountainheads of a large part of modern scholarship and science. By the beginning of this century, the German university system was the most admired in the world. Its internationally famous professors, many of whom counted among the great discoverers, scientists, and theorists of the age; its thorough critical training of students; its research-oriented teaching methods in seminars and institutes; its academic freedom, dignified spirit, and colorful folklore; and even its impressive buildings, such as libraries and laboratories, excited envy, scrutiny, and emulation around the globe. After such glory, its precipitous descent into the dark night of Hitler's era gave a chilling example of the fragility of the achievements of the human spirit.

The German university system had an unusually significant place in the history of Germany, as well. The impact of the German universities on the society was surely deeper than that of their American or British counterparts. Moving directly from lecture hall to government bureaus or professional offices, university graduates commanded the modernization of the German lands; the men who shaped its cultural and scientific life were also closer to universities than in most other parts of Europe. It was in Germany around the beginning of the nineteenth century that scientific investigation moved out of the overburdened academies of science and into the universities, beginning a process still perceptible today. More than in the relatively open societies to the west and the closed ones to the east, the German universities served as the breeding ground for a peculiar social stratum, an academic bourgeoisie (*Bildungsbürgertum*), the recruiting pool for both cultural and administrative elites. The universities also served as shelters for the emerging political and social doctrines of the nineteenth century: German professors and students were on the forefront of national oppositional leadership before 1848, just as they were to become leaders in nationalist agitation before and during the First World War. The universities' monopoly over access to the professions was also much stronger than in America or Britain and more exclusive than that of universities in much of Europe.

In informal ways, too, the German universities played an important role in national life. They were among the few places in a provincial country where the young could transcend the limits of provincialism and gain an introduction to cosmopoltian thought patterns and life-styles. The friendships and connections made at the university, both between students and teachers and among students themselves, were often invaluable in a country where regional, class, religious, and other petty social distinctions tended to discourage change and mobility. The university was often called the "republic of letters"; this republic was of the utmost importance in a country having so few liberal institutions.

Finally, the German university system is useful for a case study of the evolution of the European university in modern times. Despite the many peculiarities of German universities, the general lines of their development bear significance for the analysis of university history everywhere. They were the most brilliant and successful examples of adaptation of a medieval European institution to the demands of the age of expansion of the nineteenth century. That the German universities were the first in the world to become objects of a state science and educational policy should alone make them interesting to us today.

State, society, and university

If the history of higher education can help us gain a better understanding of the evolution of modern society, it is because higher education has evolved partly in response to the needs of society. Universities have usually been surrounded with liberties and immunities that set them apart from other social institutions, and university professors and students have traditionally resented and resisted encroachments from broader social forces. As Lawrence Stone recently put it:

> The university, like the family and the church, is one of the most poorly integrated of institutions, and again and again it has been obstinately resistant to changes which were clearly demanded by changing conditions around it. And yet, in the long run, no institution can survive indefinitely glorious isolation, and the interaction between the university's own built-in conservatism and the pressures upon it to adapt to new external conditions is one of the most potentially illuminating, but most practically obscure, aspects of the process of historical change.[3]

The traditional university of medieval and early modern Europe, and originally of America as well, was "poorly integrated" into society partly because it originated as an arm of the church and as an extension of the educational responsibilities of the family. On the other hand, it had from the start vital secular functions such as the training of agents of Europe's expanding state authority, and its corporate immunities to the everyday laws and customs of society sheltered socialization processes and intellectual innovations.

It is this dualism of the university's role that makes studying it so difficult. Whether merely a teaching institution, as it has been throughout all of its history, or a research center as well, as in more recent times, the university has required two almost contradictory things: to be supported by society and to be left alone by it. The need for support has at times been minimal, as in the Middle Ages, but it has grown to be a crucial matter in our own times and was already significant by the eighteenth century. On the other hand, *Freiheit und Einsamkeit* – freedom and solitude—are also necessary to the proper functioning of the university, as Wilhelm von Humboldt, the great German reformer, noted.

The purpose of this study is to explain how the modern German university system evolved through interaction with the forces of German society and politics. Few will deny that such an explanatory model can shed considerable light on the evolution of the German university system. For peculiar reasons to be discussed later, the traditional histories of German universities have avoided precisely this model.

It is doubtful whether one can fully understand the history of any university or higher educational system purely in terms of internal developments: It is certain that one cannot understand the German system thus. Without viewing the process of interaction, a perpetual dialectic between the university and society, the historian can obtain only a superficial and often misleading picture of the past. Furthermore, one must not be content with such abstractions as "university" and "society." One must also investigate exactly what persons and forces in both were the most active participants in the dialogues between university and society.

Rarely were universities so intimately tied to the powers of the state and the interests of social groups as in modern Germany. There are several reasons for this close relationship. First, German universities were placed under the protection of the state earlier and more completely than in other large European countries. Although this tendency was strong in the eighteenth century, it became the universal relationship between state and society in the wake of the reorganization of Germany during and after the Napoleonic wars. The lack of private universities by the beginning of the nineteenth century meant that Germany had a state higher education monopoly unsurpassed in its completeness by that of any other major European country. Not only were private universities forbidden; private contributions to public universities were neither much encouraged nor generously given. The major counterweight to the authority implicit in the state's rights as patron was the residue of corporate rights and immunities granted to individual universities in charters and statutes and by long-standing practice. Because it was in the interest of the universities to uphold these rights and immunities, it is understandable that the universities stressed them, rather than the role of the state. By the same token, functionaries of the various state educational bureaucracies often wrote and spoke as if the univerisities had no rights except those granted by the whim of the government and revocable at any time; in practice, they were much more indulgent.

Not only were the German universities nominally under the patronage of the states; the latter progressively reorganized their agencies of bureaucratic control and extended their supervision and initiative in university affairs. In this, Germany was not alone; indeed, some countries, for example France, had developed highly centralized educational administrations by the early nineteenth century. Yet there is a peculiar and interesting quality about the evolution of German educational bureaucracy. Responsibilities for higher education were allocated to the states of the Holy Roman Empire, the Germanic Confederation, and the German Reich. In some states, particularly smaller ones, this federalism softened the tendency toward greater bureaucratic control and initiative, and relations between state and university were, if not necessarily better, at least more personalized. In some of the large states, particularly Prussia, the state educational bureaucracy became quite large and imperious during the eighteenth and nineteenth centuries. In practice large states tended to set patterns for small ones. The state governments had far more control over universities than was the case in America and Britain, yet there was no central educational administration, as in France. Whereas Russia and other East European countries had centralized educational bureaucracies, their efficiency and intelligence were generally not on the same high level as Germany's.

The exercise of state authority over the universities is only one of the ways in which state, society, and university influenced each other in the course of their development. In few other countries of the eighteenth and nineteenth centuries was the life of the state so bound up with that of the university; and in few did the universities play such a prominent role in the life of the society at large.

The crucial role of the universities in the evolution of the German state bureaucracies derived from the monopoly of the former over the training of the higher personnel of the latter. The introduction and gradual raising of partly meritocratic standards of recruitment and promotion supported the function of the universities as producers of trained civil servants. The importance of the bureaucracy in the German states, in the absence of other forms of modern policy-making apparatus such as parliaments, assured the universities an indirect sort of influence over the mentality of the administrative elites. In no other country was academic training so important a prerequisite for high office as in the German states by the late eighteenth century.

Conversely, in few other countries were the universities such rich breeding grounds for political opposition to the established order. It is difficult to think of a single major political ideology of the nineteenth century that did not issue from or have decisive support in the German universities. Oppositional professors and students of many political colorations used the universities in the early nineteenth century as bases for the propagation of their ideas about a just social and political order. In many places the professoriate even provided a surrogate leadership group for the disorganized and timid German middle classes. The election of many academics to the "parliament of professors," the Frankfurt National Assembly of 1848, underscores this important role of universities in national political life.

The German universities played an exceptionally strong role in the life of the German churches, too. In most parts of Germany the clergy was better trained than its counterparts in other European countries, thanks in part to government pressure for such training and to the high standards of theology faculties from the late eighteenth century onward. The close ties between churches and states in Germany since the Reformation involved the universities, as well. The struggle against domination by church orthodoxy is a major element in the history of German universities; but even when this struggle was won, the interests of the churches continued to be represented in the universities.

Even outside the organized realm of the state, in the more diffuse and heterogenous arena of German society, the universities developed relationships that gradually broke down the walls of the ivory tower.

Because the universities were increasingly exclusive channels of access to careers in the civil service, science, and the professions, certain groups in society began to take a heightened interest in the teaching and, in the nineteenth century, research activities of the universities. More and more social groups joined the relatively narrow spectrum of university alumni and pressed the universities to aid them in their search for professional or other advantage. As elsewhere, the German universities both legitimated the social status of existing elites and conferred higher status on other social strata. The university is not necessarily a major vehicle for upward social mobility, though it usually promotes mobility to a certain degree; it has also been a means for the reproduction of elites. Given the comparatively exclusive qualities of these elites in Germany, access to them through university training gradually heightened the interest of broader social groups in such training. In many other countries, either elites were more open or access to them lay through channels other than the university – the Inns of Court in England, for example. It is therefore no wonder that groups in German society viewed the university as important to their own social position and tried to exert their influence in questions of curriculum, admissions, size, function, and style of the universities.

The universities played a significant role in the shaping of a specifically "German" society, because they were among the first institutions in Germany to foster a sense of national community. After the French Revolution, the universities acted increasingly as centers of national communication. They drew students from all across the German states and helped infuse in them an outlook broader than the traditional *Kirchturmhorizont,* the horizon limited by the view from the village steeple, which had been the characteristic mentality of many of the dozens of small German states and cities. National reviews and journals, national professional congresses, and outright agitation for national union were all primarily based in German universities beginning in the early nineteenth century.

Finally, one must consider the relationship between the development of the modern university system and the development of the German economy. The university system and the industrial economy experienced their most rapid growth and drive to maturity at roughly the same time, in the late nineteenth century. The relationships between such sectors of modern German industry as chemistry and some German universities have begun to come to light in recent studies, but the relative positions of the leading sectors of the national economy and the system of higher education are still largely unknown. What is clear, however, is that the relationships were not nearly as negligible and casual as has long been assumed. Even before the industrial revolution, the German universities had to make adjustments to modern economic conditions. For example, the universities' change to a complete money budget and the surrender of the last remnants of payment in kind had a serious effect on the future of the university system.

Questions to be asked

The central question raised by this study has already been mentioned: How did political and social forces condition the change of the German university system from its nearly moribund state in 1700 to its pinnacle in 1914? Within this broad question lie many smaller ones. First, restricting our questions to the relationship of the state and the university, we find that there are subsidiary areas involving the state's role as administrator, innovator, lawgiver, financier, and promoter of values. The universities in their turn had roles to play in the life of the state. Second, looking at the relationship between the university and society, we must ask how the latter used the former and pressed for changes to enable further use, as well as how the former resisted or accommodated pressures for change. Third, we must ask a number of specific questions about the contribution of state and society to the evolution of the university system: How was it saved from extinction in the eighteenth century; how did it achieve a breakthrough to modernity in a country that was relatively backward; how did it achieve qualitative change in times of quantitative stagnation; how did its individual parts and academic specialties develop; how did research concerns intrude on traditional pedagogical functions; and how did the structure of the teaching body alter?

The role of the German states in the affairs of their universities was not a simple one, and it changed considerably during the period under discussion. The loose rights of supervision implicit in the prince's status as patron of the university were extended gradually to include tight control of personnel appointments and finances. We shall see how the states viewed their prerogatives of regulation over such internal university matters as curriculum, enrollment, admissions and examination standards, the activities and discipline of university members, and the standing of science and scholarship. We shall ask how the administrative machinery changed, and what inducements and powers were used to control the universities. We shall see how the universities reacted to directives and requirements from the state, and what weapons they possessed and used to retain their autonomy.

What role did the state play in the introduction or retardation of change? Did the states simply administer the universities and allow them to develop organically, or did they also take the initiative without scrupulous concern for the autonomous rights of the university corporations? How strong and innovative were these corporations themselves? These questions must be asked, not only of the formal dealings between university and state, but also on an informal level. In many universities the formal machinery of decision making was either undermined by informal channels or steered by such informal understandings.

Indeed, the legal relationship between state and university, so elaborately laid down in university statutes, rarely reflected the actual relationship. Legally, most universities derived their degree-granting rights from the emperor and their moral authority from the church; whereas in fact they were much more subject to the will of the local prince. During much of the nineteenth century, one could search in vain in the statutes of many German university faculties for a legal guarantee of the right of the faculties to nominate new faculty members; yet this right was widely honored in practice.

How did the financial relationship of state and university change over the period under study? A considerable number of eighteenth-century universities lived almost totally (although very poorly) from their own resources. Revenues from university administered lands could take the form of money rents, but they were also often in the form of grains, firewood, or other natural products. University members were granted all sorts of privileges to compensate for the lack of money resources. By the middle of the nineteenth century, the state had almost everywhere become incomparably more involved, and more financially responsible, for the universities. We must ask how this increasing financial involvement affected the universities' ability to order their own finances and allocate funds where they saw fit, as well as what impact greater state generosity had on the general independence of the universities. This question becomes much more intriguing when one considers that the libraries, collections, scientific research apparatus, and laboratories of the nineteenth century far outstripped in cost the modest inherited resources of the universities.

The increasing role of the state also brought about subtle moral and intellectual changes in the university. How did the state's influence affect academic freedom, for example? To what extent did the state's role encourage, directly or indirectly, the commitment of professors and students to a more rigorous and scientific approach to their studies, or, in many cases, discourage such an attitude? What did the state try to do to improve morale, discipline, and the general level of student conduct, which was notoriously bad in the eighteenth century?

While we are asking questions about the state's role in the evolution of the university, we must not forget that the university also played a role in the life of the state – providing civil servants and regulators of many aspects of public life from sanitation to legal theory; public leaders, writers on public affairs, and political theorists; pastors and priests, the main agents of cultural diffusion and control of the rural masses; high school teachers; and a host of scholarly and scientific theories that forced changes on the political system.

The relationship between the German universities and German society was both more general and less precisely definable than that between university and state. Indeed, if one believes the rhetoric of nineteenth-century neo-humanist academics, one could almost be persuaded that the universities really were ivory towers perched too far above the muddy plain of social action and conflict to be involved in any way. Although this rhetoric sprang from the understandable desire of academics to keep the university out of direct partisan conflicts and to edify other academics with the notion of their own mental and moral superiority, it never corresponded to reality.

For in the German lands, as everywhere in Europe, identifiable social groups used the universities to maintain or change their own positions in society, and if necessary they worked to change the universities to facilitate such maintenance or improvement in their standing. Even in cases where the universities were changed by other forces than the pressures emanating from identifiable social groups, these changes inevitably affected the social groups having some stake in higher education.

There existed in Germany an extraordinarily high integration of university study, professional and civil service career patterns, and inherited social status. To what extent were the highly educated elites the product of meritocratic education? To what extent had existing elites penetrated the universities and merely used their prestige as a legitimation of their existing social privilege?

In addition to such general inquiries about the relationship among state, university, and society, some more specific questions need to be raised in this study. The most urgent, at the outset of the work, is this: How did the German universities survive the eighteenth century? That century was one of transition and crisis for most of the universities of Europe. Oxford and Cambridge survived largely on their comparatively massive wealth, but most continental academies were poor, badly attended, and threatened with extinction; the German universities were no exception and indeed provided some of the most ludicrously appropriate candidates for suppression. Still, Germany did not shut down its university system, as France did in the 1790s, nor carefully copy the new French system of higher education, as several European countries did in the early nineteenth century. Despite some experiments with French adaptations in a few German states in the Napoleonic era, German university reform took place largely under the inspiration of native models, and it began before the French Revolution.

Another, related question pertains to the rise of modern universities in a part of Europe that was distinctly unmodern in many other ways. The appreciation and fostering of a scientific temper is widely regarded as an indispensable ingredient of modernization. Yet Germany before the late nineteenth century deviated from the pattern of development of more advanced societies, such as England and France. If the same governmental elites resisted political modernization and furthered the advancement of science in the universities, then some of the more mechanical models of modernization might have to be revised. The evolution of the German university system contains many paradoxes, from the pressure of conservative elites for a modernization of higher education in the eighteenth century to the protests of politically progressive professors against synchronization of higher education with the industrial revolution at the end of the nineteenth century.

If the rise of universities committed to research and scholarly discovery appears dissynchronous with a will to general modernization, it is also dissynchronous with some pressures emanating from German society. At first glance it is puzzling that the renewal and first reforms of universities in the eighteenth century took place against a background of decreasing student demand for higher education, judging by declining enrollments. Similarly, the foundations for the practices and habits of advanced research and teaching of the early nineteenth century were laid at a time when student enrollments were comparatively stable. By the time the enrollments began to grow rapidly in the late nineteenth century, attesting to a heightened demand for higher education, German universities had largely developed the patterns of teaching and research that were already admired abroad; indeed, one can discern a certain resistance to further change and even concern about mounting enrollments among university and government officials. All this suggests that not the quantity, but the quality of students and of social demand for higher education may be the key to understanding social influences upon university development.

One must further ask how the individual parts of the universities responded to the demands of state, society, and scientific growth. Over the long run, it was the philosophical faculties that grew the most and provided the greatest innovations in teaching and research. All of the traditional four faculties— theology, law, medicine, and philosophy—grew and changed at different rates. In many ways, this growth implied a response to the internal dynamics of different scholarly and scientific disciplines. For example, the proliferation of knowledge about a given subject would lead to pressure upon the universities to institute a teaching position for a new specialist. Yet we must not forget that this process was far from smooth and automatic; universities and governments were frequently blind to the "imperatives" of development in a given discipline and deaf to appeals to erect new chairs. Decisions had to be made before new disciplines could unfold in a university setting. A few disciplines virtually died out at German universities after promising starts, simply because the state no longer looked upon them with favor.

Given the peculiar German university mixture of teaching and advanced research functions in the nineteenth century, one normally finds that pedagogical concerns outweighed other factors in the recognition of a discipline as a newly autonomous science when considerations of new university chairs and institutes arose. Why teaching and research functions should have been combined in the first place is another important question about the German system. With few exceptions, the universities everywhere in the eighteenth century were teaching institutions, pure and simple; they were rarely expected to carry out what we would call research. But by the early nineteenth century, a reputation for good scholarly research had become an important qualification for a professorship. Ultimately, research came to be integrated into pedagogy, with advanced students studying and working along with their professors on the frontiers of scholarly knowledge. The professorial career had become attractive enough to induce many bright students to follow the call of teaching, and the availability of resources and rewards for original scholarly investigation drew in many scientists.

What was the structure of the professoriate and how did the professorial career change over our period? Despite superficial continuities, including a penchant for quarrelsomeness, pedantry, and pride, the professors of 1914 were radically different from their predecessors at the beginning of the eighteenth century. What these changes were, and why they came about, are further questions this study will ask.

Historiographical and methodological problems

The questions we shall ask in this study have not been asked very often by the traditional historians of the German university system. Indeed, very few of these historians looked at the system as such. Friedrich Paulsen, the last scholar to publish a substantial history of the German university system, began his book with a quotation from the sociologist Lorenz von Stein: "Despite the high importance that German universities have for the entire people and despite the very lively consciousness of this importance, the literature about universities is precisely the paltriest in the whole field of education."[4] Paulsen lamented that Stein's statement of 1868 was still true in 1902; it is still true to some degree in the 1970s. Perhaps no other public institution has been the victim of such a large volume of uncritical writings. Only recently has this situation begun to change markedly for the better. The paucity of good historical writing about universities is beginning to yield to the research of a small but growing group of scholars, especially in America, Britain, France, and Germany. From their monographs, articles, and dissertations, a new picture of university history is emerging.

What has largely been lacking in the historical writing about German universities is not energy, devotion, interest, or support; it is a critical spirit. How ironic that the German universities have for generations taught their students to look with an open and critical eye upon every matter except the institution of the university. The bibliography of German university history is immense, but the level of critical quality, until very recently, has been disappointingly low. There are several reasons for this disproportion between quantity and quality. First is the "jubilee syndrome," a combination of local, particularist pride, celebratory intent, and unprofessional zeal. Many uni-

versity histories have been financed as jubilee enterprises, supervised and written by nonhistorians, and flawed by the heterogeneity of contributors, research objectives, and viewpoints.
As such, many of these histories are acts more of piety than of
critical scholarship. Some of course transcend the particularism or self-serving intent of collective *Festschriften* in praise of
alma mater, but even many of these are quite old and reflect
the historical standards and questions of earlier times. Nor do
we find many works that attempt to transcend the history of a
single university and to analyze the university system as a
whole; and even the few that do make the attempt are anti-
quated. Such admirable recent studies as those by Christian
von Ferber, Alexander Busch, and Fritz Ringer tend to concentrate only upon limited sets of questions, even as they survey
the scope of all German universities. Significantly, much of the
best recent work on the German university system has been
influenced by sociological questions and methods. This special
curiosity not only reflects a heightened interest in recent decades about the relationship of university and society, but
tends to arise in response to one of the most consistently glaring omissions in the work of earlier university historians – their
diffidence, not to say almost total silence, about the role of
state and society in the evolution of the university system.

Another major difficulty for the historian of the German
university system is an abundance of methodological, conceptual, and research problems. There is no widely accepted body
of theory about universities and their activities, so that the
historian confronts a forest of detail with few theoretical paths
to follow. Educational, sociological, economic, and even psychological theorists and historians have occupied themselves
far more with the institutions of lower learning, for example,
schools, than with universities. Perhaps the reason for this
paucity of theory lies in the complexity of what happens at
universities, on the one hand, and the relative smallness of
universities compared to other social, educational, and scientific institutions, on the other. Many of the new questions

being asked about universities and their history can thus be formulated only imprecisely and answered only tentatively.

Two examples may help illustrate this problem. Students at universities absorb not only the formal content of their studies, but informal lessons about life and the world. To some degree, they continue the socialization process begun in family, school, or church. Yet there is no acceptable body of theory about socialization through universities. Or consider the problem of explaining how scholarly creativity is related to the institutional setting of the university. Numerous theories of scientific discovery exist, but to some extent they are contradictory, and few of them take up the specific problem of the university setting as a factor complex.

Even if the historian were armed with a set of theories and hypotheses, testing them on the basis of existing source material would be a difficult task. The silence of older traditional university histories about such questions does not simply reflect a lack of interest in them; rather, it reflects the frequent absence in university records and printed sources of materials that could help answer them: German university archives are frequently voluminous, but much of the volume consists of materials of little use to this kind of study. Despite losses to carelessness, war, and other enemies of historical records, university archives in Germany appear still to contain the substance of past university records. State educational bureaus also kept records, although their richness varies considerably. Like the university archives, these records are filled with the minutiae of routine matters but are frequently disappointing in areas of interest to the historian. For example, professorial personnel records were kept hardly at all in the eighteenth century, and kept sporadically and with very little biographical information during much of the nineteenth. All too often, local obituary notices contained more information about professorial careers than did personnel files at the university. Many university archives are more clearly organized to aid the genealogist than the social historian. Notes were rarely kept of important meetings, whether on the level of the lowest academic collective decision-making body, the *Fakultät,* or at the level of the ministry of education. Even when the archives contain routine material that could be interesting – matriculation records of students or dossiers of professors, for example – there is often insufficient data to make a meaningful quantitative study. Finally, the university and educational ministry archives of many German states will have to undergo years of organizational and cataloging work before they can be used with systematic ease by the educational historian. The personal helpfulness and knowledge of most archivists cannot compensate for previous decades and even centuries of neglect, such as the kind that relegated the papers of Göttingen University to various wet cellars and pigeon-filled attics until only a few decades ago.

For all these reasons, the history of state, society, and university must, in the meantime, be satisfied with a method of approach and conclusions that are more tentative than author or reader would like.

In addition to methodological problems, this study has had to face a number of conceptual difficulties. In the literature of German higher education, the term "university" is usually taken for granted; a *functional* definition is hard to find. The problem of definition is not a mere bit of pedantic fussiness, for in the eighteenth century all sorts of institutions called themselves universities, from tiny moribund collections of masters and pupils not much different from a Latin school to such large, prosperous, and world-famed universities as Göttingen and Halle. Some "universities" had only one or two functioning faculties and a few dozen students; it is even uncertain whether the professors actually held their lectures. The long-term trend over the nineteenth and twentieth centuries has been toward homogenization, but even in the mid-nineteenth century large gaps separated the first and the last universities in the German system. The former had become well-endowed and diverse institutions of higher learning and research, with the finest scientists and scholars in the land gracing their chairs and important scholarly investigations being carried out by professors and students in laboratories and seminars. The latter remained quasi-medieval corporations of second-rate teachers, most of whom never considered it their obligation to do research and many of whom found it necessary to moonlight in order to make ends meet. Libraries, laboratories, and seminars were almost unheard of.

By the same token, the German state and German society, terms that will be used throughout this work, in fact changed considerably over the eighteenth and nineteenth centuries. Government attention to university affairs in the early eighteenth century was normally sporadic and, given the collegial arrangement of government bodies, not clearly assigned to particular offices. Church supervisory bodies had some say, but individual councillors of the prince or even the prince himself also intervened. By contrast, toward the end of the nineteenth century virtually every German state had a regular bureaucracy for education affairs.

German society in the early eighteenth century was still divided relatively rigidly along the lines of estates, whereas a modern class society had developed by the end of the nineteenth century. Furthermore, within that society there were numerous divisions and special interest groups. The universities had special clienteles in many of the estates or classes and virtually none in others. Yet these clienteles did not necessarily share identical interests with their broader social-category members. The "middle class" or *Bürgertum* was, for example, the major provider of students to German universities, yet only a small portion of this social class attended the university. The broader bourgeoisie was indifferent and even hostile to university education throughout much of our period, but then finally began to perceive advantages in university training toward the end of the nineteenth century. The relevant class grouping for the universities was thus not the middle class as such, but the professional, administrative, clerical, or other elites within it who benefited from education and tended to send their sons to universities, too. Similar distinctions may be observed in the aristocracy. One must also keep in mind that the size, influence, and wealth of given social strata changed considerably over the period under discussion; whole new social groups, such as industrial workers, came into being.

The specific history of German higher education has been told in terms that are not always clear. It is difficult to read anything about the educational reform movements in Germany between about 1770 and 1820 without encountering the concept of "neo-humanism," for example. This useful little label, meant to describe a reawakened interest in the study of antiquity with the purpose of cultivating the spirit, has become in the hands of many writers an elevated philosophy of life and education, a tangled Germanic concept with no clear boundaries. Other classical German concepts, such as *Bildung* and *Wissenschaft,* can also be troublesomely vague, if for no other reason than a considerable shift in meaning from the eighteenth to the twentieth century. Fortunately, most of these concepts are not essential to understanding the evolution of the German university system, and so can be avoided most of the time. Yet there are many conceptual pitfalls of which researcher and reader should be aware. Our subject, the German university system, changed considerably more than the concepts used to describe it; therein lies a problem in our understanding.

Boundaries of this study

The concentration of this work on the relationship between the university system and German states and society addresses an outstanding need in scholarly literature. It does not necessarily exclude other important aspects of the growth of universities and the change of their tasks. Some limitations have, however, been inevitable. The selection of emphases in this book, undertaken in full consciousness of such limits, has followed persuasive criteria.

The temporal boundaries of the study embrace the eighteenth and nineteenth centuries and the beginning of the twentieth, to the First World War. Although the story of the evolution of the modern German research university falls chiefly in the nineteenth and early twentieth centuries, it is difficult to overlook the evidence that the roots of serious university reform stretch back into the age of the Enlightenment. The tempo of change, in universities as in other public institutions, undoubtedly accelerated after the beginning of the French Revolution; but the changes brought about by this historic event amounted to the unblocking of a path for reform ideas already discussed well before the revolution. The relatively larger space devoted to nineteenth-century developments in this work does attest to the recognition, however, that the main evolution of the modern German research university occurred then.

The selection of a political and military event, World War I, as the other temporal limit of this study may at first glance seem an inappropriate recognition of the primacy of "political" over social and intellectual historical concerns. But World War I was no ordinary conflict; it entailed the total mobilization of resources of all combatants, particularly hard-pressed Germany. The universites were virtually emptied of students for years, and the normal evolution of the university system was seriously interrupted. That the world conflict of 1914 could have such a fundamental impact on the university system in itself shows the degree of integration between universities and German society. The universities under the Weimar Republic could not simply take up where they had left off in 1914.

The catastrophe that struck the German universities with the advent of Hitler was of such dimensions that it deserves a separate study. Hitler despised the universities. He drastically reduced the number of students; drove a large number of professors into exile, resignation, or silence; and introduced some of his own "national socialist sciences" into the lecture halls and seminars. The painful and gradual recovery of the German universities and the onset of problems in the 1960s properly belong to another history, that of the decline and transformation of the German university system in the twentieth century.

The geographical limits of this study encompass the universities of the German states except Austria. Some mention must be made of the Austrian universities, particularly as reform models during the late eighteenth century. Switzerland, too, contributed to important changes in higher education in the German-speaking world, notably in the area of technical education in the nineteenth century. Yet several compelling reasons argue for the exclusion of Austria and Switzerland from the mainstream of German university history. After an initial burst of reform activity under Maria Theresa and Joseph II, Austrian higher education policy relapsed into protracted bureaucratic immobility lasting until the middle of the nineteenth century. The main exception to this generalization lay in the area of technical education. By the end of the nineteenth century, Austrian universities began to change, but largely in the wake of innovations already introduced in the German states to the north and west. Austria and Switzerland were multinational states; and despite continuing comparabilities between their university systems and that of Germany, their systems were distinctly separate. Nobody can deny the importance of such universities as Vienna, Prague, or Basel for the scientific and cultural history of Europe. But their contributions and development took place in a social and political setting rather different from that of their sister institutions in northern and western Germany.

A further boundary of this study pertains to the type of higher educational institutions discussed. Many types of post-secondary educational institutions existed in Germany, and their importance is undeniable. Technical colleges separate from universities played an incalculable role in the education of German engineering and business elites and contributed in many ways to the modernization of the German economy. So did forestry and mining schools, military academies, and other types of higher educational institutions. But compelling reasons exist for not treating these institutions in the same way as the universities. One reason is the traditional separation of technical and university education in Germany. Until the very beginning of the twentieth century, technical schools in Germany were not recognized as being remotely equal to the universities. The latter successfully fought for a monopoly on theoretical studies, and the technical schools were supposed to restrict themselves to the teaching of practical subjects. The erosion of the line between university *Bildung* (education) and technical-school *Ausbildung* (training) is a part of our story, but the process was only beginning before 1914 and is still incomplete today. A second reason for treating the technical schools only briefly is the confusion that long surrounded their status in the vertical hierarchy of German "higher" education. Technical training schools initially served as types of secondary schools: Some actually trained schoolboys in vocational and artisanal subjects, while others trained more mature students in bridge building, surveying, agronomy, or military surgery. Cadet schools and *Ritterakademien* (knights' academies) were functionally on the same level. Thus, in the eighteenth and early nineteenth centuries, most of these schools were too much like secondary schools to be directly comparable to the more outstanding universities. In many German states, these institutions were considered to be so different from universities that they were placed under the authority of governmental departments other than the educational ministry – the commerce ministry, for example. If one included the technical schools in this study, one would logically have to include the other secondary schools, particularly the classical *Gymnasium* of the nineteenth century or the *Gelehrtenschule* (Latin school) of the eighteenth. The relationship between secondary and technical education, on the one hand, and university education, on the other, undoubtedly deserves study; but it deserves a book of its own and cannot be treated fully in this one.[5]

Some other emphases of this study must also be mentioned. It is a history of changes in the German university system: Adaptations and alterations, particularly those made in response to political and social pressures, constitute its object. It is a study of university reform, but it is also more. Many changes were made in a spirit quite opposed to reform or as the result of struggles between reformers and their opponents. Focusing on the dynamics of change, this book bypasses many static phenomena. Much of the literature about German universities deals with such static phenomena — archaic remnants, moribund practices and attitudes, and somnolent routines. Much of this type of history embraces the folklore of the university, some of it charming, some of it maddening. This, too, deserves a study, but it cannot be treated here.

A more serious and regrettable result of the limits placed on this study is the exclusion or merely cursory treatment of a number of subjects that do belong in the mainstream of university history. It proved impossible to incorporate them here. The evolution of science and scholarhsip on a discipline-by-discipline basis, for example, would require not only several volumes of treatment but the efforts of a team of specialist historians. On another level, it has proved impossible to devote much space to professorial biography. Some attempts to include prosopographical investigation of the professoriate in this study had to be abandoned for lack of a sufficient evidential base. Merely to collect information on the professoriate at Berlin University for the nineteenth century would have required several months of sustained biographical research (even if the university archive had been willing to allow such research, which it was not) and several more months for programming and analysis. The value of such studies would be considerable, but they would also require a large team of researchers and ample resources. The statistical material in this study is thus intended to be illustrative, not definitive or even sophisticated.

The life of the students has also received only passing mention. There are some good recent works on student life. But more importantly, students appear to have played a mostly passive role in the evolution of the German university system in the eighteenth and nineteenth centuries. The history of individual universities cannot be repeated here in detail; for that, there are innumerable histories of the old type. Instead, our focus shall be on the university system and some of its most influential individual components.

This work is divided into four parts, each dealing with a discrete time period. Part I treats the eighteenth century reform movements; Part II, the period of restructuring the German states in the wake of the French Revolution, which culminated in the establishment of the University of Berlin; Part III, the rise of the research university system between the 1820s and the 1860s; and Part IV, the period of the German Empire. Within these parts, I have employed an analytical approach.

Let us now turn to the first of these parts. Here we enter into a somber landscape, filled with decayed universities in the full grip of crisis and decline. German universities probably never came closer to extinction than at the beginning of the eighteenth century. Formal, empty, and frightened of new ideas, they provoked ridicule and anger even among their own dwindling band of graduates. Many of them owed their founding to the religious zeal of the Reformation, but most of them had lost touch with the important religious, intellectual, and social forces of the German states of 1700. Only slowly, painfully, and with many experiments and failures could this situation of deterioration be stopped in the course of the eighteenth century.

PART I

The eighteenth century

In the German states, as in most other parts of Europe in the eighteenth century, universities were under frequent attack. At the beginning of the century, many outstanding German thinkers, Leibniz among them, considered the universities hopelessly wedded to the past and suggested the establishment of other paths to higher knowledge and science, notably scientific academies. At the other end of the century, just before the French Revolution, literati of the German Enlightenment mounted sweeping attacks on the universities, and many called for their outright abolition. In the course of the reforms and reorganization attendant upon the French revolutionary invasions and wars, many of them were indeed suppressed. Literary attacks and actual closings have left a dark image of German universities during the "century of light."

In fact, many important changes and innovations took place quietly in a number of German universities of the eighteenth century, and it was upon the traditions of these reforms that the glories of the German universities in the nineteenth century were built.

In Part I, dealing with the eighteenth century, I shall sketch the state of German universities before reforms began to alter them; then take up the first university reform movement, which led to the establishment of new-model institutions (Chapter 2); and then discuss the second, less successful, re-

form movement, aimed at transforming existing institutions in the late eighteenth century (Chapter 3).

In 1700 there were twenty-eight universities in the German states other than Austria. Many of these had such tiny enrollments that they were barely able to function. Heidelberg, for example, had only about 80 students per year on the average (1701–5), and twenty others had less than 300 students. The most popular universities were Cologne, Leipzig, Wittenberg, and Halle (all with over 500 students), but only Halle, less than ten years old in 1700, had anything resembling an innovative curriculum. These twenty-eight universities divided about 9,000 students among them around 1700, whereas just before the Thirty Years' War, when there had been only twenty universities, they had enrolled nearly 8,000 students.1 Although each university had had an average of 400 students then, by 1700 each one had an average of fewer than 290. This situation, bad enough in 1700, was worse by the mid-eighteenth century. In the late 1760s, enrollments dropped to slightly over 7,000, and three new universities (Breslau, Göttingen, and Erlangen) had joined in the competition, giving a median student body of about 220. Some in fact were much larger (Göttingen, Halle, and Leipzig), but a few were struggling along with impossibly low average enrollments – for example, Rostock (74), Greifswald (82), Duisburg (71), and Paderborn (45).2 By the last five years of the eighteenth century, despite an intervening slight recovery in student numbers, total enrollments at German universities had sunk to about 6,000 per year.3 A few of the universities had already closed in the 1790s (Cologne, Trier, and Strasbourg), but this reduction of the fierce and debilitating competition among too many universities, rather than rejuvenating the survivors, filled them with dread that they might be next.

The crisis in student enrollments was only the quantitative sign of a deeper qualitative malaise in the German universities. Scholasticism was the method and orthodoxy the content of most instruction. Medicine was openly ridiculed, natural science was almost exclusively the province of the new royal academies, and the movements in philosophy and law that later came to be labeled "enlightened" faced great hostility. Lectures, textbooks, and teaching staff changed little, as they were expected to transmit static truths, not develop new ideas. Latin, the universal language of Christendom's intellectuals, was still the medium of instruction and publication.

The arts or philosophical faculties had deteriorated badly in many places. They served chiefly as remedial preparatory schools for those whose secondary education was not adequate for direct matriculation into the "higher" professional faculties of theology, law, and medicine. Many universities' philosophical faculties were not even very successful at this task and were receiving stiff competition in the seventeenth century from Latin schools run by Jesuits or from "academies" operated primarily for the offspring of the wellborn. These Ritterakademien offered a curriculum that was more limited, but at the same time more fashionable and practically useful, than the universities'. They stressed mathematics, modern languages, social graces, a smattering of science, and martial arts. The late seventeenth century had also brought the grand tour into vogue for the German noblemen's sons, even if, for financial reasons, it was often limited to a semester or two abroad. It was in such countries as Holland that one could learn the most about science and even natural law, two of the subjects increasingly fashionable among the upper classes.

Practically speaking, and measured by the numbers of students listening, theology and law were the important branches of university learning. In the Catholic universities of Germany, which constituted over a third of all institutions, philosophy and theology were often the only faculties. Until the late eighteenth century, they were dominated by such teaching orders as the Jesuits. In those German states where central bureaucratic administrations of a more or less despotic type had emerged, the universities had begun serving the state by training doctors of law, for the expansion of princely power, just as *they had previously trained priests and pastors for the interests of their respective churches. Theological discussion, which had fired intellectual excitement and provoked the founding of new universities in the sixteenth and early seventeenth centuries, had degenerated into sterile orthodoxy in virtually all German universities, Catholic and Protestant alike.*

The law faculties at German universities, while relatively less ossified than the theological faculties and incomparably more popular than the philosophical faculties, were nevertheless caught in a decline, compared to previous generations. The traditional Roman law that had served since the late fifteenth century as the basis of instruction and had had some relevance to the law of the Holy Roman Empire was now becoming comparatively useless as the new enlightened despots created their own legal traditions and needs. Whereas a doctorate in the laws had been regarded as almost tantamount to a title of nobility in the mid-seventeenth century, it had slipped somewhat in prestige, thanks to the lack of adapability of the law faculties to new political realities.

Finally, medical schools in most German universities were in low repute, caught still in a reliance on medical observations going back to Aristotle in some areas, and not yet in a position to incorporate some of the scientific discoveries of the age. As one Hanoverian official remarked acidly in about 1730, the purpose of medical schools was to "create ten or fifteen young angels of death [Würgengel] *so that the people may be buried methodically."*4 *Anatomical theaters were all but unknown or wretchedly inadequate at German institutions of higher learning.*

What scientific research there was tended to be carried on at the new royal academies of science. These academies, inspired by the French royal academies, were beginning to spring up in the German states after 1700, the year of the founding of the Prussian Academy of Sciences. Similar academies followed at Göttingen (1742), at Munich (1759), and elsewhere. They were a sign of royal patronage of the rapidly developing arts and sciences of the modern age; but they were also implicitly a slap at the universities and a testimony to their torpor in the pursuit of new knowledge. The academies were expected to produce useful knowledge, not the sort of scholastic subtleties that were widely considered to be the very heart of university work, particularly in the "disputations" that were regarded as the highest form of university intellectual creativity.

With a few exceptions, university professors around 1700 did not produce new knowledge. The publications flowing sparsely from their pens were in large part textbooks that merely repeated old knowledge. As long as theology was regarded as the "queen science" of the univerisites, and as long as theology was dominated by a static orthodoxy, significant changes in the arts and sciences were blocked from the German institutions of higher learning.

The cause of the universities' inability to adapt themselves and their curriculum was in large measure the corporate structure inherited from the Middle Ages. Many professors resisted innovations in the curriculum and, indeed, any and all change as an infringement of their traditional immunities, rights of self-government, and privileges. This traditional separation of the universities – complete with their own legal jurisdictions – from the rest of society implied a more serious problem than mere conservatism, however. Legally immune or not, universities are never immune to the social groups they are supposed to serve. By 1700, most German universities had begun to lose what support they had enjoyed in the broader society.

The most numerous estate, the peasantry, traditionally had the least to do with universities, although there may well have been more peasants attending them than in the nineteenth century. Nor could one say that the bourgeois estate as a whole constituted the natural clientele of universities around 1700, because one very important element of the bourgeoisie – the oligarchs and citizens of Germany's many towns – had little use for universities and certainly did not bestir themselves to maintain such institutions (although a very few, like Cologne and

Strasbourg, were "city" universities). Universities were, to be sure, predominantly "bourgeois" in their clientele and staffs, but they drew heavily on a small segment of the bourgeoisie, one Mack Walker has recently called the subclass of "movers and doers,"⁵ those who left the fixed place in life guaranteed and decreed by the German towns to join the comparatively "rootless" class of professionals, civil or ecclesiastical, who belonged to another world wherever they lived. Rather than being fixed in the carefully hierarchical world of the German towns and cities, this branch of the bourgeoisie placed itself at the disposal of the expanding professions and, above all, the new territorial bureaucratic states. In training, language, clothing, life expectations, life-style, and function, the academic "bourgeoisie" was far removed from the traditional world of the German Bürger, *as the frequent clashes between urban "philistines" and university students or professors might indicate.*

The German noble estate was as little a "class" in the modern sense as the bourgeoisie. The difficulty of including all those with noble parents and family background in one term is enormous, so much so that even today the historian has the greatest difficulty in saying anything precise about the German nobility. The geographic, political, religious, and economic differences among all those families entitled to use the "von" before their name were probably greater in Central Europe in the eighteenth century than anywhere else at any time. No scholar can be sure even of the size of this social group, except that it was larger than that of England and smaller than that of Poland or Hungary. Some nobles were working farmers, others mere seigneurs *collecting rents, still others members of princely bureaucracies, yet others court nobles. Some were poor sovereigns over tiny, but autonomous domains, whereas others were rich but servile to a territorial prince. The German language richly reflects the complexity of the German nobility, with such prefixes to the term "nobility" as "old," "new," "imperial," "territorial," "court," "country," "high," "low," "patent," and so on.*

Attitudes toward education naturally varied as much among the noble familes as among the bourgeois. The nobility, which had attended German universities in large numbers during the sixteenth and early seventeenth centuries, had deserted these institutions by the beginning of the eighteenth century – an indication that universities had become increasingly irrelevant to their needs. Young noblemen had learned to prefer the knightly "academies" (Ritterakademien) mentioned in Chapter 1. These stressed the building of character over knowledge for its own sake, in keeping with the German version of the Renaissance idea of the gentleman. The academies offered worldly breadth, rather than scholastic depth; and a grand tour or, occasionally, a short visit to a foreign university completed the ideal cosmopolitan gentlemanly education begun in the academies, especially for those noblemen bent on a diplomatic or civil service career.

Given the structure, tastes, and needs of German society as a whole around 1700, many observers regarded the existing universities as hopelessly irrelevant, too numerous for their existing clientele, and unlikely to change in such a way as to attract more and better students. Yet the very end of the seventeenth century and the first half of the eighteenth witnessed the opening of four new universities: Halle, in Prussia (1694); Breslau, in Silesia (1702); Göttingen, in Hanover (1737); and Erlangen, in the Frankish principality of Bayreuth (1743). Although Breslau was little more than a Catholic seminary, the other three universities shared a modern, pioneering spirit born of the first reform movement. Two, Halle and Göttingen, became large and prosperous despite the superabundance of universities already in existence. Both had large state governments standing behind them, to be sure, but more importantly, they succeeded in attracting a disproportionate number of the "movers and doers." They succeeded, in other words, not only because of strong government support (and control), but because they apparently appealed to certain important groups in German society.

2

The first eighteenth-century reform movement

The beginning of the first eighteenth-century university reform movement in Germany may be dated from the founding of the University of Halle. The new university came into being and took on a model character for later university reformers mostly by a set of accidents and the interaction of several strong personalities, but the response of German students to the new institution was tellingly positive. Halle was initially based upon a previously existing *Ritterakademie,* upon which was grafted a Pietistically oriented theological faculty and a comparatively progressive law faculty. Pietism was at the beginning of the eighteenth century a dynamic force in Germany, a religious doctrine stressing active faith and emotional commitment more than scholastic subtlety. Part of this activism was reflected in the reform of pedagogical training by the theologian and head of the Halle orphanage, August Hermann Francke. Just as important was the rather worldly engagement of the Pietists; their members in the teaching staff were not implacably opposed to the *vita activa* and thus did not place major obstacles in the way of other faculties. Thus it was possible to modernize the arts curriculum somewhat. One of the leading educational modernizers of early eighteenth-century Germany, Christian Thomasius, sought to combine the education desiderata of a gentleman (including riding, fencing, foreign languages, and the new sciences) with the state's formal requirements for civil service education. Thanks to this clever mixture of cosmopolitan spirit and modern legal training, Halle began attracting law students from the wealthier classes from all over Germany. It had, in the first decades of its existence, a much higher proportion of noble students than other German institutions, indicating for the first time that a university that attempted to adopt some of the new goals and methods of the time could compete successfully for the most desirable students. Nobles were among these, as they paid considerably higher fees than commoners and brought a certain prestige to the university. At the same time, Halle's Pietism exercised a considerable attraction on would-be pastors and schoolteachers.

Only when these two rather different traditions – the worldly noble and the Pietistic – came into conflict did Halle's fortunes decline. Pietism grew more conservative and orthodox at Halle, while the Enlightenment became more radical. The expulsion of Christian Wolff from Halle in 1723 was a sign that the Pietistic theologians were still in control and that they would not tolerate the most advanced philosophical conclusions of the Enlightenment. Even though Wolff was reinstated upon the accession to the throne of Frederick the Great in 1740, the damage to Halle's leadership had been done. Nevertheless, its example had not been lost on others who hoped to assume that leadership.

The foundation of Göttingen

One of the keenest rivals of the Hohenzollern kings, who had founded Halle, was the house of Hanover, recently elevated to the throne of Great Britain but still keenly interested in its standing among the other German princely houses. Even before the accession, Hanover had nurtured great-power ambitions. For the Prussians to have the most prestigious university in Germany when Hanover had none was a constant goad to pride.

Even more important was the need to build the Hanoverian state on a well-educated bureaucratic class. As early as the beginning of the eighteenth century, Hanoverian officials were clearly dissatisfied with the arrangement whereby Hanoverians were supposed to attend the university of neighboring Brunswick-Lüneburg in Helmstedt. Furthermore, their words made clear their concern for the education of the upper classes in a more "practical" and fashionable manner. As Chancellor Benjamin Beischärff complained in 1710, "Noble youth and agile geniuses," especially those destined for military careers, were damaging themselves and the state with their poor training. Law, he groaned, was "negligent, casual, and without any special application" to the realities of contemporary administrative needs. Theology was also taught in an "impractical" way.[1] Beischärff was so repelled by the universities' performance that he eschewed the term entirely and, like Leibniz and other thinkers of the period, recommended setting up "academies" instead. These would offer a broader curriculum than the *Ritterakademien,* but they would be teaching rather than research institutions.

Beischärff's call for a new higher education system went unheeded until a quarter of a century later. When the Hanoverian government did create a state university, it was modeled on Halle, retaining the forms and privileges (as well as the name) of a university. It is characteristic of the thinking of the leading Hanoverian privy counselor at the time, Gerlach Adolf von Münchhausen, that Göttingen clung to many conservative practices in form while joining in the current of curriculum modernization initiated on a large scale by Halle. Many historians have seen in Göttingen's moderation – its cautious avoidance of extremes and its attempt to combine traditional and progressive elements – the secret of its success. What were the specific elements of this Göttingen approach to university reform? In particular, what were the innovative elements, the ones that have caused many previous scholars to argue that Göttingen has an even better claim than Halle to the title of

Europe's "first modern university?" And what did the "modernity" of Halle, Göttingen, Erlangen, and subsequently reformed universities have to do with social movements and the needs of the state?

Göttingen offers the historian the clearest and fullest evidence for answering these questions. From its inception, the new university was less a "royal" than an "estate" institution, because the noble-dominated estates put up the lion's share of the operating expenses.[2] The electoral dynasty lent its moral and political weight to the enterprise, which, tradition claims, interested the culturally undistinguished Elector George II less for itself than for the prestige it would give him in his bitter rivalry with the king of Prussia.[3] The elector's diplomatic weight was doubtless useful in obtaining imperial and papal recognition of Göttingen; but the main impetus came from the bureaucracy, with strong support from the noble-dominated *Stände*.

The leading figure in the foundation of Göttingen was himself a noble civil servant trained in the new Halle legal curriculum. Münchhausen was born in 1688, just six years before the opening of Halle. He subsequently took a grand tour and studied abroad at Utrecht, like so many other noble law students bent on a high civil service or diplomatic career. The necessity of leaving Germany for the polish expected from travel and study abroad evidently struck him as odd. After a few years in the Hanoverian court system and diplomatic service, when Münchhausen became a member of the Privy Council (1728), he began agitating for the foundation of a Hanoverian university to provide gentlemanly higher education. Six years after his entry into the Privy Council, he brought about the official foundation of Göttingen, of which he was the first *Kurator*. Münchhausen also personally founded the university library and, later, the Society of Sciences. Although he became the equivalent of prime minister in 1765, Münchhausen continued to take a lively interest in his university until his death in 1770.

Münchhausen, who in effect governed the affairs of the university from his office in Hanover, faced formidable hurdles. He was opening a new university at a time when many believed universities ought to be abolished, either because there were too many of them or because they had outlived their usefulness in an enlightened age. Halle had proved that a new university could survive and even thrive, but it had to be large to be effective, and to be large it had either to lure students away from the other univerisites or to attract the sort of student who had previously avoided university education. Because nobles and wealthy students in general paid higher fees than the many ordinary "in-state" students (*Landeskinder*), Münchhausen deemed it necessary to attract a maximum of *Vornehme und Ausländer* (notables and foreigners) in order to bring money into the country and help defray the cost of the university. Yet "academic mercantilism,"[4] as this system has been called, was not the only motive for attracting nobles and foreigners. Their presence would heighten the visibility of the new university and lend it some of their own social prestige. That, in turn, would attract other students.

In seeking to attract young noblemen and ambitious but wealthy non-nobles, the planners of Göttingen did not deviate from the dreams of all university administrators. Who did not prefer rich, elegant, and well-prepared students to impoverished, provincial, underprivileged ones (simply called "paupers" in the less euphemistic language of the eighteenth century) who begged for free meals (*Freitische*) and for dispensation from lecture fees? What is remarkable about Göttingen's history (even in comparison to Halle's) is the decisive innovations made to please and attract the upper-class students. Historians have often written that Göttingen (like Halle and Erlangen) was fashionable with nobles.[5] What has not appeared clearly is the degree to which the founders of Göttingen set out to lure this class of students by a series of curricular and other reforms. Münchhausen and his aides sought to avoid a long list of university characteristics distasteful to young noblemen, while placing new emphasis on forms of education fashionable among them. Insofar as much of the "modern" movement in ideas was fashionable with the nobility, it appears that Göttingen was consciously constructed as a *modern* university in order to make it a relatively *aristocratic* university. Such a linkage of educational modernity and a social group that – especially in Hanover – has traditionally been associated with reaction will need further discussion later. First let us turn to what Göttingen's planners sought to avoid in the German university heritage and what they sought to introduce or augment.

A typical avoidance tactic was Münchhausen's insistence that theology play a quiet role at Göttingen. Münchhausen did not wish to diminish the authority of the church, but rather to avoid the acrimonious disputes among Protestant sects (e.g., Pietists and orthodox Lutherans) that had been raging in Germany since the end of the seventeenth century. The university statutes consequently forbade denunciations of teachers for "heretical" opinions.[6] Münchhausen hoped thereby to avoid the fate of Halle, which had come under the influence of an increasingly rigid Pietism. The position of the theologians was thus considerably weakened from the start, and Münchhausen sought to further guarantee peace by appointing doctrinally neutral professors of theology. The energies of students and professors could be turned to more productive (and more secular) concerns than squabbles over orthodoxy. In this negative sanction against heresy charges and other forms of exaggerated scholastic feuding, one can see the germs of academic freedom, which later in the century made Göttingen a favored residence even of nonuniversity intellectuals. Göttingen's freedom to think, write, and publish was unsurpassed in Germany. Even though the Göttingen theologians had to be good Lutherans,[7] the spirit of intellectual liberty left to them allowed Göttingen to develop into a major center of "enlightened" biblical criticism and church history.

Not only did Münchhausen cool the religious zeal of the theological faculty, he went out of his way to accommodate

Catholics (especially noblemen) who might wish to study in Göttingen. He thus made arrangements whereby Catholic students could exercise their faith. The deference Münchhausen showed to Catholic Vienna in obtaining an expensive imperial charter for the university undoubtedly sprang more from political convenience and concern for attracting wealthy Catholic students than from any particular sense of ecumenicalism.

In his selection of professors, too, Münchhausen took pains to avoid quarrelsome or overly notorious scholars, who might drive away students by their extremism. He kept the most important prerogatives of appointment in the hands of the government and its agents. Such an approach, which contrasted with the usual guildlike prerogatives of faculties to make their own appointments, might at first appear as an unwarranted presumption and a threat to academic freedom. In the context of the eighteenth century, however, it was the only guarantee against the nepotism, favoritism, and seniorism prevailing at most universities. By giving the faculty only a right to suggest candidates upon invitation, Münchhausen sought to avoid divisive quarrels and factionalism in the faculties, especially the sort that derived from conflicts of personal interest. Münchhausen was not willing to seek the advice of scholars themselves in making appointments; but he considered it wiser to rely on the advice of those he know to be relatively impartial, whether outside the university or within it. One of the by-products of this policy was the recruitment of a faculty with a superregional and even international reputation.

More important than avoiding the mistakes of others, Münchhausen and his advisers sought to offer something new and positive as an inducement to student and professors. The professors, in addition to a climate of liberal scholarly discussion and publication, received the added inducement of high salaries and the promise of high fees.[8] Münchhausen readily used the elector's political influence to obtain the release of professors from the service of other rulers (professorial mobility was still not an established principle). He paid moving expenses, arranged for professors' housing, and otherwise made an offer from Göttingen almost irresistible. Münchhausen personally supervised the recruitment of the professoriate. In general, his chief criterion was the fame of the scholar, which he knew would quickly draw attention to Göttingen. For this fame, which often derived from nationally recognized publications, Münchhausen was willing to pay the best prices in Germany.

Göttingen soon acquired the reputation it subsequently held, as one of the chief seats of scholarship and science in Central Europe. The Society of Sciences established there in 1742 made the city a leading intellectual center, one of the few in Europe to have both a university and a scientific academy. The library, which was generously endowed from the first, attracted many serious scholars, so that by the end of the eighteenth century, Göttingen probably had more learned men per capita than any other city in Germany.[9] The Göttingische Gelehrten Anzeigen retained a leading place in the literary and scientific life of Germany, drawing upon professors for most of its contributions. Although it is difficult to prove that Münchhausen's preference for publishing scholars induced the beginning of the research and publication ethic so apparent in nineteenth-century German universities, the effect was to place a premium on teachers who could also publish, and whose publications were sufficiently significant to draw attention to their institutional base.[10]

The relative weight given to the four faculties (theology, medicine, law, and philosophy), the curriculum allocations within each one, and training institutions set up outside the four faculties also shed much light on the social and political motivations in the thinking of Münchhausen and his advisers. We have already noted the relatively severe limitations placed on the traditional censorship powers of the "first" faculty, that of theology. The medical faculty, as at Halle, was relatively weak.[11]

More significant than the curriculum in these two faculties were the emphases set in the other two, philosophy and law.

Of these two, philosophy at first took a distinctly inferior place, as it always had in traditional German academic organization. The philosophical faculty remained largely an antechamber to the higher faculties, for teachers as well as students. And it did not lose its preparatory function until later in the eighteenth century, even at Göttingen. Yet the struggle for equality with the other three faculties had already begun, and Münchhausen added to the weight and importance of the "philosophical" subjects, such as history, languages, and mathematics, by his insistence that these fields were more than remedial areas for poorly prepared freshmen.

Münchhausen took special pains in the compostion of the philosophical faculty. True, he was personally suspicious of radical innovations in speculative philosophy.[12] It is also true that Göttingen did not shine as brilliantly as Halle before the expulsion of Christian Wolff, the greatest contemporary German Enlightenment philosopher. But even here Münchhausen waived his baroque distaste for Wolffianism on the pragmatic grounds that it was fashionable and would therefore draw students.[13] And although the philosophical faculty as a whole started out somewhat disadvantaged in comparison to the rights and status of the others, certain disciplines – notably history, mathematics, and eloquence – gained lavish promotion when compared to other universities. The proposed salary for one history professor, Treuer, was quite close to those of the top legal professor (Gebauer) and theologian (Rambach).[14] Münchhausen himself emphasized the importance of history, and specifically of *modern* history, in choosing candidates for professorships. This attitude pervaded Göttingen, so that even a contemporary theology professor there called history not only the "favorite science of our time" but also the proper substitute for legal studies among those "*Vornehme* and foreigners" (meaning in this context nobles, Englishmen, and Russians) whose wealth, life on country estates, and luxurious unemployment might make law superfluous.[15] Indeed, some 10 percent of Göttingen students in the eighteenth century were enrolled in the philosophical faculty – a figure far higher than the average at other institutions.[16] In this movement one can legitimately see the beginnings, or rather the refounding, of "liberal education" on the university level.

Among the offerings in the philosophical faculty, in addition to the traditional introductory course of logic, metaphysics, and ethics, Göttingen offered lectures in "empirical psychol-. ogy," the law of nature, politics, physics, natural history, pure and applied mathematics (including surveying, military and civilian architecture, etc.), history and its "auxiliary sciences" such as geography, diplomatics, science, art, and ancient and modern languages.[17]

Such a program, as it existed by the 1760s, indicates a step away from purely propaedeutic intentions and shows that the attempt to give a broad, if dilettantish, survey of useful knowledge to "*Vornehme* and foreigners" was not an empty promise. Private lectures, agreed on by teacher and student, and constituting a major source of income for the professors, presumably covered an even wider span of fashionable and useful subjects.

The backbone of the Göttingen curriculum from the start was the legal faculty. Münchhausen left no doubt about his reason for concern about this branch of learning. "That the legal faculty be filled with famous and excellent men is necessary above all, because that faculty must induce many rich and distinguished people to study in Göttingen," he wrote.[18] To some extent, no doubt, his comment reflected sober mercantilistic calculation: Law was the field that attracted the best-paying students, whether noble or not. The result would be a degree of fiscal self-sufficiency for the university and an augmentation of what we would now call Hanover's balance of payments. Yet a certain amount of class consciousness beyond deference to the merely rich can also be seen in Münchhausen's thoughts. The kind of law taught at Göttingen reflected the resentment of many German nobles against the high-handed innovations of increasingly absolute rulers and was designed to reinforce their position and rights under the laws of the moribund empire, common law, and private law.

A typical exchange between Münchhausen and a Mecklenburg *Landrat* shows the pains taken by the former to stress the aristocratic interest underlying legal studies at Göttingen. The *Landrat* asked Münchhausen about a rumor that Göttingen would teach "regalistic" law. It was, after all, the official creation of the king of England. Münchhausen groaned about the pernicious effects of such rumors, "especially as I hope to attract the rather numerous Mecklenburg nobles and to fix their predilection for Göttingen." Accordingly, Münchhausen replied that George II had personally warned the law professors that they would gain no favor with him by teaching regalistic law – on the contrary. Aside from royal indifference, the fierceness of Hanoverian noble families in defense of their liberties and prerogatives would certainly militate against regalism at Göttingen. "I do not know how people come by such allegations," Münchhausen sighed, "because they could figure out for themselves that the law professors would not act so unreasonably against themselves as to adopt regalistic principles of law, whereby they would load themselves down with odium, especially in the eyes of the *noblesse,* and would gain thanks from nobody."[19]

Thus even Roman law, which could be and was used to legitimate "princely" incursions, was taught at Göttingen in a sense favorable to the defense of *older* rights against the absolute princes. Georg Strube, whose *Jurisprudence* was used as a supplement to the introduction to Justinian's Institutions and Digest (*Pandekten*) at Göttingen, made this plain in a letter to Münchhausen. At the same time, one can see part of the motivation for the toleration of Catholics at Göttingen. "Catholics are themselves persuaded," he wrote, "that their publicists [i.e., teachers of civil law] are worthless. The principles of Thomasius and Ludewig, being much too princely, have scared them away from attending Halle; if we teach them a more convenient civil law, and one more in line with the laws of the empire, then it can be hoped that their best people will come to us."[20] Significantly, more attention was paid by the Göttingen legal faculty to feudal law, German common law, German and European constitutional law, legal history, and trial law (especially that of the two imperial courts at Wetzlar and Vienna) than to the traditional Roman fare of the seventeenth century.[21] However, it was not until J. S. Pütter was hired in 1746, primarily to teach the practical subject of *Reichsprozess* or imperial trial law, that Göttingen's legal reputation began to soar. *Reichsprozess* was a key to litigation against arbitrary administrative acts and therefore especially interesting to the nobility as a class. Pütter gave an entirely fresh practical bent to legal education unparallelled in Germany at the time.[22] He and the Göttingen school made major contributions to the codification of German law, thereby dimishing the power of pure Roman law as a weapon in the hands of centralizing rulers.

In addition to philosophical subjects for the dilettante and law for the place-seeking nobles, Göttingen offered perhaps the best training in courtly arts available at any European education institution. Dancing, drawing, fencing, riding, music, and conversation in modern languages were all offered, in addition to the regular curriculum. Riding alone was taken so seriously that one of the university's largest eighteenth-century buildings (torn down only recently) was an indoor riding hall. The stallmaster was held in such high regard that his place in academic processions came before that of the associate professors (*Extraordinarien*).[23] No doubt many noblemen decided to spend a few semesters at Göttingen principally for its potential as a courtly finishing school. Indeed, with the beefed-up philosophical faculty for the training of the mind and the various excellent facilities for the exercise of the body, Göttingen may be said to have transformed the relationship for the three "higher" faculties (theology, medicine, and law) to the philosophical faculty and the worldly arts: In effect, the new university combined the traditional strengths of *Ritterakademien* and traditional universities. Even if courtly training at the university later fell into disrepute or degenerated into mere dueling and horseracing, the new emphasis placed on the philosophical faculty remained a breakthrough and laid the groundwork for neo-humanism in the university, with its emphasis on the subjective, rather than objective, benefits of study.[24]

State, society, and Göttingen students

Earlier we noted that Göttingen, even more than Halle, was laid out along consciously modern lines. The term "modern," however, requires some qualification. Let us assume for the moment that it means the opposite of "traditional," that it had not only an etymological but a real connection with "mode" or fashion, and that the setters of fashion in eighteenth-century Germany still tended to be the nobility. Another, more Whiggish test of modernity is the degree to which, for example, the Göttingen curriculum and ethos approached that of later times. Or we can recall the Weberian association of modernity and rationalization. By any of these standards, a good case can be made for Göttingen's relative modernity.

As we have seen, the Göttingen planners evinced great solicitude toward the *Vornehme* in general and noble youth in particular in bringing about these departures from traditional curriculum and purpose. Even if Göttingen attracted more aristocrats, could these not be dismissed as a handful of dilettantes unrepresentative of the noble class at large? Or did evidence of university study increase among the nobility?

A survey of the social origins of the Göttingen student body is one way to ascertain its component of nobles. Table 1 shows the result of a 5 percent sample taken from the matriculation lists of the university at ten-year intervals. For the total sample, the average proportion of nobles is nearly 13 percent. Because contemporaries reported that impoverished nobles often matriculated under non-noble names to escape the higher fees imposed on their social group,[25] the real figures are perhaps somewhat higher. Although the noble population of the

Table 1. *Noble students at Göttingen,*
1737–97

Year	Total no. of students	% of nobles	% of nobles studying law
1737	297	10	55
1747	279	13	73
1757	183	15	50
1767	257	8	45
1777	334	12	79
1787	372	14	68
1797	366	15	62

Source: Götz von Selle (ed.), *Die Matrikel der Georg-August-Universität zu Göttingen, 1734–1837,* 2 vols. (Hildesheim and Leipzig, 1937), vol. I. The table is based on a 5 percent sample.

Holy Roman Empire is unknown, one might not go too far wrong in guessing that it was comparable to that of France, a maximum of 2 percent of the whole population.

Not only were nobles represented at Göttingen disproportionately to the population, they were also there in much higher numbers than at other universities. Other large universities had to content themselves with half as many. The noble enrollments at Strasbourg, for example, averaged 5 percent in the eighteenth century; Jena had about the same proportion. Leipzig had an average of a little over 7%, as did Heidelberg. A few small, limping universities such as Kiel and Rostock did, to be sure, have large percentages of nobles in their student bodies (up to 12% sometimes at Kiel), but these percentages are relatively meaningless as a fraction of the mere handful of students they usually enrolled (as few as eight one year at Kiel). Only Halle among the larger universities showed a similar pattern, with as much as 11% of its student body being noble in the late 1690s. Halle, however, slipped to only 7% from 1710 to 1740, and finally to 4% in the 1740s – partly, no doubt, because its aristocratic clientele abandoned it for Göttingen.[26] Many universities had very few noble students: Würzburg and Tübingen, for example, had less than 5%. Furthermore, and perhaps more important in the eyes of contemporaries, Göttingen outclassed all other universities in the number of higher nobles it attracted – princes, dukes, imperial counts, and others who owed obeisance only to the emperor himself. The wealthier nobles frequently brought along a retinue of servants and private tutors, customarily resided in relatively opulent quarters, and were given pride of place in classrooms and official exercises of the university. Thus their economic and psychological impact on the town and university was well out of proportion to their numbers, high as these were.

The vast majority of the noble students (see Table 1) enrolled in the legal faculty. Those who enrolled in the medical and theological faculties were numerically negligible, so that the remaining nobles can be assumed to have come with the intent of studying in the philosophical faculty or with nothing specific in mind (sometimes they did not list a faculty of preference). Although the philosophical faculty was small in comparison to the law faculty, the Göttingen planners lavished considerable attention on it, as we have seen. Noblemen who wanted to round out their general education probably made up a large component of the students, who in any case could later enter a "higher" faculty.

Parallel to the return of large numbers of noblemen to the universities, or rather to the most modern of them, one can discern a certain influx of noblemen in other spheres, notably in government. Hanover and Prussia, the homes of the new university reform idea, both experienced some version of this phenomenon. But the situations were different in important respects. Both states had seen conflict between strong rulers and indigenous nobilities during the seventeenth century, and both dynasties had availed themselves of the assistance of commoners trained in the law – known simply as *doctores* – in attempts to overcome feudal privilege. In Prussia, the long struggle ended with a compromise between Frederick the

Great and the nobility, the terms of which granted the nobles a safe place in army, state, and society at the price of surrendering political privileges. In Hanover, the fortuitous departure of the elector and his family to assume the British throne led to the long-term triumph of the indigenous nobility, which began to assert itself more vigorously and successfully against the bourgeois *doctores*. Not only did Hanover's estates, dominated clearly by the nobility, thrive in the eighteenth century; even the electoral civil service was increasingly usurped in spirit and personnel by the nobles.[27]

Yet the conquest of power was not uncomplicated. For one thing, many sixteenth- and seventeenth-century *doctores* had been ennobled (even though, or perhaps because, a doctorate was then considered a sort of patent of nobility), and some had attempted to legitimate their nobility by acquiring land and marrying into the older families. Another complicating factor was that a few noble families tended to predominate in the diets. Furthermore, despite the absence of the dynasty, it had not given up all claim to sanction policy decisions. A court nobility that had thrown in its lot with the electoral house continued to exist around the palace in Hanover, which did not experience the absence of its royal master as often under the first two Georges as it did under the third. Despite intermarriage and resulting family connections, there was plenty of room for competition both among the noble families and between them and the well-established families of former *doctores,* whether formally bourgeois or noble.

Besides the struggle for power, the nobles faced economic problems. Hanoverian noble estates were not large or rich enough to provide a luxurious style of life. As Hanover's major constitutional historian has said, "The existence of the upper classes rested wholly or in part on the civil service; perhaps in no other part of Germany was the civil service so often a source of wealth."[28]

As property holdings declined in importance among Hanoverian, Prussian, and probably all other German nobles in the

Table 2. Social origins and university attendance of Hanoverian central government officials (in percentages)

Office	Appointees, 1714–36 (N = 193)				Appointees, 1737–60 (N = 124)			
	Old nobility[a]	New nobility	Commoners	All appointees	Old nobility[a]	New nobility	Commoners	All appointees
All offices								
Social origin	64	24	12		68	20	12	
University attendance	45	76	71	56	76	100	89	82
Privy Council								
Social origin	83	17	0		100	0	0	
University attendance	53	100	0	59	89	0	0	89
Privy Chancellery								
Social origin	50	17	33		0	33	67	
University attendance	0	67	50	28	0	100	100	100
High Court of Appeals, noble bench								
Social origin	100	0	0		100	0	0	
University attendance	67	0	0	67	58	0	0	58
High Court of Appeals, learned bench								
Social origin	0	79	21		0	83	17	
University attendance	0	82	100	86	0	100	100	100

Exchequer								
Social origin	100	0	0		75	25	0	
University attendance	64	0	0	64	83	100	0	88
War Chancellery								
Social origin	78	22	0		100	0	0	
University attendance	29	50	0	33	73	0	0	73
Justice Chancellery								
Social origins	42	37	21		48	28	24	
University attendance	40	78	80	63	83	100	83	88
Court Marshal's Office								
Social origin	73	27	0		100	0	0	
University attendance	13	0	0	9	33	0	0	33
Household								
Social origins	86	14	0		90	10	0	
University attendance	38	20	0	32	53	25	0	50

Note: This table does not include the "secretaries" at the lower end of the bureaucratic hierarchy, an additional 135 persons. They were overwhelmingly commoners by origin and were not as well educated as the higher officials. Nevertheless, more secretaries attended universities in the second period than in the first, an increase from 41 to 56 percent.

[a] At least four generations old.

Source: Compiled from Joachim Lampe, *Aristokratie, Hofadel und Staatspatriziat in Kurhannover, 1714–1760*, 2 vols. (Göttingen, 1963).

eighteenth century,[29] surrogate sources of "honor," the essential quality of a nobleman after lineage, had to be sought elsewhere. Some writers began to stress the honorific value of a university education. A major eighteenth-century chronicler of the nobility, C. F. Pauli, for example, wrote approvingly that "noblemen frequently took academic degrees and honors and showed thereby that they were the most qualified for political posts of honor and they therefore demanded preference before their [social] equals."[30] Significantly, it was the brilliant new universities, with their emphasis on excellence and a famous faculty, that succeeded in convincing part of the nobility that some extra margin of honor was to be gained by university attendance. It is tempting to reflect on the reciprocal influence of the two concepts of fame and honor. Fame, one might suggest, was the equivalent of honor for a bourgeois scholar. The more famous the scholar, the more honor the aristocratic student derived from hearing his lectures. And though a student (noble or not) might actually learn more from a conscientious young teacher without a wide reputation, the nobleman would later wish to boast that he had studied under "the famous Professor So-and-so." Thus, in terms of money, power, and social psychology, the nobles responded to the reformed universities in a warm way.

Given the attractiveness of the civil service to the aristocracy, the traditional learnedness of the non-noble or new noble civil servants, and the lead given by some of Hanover's most prominent old nobles, it is not surprising that university attendance or at any rate a state examination based on university legal curriculum became increasingly the norm in the course of the eighteenth century, at least for holders of certain offices.[31]

The highest echelons of the Hanoverian administration became generally more exclusive in two ways between the departure of the dynasty in 1714 and the accession of George III in 1760. First, the proportion of noble officeholders generally rose. Second, the level of education for both noble and non-noble officials increased markedly (see Table 2). If one divides this period into two equal parts, 1714–36 and 1737–60, one can see the following patterns. In the first period, the members of the Geheimes Ratskollegium (Privy Council), the chief ministerial and legislative body of Hanover, were all noblemen, but 17% of them were of the new noble families (less than four generations old); the educational accomplishments of the new nobles were much greater than those of the old nobles (100% vs. 53% university attendance). In the second period, however, all the members of the Privy Council were old nobles, and 89% of them had attended a university. In the Chancellery or Geheime Kanzlei, the proportion of nobles to non-nobles (2:1) was reversed between the two periods, but university attendance rose to 100% in both cases. The Privy Chancellery was incidentally losing power during this period.

The Ober-Appelations-Gericht or High Court of Appeals in Celle was divided into a hereditarily aristocratic bench and a "learned bench"; so competition on the basis of education was probably not as keen as elsewhere. This may explain why the percentage of old nobles attending universities dropped slightly from 67 to 58 in the second period, despite an official rescript aimed at raising it. But there were nobles sitting on the Gelehrte Bank as well: It was 79% noble in 1714–36 and 83% noble in 1737–60. The percentage of noblemen with university training rose from 82 to 100, whereas the commoners all had university training in both periods.

The Justizkanzlei (Justice Chancellery) shows a similar configuration: more nobles in the upper, important offices and considerable increases in the number attending universities. The Justice Chancellery was 79% noble in the first period (42% of ancient lineage) but 76% noble in the second (48% old nobility). Of all the noblemen, 58% had university training in the first period as opposed to 89% in the second period.

In the War Chancellery, the Kriegskanzlei, where educational qualification was understandably somewhat lower, the pattern was nevertheless similar. Counselors were always noble; but whereas 22% of them had at least been nobles of recent origin in the first period, the old families completely dominated in the second. At this time, while old blood won out over new, the proportion of old nobles attending universities rose from a mere 29% to 73%.

Finally, by way of control, it might be useful to cast a glance at the court, where the supreme test was high birth and education was quite secondary. Is there any parallel to developments in the political administration? The answer is affirmative: The officers of the Household came from the ancient nobility in 86% of the cases in the first period, but in 90% of the cases in the second. Both the old and the young noble family members at court were more likely to have attended a university in the later time period, even though the increase was from a rather low 32% to 50%.

Both the nobles of the court and those of the bureaucracy often attended the *Ritterakademien* and traveled for their worldly polish. The high nobility of the bureaucracy, however, was twice as likely to take the further step of attending a university. The newer nobility was the group that had most often attended a university: Being somewhat insecure in their birth status, newer nobles were more likely than others to back it up with the status of education. As in the seventeenth century, when the bourgeois *doctores* had held many high posts in the Hanoverian government, it was the commoners, rather than the aristocrats of either type, who held the highest degrees (usually doctor of laws): Noblemen were not expected to bother with certification.

One can draw some tentative conclusions from this prima facie evidence. Clearly the Hanoverian administration became both more exclusive by birth and better educated by university attendance in the nearly half a century for which we have evidence. The amount and intensity of university study varied with the degree of nobility, so that old nobles almost never bothered with a doctorate and commoners almost always had one. This is an important point for the social and political history of Hanover, but not such a vital one for the fortunes of the university at Göttingen, which rested more on the *presence* of students than on their taking degrees. Because the bachelor's degree had fallen into disuse everywhere in Germany and the master's was more a byword for professorial venality and student abuse than a true sign of magisterial accomplishment, the doctorate had already become the only worthwhile degree. Functionally, inscription at a university and a year or more of attendance represented the German equivalent of the baccalaureate.

One could conclude from Table 2 that attitudes toward higher education in all branches of the higher civil service changed markedly from the first to the second half of the total period, even if we had no other evidence of the attitudes in government circles that produced the new university itself. Academic observers of the time, however, commented on the desire of young nobles to acquire university training, in contrast to their indifference prior to the eighteenth century. Professor Treuer, one of the original history professors at Göttingen, commented on the increasing preference of young nobles for "study and scholarship," which could pave the way for "important posts" in Hanover.[32] Late in the century, almost all persons who reached high office in Hanover had been students of the jurist Pütter in Göttingen.[33]

The nobles in the higher administration of Hanover constituted, to be sure, only a small fraction of Göttingen's noble alumni. For one thing, the size of the central administration was minuscule when compared to the noble alumni pool. For another, the holders of high posts were generally men already in the autumn of life when appointed, so that only the last few appointees before 1760 would have been able to attend Göttingen – and indeed did so heavily, forsaking such former favorites as Leipzig and Helmstedt. To take one indication, only one-third of the members of the Household from 1714 to 1736 attended universities; half the appointees for 1737–60 had done so, and over 75% of them spent at least one semester at Göttingen. The new university was also the heavy favorite among those in the other administrative posts. What is most interesting about the figures for members of the Household is that they show such an increase, particularly in favor of Göttingen. It is safe to say that Household duties did not require special legal or other training, beyond what a decent *Ritterakademie* would provide. This form of support for the university must be kept in mind when explaining Göttingen's success. In addition to a curriculum and professoriate tailored to the tastes of the nobility, Göttingen strove from the outset for a style and a set of extracurricular arrangements that would attract even those students who were uninterested in a civil service career.

The testimonial and statistical evidence points in the same direction. Göttingen was planned in such a way as to attract noblemen and other *Vornehme*. It clearly succeeded in attracting a disproportionate share of the nobles, whom one can easily recognize in the university statistics. We have also seen the concomitant rise of higher education qualifications among the ranks of higher civil servants, both noble and non-noble, during the half century in the middle of which Göttingen was founded.

Yet Göttingen hardly typified the German university system of the mid-eighteenth century. True, Halle (and then only partly by plan) shared with Göttingen the desire to have a modern curriculum and to attract the upper classes. Erlangen was also a conscious copy of Göttingen. It did have a comparatively fashionable curriculum and did attract a large number of noblemen. But Erlangen remained more of a *Ritterakademie* and a local university than Göttingen or Halle.[34] Other German universities did not rush to follow the lead of the new-model institutions. It is significant that education reform succeeded best in new universities; the old ones lacked the will to reform, or saw their interests threatened by innovation. Corporate rule by the professors meant, in general, lethargy and corrupt practices (characteristics of many corporations in eighteenth-century German life). Halle, Göttingen, Erlangen, and a few others were able to overcome such lethargy because the

state virtually ran them and intended to align university life
with the perceived needs of state and society. In other universities, however, habit and privilege often successfully beat back
attacks by enlightened (and sometimes benighted) princely
bureaucracies and ministers inspired by the second reform
movement of the late eighteenth century. Only then, when
enlightened despotism reached its zenith and the unreformed
universities (especially in Catholic states) had few defenders
left, were the principles of the new universities put into practice on a large scale. And even then, the Napoleonic wars, the
further development of pedagogical and scientific principles,
and other changes in thought and conditions revised much of
the detail of the Göttingen reform model. Indeed, given the
limited student market of the eighteenth century, Göttingen's
planners could not have even wished other universities successfully to copy their ideas; Göttingen's success, they assured
themselves, lay in its differentness. Nevertheless, Halle and
Göttingen did serve as reform models. Even though they were
atypical, the ideas for which they stood eventually entered a
second German reform tradition and worked on well into the
nineteenth century.

3

The second eighteenth-century
reform movement

By the middle of the eighteenth century, the first university
reform movement of the century was complete and moderately
successful. Three new universities, Halle, Göttingen, and Erlangen, had been founded on new principles and proved able to
float atop the ebbing tide of German student enrollments. Significantly, all three universities were Protestant, largely state
funded and state controlled, modernizing in outlook and curriculum, and designed to attract upper-class students. Their
secularizing tendencies (or at least their opposition to church
orthodoxy as the guiding principle in curriculum) helped nur-
ture new ideas about the goals of higher education, and for the
professoriate, about the search for truth, resulting in the beginnings of a neo-humanistic orientation in teaching and a modern
research ethic in scholarship. Their success spurred on a second
reform movement in the late eighteenth century, particularly in
the Catholic states of Germany. Their example led in part to a
new relationship between society and higher education.

The university reform tradition established by Halle and
Göttingen acted as a modernizing challenge for many other
established but unreformed institutions. By all three definitions
mentioned in Chapter 2, this reform tradition was a modernizing one. By the Whig definition—moving in the direction of
our own time—it was clearly modern. In contrast to the earlier
German university tradition, Göttingen and Halle taught in the

vernacular and deemphasized the rote grammatical study of ancient languages. They placed new emphasis on common and recent law while diminishing the canonical value of Roman law – a movement that has left traces on German law, even though it is a "code" law, up to the present time. They deemphasized religious orthodoxy, and Göttingen at least demoted theology to a much lower rank than it had held in centuries; it virtually lost its tutelage over the other faculties. This attention to the here and now went beyond religious questions. It encouraged a developmental, scientific approach to reality, and above all "practical" studies, in place of the static scholasticism, eternal verities, and speculation of the preceding century. History, especially modern history, augmented the study of the speeches of antiquity. Mathematics instruction took on a more applied tone. Philosophy turned its attention to problems of life and away from casuistry. Students were encouraged to read books on their own, to exercise their bodies as well as their minds, to think practically, and to develop themselves in an all-around manner that the later idealists would sneeringly describe as "shallow," but that lived on in an idealized form in the conceptions of Humboldt and other nineteenth-century university reformers.

In two other respects the Halle–Göttingen reforms may be seen as modern. In the simple etymological sense, "modern" means "de la mode," or fashionable. The success of Halle, and then Göttingen and Erlangen, in attracting the most fashionable section of German society back to the universities implied both a change in curriculum to suit the tastes of this section and, by the success of this change, the opening of a new dynamic toward university reform to suit the needs of society. In contrast to their earlier convictions, university administrators and, eventually, professors and diets were persuaded that change was a good thing – particularly if it meant growth.

In Weber's terms, rationalization is the key to modernity. In this sense, too, the Halle – Göttingen reform model was clearly modern, as the purpose was to make education *zweckrational* by introducing the subjects and educational purpose – preparation for life as well as for a wider range of careers than provided for by the medieval university – of the knightly academies. The paramount importance of law studies at Halle and Göttingen, the concomitant specialization and growth of bureaucracy in many German states, and the rise of "liberal education" in arts and sciences (a self-consciously gentlemanly form of education) indicate a meshing of the needs and purposes of the leading political and social circles with the offerings and purposes of higher educational institutions.

Over the course of the eighteenth century, the early reform ideas about an education useful for men of the world took root in some theological and philosophical faculties. The classical revival at the end of the century reflected new attitudes about the curricular uses of the classics begun at Halle and Göttingen. The latter in particular pioneered the philological seminar with the purpose of training the "taste, judgment and intellect" of the student rather than fostering a facility for producing adequate copies of classical Roman models of rhetoric.[1] What began in the seminars of Gesner and Heyne as a rationalized system for teaching the classics and defending them against charges of obsolescence leveled by more utilitarian reformers ended by pervading much of the reform movement. Neo-humanism or neo-idealism subtly redefined the image of the educated man from the rather external one of the first university reform movement to a more internal one, expressed in the concept of *Bildung*.

At first the neo-humanistic seminars were attractive to students bent on teaching careers or the ministry, and as such they appealed to young men from the poorer sectors of society. In the midst of social betters trained principally in courtly arts and law, these students gained a new respect for their own fields of study and a heightened prestige as contributors to a reinterpretation of the classical and biblical worlds. They could begin to look askance at the richer and more aristocratic law students for the mundanity and shallowness of their man-of-the-world training. By the end of the eighteenth century, many noblemen themselves had begun to accept this "deeper" vision of the purpose of university education, as the case of the Humboldt brothers demonstrates.

Much of the criticism of the Göttingen model in the late eighteenth century came, indeed, from men who accepted many of its reform premises but criticized it as being too utilitarian. From the viewpoint of philosophers becoming more and more idealistic, of philologists insisting on more scientific rigor and specialization, or of theologians wishing to arrest the march of materialism, such criticisms (many of which came out of late eighteenth-century Göttingen and Halle themselves) are understandable. Yet it is debatable whether neo-humanism and idealism should necessarily be associated with modernity. In some respects, the revival of classical studies – even though on an incomparably more scientific basis – can be regarded as a rejection of some aspects of modernity incorporated in the German Enlightenment and in the early Göttingen reform model. The fact that Göttingen, in the late eighteenth century, was a leader in the philological renaissance should not surprise us.

For the rise of neo-humanism at the very university that stressed *modern* curriculum was in itself a response to the noble-oriented curriculum of Göttingen's first decades. Rather than do away with the classics as an outworn relic of bygone ages, Göttingen was able to invent a new pedagogical purpose for studying them. The resultant rejuvenation of the philosophical and theological faculties was one result, and it was a weighty one for the fate of German universities in the Napoleonic era and after.

The renewed vigor and hope injected into the idea of the university by the success of Göttingen and the partial success of Halle and Erlangen as modernized higher educational institutions had a marked, if not revolutionary, impact on other German reformers. These successes encouraged those who still believed the German universities could be reformed and saved from extinction. Such people were still probably not a majority among either civil servants or the rapidly expanding literate public, however. The funds and energies of the state were often directed elsewhere, as a series of costly and widespread wars and recovery programs distracted the German rulers. It is notable, for example, that Prussia, which came close to extinction in the Seven Years' War, paid little attention to educational reform until the time of protracted peace in the 1770s and 1780s. Yet although the civil service was too poor and distracted, usually, to effect sweeping or lasting university reforms, it was not yet forced to extinguish the weaker universities; this process came about only with the cataclysms of the Napoleonic wars. The universities themselves were often content to muddle along. Though students rioted a good deal toward the end of the eighteenth century, they were not usually rioting for "structural change"; the professoriate was little inclined to generate reform from within and quite inclined to frustrate and sabotage reform from without. Finally, although university conditions became the subject of an increasingly heated public debate during the last quarter of the century, the advocates of university abolition and a fresh start on higher eduction were impotent to effect the changes they demanded.

On balance, then, the late eighteenth century appears to have been a time of relatively little change in German higher education. The more dramatic events of the Napoleonic period, including the definitive destruction of many old universities and the founding of influential new ones, such as Berlin and Bonn, overshadow the last decades of the eighteenth century in significance. Yet one cannot pass over these decades in silence. There were important alterations in bureaucratic and public thinking about universities that helped prepare the ground for events at the beginning of the nineteenth century. In the very failure of both university reformers and university "abolitionists" we may learn much about the emerging new dialectic between states and educational institutions. The fact that the reformers scored some points and the abolitionists, by their own efforts at least, gained almost none indicates that the reform tradition was alive, if not yet mighty, a generation or two before the more notable reform epoch around 1810. It might well be argued that the reform tradition was nothing new when Berlin and Bonn were founded and numerous other universities revamped. It was a slow product of the eighteenth century rather than the sudden result of the French Revolution. The conjunction of the reform movement and the external upheavals brought on by the Napoleonic wars brought about one of those historic movements allowing reform to be carried out. In the next chapter, we shall see whether the Prussian reform movement, in particular, was as simple and pure as German university ideology has painted it, and as untouched by the eighteenth-century reform tradition as the heirs of German romanticism have claimed. In this chapter, let us see what that reform tradition was, where its strengths and weaknesses lay, and what effects it had upon the German university system. Then we can better see how this reform tradition, which one can also call the second eighteenth-century reform movement, worked itself out in some of the smaller German states both before and after the upheavals caused by the French Revolution.

The continuing crisis of universities

Despite the evident ability of reformed universities to attract enough students – and often students from the higher social ranks – to maintain themselves easily, the rest of the German universities continued to suffer from poor enrollments. The situation went from bad to worse toward the end of the eighteenth century. Total enrollments in German universities had fluctuated between eighty-one hundred and just under nine thousand between 1700 and 1755; the averages declined by as much as a thousand a year from then until the beginning of the French Revolution. During the years 1791–5, total enrollments fell below seven thousand for the first time in the century; in the last five years of the century, they fell below six thousand. The decline continued until, during the upheavals of the last phase of Napoleonic imperialism in Central Europe, 1811–15, they fell to just under four thousand nine hundred.[2] This monumental decline in student population between 1700 and 1815, which came close to halving the student bodies at a time when general population had grown strongly, has prompted some writers to describe the situation in catastrophic terms.[3] One must, of course, take into account the military disruptions of university life. War had always brought with it some large declines in enrollment as universities were beleaguered, cut off, or closed down and students went off to war. The dramatic recovery of German university enrollments immediately after the peace of 1815 should recall this fact to mind.[4] Nevertheless, despite the aggravating factor of war and upheaval, the decline in enrollments, even when adjusted, was real and seemed even worse because the trend ran counter to the movement in size of the general population.

Characteristically, the secular decline did not affect all universities with equal force. Halle, Leipzig, and Göttingen, which had been among the five largest universities throughout much of the century, lost a far smaller percentage of their students to the general attrition than did others and were able to protect themselves better from criticism as a result. On the other hand, Cologne, which had been the fifth or sixth largest university in the early eighteenth century, lost half of its student body by the late 1770s and was no longer viable when it was closed in 1798. Jena, which had been very large in the early part of the century, counting between a thousand and fifteen hundred students every year, had declined by the 1700s to well under four hundred a year. This situation prompted reform efforts that temporarily reversed the trend, as we shall see. Many other universities, which had not been particularly popular to begin with, were not so fortunate. It was difficult enough to justify the continued existence of a university such as Duisburg when it had one hundred students a year in 1700; it was simply impossible when it had between twenty and thirty in the years just after 1800.[5]

Numerous explanations have been advanced by various students of the eighteenth-century university for this crisis of enrollments. The most often heard, that the universities were increasingly backward and irrelevant in an age of *Aufklärung* and therefore alienated their natural clientele, the young, is superficially convincing if only because the basic premise is partly correct. Many universities were behind the times intellectually, and they received much well-deserved derision from Enlightenment writers. It does not necessarily follow, however, that this backwardness alone explains the declining student enrollments. Even progressive universities suffered some losses in the late eighteenth century. Because most students attended universities in order to advance their careers, they often had little choice but to attend, no matter how outdated the course of instruction. Another source of student rejection of the university may have nothing to do with alienation: Schools were slowly improving in Germany during the eighteenth century, and this improvement undoubtedly contributed to the decline of the universities' role as remedial educator, particularly through the crumbling *Artistenfakultäten* (faculties of arts). These were often the faculties hardest hit by enrollment decreases.

One may legitimately posit an ideal-type difference between these *Artistenfakultäten* and the reformed *philosophische Fakultäten*. Although the terms remained virtually interchangeable in the early eighteenth century, the "philosophical faculties" gradually emerged as closer to the institution of the same name at Göttingen than to the more schoollike faculties of arts. Declines in other faculties were not greatly out of line with overall declines, and one faculty, that of medicine, actually registered gains – perhaps the only sign of a direct influence of the Enlightenment on student curricular choices.

Purely economic explanations of enrollment decreases are also questionable, because the prosperity of the German states apparently increased. If anything, economic arguments could be used to explain declines in university enrollments by suggesting that slightly more opportunities existed in the private economic sector than in the early eighteenth century. Not poverty itself, but the belief that a university eduction will do little to justify the expense, has apparently been a decisive factor in keeping young men of humble means from the university throughout modern times.

The question of careers must also be raised. Did potential students decide to stay away from the university because they believed it would be a waste of time even as a portal to professions and the civil and ecclesiastial service? Henri Brunschwig has pointed out that in Prussia, at least, the university graduates were becoming desperate at the end of the eighteenth century: There were not nearly enough positions to go around, and access even to these few careers was not based solely on talent and merit.[6] Governments did much in the late eighteenth century to discourage aspirants to civil service careers and to increase norms and regulation of the "free" professions. In Prussia alone, formal examinations supervised by a permanent commission were prescribed for access to higher civil service positions in 1770 and 1775. Examinations for physicians were tightened progressively from 1789 on. Though the civil service and judicial examinations tended to encourage university study, they were still based more on experience acquired on the job than on academic theory.[7] At Halle, the major Prussian university, the enrollments in the law faculty rose from decade to decade after the institution of state examinations for civil service and judicial offices in 1770.[8] Medical enrollments also increased all over Germany at the end of the eighteenth century, even as governments moved to tighten regulation of the profession. Brunschwig may be on the right track in linking the blockage of careers to talented people with the genesis of the "romantic mentality," but it was still university graduates who were thus afflicted with frustration and restlessness. Government efforts (such as those by the Wöllner regime in Prussia under Frederick William II) aimed at reducing university populations indicate that some civil servants believed there were still too many educated men for the needs of society *despite* the decline in enrollments of the last half of the eighteenth century. Similar complaints would be heard again from the German bureaucrats in the period after 1815, when enrollments rose dramatically. In other words, although one may legitimately speak of a "crisis" for the universities in not having nearly as many students in 1800 as in 1700, the universities were still evidently overproducing professional people of all types, from clergymen and lawyers to doctors and literary men, judging by the low esteem and equally low incomes of the university-trained professional class even as late as 1800.[9]

One contemporary estimate recorded more than a 100 percent increase in the number of authors living in Württemberg (from 120 to 285) between 1774 and 1790. During the same time, the number of university graduates was estimated to have increased by about one-third.[10] Although prices had doubled in Württemberg between about 1740 and 1790, salaries for the largest group of university graduates, pastors, had not kept pace, and 59 percent of these earned less than 600 gulden per year.[11] From the point of view of conservatives worried about discontent among the unemployed intellectuals, or from that of government officials attempting to match supply of offices with demand from graduates, the decline in university enrollments at the end of the century was not severe enough.

The crisis of enrollments, then, was a crisis felt more by the universities than by the states; its causes cannot be identified with precision. It is important to note that it was the smaller and weaker universities that were most strongly affected by it. These were precisely the universities in which reform had not taken place and which drew on much more circumscribed and parochial geographical bases, had small and obscure teaching faculties, and often had little property.

Because the student body at the end of the century became more and more aristocratic as it decreased in size (judging by the partial figures available so far[12]), one reasonable explanation of the decline is that the less wealthy students were the ones most likely to turn away from university attendance. Not many universities could offer 100 scholarships plus 140 *Frei-tische* to their student bodies, as Göttingen could after 1760. Even so, for each student enjoying some form of financial aid, there were two paying their own way at wealthy Göttingen.[13] Rising prices made university attendance progressively more difficult even for those with financial aid. The increasing competition for civil service posts and the continued advantage held by nobles (particularly if they also had university training) in that competition would tend to discourage the poor; so would the mounting difficulty of obtaining parishes, university posts, or other careers in an overcrowded market. Finally, many poorer men who came to the university for essentially secondary education had more alternatives at the end of the eighteenth century. Because the poorer and less well-connected students, those who had the least to hope in life from preferment and fortune, were the ones who most depended on a university education to help them overcome their deficient local secondary education and qualify them for state and church jobs and free professions, the opening of other secondary institutions and the limiting of opportunity in the civil and ecclesiastical service must have discouraged them more strongly than children of more well-to-do parents. And it was precisely the poorer students who had traditionally preferred the smaller, more localized universities everywhere in Germany, but most particularly in the Catholic states. Thus it would not be surprising if the crisis of enrollments fell most heavily upon the small, unreformed Catholic universities, and the evidence indicates that this was the case.

The second eighteenth-century reform movement

The second reform movement, or the set of responses to the crisis of the universities of the late eighteenth century, differed somewhat in quality from the first, that of the era of Thomasius and Münchhausen. As noted in the last chapter, the earlier reform tradition had not been purely a movement of the Enlightenment but contained many impulses of the late baroque age, such as the stress on personal qualities rather than narrowly conceived expertise.

What distinguishes this second movement from the first? It affected universities that had already been in existence long enough to have developed a corporate identity and, to a large degree, a conservative resistance to change. It was frequently taken up by governments attempting to revamp education, along with other aspects of public policy and administration. In spirit it was akin to the radical Enlightenment reform thinking of Josephinism, aiming at the elimination of various abuses and the creation of order and regularity. In the Catholic states, it attacked the stranglehold of teaching orders, such as the Jesuits, on university education. And in all too many cases, the governments (especially in the church principalities) proved too weak or the university corporations too strong to allow the second reform movement more than a modicum of success.

In many ways, to be sure, the second reform movement resembled the first: increased state control, the breaking of religious orthodoxy, the introduction of a modern curriculum, and the training of competent, worldly students for the professions. As in the case of Halle and Göttingen, the reform efforts of the late eighteenth century took place against the background of strident criticism of existing university conditions.

Criticism and reform efforts emanated from three major quarters in the late eighteenth century. First and most feebly, they came from within the universities themselves. Some professors were aware of a "crisis" in higher education and contributed their ideas both in private memos and in published works. There was no lack of insight about the problems of the German universities: backward curriculum, lazy and corrupt professors, students interested only in quick degrees as passports to jobs, student dissoluteness, lack of money, a multiplicity of self-duplicating institutions – these complaints recur again and again in the ritual incantations of what was wrong. But professors also wrote to defend the universities against attack, even at such intellectually leading institutions as Göttingen. Students took little active role in university politics, as they did at the end of the Napoleonic wars. Even so, there were many signs of student unrest, such as the serious rioting in Halle in 1796 and 1797. The emergence of the *Burschenschaften* or reformed student fraternities after 1800 was also indicative of ferment and dissatisfaction among students. For the first time, the rough and fundamentally antiintellectual values of the old student *Korps* were coming under attack.

A second source of criticisms was the official bureaucracy, either civil or ecclesiastical, charged with responsibility for the universities. The increasing flow of rescripts and orders aimed at reforming university abuses attests both to government awareness of problems and to the failure of previous government decrees to affect the abuses. The Württemburg government, for example, issued a rescript to the professors at Tübingen ordering them to make suggestions for the "amelioration of conditions at the university" in 1767. In the 1780s and 1790s the Landgrave of Hesse and his ministers compiled a huge dossier of complaints about the University of Marburg. The catalog is quite like that everywhere in Germany: abuse of vacation periods, professors not managing to get through their courses, students taking only the basic courses needed to get a job (*Brotstudium*), and so on. The faculty's response to these government reform initiatives was predictable. Marburg's Professor Bering, for example, admitted in his response that things could be better, then proceeded to fill the rest of his memo with praise for what Marburg was doing well.[14]

A third, and most vocal, group of critics was increasingly to be found among pedagogical reformers and other intellectuals outside the universities. They used the rapidly expanding public market in pamphlets and books to raise the issues of educational policy that had begun to sweep Europe, particularly after the appearance of Rousseau's *Emile* (1762), a book that excited the public imagination in Germany even more than it had in France.

In studying the efforts of university professors themselves to effect reforms, one encounters many frustrating examples of good ideas held back by the vested interests of the university communities. The relative ease with which Göttingen and Erlangen were able to adopt a modern curriculum and attract good professors had much to do with the very lack of these vested interests – that is, a torpid faculty jealously guarding its prerogatives – at the new universities. The professorial critiques were not often published, but rather found their way into university and state archives. One of the most extensive published works, and one that began a tradition of similar public critiques by professors, was the fairly moderate examination by the Göttingen professor Johann D. Michaelis.[15] More common were the *Denkschriften* composed by professors, read by other professors and sometimes state officials, and then forgotten. A good example of this genre is the lengthy memorandum of the poet Christoph Martin Wieland, who spent a few frustrating years as a professor at the University of Erfurt (1769–72).[16] In addition to making the usual complaints about the financial condition of the corporation, the laziness and immorality of students, and the irregularity of classroom teaching, this already well-known author proposed reforms to increase the scholarly seriousness of the faculty members themselves. Despite expressions of concern from the officials of the Archbishopric of Mainz (who supervised the university), lack of money and professorial opposition frustrated this and other Erfurt reform proposals.

What limited success professors had in persuading their universities to carry out needed reforms almost always came as a result of their good connections with state education ministries or with the rulers themselves. In this context, a good example might be that of Professor Achateus L. K. Schmid of Jena. When the professors of that universtiy had been asked by the governmental authorities to propose desired changes in 1751, they had been unable to propose any beyond the enforcement of the old regulations. In practice their "reform" proposals tended in the direction of limiting competition for the income and prerogatives of the full professors by such measures as enforcement of religious orthodoxy, prohibiting subjects of the Thüringian states from studying anywhere else, and reducing the number of lower-ranking professors, who lured fee-paying students from their classrooms. Schmid, one of the few Jena professors to see the need for reform, was appointed to a government commission in 1766. He drew up the first comprehensive budget in the history of the university; raised faculty salaries, hoping to induce faculty members to limit their time-consuming dependence on outside sources of income (e.g., giving legal opinions or teaching school); and tried to break the notorious nepotism of the senior professors (one of his "radical" proposals was to count the votes of faculty members belonging to the same family as only one vote).[17]

Another example of reforms carried out through professors and government working together (sometimes against other professors) can be cited in the career of Gerard Van Swieten at the University of Vienna, which quickly became a model for other universities in Catholic Germany, particualrly in the field of medicine. Van Swieten had studied at Louvain and Leyden. His connections with Maria Theresa and her family (as court physician) led to his being invited by the monarch to propose reforms for the medical faculty. These included increased salaries, stricter control of the faculty by a representative of the government, removal of church influence from professorial appointments, and a more rational, bureaucratic system of administration (with Van Swieten himself appointed royal director or curator of the medical faculty).[18] These 1749 reforms were followed by others inaugurated by Van Swieten with the aim of limiting even further the freedom of university professors and of regularizing instruction and regulating it in minute detail, even to the extent of prescribing to the professors what textbooks they must use.

These were modest reforms, but even they would have probably been defeated had it not been for support from powers outside the university in the state bureaucracy. Let us now turn to this second source of reform thinking in the late eighteenth century. In many German states, the crowned heads and their advisers increasingly took on the role of radical reformers, not only in education, but in every matter of public interest. Some of the most dramatic attempts at reform took place in Catholic states that had for generations allowed their universities to vegetate in peace. But in and after the 1760s, many Catholic princes began to press for reforms. They were inspired by the example of Austria, where an increase in the pace of serious university reforms began after Joseph II became coregent with his mother in 1765 and continued until Joseph's death in 1790.

In the case of the University of Vienna, which became one of the leading models for reforms in Germany, the purpose of change was threefold:

> To set up the institutions of study without exception as purely secular organizations by removing all remnants of ecclesiastical tendencies; to declare them . . . primarily and ever more exclusively to be serving the purposes of the state and the civil service; and to use the school as a means of inculcating reforms throughout the territory of the state, in opposition to the church, because the reforms were not regarded as secure or even complete.[19]

In contrast to Göttingen, however, Vienna was placed under a rather rigid state control: Professors were not supposed to deviate from the exact curriculum prescribed by a government commission. The system bore many of the traits that later came to be associated with the Napoleonic university system in France, and full academic freedom and university self-government were not to return to the university until the middle of the nineteenth century.[20] In their harsh attitude toward the power of the Jesuits and in some of their reorganizational thinking, reformers in Germany sometimes copied the Austrian reforms; but they equally often attempted to introduce the kind of freedom of teaching and research associated with the reformed Protestant universities. Indeed, many of the German reformers and the new teaching staff brought in to inject new life were Göttingen alumni.

Consider, for example, the University of Trier. It was opened to reform in the 1760s by Nicholas von Hontheim, the suffragan bishop of Trier and prochancellor of the university. Hontheim was also the author, under the pen name "Febronius," of one of the century's most lethal attacks against papal authority. Hontheim introduced the philosophy of the Enlightenment into the curriculum and placed Göttingen graduates on the faculty.[21]

The University of Mainz, also in the Rhineland, witnessed several reform attempts in the period 1760–90, particularly under the influence of the leading spirit of the educational bureaucracy, Baron A. F. von Benzel, who eventually became chancellor of the archbishopric. Like many other servants of Catholic princes of the time, Benzel was an enemy of the Jesuits, who had controlled Catholic university education up to then. In addition to supporting the dissolution of the order in the German states in 1773, Benzel hired Protestant professors and allowed Jews and Protestants to take degrees.[22]

Other moderately successful reforms in Catholic universities could be mentioned briefly. Würzburg, perhaps academically the best German Catholic university, was constantly being modernized by the ruling Schönborn family and was heavily reformed under the influence of F. L. von Erthal, a leading minister, in the 1780s and 1790s.[23] Baron Franz von Furstenberg, the chief minister in Münster, put his stamp on the newly created University of Münster in 1773, significantly the year of the suppression of the Jesuits. Münster's curriculum tried to combine the ideas of the Enlightenment with Catholic faith, and for a time it was considered one of the best universities in Catholic Germany.[24]

The first curator of the new University of Bonn, Baron F. W. von Spiegel, was not only a Göttingen graduate but a Freemason, empowered to introduce Enlightenment philosophy by his patron, Elector Max Francis, youngest brother of Joseph II.[25] The Bonn academy was raised to the status of a university in order to provide a modern education to the future clerics and state employees of the Archbishopric of Cologne and the surrounding area. The motives have a familiar ring: to prevent local students from attending "foreign" universities (particularly better Protestant ones) for ideological as well as financial reasons; to provide a fashionable, enlightened curriculum (the University of Cologne, the nearby rival, was considered a bastion of backwardness and obscurantism); and to enhance the prestige of a powerful prince at the expense of rivals (in this case, the City of Cologne and its decrepit university). As in the case of the founding of Göttingen, funds were conveniently available (funds for Bonn came from the confiscated property of the suppressed Jesuit Order), and powerful personalities in the government, such as Count Karl Belderbusch, took a strong personal interest in university matters.[26] The planners of Bonn were strongly and consciously influenced by the models of Göttingen and Vienna.[27]

Yet for each university that attempted reform in the decades just before the French Revolution, there were many others where no initiatives for change occurred or where conservative resistance by professors prevented full reform. The frustration of the government of Weimar in dealing with Jena well illustrates the dilemma of reform-minded bureaucracies elsewhere. Goethe, who advised the Saxe-Weimar government on educational matters, also mocked and laughed at the backward usages and corruptions of Jena. Goethe's patron, Grand Duke Charles August, called upon friends in the university, such as Professor Justus Christian Loder, to keep him informed of the true state of the university and to carry out the government's will as far as possible. The formal channels of university governance were ignored insofar as possible by the officials in Weimar. Indeed, reform of Jena was impeded even further by the peculiar copatronage over the university of all major Thüringian princes, none of whom wished to increase their financial commitments any more than to give up their jealously guarded "rights" as patrons. Miraculously, the Weimar officials often managed to circumvent this suspicious and niggardly attitude

of the other Thüringian states. Even so, despite the good will
of the government and the excellence of such ministers as Goethe, the dead hand of tradition could only be squeezed, not
broken, at Jena. The older professors continued to defend their
privileges. New appointments, especially of brilliant younger
men, such as Fichte, the Schlegels, Schelling, and Schiller, only
undermined their already tenuous hold on the loyalty of their
students, who would surely abandon second-rate teachers
when given a chance to follow a real star with their notebooks
and lecture fees.

In the end, reform at Jena resulted in a sort of cold war
between the Weimar government and the older Jena faculty
members. The latter blocked much change, but the former
increasingly ignored them. In order to get around the faculty's
right to nominate full professors, the government appointed
mostly *Extraordinarien* or associate professors, positions the
government funded and therefore controlled. Thanks to this
unremitting pressure from the enlightened ministry of Saxe-
Weimar, Jena improved and became for a short time at the end
of the eighteenth century one of the intellectually leading universities of Europe, particularly in philosophy. But the gains
were temporary, for the university was not thoroughly reformed. Professors continued to fear the loss of their income
and power and even resisited government efforts to improve
discipline and the moral tenor of student life, which was disso-
lute and sometimes violent, because they feared discipline
would drive the students (and their fees) away to other, more
easygoing schools.

The reforms emanating from the bureaucracy were very
often motivated by practical considerations, no matter how
fashionably enlightened their tone might be. A very strong
utilitarian current was perceptible in the thinking of most "enlightened" bureaucrats by the 1780s and the drift of their
thinking was toward changing or even abolishing the traditional university model in favor of the specialty school. Technological advances had brought about the foundation of the

first technical schools in the eighteenth century, and much of the reforming effort directed at the universities strove to upgrade specialized education in medicine and law. With the decline of theology as the "queen science" holding together a scholastic curriculum, reformers could seriously question whether there was any point in the "unity of knowledge" that gave the universities their organizational form and raison d'etre.

The Berlin Mittwochgesellschaft, a secret society of intellectuals and civil servants, debated in 1795 the question whether universities should be abolished. The argument against universities was similar in most respects to the ones used by Campe and other radical abolitionists of the time discussed later in this section. The main advocate of abolition, Pastor J. G. Gebhard, argued that what universities did at all well could be done better in specialty schools and that the universities caused so much damage to the moral well-being of students that they could not justify their existence.[28] Significantly, most of the society's members who took a written position disagreed with Gebhard. Although they admitted that many weaknesses and abuses existed, they were not in agreement about how to solve them, except that abolition was not the answer. One of the main ideas for reform concerned university members' immunity to prosecution by the civic courts and the laxity of university courts, both of which resulted in scandalous student crimes that virtually went unpunished. Another area of concern was the monopoly of the faculties over certain fields of knowledge and, in particular, the traditionally leading role of theology and the subordinate one of philosophy. Most of these men shared the view of Kant expressed in his *Streit der Fakultäten* (1798) that the philosophical faculties had become important enough to deserve equality. The main respondent, Dean (*Probst*) Teller, demanded specific reforms:"The monastic division into faculties, in which philosophy walks behind like a handmaiden, should cease; everyone should be able to lecture on whatever he wants; students should be subjected to regular civil jurisdiction; and those who want to attend the university should be tested more carefully as to their talents and prior knowledge."[29]

At the same time, however, the members defended the universities as useful institutions, not only because they were the best and most convenient way to transmit a knowledge of the arts and sciences (members ridiculed the idea of autodidacticism), but because the arts and sciences were so dependent on the universities that they "would fall without the latter."[30] If this collection of comments by Berlin intellectuals and high government officials (including Nicolai, Biester, and Svarez) is typical of the attitudes toward universities at the end of the eighteenth century, one can see that general dissatisfaction and a widespread criticism of the institutions of higher learning did not necessarily rise to the point of calling for abolition; instead, reform was the word most employed in this particular debate.

While the state officials pondered the traditional form of the German university and weighed other ways of transmitting a modern higher education, some German publicists went even further in their demands, especially in the last decades before the French Revolution. So great was the interest in pedagogical reform that entire journals sprang up to service the public's interest. One of the most interesting of these was the *Allgemeine Revision der gesammten Schul- und Erziehungswesens,* published in Hamburg from 1785 onward. The contributors, who included Johann Heinrich Campe, were mostly students of the new pedagogy exemplified by the reformer Basedow, whose *Philanthropinum* school had provided a controversial model for radical pedagogical reform. Most of the efforts of the reformers and critics associated with Campe dwelt on the elementary and secondary schools, but they did take time to denounce roundly the abuses of the universities and often called for their abolition.

Campe himself opened his major critique of the German universities with the question, "Do universities do more good than harm?" He clearly believed the answer to be no. Universities, Campe maintained, ruined the morality of students: "The best young people are, if not destroyed completely, at least made wild at universities and return from them weakened in body and soul and are lost to themselves and the world." He was clearly pessimistic about the very possibility of reform: "To change the nature of the universities means to abolish them." Campe dismissed the argument that students from different classes learned to live and work together at universities; rather, he said, the poorer students learned to ape the richer ones and thereby made themselves miserable. Whatever is learned at universities, he argued, could be learned outside them, more cheaply and conveniently, and without the ruination of morals. Academies of science could better deal with the propagation and discovery of truth, but even they were not necessary, because genuine scholars could work without such organizational frameworks.[31]

Mockery of the traditional German universities became almost a staple of the budding German literature of the period, from such long-winded early novels as Salzmann's obscure academic epic, *Karl von Karlsberg,* to such world-renowned pieces as Goethe's *Faust.* Added to the traditional denunciations of abuses cataloged by earlier critics, however, were suggestions for alternative forms of higher education that would liberate the student soul from the purgatory of a meaningless pedantic curriculum and would train the mind for the practical tasks of later life. Aware of the difficulty of reforming the universities, and seeing virtually no good in them, radicals of the 1780s urged their dissolution. The most eloquent defenders of the university idea were, significantly, professors and alumni of the new, reformed universities, notably Göttingen.[32] Their influence was not insignificant, considering that many later university reformers (such as Wilhelm von Humboldt) had been strongly impressed with the viability of modernized universities during student years at Göttingen. Those who tried to explain and justify the university as a type of educational institution were, to be sure, on the defensive in the late eighteenth century; but in contrast to the situation at the beginning of the century, the universities had at least some defenders.

The German professoriate

The professoriate, as we have already seen, was not noted for leadership in the movement to reform German universities, although many of the counterattacks against university abolitionists did originate from professorial pens. Would it be fair to conclude that the professoriate was entrenched in a conservative posture, unwilling and unable to change age-old customs even when they had become corrupt? Such a conclusion, however warranted on the surface, would obscure certain developments that were in effect favoring the emergence of a new kind of professoriate. The crisis of the German universities, given a final acceleration by the external events of the Napoleonic wars, coincided with the crystallization of new attitudes toward higher education, science, and philosophy, so that there was a new intellectual cement ready to rejoin the pieces of the shattered German university system after the blows of French armies and decrees. Both inside and outside the professoriate there were men who adhered to a conception of the teacher–scholar more attuned to today's notion than had been the case among earlier eighteenth-century thinkers. Even though this conception had by no means won out in the academic world, one can perceive the beginnings of its spreading influence at the end of the eighteenth century. (Some of the most precise statements of this new conception of the duties of the professoriate will be discussed in Chapter 4 in connection with the debates preceding the founding of the University of Berlin.)

The size and growth of the professoriate in the late eighteenth century are difficult to determine exactly. The full professors numbered 658 in the non-Austrian parts of the German Empire in 1796 (791 including the six Austrian universities), according to one estimate. In 1758, twenty-four German universities (excluding Austrian ones) for which data are available had a total of 539 *Ordinarien*.[33] This figure constituted a 22 percent increase in thirty-eight years; some universities as much as doubled their chairs for *Ordinarien*, whereas most grew only slowly and some actually had fewer full professors. The full professors of the Prussian universities increased about 35 percent between 1775 and 1804.³⁴ The total of all professors, including *Extraordinarien,* is uncertain, but there are good reasons to suspect that many universities shared the tendency of Jena and Göttingen to appoint more men of this rank: There was an increasing supply of qualified applicants, it cost much less money, and it often brought a fresh breeze of new thinking into the musty halls of the corporate *Ordinarienuniversität.*

One estimate holds the number of extraordinary professors to have been about 86 in 1758 (with only 38 *Privatdozenten*); by 1796, the number had grown to 141 *Extraordinarien* (and 86 *Privatdozenten*) in all German universities. Even so, together they constituted only about one-quarter of the teaching staff in 1796, whereas they would be one-half by 1840.³⁵

The turnover rate among "extraordinary" professors was considerably higher than among full professors. The university archives of Germany indicate that several appointments to the junior rank were made for every one to the senior rank. This was because the extraordinary professorship was not really a secure rank in the academic hierarchy. It served two major functions for its holders: It was either a waiting post for a full professorship or a second job next to some activity in the wider community. Almost no *Extraordinarius* could live on his salary and fees at the end of the eighteenth century. Thus the rank was subject to a number of pressures that caused higher turnover. Some *Extraordinarien* left their posts in order to take full professorships, sometimes outside their own institutions, but more typically within them. The process of *Aufrücken* or moving up as full professors died, retired, or left was a hallowed practice of German universities. Even as late as the late eighteenth century, more than half the associate professors went on to become full professors at Tübingen in this manner.³⁶

The vast majority of full professors at Halle also came up through the ranks in the last decades of the eighteenth century, and most were locally recruited at that. Quite typically at

Halle, a young man would be recommended (or even would recommend himself) for an *Extraordinarius* position; commonly, the most important question asked would be whether he had good *Applaus,* that is, was a good and popular lecturer. When a full professorship opened (usually not too many years later), the *Extraordinarius* would apply for it and often receive it; nationwide searches were the exception even at the end of the century. A few examples from Halle may give some flavor of the process. S. F. G. Wahl, previously a school rector, was appointed associate professor of Oriental languages at Halle in 1788 after being recommended by the Prussian Oberschulkollegium and the Department of Foreign Affairs. The former had been impressed by the textbooks Wahl had submitted to it in his pleas for a job, and the latter pressured Halle to hire him because the department wished to improve the teaching of Persian and Arabic to better relations with the Near East. J. C. Bathe was appointed to an associate professorship in law in 1788 because, as a local attorney, he had given some lectures and was good at it. Nine years later, he was appointed to a chair. J. K. L. Mencken, another lawyer, began as a tutor to local boys preparing for state legal examinations, petitioned the Oberschulkollegium in Berlin to give him a professorship, and received one in 1787; he was promoted to a chair in 1789, not because of any merits as a scholar or writer, but because he was being rewarded for his work with the Prussian Administrationscollegium.[37] Some of the careers of these "extraordinary" professors were indeed odd. Consider J. C. C. Rüdiger, an assessor in the state salt administration in Halle, who partitioned repeatedly for an appointment as an associate professor. He was turned down several times but finally received the desired appointment and, in the same year, was promoted to full professor (on the death of a senior colleague). The historian of the university notes, however, that Rüdiger was a wretched lecturer, knew little about his subject (economics), and finally went mad.[38]

The archives of other Prussian universities in the last two

decades of the eighteenth century reveal a similar pattern. At Königsberg, the government had forbidden professors to hold *Nebenämter,* or second jobs, in a well-meaning effort to force the professoriate to pay its full measure of attention to academic affairs; but the government did not take the next logical step and increase the salaries of the professors. At Königsberg toward the end of the century, four hundred thaler was the highest salary. In one typical recruitment action, a local lawyer, A. W. Heidemann, applied repeatedly for the fourth chair in law and as late as 1802 was offered a salary of 68 thaler.[39] Sometimes, when the local representative of the government was a strong personality, the normally slack and rather inbred recruitment process received an injection of orderliness, as was the case with Erlangen University's appointments around the beginning of the nineteenth century, while Hardenberg was the Prussian governor of Bayreuth. But even there, the applicants' scholarly and research accomplishments were not usually the most important criteria for hirings.[40]

Even at Göttingen the principle of selection according to scholarly merit as a prime criterion was not absolute in the late eighteenth century. A prosopographical study of the members of the university's philosophical faculty in 1765–6 has shown that Göttingen professors published heavily, but that many of their publications were "works which the nineteenth century would never have called *wissenschaftlich.*"[41] The average number of publications by the nineteen philosophical faculty members for whom information was available was five at the time of first appointment and about ten at the time of promotion to full professor.[42] But the quality of these publications was uneven, consisting of such diverse works as collected sermons, encyclopedic compendia, disputations, and literary works. Steven Turner concluded that at most eight of the nineteen professors he studied could be considered to have met the standards of later, nineteenth-century scholarship, that is, to have advanced the frontiers of knowledge through the application of critical methods of research and analysis.[43]

At about the same time, Wieland considered less than one-quarter of the philosophical professors at Erfurt to have achieved any fame through their writings; at Ingolstadt, two-thirds of the members of the philosophical faculty had published little or nothing.[44] Good teaching and such collegial values as popularity in the university or what we would now call "service" were obviously just as important as scholarship if one looks at *all* the professors.

On the other hand, one probably receives a distorted impression from the activities of members of the philosophical faculties at the middle of the eighteenth century. It was still the junior partner in the university, lacking prestige, paying the lowest salaries, and attracting the fewest students.

In the other faculties, theology, medicine, and law, nineteenth-century standards of *Wissenschaft* would have left these fields appearing somewhat "unscientific" even in the early nineteenth century. Yet it would be incorrect to say that there was no increase in the quality and quantity of useful studies and even discoveries in the late eighteenth century. Law was still a systematic rather than a scientific, discovery-oriented discipline in 1800, on the eve of the development of the historical school of law. To some extent, this is still true of legal studies today. But the very systematization of legal studies was a step forward, and many of the complaint of observers around 1700 about the lack of system and practical application in legal studies had been answered a century later. Legal faculties throughout the century had "found" law in the sense that they were often asked to serve as *Spruchkollegien,* pooling their expertise to give governments and sometimes private individuals opinions on legal questions. These opinions were held in high regard and influenced the evolution of German law. Even though various German governments attempted to restrict the activities of these *Spruchkollegien,* starting in the 1750s, they continued to operate successfully down to the time of Napoleonic conquest.[45]

The activities of eighteenth-century university theologians, while largely mired in tradition, did produce a revolution in the interpretation of sacred texts and church history; indeed, the basis of excellence of early nineteenth-century philosophical inquiry (philology, history) was laid by the work of certain theological seminars such as those as Göttingen and Halle.

In medicine, the end of the eighteenth century witnessed a number of respectable developments in clinical practice and discoveries important to better health care. Yet medical men still tended to transmit these discoveries and techniques as much in their textbooks and clinical demonstrations within the context of university teaching as in publications in medical journals, which were still poorly developed as a forum for scientific discussion.

Undeniably, then, the professoriate at most German universities at the end of the eighteenth century compares unfavorably with the professoriate two or three generations later, if one makes scientific publication the main criterion of scholarly activity. Yet the relative lack of large, well-organized disciplinary communities and specialized journals intended to serve them does not in itself suggest that there was no growth in scientific and critical scholarly activity in German universities. Although this lack inhibited publication, it did not necessarily imply the absence of scholarly exchange. Late eighteenth-century scholars did travel and speak to their counterparts elsewhere, and they sent manuscripts to one another. Creative scholarship and scientific inquiry were certainly made more laborious and isolated activities by the lack of convenient national journals for specialized publication, but they were certainly not rendered impossible.

A necessary step prior to the establishment of professionalized, academic journals was the creation of journals of a more general sort and the cultivation of a public interested in advances in science, scholarship, and the arts. In this area the late eighteenth century witnessed considerable activity, and the universities, far from showing hostility to these new journals, were rather inclined to serve as their backbones.[46] Many of the leading serious journals of late eighteenth-century Germany had some connection with universities. The *Göttingische Gelehrten Anzeigen* was one of the most important and durable. But many of the other new journals that sprang up after about 1770 had connections with the universities. One of the first new ones, the *Deutsche Merkur,* was founded by Wieland in 1773 after he had given up trying to reform the university of Erfurt. Göttingen professors had a large hand in the journals *Staatsanzeigen* and *Göttingisches Historisches Magazin.* Leipzig professors wrote for the *Deutsches Museum.* Cotta's important *Allgemeine Zeitung* was first established in Tübingen in 1798. These journals were an important forum and often a means of gaining a reputation both for the university and for the faculty. Jena's *Litteraturzeitung,* for example, founded in 1785 by Professor Schütz, was "the common organ of the younger Jena professors . . . [and] regarded its task as being to make known Kantian philosophy and, more generally, modern currents of intellectual life, and to criticize new works from this point of view."[47] The journals also constituted an important source of income, particularly for the younger teachers. That they had to write for a living rather than pursue research pure and simple is perhaps regrettable (as nineteenth-century observers remarked), but the intellectual demands placed on young professors, the encouragement given to creativity by literary activity, and the possibility of earning a living by doing something connected with scholarship rather than schoolteaching or professional practice must not be dismissed as unimportant in the shaping of new ideas about the university professoriate.

There were also increasingly some substitutes for the later, professionalized public forum of the discipline community toward the end of the eighteenth century. The multiplying literary and intellectual salons of many German cities offered places where ideas could be aired, exchanged, and criticized. Goethe's home in Weimar served as a nationwide clearinghouse of ideas and of social connections between learned men and potential benefactors; quite a few young academics launched their professorial careers or furthered them dramatically as a result of contact with Goethe's intellectual court. The city of Berlin and indeed all German towns with any self-respect had reading circles that served as the focus of local intellectual life: Readers of different social strata (but primarily the nobles and burghers) and even different sexes met there. Berlin's more famous ones included the Monday Club (founded by Nicolai, Lessing, and others), the Society of Friends of the Natural Sciences, the Monday Society, the successive Wednesday Clubs, the Friday Club, and the Society of Friends of Humanity, all operating in the 1790s.[48] We would today regard these circles and salons as "interdisciplinary" at best and quite amateurish at worst, in terms of today's scholarly and scientific values; but our own values and methods are to a large extent a response to scientific and scholarly specialization, a phenomenon that occurred almost in geometric progression in the late nineteenth and twentieth centuries, but that can hardly be expected to be found around 1800. Instead, intellectuals still believed in the unity of all knowledge, and so they saw nothing unprofessional or damaging to the progress of *Wissenschaft* in discussing their views over wine and tea at the salon of some German grande dame.

The professorship was still not a fully developed career at the end of the eighteenth century, but it was tending in that direction. Since the early part of the century, standards for admission to the professoriate had tightened somewhat. *Habilitation* was beginning to be taken more seriously, at least at the best German universities, and was no longer a mere formality (retained mostly to bolster the power of the faculty and to yield fees), as it had been around 1700. The number of *Privatdozenten,* not to mention their quality, had probably increased slightly through the century, and *Extraordinarien,* too, were increasing in number. Many of the full professors came from these positions, which meant that a certain career pattern can be observed. Yet it is hard to discover to what extent criteria for movement up the professorial hierarchy were hardening. University archives contain reviews of the qualifications of younger and middle-aged scholars for professorships that do sometimes mention the scientific standing and publications of a candidate, but not as often as the qualities of the candidate as a teacher. Even a full professorship still did not pay enough, on the average, to make it a career objective par excellence. One can thus agree with Alexander Busch when he writes of the late eighteenth century: "A university teacher, and certainly a *Privatdozent,* but also a clergyman, lawyer, or doctor was that only secondarily. Primary stood his character as a savant [Gelehrter], who earned his living in various professions and did not require the activity within the walls of the university in order to show that he was a savant."[49] Yet despite the very looseness of the characteristics that sociologists identify with professions, the professoriate at the end of the eighteenth century was somewhat closer to professional status than it had been a century before, and at some universities, notably Göttingen, the signs of change were very strong indeed.

The universities and the economy

Whatever the variations and degree of gains, the eighteenth century does not appear to have been one of economic boom in Germany. Still primarily an agrarian society, Germany had to face the cruel Malthusian problem of a rapidly growing population and a relatively slow-growing food supply. Despite considerable efforts by the German states to stimulate commerce and manufactures through mercantilistic policies, and despite some successes with these policies, the German population and the German states were still poor at the end of the eighteenth century. Costly wars, crushing taxes, and all sorts of economic restrictions conspired to brake economic development, even though the enlightened bureaucracy was increasingly persuaded that something must be done (and turned to Adam Smith for relief in the late decades of the century).

Considering this general economic situation, the ill repute of

unreformed universities did nothing to encourage greater outlays of money so sorely needed elsewhere. Yet lack of money
was what most university professors and administrators identified as the root cause of all the universities' other troubles.
Various professors at the University of Rostock responded to a
government rescript ordering them actually to hold their public lectures (those free of fees) with the complaint that their
salaries, low as they were, were seldom actually paid. Thus
professors at Rostock (and many another university) were
obliged to concentrate on their "secondary" jobs, practices,
and so on, in order to survive.[50] Even when the salaries were
paid more regularly, they were inadequate. Given the considerable rise in prices throughout the century, a stationary university budget meant an actual worsening of financial conditions. Prussia increased its outlay for all its universities from
only twenty-six thousand thaler in 1697 to thirty-three thousand at the death of Frederick the Great in 1786, and even the
ten thousand thaler added to the state university budget in the
next year did not solve the basic problems.[51]

At Leipzig University, still one of the largest and most prestigious in Germany, the total budget for professorial salaries was
just under 3,000 thaler in 1765. Leipzig had something over
forty professors at that time (nearly half of them in the philosophical faculty, which received under 1,000 thaler in total for
salaries).[52] Full professors with some time in rank (e.g., the
"first" and "second" professors in a given faculty) received
between 100 and 180 thaler at this time. A quarter century
later, salaries had not increased appreciably. The top Leipzig
professor received a salary of 224 thaler; others received salaries in the low 100s. Of course fees and fringe payments of
various kinds increased these amounts by two or three times.[53]
The salary budget constituted more than half the state's outlay
for higher education at most universities until well into the
nineteenth century. Even doubling Leipzig's salary budget to
arrive at something like total state outlays, one achieves the
figure of only 6,000 thaler or a little over 1,000 pounds sterling.

At Göttingen, the professoriate was better paid than at any other university. Rough budget drafts for the first years show that Münchhausen was reckoning with outlays for salaries ranging between 17,000 and (later) 23,000 thaler.[54] The latter figure was close to the entire amount of the Prussian state budget for *all* its universities at the same time. Nevertheless, even relatively well-funded Göttingen was poor compared to some universities abroad. Paulsen, for example, estimated that Oxford had at least one hundred times the annual income of Halle in the eighteenth century, and Halle was one of the best-funded German universities after Göttingen.[55]

One must, of course, be aware that the eighteenth-century universities were still not thoroughly integrated into the financial existence of the state, or even into the money economy. Most universities drew income from land and other forms of endowment. Until late in the seventeenth century, university professors had lived largely from prebends and fees, not their salaries. Even as the prebend system died away and the state intervened more and more in the financial (and of course administrative and political) life of the universities in the course of the eighteenth century, the older universities still relied heavily on their endowments of various kinds. Göttingen was in fact the first German university to have no endowment at all and thus be totally dependent on state budgets and student fees for its maintenance.[56]

It is not easy to describe university economics in the eighteenth century with any high degree of accuracy. Professorial salaries and state outlays for them constituted only a part, and in most cases a minor part, of the universities' financial affairs. The complexity of their finances derives from the mixed system employing both aspects of the modern and residues of pre-money economies. Many universities in the eighteenth century still remunerated professors with goods and privileges, for example, in addition to salaries, fees, honoraria, and other forms of money income. Firewood, food products turned over to the university by a tenant farmer, or licenses to the professors to maintain beer and wine cellars for public sales were examples of common nonmonetary remuneration. These rewards fluctuated from year to year in many cases (for example, depending on the size of the harvest), and so their worth as a total part of the university's finances cannot be calculated precisely. Moreover, university financial records in this period were not well kept. Judging by the hefty correspondence from university professors begging for salary increases or bonuses, which constitutes the vast majority of letters in professorial files of the eighteenth century, the rewards for teaching, whether in money or in kind, were far from satisfactory.

Not only the size of university budgets (always too small) but the confusion and inefficiency of this traditional mixed system led to dissatisfaction. The costs of running universities were increasing in the eighteenth century, and the universities were unable to increase their income from their endowments. Overseeing their finances was not easy, owing to the complexity of accounts, and the bother of administering these was increasingly unwelcome to the universities. For these reasons and because dependency on increasing government subsidies seemed to offer the only way out of financial need, the states demanded and the universities gave up without much struggle the right to administer university finances.[57]

Turning to the state for salvation from economic perils of the time constitutes one of the most important results of the general university crisis of the eighteenth century. Although it did not destroy the "corporate" nature of the German universities, it weakened it in vital ways. From the late eighteenth century on, state involvement in financing and administering universities grew rapidly. The professoriate no longer had the wide-ranging freedom to decide its own affairs autonomously, as it had enjoyed when the university was a "corporation" more closely tied to the church than to the state. In appointments, curriculum, regulations for students and faculty, criteria for awarding degrees, discipline, and other areas of university life, the state gained the upper hand as a result of the universities' poverty and inability to overcome it without the aid of the *Polizeistaat* or paternalist state. The professor was more and more a civil servant (though a peculiar one) and less and less a member of a *Korporation*. Many of the struggles between university faculties and governments in the early nineteenth century were to be over corporate rights, such as the right of the professors to suggest candidates for chairs. In the late eighteenth century, however, such struggles were rare. Because governments did not yet view universities as subversive of the status quo, they did not control their intellectual life very strictly. Instead, the states were beginning to clean up university finances and see to it that the campuses were run in an orderly, bureaucratic manner. Attacks on certain corporate abuses in certain of the universities were also clearly an aid to the long-range improvement of teaching and upgrading of the prestige of research.

One interconnection between the universities and the broader economy ought to be stressed, if only because the debate about it tended to set the tone for the nineteenth century. The doctrines of mercantilism had become so pervasive in the German states that by the time governments began assuming more responsibility and administrative control over the universities, the governments tended to regard universities at least partially in utilitarian, cost–benefit terms. We have already seen an example of mercantilistic thinking in the previous chapter in connection with the calculations surrounding the foundation of Göttingen. Michaelis, for example, listed the *Cameralnutzen* (cameralistic advantages) of founding Göttingen as the best reason to go on with the project. Religion and the sciences were already looked after well enough, he reasoned, but other universities did not improve Hanover's balance of trade.[58] Toward the end of the eighteenth century, governments no longer thought of universities so much as mercantilistic enterprises; but they did begin to think of them as a part of the broader economy in other ways. The link between education and economic prosperity was being explored. As utilitarian and secular thinking about higher education replaced traditional and religious justifications, the university came to be viewed by many governments as more or less a collection of specialty schools conveniently located in the same place. Indeed, it is safe to say that the dominant organizational mode in higher education at the end of the eighteenth century was that of the specialized school. Not only were universities facing competition from entirely new types of schools (military, medical, and technological) founded in the late part of the century, but they were under pressure to reorganize themselves and justify their curriculum as contributing "useful knowledge" that would advance society and produce wealth.

University and society at the end of the eighteenth century

As we have seen throughout this survey of eighteenth-century German university life, it was characterized by ongoing lethargy, decline, and frequent crises. Taken as a whole, German universities were losing students, facing chronic financial problems, coming under increased attack from public opinion, and showing limited willingness to change. Against this somber picture, however, we saw contrasting flashes of reform. The will to change was present, if not predominant or always successful. Reformed universities, such as Göttingen, Halle, and Erlangen, suffered less from the general university crises than unreformed ones. Many of the latter were swept away in the hurricane of change inaugurated by the French reorganization of Germany. Yet many others survived, either because, like Göttingen, they warranted respect even in the eyes of the French conquerors, who had abolished their own decayed universities, or because they bowed to the need for reform and busied themselves at last in that direction. The French themselves did not carry out these reforms: Indeed, they simply shut the German universities in the Rhineland conquered in the first wave of attack on the empire. It was the Germans themselves who carried out these reforms after 1800.

One of the most intriguing questions about university history in this period of Napoleonic conquest is why the Germans chose a future for their system of higher education different from that of the French. The obvious and simple answer is that the Germans had more confidence in the possibility of reform and in the necessity of retaining the university format. State and society endorsed the universities, although often grudgingly and on condition of significant changes. In Germany the universities had become more and more state institutions, even in the church states, whereas in France their continued connection with the church had exposed them to danger from the claims of the revolutionary state. Equally important, however, was the degree of support from German society or, more specifically, important elements in it.

As we have seen, the German nobility took a positive attitude toward at least the reformed universities. Their patronage, connected with pressures from governments, undoubtedly raised the attractiveness of university education for certain strata of the bourgeoisie, as well. There were definite limits to the potential for aristocratic patronage and interest, and many of the pioneering traits of reforming universities cannot be traced from them. The institution of the seminar, which eventually came to be a hallmark of German university education in the nineteenth century, owed more to the needs of bourgeois theology students than to those of the nobles. And the majority of law students and cameralists remained non-noble in social origin. It is also difficult to make an argument for any special class origins of neo-humanism, or of the revival of the philosophical faculties, an area in which late eighteenth-century Göttingen was a leader. Neo-humanism may well have had a social character, especially with the generalization of *Gymnasium* education among the bourgeoisie in the nineteenth century, but it cannot be proved that it had a *class* character, adhering to only one class.

What one can argue is that many new universities were founded with the role of nobles and other *Vornehme* as a sine qua non for their existence. One may also argue that Göttingen, at least, succeeded beyond the wildest dreams of its founders and ultimately served as the model for more "bourgeois" institutions, such as the University of Berlin. Yet the formula that won the admiration of Humboldt and other later reformers (many of whom had attended Göttingen) had been created especially to attract nobles, and the style of academic culture it stood for was on a much different level from that of the traditional university. If Göttingen became a model for general university reform, it was not because the university gave up its noble-tailored curriculum, but because the non-noble students attended it with this style in mind. Michaelis could argue in the 1760s that financially poor students should be *discouraged* from studying at the university, because, in effect, the employment market was too narrow to accommodate them afterwards. But he was careful to rule out *excluding* them. He gave as his reason the unhealthy effect exclusion would have on social cohesion – on the "useful emulation of the wealthy."[59] In throwing out this casual explanation, which must have seemed obvious enough to eighteenth-century pragmatists, Michaelis delivered a clue to the success of reformed universities in drawing new support.

The new middle class of eighteenth-century Germany, which Mack Walker refers to as "movers and doers," was departing from the standard pattern of middle-class higher education in its way almost as much as the nobles who attended Göttingen. Although it is hard to imagine that Münchhausen and other members of the exclusive old nobility of Hanover would have desired it, Göttingen forged a new kind of education that was able to bend the edges of *Stand* limits and prepare the way for a new stratum in German society. This stratum, too small to be a "class," nevertheless achieved a commanding position in Germany through its manipulation of the administrative system, specifically the state, the church, and the professions. Wilhelm Roessler has pointed out the rise of this new stratum (which he calls, too vaguely, the "educated class") and has argued that the aristocracy was the first provider of its members in the early eighteenth century. He sees in the fusion of the "scholarly" and traditionally "ruling" classes the beginnings of a "rationalization" of noble authority in the form of systematic administrative training.[60] Roessler further argues that the self-image of the new middle class (which was primarily responsible for the revival of German culture in the late eighteenth century) set it apart from the traditional middle class, and that it emulated the nobility more than any other class, not only in domestic architecture, servant employment, and so on, but in a cosmopolitan knowledge of the world and life-style.[61]

Much contemporary evidence from the late eighteenth century itself argues that the perception of social distance between the nobility and at least the "new" middle class, and therefore the barriers to a degree of emulation, were diminishing. Göttingen professors themselves remarked on this phenomenon.[62] Contemporary literature such as Goethe's *Wilhelm Meister* indicates that the new *Bildungsbürgertum* regarded *education* as the most promising path toward a narrowing of social distance between itself and the nobility it admired. Although one cannot argue that social distance diminished in fact (we simply do not know about intermarriage rates and other such indicators), the perception of narrowed distance has interesting connotations for the history of higher education. A generation or so after the opening of Göttingen and a generation or so before the opening of Berlin, university training had become fashionable again. Its ideology was that of professional training coupled with "modern" social and literary graces, practical utility with social exclusiveness. The broad middle class did not yet give its allegiance to the new reformed university, judging by the conjunction of stagnant enrollments and rising population. Indeed, purely utilitarian voices clamored for the dissolution of the traditional university form into more professionally channeled school (as actually happened in France after the Revolution). The main rationale for retaining the university format centered on the humanistic function of the philosophical faculty, which had already begun its meteoric rise at several reformed universities.

The philosophical faculty at Göttingen, for example, was preeminently responsible for the shift of emphasis in "gentlemanly" education from external to internal values, from *galant,* "modern" dilettantism to a serious philosophical commitment to *Bildung.* This process cannot be discussed here. One should keep in mind, however, that the urgent preoccupation of the later Berlin reformers with "philosophical" training at both the *Gymnasium* and the university levels ran in somewhat the same direction as that of the Göttingen reformers decades before. The differences must not be forgotten. But the notion that there was a *Bildungsgut* or fund of knowledge and thinking techniques, which every "truly educated" man must have, ran counter to the purely professionalizing tendencies of many Enlightenment institutions (and those set up by Napoleon in France). The Berlin reformers, to be sure, suppressed crass references to the *class* they wished to attract, and seemed generally less conscious of social divisions than their predecessors at Göttingen. But the type of study they proposed to make obligatory for the future *Bildungsschicht* tacitly implied leisure, solid (and expensive) schooling, and early exposure to a refined life-style. These were the characteristics of noblemen and children from wealthy and educated families. Even a casual glance at matriculation lists of the eighteenth and nineteenth centuries shows how drastically the poorest class of students, *pauperes,* dwindled over time. Seventy-three years after the founding of Göttingen, the founders of Berlin University spoke and wrote of an educational ideal that was far from a copy of Göttingen's. Yet the purposes and aims they set were almost unthinkable outside the context of earlier university reform. Above all, the lofty tone of the Berlin reformers contrasted with the practical one of Münchhausen. The former had so internalized and idealized the benefits of university education that they now called it "noble" in the moral sense. Nor was the titled aristocracy so conspicuous in Berlin, overwhelmed as it was by the crushing size of Germany's largest student body. Yet Berlin was far from being the foundation of a resurgent middle class. If its founders thought less in class terms than had the men of the early eighteenth century, it was because they had learned the thought habits of the "educated class," one composed of both nobles and bourgeois, dedicated to the administration of the state and organized culture, and hostile to the "philistine" and ordinary style of both the commercial bourgeoisie and the crude titled bumpkins of East Elbia.

The tremendous aura of prestige that surrounded universities in Germany from the founding of Berlin on was not merely a reflection of their scientific achievements. Equally, it derived from their association with the small elite class that directed, supervised, and initiated so much through the bureaucratic structures of the German states. It is likely that these states would have developed some other higher educational system equally serviceable to the reigning bureaucracy, had the Göttingen reform model with its stress on gentlemanly, philosophical education not been available. They could have set up specialized schools, as in France, to train their elites and create a shared ethos among them. The end results for scientific and scholarly achievement might have been far less, but German elites might have been somewhat more open. The salvation of the German universities, even though it cost the price of reform, was possible partly because a few German universities had been able to ally themselves with powerful social forces and meet their needs. Few universities elsewhere before 1789 had been able to do this. The long-lasting impact of German universities on educational systems abroad is well known. It should thus give cause for thought that the origins of the modern university system in Germany appear to have been bound up with an attempt to stabilize and legitimate the rule of the more flexible part of the aristocracy with the aid of a small elite recruited from the middle class.

PART II

The Humboldt era

4

Revolutionary upheavals
and the rise of Berlin

The modest progress of university reform in the German states in the later eighteenth century yielded to a period of catastrophic change in the era of the wars of the French Revolution and Napoleon beginning in the 1790s. Three basic responses to the problems of universities emerged at this time, all of them significant for the German university system of the nineteenth century.

One response to the French Revolution was a growing suspicion and hostility toward reform among many governments. In the Rhenish church states, in the Austrian domains after the accession of Francis I, in Prussia under the Wöllner regime, and elsewhere, cultural policies swiftly became more conservative; and rapid change, in the universities as elsewhere, became unfashionable. Where reform measures had been introduced, as for example in the new University of Bonn or at Jena, they were abandoned or attenuated.

A second response was to close universities, especially those that had been chronically weak. French occupation armies, reflecting the hostility of the Revolution to universities, forced some of these closings; German authorities, often in the wake of the rapid territorial reorganization of the German states, closed others. Trier, Cologne, Strasbourg, Bonn, and Mainz were early victims of closings. Erfurt, Wittenberg, Frankfurt/

Oder, Helmstedt, Herborn, Altdorf, Bamberg, Duisburg, and Fulda followed after 1800. Frankfurt/Oder and Wittenberg were consolidated with Breslau and Halle.

During the first decade of the nineteenth century, a third response, that of renewed reform efforts, succeeded the more negative ones. In such newly expanded territorial states as Baden and Bavaria, older universities (Heidelberg, Freiburg, and Ingolstadt/Landshut, for example) were reformed. In Prussia, which had lost Halle, a new university was designed for Berlin and an expanded one for Breslau, and Bonn was revived in a new form after 1815. Even the French preserved the universities of Göttingen and Halle in their new satellite state, the Kingdom of Westphalia, where educational reform was a major objective of the regime.

The rise of suspicion about the political views of university members was a new factor in German academic life, as was indeed the rise of political consciousness in the universities themselves. Perhaps the most celebrated case of the time was that of the Mainz "Jacobins," led by Andreas Joseph Hoffman and Georg Forster, both members of the university staff. As the electors' government favored the settlement of conservative French emigrés in Mainz and began to persecute such radical Enlightenment writers as Hoffman, one of the first essentially secular political struggles between government and university professors took place. The fact that Hoffman and Forster later served as president and vice-president of the French-supported Mainz republic did nothing to lessen the suspicions of other German governments about the potential radicalism of universities. Although professors and students elsewhere remained mostly passive and loyal, the germ of a tradition of suspicious watchfulness over the universities for political reasons had been planted and was to flower after the defeat of Napoleon.

The closing of universities also had important consequences for the system of higher education as a whole. Although most of the institutions shut down had been weak or moribund to begin with, their elimination reduced the competition for students among the stronger universities and led to a streamlined regional base for most of the survivors. Most of the universities closed had simply lost their traditional political base, as in the cases of imperial free cities' schools (such as Strasbourg and Nürnberg's university at Altdorf) and those of some ecclesiastical territories (e.g., Fulda, Erfurt, and Würzburg).

Despite the initially conservative wave of reaction to the French Revolution in many of the German states, the triumph of Napoleon in Germany after the beginning of the nineteenth century ultimately led to a resuscitation of the tradition of enlightened absolutism, at least insofar as the administration and consolidation of many surviving German states were concerned. In the newly enlarged South German states, and after the devastating impact of the defeat of Jena even in Prussia, traditions were swept away in a flurry of reforms. In Montgelas's Bavaria, in Reitzenstein's Baden, and in the Prussia of the Stein–Hardenberg period, universities, too, were caught up in the sweep of change. The ancient Bavarian university of Ingolstadt was physically removed to Landshut and given new forms and spirit; the university of Heidelberg, which had resisted virtually all reform in the eighteenth century as a part of the Palatinate, was drastically renovated as a part of the expanded state of Baden beginning in 1803. And Prussia went even further, creating its own models of the reformed university in Berlin and, later, in Breslau and Bonn. Other universities carried out reforms more cautiously, but in a much more aggressive spirit than had been the case in the previous century.

The significant changes in the German university scene in the generation after the French Revolution were thus an integral part of the sweeping political and social changes taking place all over Central Europe. Coming on top of the more modest evolution of the eighteenth century, these changes implied the breakdown of the universities' location as autonomous corporations in a hierarchical, semifeudal society of privilege and tradition and showed the way to a new position within the emerging modern state and bourgeois society. Rather than being abolished along with other vestiges of the ancient regime, as their French counterparts had been, the stronger German universities survived in a new and more modern form to lay the basis for the nineteenth-century development of the research university. Even though French influence on German higher education was profound, particularly in the area of specialty schools, such as the later technical colleges, it did not result, as in France, in the sundering of research and pedagogical functions.

The survival of the German university system owed much, in fact, to reaction to the French Revolution, rather than emulation of it. The nationalistic, conservative, and neo-humanistic ideologies that developed strongly for the first time in the German states in the wake of revolutionary and Napoleonic challenges tended to favor the retention of the university as an institution. For the "reform conservatives" (as Epstein has called them[1]), the universities combined tradition with a proved ability to change slowly in response to altered social conditions. For the young nationalists, universities were a rallying point. And for the neo-humanists, the university fulfilled an essential function that mere specialty schools and academies of higher learning could not—the furtherance of individual personal development through application to creative thought. The neo-humanists in particular provided strong arguments for the retention of the universities and an ideological basis for the later evolution of the universities into research-oriented institutions (which they had not yet become by 1800).

The retention of the university model in the German states also owed something to the financial condition of the German states, which was none too good during the Napoleonic period. German bureaucrats were certainly not unimpressed by the well-endowed new *grandes écoles* established in France, but they did not have the means to set up research institutions separate from training academies. As we shall see in this chapter, the very idea of establishing a new university in Berlin was conceived in part as a means of saving money, because members of the Prussian academy could be used for part of the teaching force, and existing collections and research apparatus could be placed at the disposal of the new institution. As the slow and often painful growth of research institutes and seminars at universities before 1860 shows, the German states were hesitant, for financial as well as policy reasons, to commit themselves as deeply as France to separate research institutions, preferring instead to let them develop in the relatively less expensive, preexisting setting of universities.

The decision to retain and reform some German universities was also carried out in a rather diffeent political structure-field from that of France. Germany had no parliamentary institutions during the reform era such as France had had at the time of the abolition of French universities. German public opinion thus had no forum for influencing policy. Nor was the reorganization of higher education carried out by a high-handed military dictator, as happened in the newly founded French system under Napoleon. In the German states, typically, the university reforms were carried out by the traiditonal royal bureaucracy, that is, by graduates of universities who tended to look back on their educational experience with a certain positive attitude. The university professors themselves, as in the eighteenth century, did not push themselves forward into the vanguard calling for reform. But the traditional professoriate was undoubtedly shaken in its complacency and was in no position to put up much resistance. At the same time, the German bureaucracy could count upon the talents and insight of a vocal minority of German professors who did recognize the need for reform and evolved a new ideology of higher education. At no time in the eighteenth century or the later nineteenth were so many reform ideas produced by members of the German professoriate (one need only mention such names as Schleiermacher, Fichte, and Schelling).[2] The bureaucracy, in contrast to that of other periods, was willing to listen and even act on their ideas.

In the wake of all this ferment, a considerable debate about universities took place in the German states.

Utilitarian and neo-humanist reformers

It might be fair to characterize the various parties in the debate about higher educational reform as falling into three major groups, depending on their view of the purpose of education in general. The oldest and most conservative position was maintained by many university professors and was associated with an orthodox clerical position: The object of education was to pass on a tradition of right belief through the use of traditional pedagogical techniques such as the disputation in Latin. Although by no means restricted to theological faculties, this viewpoint usually had its staunchest defenders there, partly because more experimental approaches threatened the primacy of theology. A second attitude might be called utilitarian. This viewpoint defined the purpose of education in a pragmatic way, placing greatest emphasis on the training of young men in skills useful in the professions, the state, and the church. Its major protagonists were found in state bureaucracies and in the law and medical faculties, though not exclusively there. A third pedagogical party, and one that became increasingly powerful in the closing decades of the eighteenth century, defined the purpose of education in a more subjective way. For this group, the aim of education was to help unfold and realize the full potential of the personality. It could hardly be said that this movement found its university home in the philosophical faculty, because this was still usually the feeblest of the faculties in the eighteenth century. But the subjects most closely associated with it – philology, classical studies, history, the natural sciences, and philosophy itself – were core disciplines for the arts and sciences. Stressing the lifelong development of the individual as it did, this group had the least direct commitment to particular forms of education, including the university. Yet its demands led to the regeneration of the philosophical faculty and the redefinition of the idea of the university finally incorporated in the new institution in Berlin.

As had been the case earlier in the eighteenth century, the

regeneration of the universities was less the result of reform movements emanating from the professors than the product of external circumstances. Nor was the modernization of the university system the sole outcome of intellectual movements. Despite reform attempts by various princely governments, including those in the Catholic states, the system of German universities was far from being on the road to a new era in 1790. At best, the radical pedagogical reform movement of the late eighteenth century, deriving in part from Rousseau, Pestalozzi, Basedow, and others, weakened the public support for the status quo without transforming the basic abuses of most universities. The successes of Halle, Göttingen, and a handful of other institutions were a spur and an embarrassment to the declining institutuions, but the latter were still in business. It took the catastrophic intervention of French armies and the territorial reorganization of the old empire to close down many of the less illustrious universities and pave the way for renewal.

Although the utilitarian and neo-humanist reformers shared the same enemies, they carried out changes with somewhat different end goals. The South German states adopted a utilitarian approach during the major reform period right after 1800, although they altered their objectives and came closer to the neo-humanist position with the passage of time. In Prussia, although utilitarians also attempted to carry out university reforms, they were overwhelmed by events and forced to yield the field to the neo-humanists.

The initial university reforms in South Germany (notably in Baden and Bavaria) had the character of an organizational shuffle, a drive to greater secularization, and an emphasis on the role of the universities as training grounds for good state and ecclesiastical servants. The admiration of such South German ministers as Baron Sigismund von Reitzenstein in Baden and Count Maximilian von Montgelas in Bavaria for Napoleon's reorganization of France led to considerable imitation.[3] In Heidelberg and Landshut, for example, the old division of the university into faculties was at first abolished or made meaningless by the introduction of "sections" for philosophy, history, mathematics and physics, and so on. Cameralistics were pressed with great force, betraying the heavy investment of both states in well-trained administrators for their newly aggrandized states. Religious squabbles were minimized by the affirmation of tolerance, a commodity conspicuously lacking from both Heidelberg and Ingolstadt during much of the eighteenth century and a reason for their intellectual backwardness. The abolition of the Jesuit order and its stranglehold over instruction at the Bavarian university in 1773 had still not been enough to promote a fully modern curriculum; and one of the reasons for moving the university to Landshut in 1800 was to free it from remnants of "obscurantism."[4]

The Bavarian and Badenese reforms had the immediate effect of increasing enrollments – in Bavaria, by over 75 percent compared to the 1790s. At Heidelberg, by 1808, there were about 440 students in all, a respectable number. Most surprisingly, nearly three-quarters of these matriculated in law or cameralistics. Students enrolled in the philosophical faculties at both universities constituted only a tiny proportion of the whole, indicating that as yet neo-humanists ideals had not taken deep root in South Germany.[5]

Rationalist–utilitarian reformers could be found in North Germany, as well. In Prussia, plans had been discussed since about 1800 for the reform of Königsberg University and the creation in Berlin of an *Allgemeine Lehranstalt* (general teaching institution) as a loose agglomeration of institutions, some already existent (veterinary and medical schools), some to be created. The term "university" was avoided by the Prussian minister, Beyme. Reflecting the same distaste for traditional university organization and interest in specialty schools that French educational planners held dear, the Beyme ministry talked much but acted little. In the end, the reforms of Königsberg were left half finished and the plan of an *Allgemeine Lehranstalt* transformed into the idea of the University of Berlin as a result of the crushing Prussian defeat at Jena in 1806.[6]

The attitudes and plans of the utilitarian reformers, whether carried out in full or not, aided in introducing a degree of financial security, state control, and orderly teaching processes into university life. The reduction in the autonomy and in the hoary traditionalism that resulted for the universities constituted an important step in the restoration of many universities to new vigor and effectiveness. It is true that the ideas of the utilitarian reformers were not philosophically profound. Reitzenstein, Montgelas, and Beyme regarded universities as producers of civil servants, clerics, and doctors, and they acted out of a conviction that the universities were simply not doing their job well. They have often been belittled in German university histories for their rationalist "shallowness" in contrast to the high thinking of the neo-humanists. Yet the reforms they carried out, mundane and even mechanical as they often were, laid a new foundation for the survival of the universities. Neither teaching nor research could flourish in German universities so long as professors were forced to moonlight, omit lectures altogether, or stretch lectures out over several semesters. The ability of students to learn could not be heightened so long as student abuses such as drunkenness, gambling, dueling, and absenteeism not only went unchecked but were actually condoned by the lax discipline that was traditional under university rights to legal immunity from civil courts and to privileged jurisdictions. The utilitarians' reforms could not overnight transform the German universities into great centers of research and teaching, nor did they aim to; but they did effectively erase many of the most heinous abuses and silence those who had called for the abolition of universities. The utilitarian reformers gave the universities a static base upon which to stand. But they were unable to give it a dynamic idea for its further development. For this the ideas of the neo-humanist reformers had a solution.

It is commonplace to say that the reform of German universities around the beginning of the nineteenth century took place under the aegis of "neo-humanism." Certainly the creation of the neo-humanistic Prussian *Gymnasium* system justifies such a claim for the educational system as a whole. And just as certainly, the breakthrough of the philosophical faculty, especially in its role as interpreter of classical antiquity, to a position of equality with the three traditional professional faculties of theology, law, and medicine can be dated from this time. Yet what is usually meant is that the reformers tended to belong to the third of the partisan groupings at the beginning of this section – those for whom the aim of education was personal development. A generalized admiration for the world of classical culture linked many of the leading thinkers of the day, all the way from Goethe's intellectual court in Weimar to the philological seminars of Göttingen and Halle to the educational reformers grouped around Wilhelm von Humboldt in Berlin. The renewal of German universities took place amidst a generalized respect for a certain kind of learning oriented on the development of the individual personality.

This did not mean that the neo-humanists were utopian dreamers, however.

The top men in the Prussian reform bureaucracy formulated a program combining legal and political-science studies with philosophical–historical general education that they had personally experienced at the universities of Göttingen and Königsberg under Pütter, Achenwall, Kant, and their disciples and that they had learned above all from the new philosophical and economic doctrines of Adam Smith. In contrast to the tendency of later historiography to interpret the Prussian reforms as idealistic and neo-humanistic, one must emphasize that they laid weight on the importance of *Staatswissenschaften*.[7]

It is this compromise position between the radical pedagogical reformers and the pedestrian advocates of specialty schools that characterized the neo-humanists.

After a century more or less of the debate between the "classics" and the "moderns," a peculiarly German synthesis had taken place and was increasingly used as the philosophical justification for secondary and higher education. The classical curriculum of the university, based on the medieval reception of Aristotle and the formal study of classical languages, had lost much of its meaning in the course of curriculum reforms such as those of Göttingen. The introduction of modern subjects, the use of the vernacular, and a turn toward stress on the content rather than the form of classical texts had taken the place of the traditional scholastic approach. Goethe's own intellectual career might be said to reflect this shift, moving as it did from the profound concentration on purely modern subjects in the Germanic language sphere (Götz von Berlichingen, Werther) in the 1770s to an intense preoccupation with the classical world and natural science by about 1800. The universities of 1700 had taught both classical literature and natural science in a formal, fixed way. Neither Winckelmann's open-ended curiosity about the classical past nor Goethe's scientific interests could have been accommodatd in such a system. By 1800, however, universities had changed enough so that a discovery-oriented attitude could gain a foothold. The philological seminar of Gesner and Heyne at Göttingen produced some of the best classical research of the century, and the movement of *Naturphilosophie* took the study of natural phenomena well beyond the bounds of traditional Aristotelian models, even if in directions that the history of science tends to regard as wrong.

Neo-humanism and society

The social origins of support for neo-humanism are somewhat ambiguous. As we have seen, the decidedly new element in German higher education in the early eighteenth century lay in its renewed appeal to the socially leading elements of the student body – the aristocracy and the wealthy patriciate, the *Vornehme*. At Halle and Göttingen, the professor ideally became more *vornehm* himself, teaching values and subjects of use to his most socially respectable students. By the end of the eighteenth century, certain emphases had changed, even at Göttingen. The noble and *vornehm* student was still cultivated, but fashions were beginning to change in the curriculum. Alongside the stress on worldly and practical subjects, such as law, a new interest in the internal values of classical antiquity had grown. It was thus not completely anomalous for an aristocratic student like Wilhelm von Humboldt to enroll in the theological seminar at Göttingen – not because he wished to become a pastor, but because that seminar taught the newly fashionable classical sciences in an unparalleled way. The grand tour, the classic finishing school of the wealthy and aristocratic student, was beginning to have a corollary – the tour of discovery of the ancient world and, for some, of the mysteries of nature. For a small minority of aficionados the research of time past and of infinite Nature held an excitement far beyond the then standardized trips to Holland and France. It was a personal voyage of discovery, dictated to some extent by fashion, and accessible only through preparation by savants. As E. M. Butler has pointed out, this voyage was almost exclusively intellectual.[8] Few of the Grecophile Germans actually went to Greece, nor would they have found what they were seeking even if they had, considering the state of contemporary Greek culture. Visiting Rome was an experience for the historically initiated, not an empirical exercise for the eye and ear. With the shift of pedagogical object from the glories of the contemporary European state and society, which still animated the founders of Göttingen, to the more imaginary constructs of the ancient or, for a few, the abstract glories of science and philosophy, higher education at its optimum changed meaning. It was not solely preparation for the real world of court, bureaucracy, and affairs – a major step taken by Halle and Göttingen – but preparation for a lifelong voyage of personal development. No university ever has fulfilled such hopes, and probably none ever will. But the very expectation that it should changed the tenor of pedagogical thinking in Germany.

The neo-humanists held a vision of the university that was not closely tied to the interests of a single social class. The changes they strove to bring about were not directed so clearly at the nobility, for example, as those introduced by the founders of Göttingen. Nor could the neo-humanists be described as carriers of exclusively bourgeois values. They did share some parts of a bourgeois ethic when they emphasized hard work, self-sacrifice, and self-improvement; but they also explicitly decried certain other values of the German middle class, as we shall see later. One can much more readily seek the social grounding of neo-humanist thought in a stratum, rather than a class: the sizable bureaucratic–professional elite, recruited from both the bourgeoisie and the nobility, but fashioned over the course of the eighteenth century into an influential, separate, and relatively cohesive level of society.

Although the position of the aristocracy had still been secure enough at the time of the establishment of Göttingen to warrant considering it as the driving element of reform, this was no longer true by 1800. The position of the court nobility, which had never in any case had much use for universities, was severely shaken by the time of the French reorganization of Germany. The noble landowner was threatened by the widespread agrarian reforms in Germany.[9] The noble officer found himself serving next to the bourgeois officer of the Boyen-Scharnhorst reforms. The security of noble estates itself was undermined by the increasing salability of noble lands.

One of the few remaining bastions of the nobility was the princely bureaucracy. Here the trend seems to have been away from the learned bourgeois in the highest positions of state, and toward the learned noble. Whatever gains the tiny and weak industrial and commercial bourgeoisie of Germany may have made during the Napoleonic period – and there is evidence of such gains – the bureaucracies of the leading German states seem to have passed from the hands of the bourgeois or newly noble to those of the educated old nobles. Many of the first ministers of the time, such as Stein, Hardenberg, Metternich, and Montgelas, were university-trained men of considerable social parts. They had often attended the universities that had set up curricula to attract their class – Göttingen,

Strasbourg, and so on. And they worked with officials, noble and non-noble, who had shared this same educational background. They and other state servants had gone through the educational system of which Göttingen was the apotheosis. They and their fellow bureaucrats formed a group united by a common state service ethic, tempered by a certain sense of belonging neither to the class from which they had sprung (whether bourgeois or noble) nor to a special region. Having gone through their university years in the most pleasant possible way, courted by professors and untouched by the misery of ordinary student existence, they had no reason to share the disdain of the bourgeois public for the university as such.

Neo-humanism has always been regarded as a manifestation of the self-consciousness of the German middle class; and one can hardly ascribe its social origins to the peasantry or the nobility as a whole. But upon closer investigation, the bourgeois quality of neo-humanism becomes slightly nebulous. Its originators were mostly bourgeois people, but it was not therefore a clearly bourgeois ideology. Its emancipatory and progressive traits aimed at the individual and called upon the internal strengths of the personality rather than aiming at the collectivity and calling for the external restructuring of society for salvation. The insistence of the neo-humanists on education and self-development as the primary marks of a true *Mensch* tended toward a form of elitism that excluded the values of a majority of normal burghers. The pursuit of wealth or other mundane signs of fortune characterized the values of these burghers, in the eyes of the neo-humanists, and they rejected such values out of hand. Thus, in important respects, neo-humanism was an elite bourgeois ideology directed against a common bourgeois value system. It appealed across class lines to men who possessed the precondition of a certain leisure and the will to self-development and cultivation. And because the key to its program lay in education, it appealed most strongly to the bureaucratic–clerical–professional body of university graduates.

It was this group of university graduates, some noble, some bourgeois, that saved the German university system from the extinction that many thought it deserved around 1800. Had the princely bureaucracies listened to whatever there was of "public opinion" in the late eighteenth century, they would probably have abolished the universities along with serfdom and other relics of the Middle Ages. Certainly the reports from the universities themselves gave little reason for keeping them on. The only good justifications of universities emanated from Göttingen and a handful of other institutions, and it was fortunate for the university system that so many of those called to power graduated from reformed universities. Humboldt, for example, had been equally exposed to the arguments against and for the German university. His youthful tutor, J. H. Campe, was one of the most vociferous champions of suppressing all universities. Yet Humboldt had been awakened to the value of university instruction when he attended Göttingen, and as the appointed head of the educational bureaucracy in Prussia, he never wavered in his determination to keep universities – on a reformed basis.

It should also be emphasized that the neo-humanists were not the only group having a say in university reform. It has been the pleasure of nineteenth-century German chroniclers of university history to write as though "idealism" shaped everything. Such was never the case. Instead, the neo-humanists insinuated a certain ideology into discussions about the university that ran parallel to, but did not necessarily itself dominate, university reform. Although various neo-humanistic tracts, such as the reform proposals of Fichte and Schleiermacher, have come down to us as the most ringing arguments for the restructuring of university education, there is no reason to believe that most students, professors, and educational bureaucrats were more swayed by them than by more mundane considerations.

One of the most significant of these considerations was an apparent shift in student interest away from the theological faculty and toward the other three. The tight employment market for theological candidates evidently acted to discourage students from taking their degrees in theology. At the same time, enrollments in more secular studies increased in the last part of the eighteenth century. This shift, undoubtedly welcomed by many educational authorities, had important consequences for the universities, and in particular for the philosophical faculties. For the latter, it delivered further weapons to use in their fight for equality with the other faculties. It was no accident that the philosophical faculties were the ones where many of the fundamental new approaches to scholarship arose: They were seeking self-justification against criticism and suspicion from the traditional faculties.[10] The struggle for a secular, verifiable method of scientific discovery was fought not only by the "hard" sciences but, even more so, by the humanistic disciplines, with their anthropomorphic concerns, against the otherworldly visions of traditional Christian orthodoxy. The new methods of studying the humanities had, to be sure, been evolved to a large extent in the theological seminars of Göttingen, Halle, and other universities. But these universities had shown a progressive distaste for priests and an increasing interest in laymen. The final step for neo-humanists was to try to escape theological control altogether by settling the study of humanistic culture (and science) into the rising philosophical faculty. Neo-humanist secondary schools (the *Gymnasien*) would have to see to the propaedeutic functions previously assigned to the philosophical faculties; likewise, the teachers in these new schools would have to be trained in *Wissenschaft* by the philosophical faculties themselves. The humanistic and natural sciences aided each other and dragged the theologians, lawyers, and other more conservative professors with them in the long run.

The further secularization of higher education reflected a diminution of the attractiveness of clerical careers. Whatever their abuses, the Protestant and Catholic churches of Germany were concerned in the eighteenth century to staff their parishes and maintained support for poor students who would later become vicars. By the end of the eighteenth century, this policy was insufficient. The secular trend struck by such universities as Göttingen was followed by other institutions, where theology enrollments dropped markedly. From 1770–80 to 1800–10, theology enrollment dropped from 32 to 20 percent of total enrollments in Erlangen, 26 to 21 percent in Göttingen, 60 to 45 percent in Halle, and 72 to 50 percent in Tübingen. At the same time, law enrollments frequently increased.[11] The message is clear: The most under-rewarded profession, that of the curé, was being abandoned, while that of the most rewarding profession, law (government), was being inundated. Medicine, the faculty in which one could most easily study modern science, was making gains comparable to law's.

As they are today, law and medicine were the most costly studies for students. One can therefore reasonably hypothesize that the student body was becoming richer and coming from a more well-to-do background than had traditionally been the case. The increase in percentages of students studying in these more costly faculties at a time when enrollments in general were decreasing would further support the argument that the German student body was coming from a wealthier sector of society.

Yet the urban, mercantile middle class as such was not the source of this new type of student. The pedagogical aims of the urban bourgeoisie ran along the lines of replacing the moribund Latin schools. The reform movement of the middle class was pressing for a class-oriented type of education that would break with the traditional inculcation in formal school Latin. Inspired by late-eighteenth-century ideals of utility, these circles pressed for more practical education in the town, ending in the town, to prepare their children for the tasks of commerce. Just as the Enlightenment had liberated the German nobility from the tutelage of the *Ritterakademie,* it gradually began to free the urban bourgeoisie of its affection for the formal Latin school. The difference for the small urban middle class of Germany was that this liberation further undercut its tenuous ties with the universities. The great commercial cities of Germany had always been fairly hostile to universities. Once they began to reform their schools in a more practical sense, there was even less reason for them to send their children to universities, which taught them nothing they needed to know.

Most traditional and many contemporary students of the German universities have ignored or denied the problem of so-cial and political influences on the foundation of the new uni-versities. Even those who have not done so generally have seri-ous difficulties. Marxist university histories emanating from East Germany, for example, use a model far too simple to be very helpful. One of the few recent attempts to view the German university tradition in a sociological light, by Helmut Schelsky, finally resorts to the Mannheimian escape, classifying the founding fathers of the University of Berlin, for example, as socially *freischwebend*.[12] This is surely going too far. With few exceptions, the neo-humanists hoped to banish *Brotstudium,* studying for the sake of a career, from the university. In practice they would have banished the poorest students thereby. Stu-dents were to study for the sake of *Wissenschaft;* or, to be more precise, *Wissenschaft* was to be the method and means of achieving a cultivated personality. The notion of *Lernfreiheit* for the students aimed at substituting an internal motivation for study (curiosity, interest) for the usual external ones (career, passing exams). Fichte was one of the few innovators who real-ized that even stronger guarantees had to be built against the temptations of *Brotstudium*: Students, he proposed, must be given financial support throughout their studies and a guaran-tee of employment in the civil service afterwards, regardless of their performance *at the university*. Fichte also proposed that students wear uniforms so as to obviate and erase the external, pre-university social distinctions. But others were not so radical in their proposals. Schelsky admits that Humboldt's

own life-style – as a tolerably well-to-do nobleman, although interested in state sinecures, able to live for his own cultural interests and his aesthetic self-enjoyment – also went into his university conception . . . The "unforced and non-purposeful" sociability of the university would probably have been most complete for him if well-to-do, nonprofessional, and cultivated men with experience of the world, who devoted their lives to matters of science and art for their own sake, could spend a part of the day in stimulating conversation with each other and with young people who could hope to achieve a similar existence.[13]

Certainly this kind of existence correctly reflects Humboldt's own happiest life experiences—the years he spent in Weimar and Rome, with few or no official duties, many cultivated friends, and much stimulating talk. Just how the students at such a utopian educational institution were to acquire the means to achieve an existence similar to Humboldt's was not clear.

To be sure, the social considerations of the neo-humanist reformers were fairly open for their time; like Napoleon, they believed that education and careers should be open to talent. Fichte, as usual the most radical spokesman, despised all students who came to universities for utilitarian, professional reasons—whether the lowest peasant or the highest lord in the land. The social standing of the student *outside* the university was clearly a consideration secondary to his intellectual and moral standing *inside* the university. Yet given the expectation of thorough training in the classics *before* arrival at the university, the absence of an extensive scholarship program, and the failure to do away with the preprofessional aspects of university training, the university that emerged from the neo-humanists' plans was an elite institution in more than an intellectual sense. Despite the avowed hope of making philosophy (and its faculty) the queen science, Berlin's largest faculty the semester of its opening was medicine. Medicine and law tended to be the largest faculties by far for several decades, sometimes followed closely by theology.[14] The statistical categories used in Lenz's history of Berlin are too crude to answer many of today's questions, but they clearly indicate that 72 percent of the students matriculated at the university in 1810 came from families in the higher civil service, church, and free professions (47 percent) or in commerce and agriculture (25 percent), the rest being sons of lower officials, schoolteachers, small farmers, and artisans.[15] From then on, the percentage of poorer students sank gradually to about 20 percent in 1840.

There was also a strong note of loathing and distaste for the bourgeois world in the writings of many of those who helped plan a new university for Prussia. In the minds of Fichte, Humboldt, and others the demands of the utilitarian reformers (who thought of abolishing the university and replacing it with practical specialty schools) played directly into the hands of the mindless, materialistic, and pragmatic commercial middle class. Fichte's ultimate social vision included the rule of the academics (who would have a monopoly in the state) over the rest of the *Volk* – a revolutionary idea implying the supplanting of the old birth elites by a consolidated elite with a common experience of high education. Fichte and even Humboldt intended to produce, if not philosopher–kings, philosopher–bureaucrats to rule Prussia. Taken to its extreme, this program had to do not with reshaping the university to meet the needs of contemporary society, but rather with reshaping society through the university. While Napoleon ridiculed and punished the *ideologues* in France, Prussian intellectuals were bandying about terms such as *Geistesaristokratie* and looking to the new university as the source of it.

To be sure, the influence of Fichte and the more radical neohumanists on the actual development of a new university in Berlin was far from decisive. If any one of the reformers could be said to have dominated the new Berlin University in its decisive phase of initial development, it was the theologian Schleiermacher. A comparison of Schleiermacher's memorandum concerning the guidelines for the new university with that of Fichte clearly shows that the former was more accommodationist, pragmatic, and respectful of certain older traditions of the German universities than the latter. Schleiermacher, not Fichte, was chosen to head the commission that in effect called the new faculty to Berlin and administered the erection of the new school. Fichte, although appointed first rector of Berlin, quit after a semester – over a conflict with faculty members more tolerant of traditional student abuses than he. The opposition to Fichte's stern line was led by Schleiermacher. Wilhelm von Humboldt himself held office in the Department for Church and School Affairs only a short time (in 1810); his replacement, Schuckmann, was later raised to the dignity of minister. Schuckmann probably reflected the thinking of the king and the Prussian bureaucracy better than Humboldt and was, in Humboldt's sneering words, filled with utilitarian projects of the Enlightenment.[16] It is important to remember that unlike Göttingen, none of the new Prussian universities was shaped in its first decades of existence by the men who had conceived of the "model." All too often, historians have assumed that the ideas of Fichte, Humboldt, or Schleiermacher were simply translated into practice, but this was far from being the case.

In conclusion, the neo-humanist reformers may be said to have had a relatively well-to-do student clientele in mind for the new-model university. On the other hand, they did not aim their reforms so openly in the direction of one social estate as had been the case in Göttingen three generations before. Although the proposals of Fichte contained a certain liberality, stressing that ability, not birth, should determine who went to the university, they also foreshadowed the creation of a new elite of university graduates. Despite such overtones of equal access, however, the more frequently heard theme of the leisured, vaguely aristocratic ethos of self-development via the pursuit of scholarship had little in common with the practical and hard-headed thinking patterns of the commercial bourgeoisie, let alone those of the artisans and peasants.

It is not possible at this point to analyze carefully the social composition of the student body at the new University of Berlin.[17] Lenz's estimates would indicate that the proportion of truly poor students was small and became even smaller as time went on. And evidence from studies on other universities indicates that the middle and lower-middle strata of the bourgeoisie comprised a larger percentage of students in times of high enrollment, but they were also the first to depart when various factors made a university education seem too expensive. Nobles, to some extent, held their own as a proportion of the student body. The appeal of the reformed universities after 1815 was very strong: Berlin, Bonn, Breslau, and Munich alone drew about 40 percent of all students. Whether they were drawn from admiration of neo-humanist reforms or because of a return to peaceful conditions and a dearth of young men trained for civil service jobs, one cannot say with certainty. The growth of the student body did not coincide with the wishes of many reformers, however, and governments began to worry in the 1820s about an oversupply of educated man and to take measures to make a university education harder to get.

The neo-humanist and utilitarian reforms had made the affected German universities stronger, financially better off, and organizationally more modern, and had raised the prestige of university study. The universities also tended to become financially and academically more difficult to get through, with fees and entrance requirements rising dramatically after about 1815. In social terms, the reforms of the Napoleonic era ended by augmenting the appeal of the universities to a social elite and firmly fixing a university education as one of the most important acquirable badges of membership in that elite.

New concepts of research

In the light of changing social ideals about the function and purpose of education at the turn of the nineteenth century, reigning notions of the best teaching methods and the calling of the teacher itself changed as well. They did not change as abruptly as some scholars, bent on heightening the contrast between eighteenth- and nineteenth-century modular types, might lead one to believe. There was no sudden break, but a steady evolution over more than one generation.

It is tempting nevertheless to revert to type-images, as contemporary literature often did, to describe the differing ideals of the pedagogue. A *university* teacher ought, of course, to possess competence in his field and the ability to communicate his knowledge to his audience. This is a minimum requirement everywhere, even though it has never been fully met everywhere. The university teacher, furthermore, was often expected to be more than competent; he was to be *gelehrt,* or very learned. The most conservative defenders of the scholastic university (whose defense was more likely to come through obstruction *in situ* rather than written replies to critics) asked little more of the professor than this. Then some early university reformers of the Enlightenment, like Münchhausen, added the second desideratum that at least some of the professors should be reasonably famous publishing scholars as well. In other words, their scholarship was to be not only passive, as among the *Gelehrten* of the traditional university, but active as well.

Nineteenth-century critics of this new kind of scholarship pointed out that the new standard resulted in a sort of encyclopedism, with scholars hurrying to collect mounds of undigested information and publish hastily written textbooks. To compare these works to the more substantial and subtle achievements of nineteenth-century "scientific" scholarship and research is automatically to belittle their significance, however; their existence and nature constituted a break with earlier traditions of scholarship and helped redefine the role of the university professor.

Finally, the third vision of the academic teacher's role emerged partly as a reaction to the Enlightenment view. It regarded *Wissenschaft* as the highest calling of the scholar and as a useful, even integral part of the life of a good university teacher. This view has come down to us today in the form of clichés about "teacher–scholars," those multifunctional humans who ought to excel in both the discovery and the transmission of knowledge. This canon was firmly established in the German universities during the nineteenth century, but its origins stretch back into the late eighteenth century.

The dynamic, evolutionary ideas underlying this new conception of the teacher–scholar motivated other concepts of this restless age – such as *Naturphilosophie,* Fichte and Hegel's philosophy, or Goethe's botanical theories. For them, the active pursuit of *integrated, meaningful,* and *pure* knowledge was the highest calling of man. Knowledge, like the world, was coming to be seen as caught in the process of development. Instead of a fixed body of unchanging truth, the teacher had to pass on an almost infinite curiosity about the unknown or half-known, along with the tools necessary to pursue the search long after leaving the university. This process of personal evolution, of self-development to the limit of one's capacities, was the real goal of higher education, which would thus perpetuate itself long after the student had left the classroom. As for the teacher, who would stay back in the classroom, his passing on of habits of inquiry and tools for research, plus his living example of a *wissenschaftlich* approach to life, was at least as important as the discoveries of his own personal research or the content of his lectures. Fichte and Humboldt even regarded the university lecture as a loose first reading for the lecturer's ideas, followed or interrupted by critical objections or encouragements by students. The university lecture, then, would resemble in some ways a serious-minded soirée in a Berlin salon. The *subjective* value of the scholarship involved weighed at least as much as the *objective* value of the scholarly achievement, or the "contribution to knowledge," itself.

Indeed, the philosophical categories of the neo-humanist reformers allowed little room for the idea of a "contribution" to knowledge, because they criticized the Enlightenment exactly for its preference for "collecting" facts as though knowledge were a mechanical mosaic instead of an organic whole. Fichte's demand that philosophy be installed as the leading, coordinating science in the university took its justification from this strong tendency of the neo-humanists to look upon knowledge holistically. The idea that differing disciplines (e.g., today's natural sciences and "humanities") should have different methods and reigning assumptions was foreign to them. At the same time, there *were* some forms of knowledge the new type of teacher–scholar was not supposed to care about: The merely practical, applied, or useful branches of knowledge, or instrumental *Brotstudium* in the pure sciences, were despised. An almost religious sense of a mission to search for the riddles of man and the universe was too high to sully with concern over the better mousetrap. One result of such thinking was the sundering of "technical" and "theoretical" education in the nineteenth century.

Thus when Wilhelm von Humboldt spoke of the university as a place where both teachers and students could "devote themselves to science" (*der Wissenschaft leben*), he meant something radically different from the later positivist or empirical construction of those words. *Wissenschaft* and further discoveries emanating from it were the instrument, not the goal, of the scholar. The full development of the personality and of a supple, wide-ranging habit of clear, original thinking was the goal. Humboldt and the Prussian reformers had every reason for demanding these capacities, and not merely in the name of the sovereign, cultivated personality. The defeat of the Frederickian "machine state" in 1806 had driven home the point that officers and civil servants trained "by the book," in the rigid, professional application of specialized expertise, simply caved in, confused, when confronted with new and unusual situations. Expert training was not to be abolished; but it was to be underpinned by a sounder foundation of general, theoretical education and habits of independent thought aroused and shaped by *Wissenschaft* in the universities. In no sense was *Wissenschaft* regarded as an alienated product of human endeavor. In whatever terms it was expressed – Fichte's search for absolute truth, Humboldt's "devoting oneself to science," or even the romantic poet's search for the elusive "blue flower" – the *search* was paramount.

This attitude toward scholarship was in fact an ideal one. Those who have recognized this fact (and the bulk of self-congratulatory jubilee literature on German university history ignores it) have either smiled at the arrogance, utopianism, or impracticality of institutionalizing this *Wissenschaft* ideal in the university or have berated corrupt, bourgeois, materialistic "society" for not living up to this Platonic dream. What has not been fully explored is the tension between the necessary political dimension of their plans and their social utopia. Fichte, the most radical of the new theorists of the university, stumbled on this tension most sharply. The new-model university, he conceded, could not come into being as anything but a state-supported institution. Yet the state was imperfect, pandered to the pressures and needs of society, and kept insisting on the production of narrow expertise. Such niggling materialistic thinking in the bureaucracy was exactly what the *Wissenschaft*-soaked graduates of an ideal university would presumably clear away in time.

Thus a vicious circle was formed. For education to effect a social utopia, to create a society in which the morally and mentally "best" ran society, the state had first to assert its utopian leadership by setting up a university that flew in the face of many of the needs perceived by large segments of society and the state bureaucracy itself. Fichte could not overcome the problem that the state was at the same time unreformed initiator of the utopia (through a new educational system) and reformed beneficiary of the new ideals.

Fichte and the other neo-humanists in effect renounced the idea of a new, *private* institute of some kind that might have been able to achieve the ideal of scientific higher education on a purely voluntary, limited basis, because only the state could provide the means to support such an enterprise (the idea of private support had actually been discussed around 1800). The idealist–humanistic reformers, even Humboldt, the author of a tract arguing against state authority in the 1790s, surrendered support of education to the state; their only hope that this control would lead to a Platonic ideal and perhaps even a moral revolution in the bureaucracy itself lay in the naive demand that the state ignore social pressures and jump over its own shadow.

In the end, the high ideals of Fichte, Humboldt, and the other neo-humanists did not prevail. Their ideas left a certain residue in the University of Berlin, to be sure, and a vast impression on the rhetoric of all German universities – indeed, on the entire modern ideology of higher education everywhere. But there were very many remnants of the utilitarian viewpoint of the Enlightenment, and the older orthodox viewpoint, not only in the Prussian bureaucracy, but even within the professoriate.

The professoriate at the university at Berlin does not appear to have been recruited in any substantially different way from that of Göttingen. A special commission was chosen by the state to staff the new University of Berlin. "With such a political purpose behind reforms, educational bureaucracy had not the least intention of leaving the universities to their own devices, as subsequent talk of the Humboldtian idea of university autonomy would have it. Humboldt created the personnel conditions for the new university by a very decisive policy of recruitment, often against the resistance of universities and faculties."[18] Nevertheless, many of the great contemporary teacher–scholars (such as F. A. Wolf) would not come. Many who did join the faculty were already on hand as members of the various institutes in the city that were now grouped under the university, or as members of the academy. Members of the latter institution, with its stress on pure research, had been recruited not on the basis of teaching talent, but more along the lines of scientific fame – the same criterion Göttingen had often used in seeking full professors. There were still too few signs of the professionalization of *Wissenschaft* – for example, professional societies dominated by a prestigious in-group – and too many signs of old-fashioned recruiting practices – such as personal contacts, influence in governmental circles – for a more modern kind of pattern to emerge. To be sure, some disciplines were tending to group around nascent research institutions, such as the philological seminars of Göttingen or Halle. But even here, as in the eighteenth century, it was more often a good word from a prestigious teacher, like Wolf, sometimes against the contradictory advice of an equally prestigious teacher of another likely candidate, rather than the more general objective standard of discipline prestige, that tipped the scales in appointments. It is symptomatic of the confusion of standards at this point that attempts had been made to attract Schiller to Berlin before his death: Schiller had fame and, backed by the Weimar circle around Goethe, an almost prophetic stance in the world of letters. But his professorship at Jena (in history!) had been more a sinecure than a choice based on professional standing.

In many ways, the idea that a university professor ought to publish his research findings (an obligation that few participants in the university reform debates around 1800 regarded as categorically binding on all professors) owed as much to the traditions of the Enlightenment as to the reigning notions of the neo-humanists. The latter, to be sure, placed a high value on *Wissenschaft* and on certain features of criticism and discussion that resemble more recent concepts of liability to professionalized scientific control. The weakness of the neo-humanists for personal, oral discussion, however, reminds one more of Renaissance sodalities than of modern professional meetings. The publication standards of professors touched by the Enlightenment not only sprang from a desire for personal fame beyond the confines of the university but also reflected the Enlightenment's passion for "publicity" and popularization. By contrast, the penchant of many idealist reformers for the "free lecture," in which the speaker (professor) literally unfolds and develops his ideas as spontaneously as possible before an audience that is supposed to "think along" and criticize, deviated from some of the concepts of sound scientific method of both the Enlightenment and the later nineteenth century. These concepts tended to cling to the distinction be-

tween the teaching and research function; and a healthy skep-
ticism about the possibilities of a perfect fusion of these functions in one person pervaded the writings of the Enlightenment
on the subject. For the neo-humanists, on the other hand,
teaching and the pursuit of truth tended to be fused. The ideal
lecture would resemble a form of communal brainstorming,
with teacher and students inspiring and correcting one another
toward discovery. The idealists' loud demands for academic
freedom for professor and student, including freedom from all
such scholastic constraints as examinations and fixed curricula, were more a reflection of the desire to create a free arena
for the untrammeled oral expression of ideas and inspirations
than, say, an expression of the Enlightenment's ideal of the
right to free expression in print.

To some extent, the Berlin Academy continued to represent
this Enlightenment tradition, with its habits of publication of
scientific research results for critique by and for the general
information of the scientific community. It is significant that
both the utilitarian bureaucrats of the Prussian government
and the founding fathers of Berlin University were dissatisfied
with the academy, although for very different reasons.[19] The
royal government complained that the academy did not exert
itself enough in the direction of applied science and practical
innovations, whereas the neo-humanists had some difficulties
defining its proper role in the holistic educational system they
were trying to fuse together from heterogenous elements. They
were ambivalent about the separation of academy and university rather than hostile to the academy as such.

The eighteenth-century academies all over Europe had not
been conspicuous in their association with universities, and in
London and Paris, for example, they fulfilled entirely separate
functions. The major exception was the Göttingen Society of
Sciences, set up as a formally separate body in Göttingen but
with an informal association with the university, and located
in Göttingen frankly because of the proximity of the already
existing university facilities. The situation in Berlin was re-

versed, in that the Prussian Royal Academy of Sciences pre-dated the university by over a century. The net result of nego-tiations was that the academy kept its separate legal identity, but it had to enter into some sharing arrangements with the university: Academy members were allowed and encouraged to lecture at the university, and certain collections and insti-tutes were used by both. In practice, the older, more famous scholars of the university and the members of the academy who liked to teach formed an overlapping pool of scholar–teachers, whereas many members of the academy and the less research-oriented or younger members of the university staff had less contact with the institution to which they were not attached. This complicated ad hoc arrangement blurred the issue of the location of responsibility for "research" and, as at Göttingen, left the matter lying heavily along the lines of per-sonal interests and qualifications of the researchers.

In theory, younger teacher–scholars at the university could work out their ideas in the daily dialectic of lectures and semi-nars; the academy, which generally appointed its members late in life (though not so much so around 1810–20), might pick among these professors once they had arrived at a high stand-ing. In practice, much of the important scholarly work at the university came to be done in the seminars, rather than in public lectures, and these were dominated by the senior profes-sors; academy members, on the other hand, were not able to run and dominate ongoing seminars. Both practically and philosophically, the academy had evolved to a point where it could hardly be integrated fully with the new university. It was specialized, advanced, geriatric, to some extent honorific, and much less interested in professional socialization than in the social control of science. The university was caught in a tense dialectic of general scientific education and specialized re-search, a Socratic relationship between freshmen and profes-sors at various levels of scientific accomplishment, relatively youthful, and not at all honorific. Whether for the *Brotstudent* or the rarer budding scientific mind, the university was caught up in the function of professional socialization. University professors published for the free market in ideas, whereas the academy published findings it had already passed upon and thus lent a certain official character to. Still, because the Berlin Academy lacked the authority (and even the desire) to act as a national arbiter of science and culture, as the Paris Academy had tried to be, its position vis-à-vis the local university (and others) was bound to diminish in the course of the nineteenth century. In 1810, however, such a development was far from obvious, particularly as both the idealist university founders and their more pragmatic successors stressed, respectively, the aesthetic and character-building aspects of *Wissenschaft* (rather than science for its own sake) and the practical education of nonresearching professionals.

The decision to locate Prussia's new university in Berlin was made mostly on practical grounds, partly in order to utilize the various institutes and collections already available and thus save the state the expense of duplication. This was also a motive for moving the Bavarian university to Munich in 1826. From the point of view of social control over students, many of the founders of Berlin had grave doubts about the suitability of locating a university in such a large city. Thus it was somewhat accidental that Berlin became the first large European city to have an outstanding academy and an outstanding university within a stone's throw of each other. One can only speculate how this somewhat accidental and pragmatic juxtaposition of full-time researchers and university teachers encouraged a competitive atmosphere in the area of research; only Göttingen had previously experimented with such a dualism. (The later Royal Saxon Academy remained a private undertaking until the 1840s, so that any competitive element in the city of Leipzig was on a different plane.) Surely the presence of the academy, the government, and an admirable assortment of institutes and collections lent the new university and its faculty a challenge lacking in the more monopolistic confines of provincial universities. Nor were students as free to exploit their juridical privileges or their numbers to lead the "free," that is, licentious and often terroristic, life-style they had sometimes enjoyed in small university towns in the eighteenth century. Students and professors alike led a much more diffuse and varied life in Berlin than in the traditional corporate confines of tiny university towns.

The role of the student

The thoughts of the founders of the University of Berlin about the proper role of students in the university had a fundamentally new character when compared to the thinking of most eighteenth-century writers. All the statements by Humboldt, Fichte, Schleiermacher, Schelling, and Steffens emphasized the key role of the philosophical faculty – the arts and sciences in today's parlance – in the education of the students. To a man they stressed the chief function of the university as the inculcation of unified principles of scientific inquiry. They did not see it as the ideal function of the "higher" three faculties to be utilitarian, practical, or (as they often said) artisanlike institutions for the adequate preparation of practicing lawyers, preachers, or surgeons: How to draft a brief, write a good sermon, or treat a wound should not represent the highest concerns of these faculties, in their view. For such matters one could become an apprentice somewhere, rather than attending a university.

There was of course nothing really new about attacking the practical side of the training given in the higher faculties: Medieval education theory had also stressed the theoretical side of these disciplines, to the extent that medical schools (an extreme case) in the early eighteenth century had not bothered to teach much practical medicine. The Enlightenment, however, had reversed this trend, and practical training had made strong inroads in all three fields by the end of the eighteenth century. The founders of Berlin were thus trying to revive an old idea in reintroducing theory as the major concern of the university. The philosophical faculty, which had sunk to its nadir by the early eighteenth century, had recovered enough by 1800 that many regarded it as the core of the university curriculum. The success of Göttingen's philosophical faculty had proven that this could be the case; Kant's *Streit der Fakultäten* had amounted to a declaration of independence even before 1800. By demanding that all university students have a fundamental grounding in the unified theory of modern *Wissenschaft,* which was the proper bailiwick of the philosophical faculty, the Berlin reformers were doing more than raising the level of prestige of the philosophical faculty and its teachers within the university (although they were doing that as well). They were explicitly raising the demands on students, who should henceforth be able to grasp the principles of the cosmos as well as learn specialized techniques for dealing with some of its limited, everyday problems.

On the surface, such demands are hard to dispute, particularly because the philosophers of 1800 were still confident of mastering the secrets of the universe and believed in the unity of knowledge and a great chain of being. The demands of the individual scientific disciplines were still relatively unspecialized, compared to a century later. The dominant figures in the higher faculties at Berlin were all men who believed to some extent in the unity of knowledge – Schleiermacher in theology, Reil in medicine, and Savigny in law. The obstacles to a unified philosophical approach to the principles of science were viewed as lying more in the weaknesses of men (laziness, materialism, faculty jealousies) than in the difficulties of discovery. It would take another two or three generations of scholarship before the practical and philosophical difficulties of the search for unified principles became painfully clear.

For the students, however, the attitudes of the founders of Berlin implied a much more severe set of standards than was common in German universities. First, only the best graduates of only the best secondary schools (the *Gymnasien*) were considered for admission by Schleiermacher and others. The thinking of the reformers assumed that all the necessary basic, passively learned knowledge, the foundations of pretheoretical education, would be strongly present in the entering students. The screening process being imperfect, many of those admitted would have to be told to go away, according to Schleiermacher. Only those who consistently showed themselves to be capable of grasping the higher principles of *Wissenschaft* would be allowed to stay and continue their studies, whether in the philosophical or other faculties.

Scholarships should be granted solely on the basis of promise, and in principle the wealthy should have as good a chance for financial support as the poor (argued Schleiermacher and Fichte). The reformers were keenly aware that university training of this caliber would be suited only for an "aristocracy," and they expressed their contempt for what they themselves regarded as bourgeois virtues and the instrumentality of bourgeois approaches to education. Because the reformers were relatively unconcerned about "schoollike" controls and regulations of intellectual growth (e.g., formal examinations), they seemed to count heavily on the professors' personal ability to discern talent and genius on the spot (a procedure that, as Schleiermacher said, required very frequent personal contact with the students). Socially speaking, their criteria heavily favored the very nobles, *Vornehme,* and wealthy foreigners that Münchhausen had hoped to attract to Göttingen with a comparable stress on the philosophical faculty. Leisure and means were at least a precondition for obtaining the type of school education that they envisioned as a prerequisite for entry.

At no point did the Berlin reformers concern themselves with either the availability of enough "talented" students to fill their university or the responsibility of the university to Prussian or German societal needs. They simply assumed that there would be enough geniuses born, with enough money and leisure behind them, to fill up the lecture halls. They further assumed that this casual attitude toward professional training would result by itself in enough doctors, lawyers, and clergymen to fill the needs of Prussian society. Humboldt, for example, spoke of the "blessings" that a scientific sort of education would "pour out upon" society. Against the background of eighteenth-century complaints about the overproduction of such specialists by universities, perhaps such a casual attitude was justified at the time; and nobody would dispute that a doctor, scientifically educated to be curious and able to keep abreast of the latest findings in medicine, would be a better physician than a man whose total competence rested on memorized ideas and procedures and who resented every further scientific advance in medicine as a challenge to his expertise. Yet the national health (or some other effect of high-quality university education) was not at all prominent in the thoughts of the Berlin reformers. They were interested in the cause, as they repeatedly said, of science itself.

In these principles one can discern the roots of some of the most worthy attitudes toward students in modern research universities. The reformers shifted attention from the average to the most qualified students, opening the way for the creation of a double kind of student citizenship. The egalitarianism of the reformers on the point of student–teacher relationships furthermore presupposed that the teacher's effectiveness would be heightened by his becoming more a *model* and less a *disciplinarian* for the student. Only those students who could or would follow the professor into the intricacies of his current scientific activities were deemed to be really performing as expected; the rest were relegated to the (always onerous) status of *Brotstudenten*. The eighteenth century had known its *Brotstudenten,* too, but they were by and large the least diligent students, those who did almost no work; by the definition of the Berlin reformers, even a hardworking student who did not have the right attitude toward science fell into the same category. This raising of expectations from the students would intensify throughout the nineteenth century, but not always in the sense the Berlin reformers themselves would have wished.

Just as these attitudes set up different classes within the student body, they tended to set the student body as a whole off from society and to increase the degree of social (if not ethical and legal) responsibility of the students. Throughout the eighteenth century the word "student" had retained a somewhat dubious flavor; students could be, and all too often were, loafers, ruffians, and vagabonds living under the protection of the "republic of letters." Jena, well known to many of the reformers from personal experience as the academic problem child of Goethe and his friends in Weimar, had the reputation as the dueling field of Germany; Halle, Prussia's pride before Berlin, had seen very serious student riots in the 1790s. One can hardly blame the reformers for wishing to replace this kind of behavior with a student ideal aimed at higher principles, and many of them believed that such an attitude, once inculcated in students, would make the problem of student rowdyism go away in time. Yet this hope, where successful, succeeded in attaching to the student, both during and after university study, a status above that of normal citizens. Not that academics had ever been closely coordinated with other levels of German society; but from this time on, their elevated status was supported more by a claim to higher knowledge than by the corporate immunities and estate distinctions that were crumbling away in Germany around 1800. Once the utilitarian ethic of university training yielded to idealistic justifications based on the pursuit of science, the functionally specific expertise of the graduate was elevated into the functionally diffuse prestige of the "scientifically educated man." The paltriest *Brotstudent* benefited from this prestige syndrome as well as the truly gifted and scientifically sophisticated one, once both emerged into the outside world.

As mentioned, the founders of the University of Berlin simply assumed that there would be enough students to support the university, and they were right. From the students' point of view, Berlin had many attractions. Theologians came, at first, because the traditional Prussian theological bastion, Halle, had been lost (and some of the best theological talent was in Berlin). Already preeminent in medicine in North Germany, the Prussian capital continued to attract medical and scientific students, who had the added advantage of being able to do clinical work in a large urban hospital (the Charité, attached to the university). Law students could look forward not only to being taught by interesting professors, but to being near the heart of Prussian government. A trend that became well established in the nineteenth century was already developing: The majority of Germany's law students were gravitating to large urban universities such as Berlin, Leipzig, and later Munich. From the pedagogical point of view, there is no reason why a tiny university could not provide as good a legal education as an urban center. But Berlin offered the spectacle of the law made and applied on a grand scale every day. For the scientists in the philosophical faculty, Berlin offered its collections and laboratories. For the humanists, it offered nationally known names, libraries, and the active literary and philosophical atmosphere outside the university. Judging from the average age of students, Berlin from the start attracted disproportionate numbers of students in their final years of preparation, making it functionally, if not formally, analogous to what in America later came to be called a graduate school. Göttingen had served the same purpose in the late eighteenth century.

In many respects this development ran counter to the intentions of the founders of Berlin University, who had stressed the *general* knowledge, based on fundamental philosophical foundations, that the *Allgemeine Lehranstalt* was to provide. In practice, Berlin became a highly specialized university decorated by some general theorists (like Hegel), rather than a seat of general knowledge integrated by universal philosophy. The same held true of other reformed universities. This was not, of course, an accidental development: It was a compromise between the somewhat utopian and elitist views of the neohumanist founders and the utilitarian demands of the traditional university in general and the Prussian government in particular. For after the ringing statements of Humboldt and Fichte, the former left office within a few months, and the latter resigned angrily as first rector of the university after a few weeks; and the representatives of utilitarianism (e.g., Schuckmann, the successor of Humboldt) and compromise with the older university ideal (e.g., Schleiermacher) had to grapple with the realization or even undoing of the original conceptions of the university reformers.

Considerations of attractiveness were not lost on the founders of Berlin, although they expressed themselves in much more elevated terms than the neo-mercantilistic ones of the founders of Göttingen. Leaving aside for the moment the highly utopian writings of Fichte, one can discern in the writings of other university reformers a desire to assure the viability of the university by making it attractive to a large number of students. Schleiermacher, a more moderate spokesman, a compromiser in matters of curriculum and rules, believed that excessively strict discipline in the manner of Fichte's demands would drive students away. In the matter of duels, for example, Schleiermacher believed that boys will be boys and that the proved mildness of academic courts was advantageous in dealing with student excesses. His colleagues in the university senate (delegates of the full professors of the faculties) sided with his views. Schleiermacher believed that Fichte's ideas were altogether too utopian and that students would be repelled by such a strict interpretation of their duty to science. He gladly tolerated the "special schools" of the three higher faculties, hoping only that the philosophical faculty would carry the burden of the new spirit of education.

Berlin's founders did not have to concern themselves as much with the mercantilistic questions of survival as did the founders of Göttingen. The dissimilarities of their situation are striking. Göttingen opened its doors as yet another institution facing the stiff competition of an already overextended system of universities. It had to tailor its curriculum in such a way as to outbid these other entities. By the time Berlin came into being, the number of competing institutions had shrunk considerably. Above all, the Prussian subjects, who might be ordered to attend their own state schools, had up to the opening of Berlin only the faraway and not terribly distinguished university at Königsberg (really the state university of East Prussia) or the University of Frankfurt/Oder, which was already on a "die-off budget," as the Prussian bureaucrats put it. Within the Prussian lands, there was no university that could compete with Berlin, if the latter were at all able to put together a decent faculty. Housing was no problem. The medical institutes already in Berlin accounted for a considerable number of students. The academy guaranteed a reasonable number of solid academics who could give public lectures in various fields. For all intents and purposes, as of 1810, Berlin would be the only major university outside Austria that was not dominated directly or indirectly by the Napoleonic system (which, to be sure, gave a good deal of room to the traditional universities and did not always try to refashion them in the image of the French *université*). Prussia being a much more populous country than Hanover, with far less university competition, the Berlin founders did not have to concern themselves as overtly with the problem of luring students to their doors. Finally, the Prussian bureaucracy, unlike that of Hanover in 1734, was shaken in its self-confidence to the point of looking to the university founding as a means of regaining, not just augmenting, its prestige.

Just as the Berlin founders did not have to worry too much about filling their lecture halls, and for the same reasons, they did not evolve as clear a set of priorities as the founders of Göttingen. There was no Münchhausen to set a personal stamp on the university and carry it through for decades. As soon as the crisis of the Prussian state passed in 1815, counter-influences (particularly politically motivated ones) could reassert themselves.

But for all the ideological pronouncements, the massive state support, the favor of the historical moment, the great names on its faculty, and the high standards of its students, Berlin did not achieve overnight its magnetic power over German university and scholarly life. Berlin prospered not so much because the university incorporated Fichte's ideals as because it rejected them in practice. The aims of the university reformers were not clearly achieved with a single stroke in their lifetimes, and different aims evolved over the next half century. Formally and outwardly, the ideas of the Berlin reformers had a disappointingly small immediate impact on German university life. Outwardly, the new university resembled the best traditional German universities, with a full panoply of bureaucratic regulations from entrance to departure.

Even in the "age of Hegel" there was no single unifying vision dominating the entire university, and certainly nothing like the reign of pure philosophy envisioned by Fichte. Hegel may have had an inhibiting effect upon the development of specialized research at the university, because his system and his allies in the Prussian ministerial bureaucracy tended to perpetuate the notion of and to favor advocates of the unity of knowledge in philosophy. But Hegel's hold on other fields than his own was proved to be short-lived; perhaps never has such great intellectual influence been dissipated so rapidly as after his death. Medicine, law, and even various divisions of the philosophical faculty went their own ways. In the area of research and publication, Berlin professors merely continued the traditions already established in the better universities. Berlin was not always able to draw away the best talent in Germany, nor did its academic allure necessarily appeal to all types of students.

At the same time, one must not deprecate too much the influence of the founders of Berlin. They provided a powerful ideological foundation that, if it was not fully implemented, could nevertheless be exploited for arguments. The later development of the University of Berlin, particularly after 1848, would take place with reference to the writings of the original founders.

State and university

Anyone who sets up a new university under the auspices of the state must be keenly aware of the advantages and dangers of living under such a patron. The founders of Berlin were no exception. Mention has already been made of Wilhelm von Humboldt's shift within fifteen years from being a champion of the freedom of the individual to being a champion of state regulation in culture. In the meantime, of course, the state had changed from an arrogant and (at times) even obscurantist body to a collection of shaken bureaucrats willing to consider liberal innovations. The central weakness in Humboldt's own thought was the assumption that the state is a moral force rather than merely the expression of the will of the king and a few hundred arbitrary central bureaucrats. Humboldt was perhaps as unwise to give up solid guarantees to the university or immunity from the state as Schleiermacher was wise to insist on them. But in neither case was the practical result much affected. As German academics discovered during the Hitler period, and for that matter as American academics learned in the McCarthy era, no constitutional guarantees can stave off a determined effort to mold universities in a certain political direction. As Niebuhr wrote in 1815, "Freedom rests disproportionately more upon administration (*Verwaltung*) than on the constitution (*Verfassung*)."[20] Where constitutional theory was weak, as in ancient Rome and modern Prussia, this was especially true.

It is symptomatic of the lack of a continuous policy of higher education that the administration of educational, ecclesiastical, and scientific affairs was often lumped together in the German states. Also symptomatic were the sporadic and shifting views of the ministers and bureaucrats responsible for cultural policy. From 1795 to 1825 – that is, fifteen years one way or another from the founding of Berlin – Prussia's cultural policies were set successively by the regimes of the clerical obscurantist Wöllner, the Enlightenment utilitarian von Massow, the dilettante, gentleman–bureaucrat Beyme, the neo-humanist Humboldt, the utilitarian Schuckmann (with effective opposition from or-thodox–conservative circles), and the vaguely idealistic but mostly pragmatic von Altenstein. With Altenstein's appoint-ment, personnel turnover in the Prussian ministry stopped until the 1840s, and Altenstein negotiated a careful path through the tense terrain of political reaction after 1817, yielding when nec-essary to the growing power of a conservative–orthodox lobby that stretched from university seminars to Junker estates, but also scoring minor victories for modern scholarship and the spirit of free scientific inquiry and making compromises to "avoid worse." Thus one might be able to describe Prussia and other large German states as having a reasonably rational and secular cultural bureaucracy after 1817, although one can argue whether its improvisatory actions constituted a single-minded cultural policy. Yet it was before this time that the major new universities of Prussia had been conceived and planned.

As we have seen, it is misleading to describe the reform *movement* typified by Humboldt and his allies as coterminous with the educational policy of Prussia. The reformers were often beaten and frustrated, partly by other reformers of a more utilitarian bent, partly by forces hostile to all reform. The resulting functional compromises produced the new uni-versities. The new universities of Berlin and, to some degree, Heidelberg and Munich, more than the rhetoric of the re-formers, constituted the main influence on the later course of higher education in Germany.

The situation of Prussia at the time of the founding of Berlin and Bonn universities was truly labile. Before the defeat of 1806, plans for a central university – or rather a "general edu-cational institution" – in Berlin had been discussed vaguely, but there was never enough money to implement them. Com-parable reform plans in other states had also proceeded haphaz-ardly before the Napoleonic period. The major reason for the decision to move ahead was the drastic alteration of the politi-cal world by Napoleon and, in Prussia's special case, the shrinkage of the university landscape as a result of Napoleonic annexation. When Frederick William III spoke of "replacing physical force with intellectual force," he was doing more than providing an uncharacteristic quotation for later nationalist historians or a ringing call to intellectuals to come to Prussia's aid. He was recognizing the facts of life: Prussia needed some inexpensive cultural prestige to offset the loss of its expensive military prestige, and it needed some centrally located university to train officials, doctors, and clergymen. The presence in Berlin of various scientific institutes and the academy meant a financial saving more than a chance to introduce a research orientation into a new university. For all intents and purposes, the Prussian government could have simply transferred the University of Halle faculty to Berlin – an idea that was considered but finally rejected as a provocation to Napoleon. The reorganization and rejuvenation of other states, such as Baden and Bavaria, similarly dragged the universities along in their wake. High politics forced the governments to abandon continuity and forced them onto an even more innovatory course.

Another political factor that influenced the shape of German higher educational policy was the two-edged sword of French example. In southern and western German states, the initial impact took the form of copying limited aspects of the French system – such as reorganizing "faculties" into "sections" and centralizing authority. These reforms would later be altered in the direction of the Prussian model, however. Prussia was torn between adopting the centralizing principles that had proved so effective in France and creating a "German" counterexample that would set Prussia off from the French-dominated German states to the west and south. Following the reorganization of the Prussian governmental apparatus with its new central, specialized ministries in place of the older, regionally organized departments, educational administration was centralized and unified as never before. Given the reduction of Prussia to a compact state east of the Elbe in 1807, there was a certain logic to creating a central superuniversity in Berlin. On the

other hand, such centralization could easily lead to regimentation of the university. It was the highly hierarchical, centralized French *université impériale* of which Schleiermacher was
thinking when he entitled his thoughts on university reform
"im deutschen Sinn," hoping to save what diversity and intellectual liberty there was in the Geman universities from stulti-
fying bureaucratic regimentation and control.

The secular trend of university–state relations in the German territories had been toward an increasing role for the
state, as we have already seen. Many universities had powerful
"curators" appointed by the royal government; and in many
cases they behaved like government commissars. The more the
principles of enlightened bureaucratic despotism spread over
Central Europe, the more central authority interfered with the
traditional self-government of the university corporations.

Anyone acquainted with the "reform era" after 1806, the
ideas of Baron vom Stein on self-government, or the youthful
writings of Wilhelm von Humboldt on the limits of the power
of the state might expect that this trend toward centralized
state control would have been reversed. Such a reversal did not
appear, however, and the reform era ended in Prussia (and
elsewhere) with a heightened degree of state power over the
universities and all other aspects of public education. This development was not solely the consequence of the undoing of
"Stein–Hardenberg" reforms by later reactionary ministers.
Humboldt himself designed the machinery of domination for
the Prussian state. His reasons for doing so were consistent
with his pedagogical outlook: The object of the state's concern
should be the freedom of the individual to develop his full
potential, not the independence of the university or its faculties
as corporations. In this, utilitarians and neo-humanists agreed.

The creeping dominance of the educational bureaucracy can
be seen in a host of examples. In the many large and small
reforms of German universities from the late eighteenth century to the founding of the University of Bonn, the fiscal independence of the universities finally ceased to exist for practical

purposes. University endowments such as those that continue to exist to this day in the Anglo-Saxon world ceased to be a major source of income for modernized universities (even Göttingen had not been given an endowment). Despite some discussion about creating a permanent endowment for the new University of Berlin, the new and reformed universities in fact wound up being dependent on the state budget for most of their capital and operating expenses. As the need for new facilities such as laboratories, clinics, and collections increased; as professors demanded more than nominal salaries; and as the German states were able to place their finances on a sound footing undreamed of in the eighteenth century, the need and possibility for government subsidies increased.

The governments were able to use the leverage of the purse in many ways. If the state paid higher subsidies to create more attractive professorial salaries, for example, it also insisted that the new professors be really worth the investment. This concern led to a much more careful scrutiny of the candidates for positions and frequent disregard of the wishes of the faculties. Many of the great names of the first decades of Berlin's history were forced on the reluctant faculties by the Ministry of Education—among others, Hegel, Savigny, and Ranke. Some of the most disreputable professors were also picked by the ministry against the wishes of the faculties, so that one must be careful about generalizing on the benefits of government control. Government interference dampened (but did not quench) the small-minded partisanship of professorial groupings at chair-vacancy time, and it reduced the widespread venality of the eighteenth-century professoriate and such abuses as open nepotism. At the same time, the state introduced its own kind of biased patronage.

The end of the reform era

Between the French Revolution and the Congress of Vienna, German universities had undergone a series of shocks and changes unparalleled since the Reformation era. Many had not survived the ordeal. Many others had been thoroughly reorganized and infused with a new spirit. A few, to be sure, lingered on in their old ways, such as Kiel, Leipzig, Marburg, and Giessen, yet they all stood under the threat of competition from the reformed and newly established universities of other states. The reform era did not end in 1815 but continued down to the year of the Carlsbad Decrees, 1819. During these four postwar years, Prussia established a new university in its recently annexed Rhenish provinces. Bonn, unlike Berlin, was a sort of outpost of Prussian *Wissenschaft* in a predominantly Catholic and heavily populated province. Its creation was an outright act of state, as important to the Prussianization of the Rhineland as the posting of troops. As if to continue the traditions of the enlightened Rhenish electors of the late eighteenth century, Berlin restored the university in Bonn as a counterweight to the clerical bastion of the city of Cologne, as a sort of intellectual fortress in hostile terrain. In the struggle against the Cologne clergy, which culminated in the religious cold war of the 1840s, Bonn was to play an important part. But it was planned as a provincial university, not as a peer to the University of Berlin.

The year after Bonn opened, the Prussian reformers were finally driven from office, and the era of deep reaction set in all over Germany. Ironically, it was the political oppositionism of the universities, particularly of the students, that provided the grist for the mills of reaction. As centers of German culture, the universities had played a prominent role in the propagation of German nationalist thinking and resistance to Napoleon. The *Burschenschaft* movement had come into existence as a spontaneous student accompaniment to the general reforms being carried out in the universities. With its murky idealism, devotion to a more dignified and intellectual role for students and to German nationalism, and acceptance of neohumanist ideas about the liberty of learning and teaching, it constituted a nascent threat to the policies of Metternich. The

Wartburg Festival and the assassination of the poet Kotzebue by a student finally provoked the frightened German governments to agree to Metternich's demands for stricter controls over the universities, adopted at a meeting of the German states in Carlsbad in 1819.

In practice, the most important stipulations of the Carlsbad Decrees did not necessarily damage the universities. The orthodox and conservative professors welcomed the new "plenipotentiaries" that each government sent out to its universities, but not all the new plenipotentiaries were reactionaries. Most of their activity was directed against student rebels, and their activities against the freedom of professors to teach and do research was sporadic and varying from one institution to another. In quite a few cases, the plenipotentiaries became actual furtherers of the universities' causes and interceded for them with the central bureaucracies.

Nevertheless, the Carlsbad Decrees introduced an element of intimidation into the universities that conflicted with the hopes of the neo-humanists for complete liberty. Schleiermacher at Berlin, Arndt at Bonn, Rotteck and Welcker at Freiburg, and many others were subjected to intimidation and harrassment throughout the 1820s. Some more radical professors, such as the student leaders Oken and Luden, suffered even more. The Carlsbad Decrees meant a defeat of some of the ideology of the neo-humanists, and in many ways that defeat constituted a return to the intense regulation that had been such a conspicuous part of the utilitarian approach to university reform.

The Carlsbad Decrees signaled, but did not themselves constitute, the end of the reform era. They coincided with the elimination of the last reform governments in most German states. Yet despite the onset of general political reaction and conscious efforts to bolster the authority of monarchy and orthodox Christianity, the organizational and fiscal reforms of the preceding era were not undone. The philosophical faculties did not immediately grow rapidly in numbers or influence, as the neo-humanists had hoped; but the other faculties contin-

ued to prosper and develop. If the rapidly mounting enrollments in the German universities are any indication, German
society endorsed and supported the reformed universities. Enrollments virtually tripled between 1805–10 and 1830.[21] Indeed, considering that some 44 percent of all students in 1830
were enrolled in theological faculties, one can perceive a direct
connection between the growth of student bodies and government policies favoring the churches.[22]

The reforms of the Napoleonic age accomplished several
major changes of permanent importance. First they eliminated
the chronic problem of oversupply of universities and the consequent weakening of all of them. The cleaning of the thicket
could have been even more thorough, for there remained a
host of small, weak institutions that could only subsist until
the enrollment boom of the late nineteenth century. Remark-
ably, however, the dozen largest German universities attracted
a fairly constant 75 to 80 percent of all German students right
through the nineteenth century, and the five largest universities
(usually Berlin, Leipzig, Munich, Halle, and Breslau) normally
enrolled about half the students.[23]

A second major result of the reforms was the fiscal security
given the universities. They were far from being wealthy or
even adequately funded by 1820, but at least they could count
on receiving what they had been promised. This calculability
aided the teaching as well as research functions of the universities by reducing the need for professors to hold second jobs
and by making the academic career attractive to talented
young people. The reserve pool of academic talent was incidentally further enhanced by the expanding institution of the
private lecturership (*Privatdozentur*).

Third, the price paid by the universities for state funding
was significant. The universities ceased to be wholly autonomous corporations and had to accept considerable government
regulation. Budgets, professorial appointments, supervision of
discipline, and responsibility for seminars and institutes were
now affairs of state. Although the traditional structure of uni-

versity self-government (as a rule, government by the full professors) was retained, the rights and duties of rectors, deans, senates, and faculties were diminished. Such traditional privileges as student immunity from draft into the armed forces and a certain amount of regular police and court authority were retained, but student discipline was markedly tighter after 1815. Student autonomy was thus reduced in practice, and students were carefully watched by the plenipotentiaries and their superiors down to 1848.

The secularization of the German universities was another reform that the period concluded (although it had not initiated it). Despite government attempts to restore the churches to their previous prestige in reactionary Germany, the theological faculties that spawned clerics for the churches did not regain their former power over the other faculties. Although many theological controversies spiced the period after 1815, it was often among the theologians themselves that the controversies raged. Rather than a united theological orthodoxy fighting to control the rapidly developing sciences and humanities, the proponents of orthodoxy had to fight just to maintain control of the theological faculties.

Aside from these organizational reforms, perhaps the most important change consisted of the revolution in attitude toward the universities accomplished during this generation. Indifference or outright hostility had yielded to admiration for and hope in the renewed universities. In the thoughts and writings of Herder, Fichte, Schleiermacher, and Humboldt, not to mention the practice of a small but growing band of teachers and students, the organic–evolutionary view of human nature and the quest for knowledge had created a new ethos for university education. This neo-humanistic view encompassed at least the preconditions for the transformation of the universities into places for research as well as teaching, for self-activated discovery as well as rote learning.

PART III

The German universities and the revolution in Wissenschaft, 1819–1866

The excitement of the Napoleonic era had resulted in the most extensive changes on the German university scene in many decades. The closing of marginal (and usually backward) universities; the opening of new ones of tone-giving importance, such as Berlin; and the reorganization of surviving universities all brought new ferment into higher education in Germany. Likewise, the defeat of Napoleon indirectly led to a period of political reaction, clerical resurgence, and high-handed bureaucratic rule in the German states; these could hardly pass the universities by without an impact. The hopes of the Humboldt–Schleiermacher–Fichte group of neo-humanists were largely disappointed during this period; but so were the hopes of most people who had a vision for the universities.

In many German states, however, political reaction and the purging from the universities of "subversives" coexisted with more concessions to the universities' needs than had been made in the eighteenth century. The philosophy of Hegel, for example, seemed to reflect the bewildering crosscurrents of the period: dynamic and rationalistic in fact, status quo oriented in politics, and religious in sentiment. The German university system of the period of reaction, during roughly the years

1819–40, was beset by confusion and contradiction. It was an age in which universities had to work quietly under the watchful eye of political commissars established through the influence of Metternich and an age when charlatanism and bitter feuds were not uncommon. Yet it gave birth to the first generation of "scientists" that we would recognize as such and trained Ranke, Marx, Bismarck, Strauss, Liebig, Helmholtz, Schleiden, Johannes Müller, and a host of other remarkable men of the century.

The second half of the period, from roughly 1840 to 1866, was even stormier in some respects. It was during this period that the ideal of Wissenschaft *was extended beyond the confines of a few innovative universities to become the leading principle of German universities. It was also the period during which the German professoriate took its most strenuous role in leading political opinion outside the universities, constituting itself as virtually the most articulate and influential "loyal opposition" to reigning political ideas. The confidence necessary to take up such a position reflected the heightened prestige that* Wissenschaft *had come to bestow upon the professoriate. The growing preoccupation of state educational bureaucracies with such extra-university matters as public schools, religious policy, and the struggle for national unification tended to weaken resistance to the professoriate within the administrative machinery. If the Prussian experience is any accurate guide, universities were often left to their own devices while ministers struggled on other fronts; and what energy even the most reactionary educational ministers could muster was often enfeebled by a solid front presented by the professoriate and, one suspects, by the sympathies for the professoriate within the bureaucracy itself (trained as it was by this self-same group).*

The triumph of Prussia in the wars of 1866 and 1870 ended this long period of gradual change and brought about the direct or (through emulation) indirect triumph of the Prussian university model throughout Germany. By this time, older sociopolitical motivations of university reform (whether the aris-

tocratically–bureaucratically initiated reforms entailed in the founding of Göttingen or the more complex combination of humanistically inspired ideals and politically and financially motivated expediencies of Berlin and Bonn) had faded into irrelevancy. After 1866, the Prussian educational bureaucracy had only to extend the successful principles of its own universities (shared to a large extent among educationally and scientifically advanced circles outside Prussia) to newly conquered institutions.

The story of German university reform before 1820 was often the story of state intervention and new foundations, as we have seen in the cases of Halle, Göttingen, Berlin, and Bonn. From 1819 to 1866, changes of equal significance took place, but they were much less dramatic than the founding of new-model institutions. If one discounts the moving of the Bavarian university to Munich in 1826, there were no new universities after Bonn and before the reestablishment of the University of Strasbourg in 1872. The only new foundings in higher education during this period involved technical schools, which significantly could not obtain recognition as equal to the existing universities. The establishment of such schools reflects favorably on the persistent tradition of pragmatism and openness to technological thinking of German bureaucrats, but it does not prove that educational bureaucracies were embracing educational change per se. Certain aspects of technical education seemed necessary to the preservation of the state; the bureaucracy tried to resist as best it could the manifold consequences of innovation in the cultural and educational field, even though the necessity of the change itself was recognized.

The educational bureaucracy, despite its enforced loyalty to the deeply conservative principles of the German monarchs, could not fulfill its primary function of maintaining the monarchy without making certain changes. The fundamentally modernizing forces of public schooling, technical expertise, and university Wissenschaft were accepted because the rationally oriented principles of day-to-day administration favored the augmentation of the power and prosperity of the monarch's state. Inadequate as this perspective was from the point of view of progressives, it did not exclude improvement. The professoriate could thus play on this basically approachable attitude in the bureaucracy as long as it did not challenge bureaucratic rule, preach social or economic revolution, or direct challenges to the monarchical principle. For the leading element in German academe in this period, goals, methods, and ideology were much more unified than for their counter-players in the state service. In Prussia, for example, the political coloration and moods of the various ministers of culture varied considerably, along with their willingness to interfere in university affairs. Altenstein (to 1840) tended to be a moderate friend of the universities; Eichhorn was an enemy, but a distracted one (as was so often the case with Frederick William IV's advisers); Raumer, in the 1850s, was tough but not irrational.

Despite the attempt to impose a common hard line on all German states through the Bund, *the worst consequences of political reaction were sometimes attenuated by the federalization of the higher educational system: The Göttingen Seven, expelled from Hanover in 1837 for their political protests, managed to find other fields for their academic expertise in other German states; the same was true of professors expelled from Leipzig in 1850. German professors in many fields had achieved a species of "national" organization and communication by the 1840s and shared a common antipathy to arbitrary meddling by the state in the "republic of letters," or, as the chastened political thinking of the time preferred to put it, in the* Reich der Wissenschaft. *The professoriate led the country in thinking of national political issues, because they had an ideology that permeated all corners of the German states, a faith in* Wissenschaft *to provide answers to Germany's problems.*

Clearly the story of movement in the German universities devolves in this period from the offices of state officials like Münchhausen and Humboldt, or even from the Berlin salons of 1807–10, to the world of the professoriate. A careful exam-

ination of the published literature and of the ministerial archives yields the same result: If the state was actively engaged in
the evolution of the German university, it was engaged without
the weapons of memoranda, directives, and other written
sources. Previous historians who have been privileged to consult both university and ministerial archives have usually relied
on university archives: The ministerial records are scanty, casual, and full of lacunae. This does not imply that the ministries
were inactive; but their activity seems to have been sporadic,
rather confused, and confined to the obligatory taking of positions on matters referred to them from the universities themselves. In an era of relative nongrowth, there were few new
chairs and few opportunities to fill old ones. Much of the material in ministerial archives consists of reports of political activities among students and (rarely) professors, dispositions of
Bund plenipotentiaries, and other matters that one would be
inclined to call "disciplinary" were it not for the importance of
the German universities as breeding grounds for political opposition. The vast bulk of the files pertains to financial questions
(for example, shall professor X be given a salary increase, first
through seventh petitions). The quiet drama of change in the
German university system either passed over the heads of the
administrative officials, or they simply did not record it. Other
evidence (for example, memoirs of leading professors) would
indicate that a great effort was made to keep the government
bureaucracy lethargic and, by manipulating and soothing their
naturally quarrelsome colleagues, to keep disputes "in house."
Whereas eighteenth-century faculty meetings had often resembled free-for-all battles, mid-nineteenth century affairs were
better managed by the faculties themselves. Nor did the leading
professors of the period 1819–66 always get their way with the
ministries: An astonishing number of battles were lost, yet the
war was won. The professoriate, facing a static and cowed
student body, and generally willing to appear cooperative with
local political emissaries of the government, reigned supreme in
the majority of university towns. With the new prestige of Wis-

senschaft *behind them, the professors could confront the state educational bureaucracies on something less than a subservient footing. And the bureaucracies, grateful for* Mass und Ordnung *(measure and order) imposed on the students, were occasionally willing to open an ear to the needs of the professoriate. State bureaucracies could not help admiring and fearing such figures as Hegel, Ranke, Liebig, Mohl, Dahlmann, and Schleiermacher.*

Another factor that makes this period particularly the period of professorial history is the relatively quiescent role of the student body in German universities.[1] *After a brief upturn in the wake of the Napoleonic period, enrollments at all German universities slumped in the 1830s and did not rise significantly until after 1870 (see Table 3). In fact, there were absolutely more students enrolled in German universities in 1830 than in 1872, despite the phenomenal increase in population in the German states during the same period.*[2] *The combination of static enrollments with booming population growth might seem puzzling at first glance. One consequence was a tendency for the social origins (income, status) of university students to rise throughout this period. The need for civil servants did not expand markedly; after 1830 or so the secularization of church property and semibureaucratization of parish priests and pastors did not lead to an expansion of opportunities for clerics;*[3] *and the need for physicians did not evidently induce more students to take up medicine until after 1850 (and even so, many medical students may have been attracted by the scientific training of the faculty without reference to the intention to practice — medical science was still in its infancy). The great gains were in the "philosophical" faculties, to which all sorts of motives must have impelled students to turn their attention. The expansion of secondary education, especially* Gymnasien, *offered careers for "philosophers": Many a youth who would formerly have followed a theological course of studies now heeded the call of science and humanities. Many a student destined to attend the university to prepare for a*

Table 3. *Approximate student
enrollment in German universities,
1819–70*

Year	Total enrollment
1819	7,378[a]
1825	9,876
1830	15,838
1835	11,899
1840	11,518
1845	11,892
1850	11,169
1855	11,969
1860	11,883
1865	13,499
1870	14,134

[a] Estimated average for years 1816–20 and
1821–5; excludes Berlin and Bonn. The
former had about 850 students in 1817 and
about 1,700 by 1825. Bonn had over 900 by
about 1825.
Source: Franz Eulenburg, "Die Frequenz der
deutschen Universitäten von ihrer Gründung
bis zur Gegenwart," *Abhandlungen der philologisch-historischen Klasse der Königlich
Sächsischen Gesellschaft der Wissenschaften*
24 (Leipzig, 1906), treatise 2, pp. 164–5,
303–5.

*calling instead succumbed to the siren call of pure learning
emanating from the philosophical faculties: Thus Ranke,
Marx, Heine, and dozens of other intellectual luminaries of the
mid-nineteenth century were rescued from the professions for
which their parents intended them.*

*The introduction of higher standards of teaching and re-
search in the German universities, for which humanists and
scientists agitated in the name of* Wissenschaft, *was indirectly
aided by the German states' suspicious attitudes toward political radicalism and fears about the creation of a restless academic proletariat. German governments strove to limit the ad-*

mission of students to the universities. Prussia's introduction
in 1834 of the Abiturzwang (school-leaving certificate based
on examinations), later copied by other states, assured that
only a diligent minority of Gymnasium pupils could enter universities. The measure was intended to reduce the number of
ill-prepared students, including those who sought university
training chiefly as an entrée into a civil service position or for
want of any better employment after school. The result was to
raise the quality of students and their ability to undertake
serious scholarly training. Another result was to eliminate the
remedial-education function of the philosophical faculty and
to make it the equal of the three professional faculties. The
prestige derived from Wissenschaft, which precisely the philosophical faculty at this time was beginning to reap, no doubt
saved it from the logical consequences that the Abitur decrees
would have had in the eighteenth century: the elimination of
the Artistenfakultät as a redundant organ of the university. At
the same time, one wonders whether it would have been possible to impose an Abiturzwang earlier than the 1830s, because
the level of education available in the secondary schools would
probably have prevented many candidates from passing the
requisite examinations. Thanks to the rising standards of the
arts and science faculties over the preceding half century, Prussia and other states were able to assume a higher standard of
instruction in the schools because of the production of better
schoolteachers by the universities' own efforts. The relative
growth of the philosophical faculties thus in the end benefited
the entire university system: Not only candidates for philosophy degrees, but those for all other faculties, had gone through
comparatively rigorous introduction to Wissenschaft through
their university-trained high school professors.

Other factors, too, contributed to the relative decline of students per unit of population in Germany. Prolonged economic
difficulties characterized the bulk of the period 1819–66: a
trade depression in the 1820s, the uncertainties of 1830–2, the
hunger and social unrest of the 1840s culminating in the revo-

lutions of 1848, topped off by political turmoil and wars in the 1860s. Despite the nascent industrial growth of the 1850s and 1860s, the new wealth benefited a class that did not yet send its sons to the university in large numbers. In the traditional fields of employment for university graduates, opportunities did not exist even for all the relatively small numbers of graduates: The 1840s witnessed a situation in the bureaucracy that greatly handicapped the careers of young civil servants and led to open discussions about overproduction of learned men. This very competitive environment no doubt made the life of science even more attractive while at the same time making competition for the relatively static number of professorships keener than ever.

Despite the relative fixity of student enrollments and university chairs, watchdog suspicion of political subversion by the states, and economic difficulties in this period, one positive fact stands out. The decline and "crisis" of the German universities, so widely discussed in the eighteenth century, had been stopped. The very fact that the states took a keener interest in the universities (if even a suspicious one) undoubtedly contributed to their stabilization. The fiscal and administrative position of most universities gained solidity as a result of the general administrative reorganization of most German states by 1820. The streamlining and modernization of government that took place in such states as Bavaria under Montgelas, Prussia under Stein and Hardenberg, and others not only made the states more efficient patrons of the universities; it made most universities abandon many of their inherited corporate, autonomous traditions. Almost everywhere, the autonomous holding and administration of university endowments in land, economic privileges, and money endowments yielded to state regulation by the 1830s. Gone were the quaint, complex, always inefficient, and frequently corrupt fiscal habits of the eighteenth-century unreformed universities: the monopolies (which in some places had granted professors the right to sell wine and spirits), the payments in kind (such as firewood and foodstuffs), and the poor or corrupt administration and fluctuating income from the universities' corporate holdings.

Although the state was rarely lavish in its support of the university during this period, it was not usually arbitrary, unpredictable, or corrupt. Thus the universities, in surrendering their ancient corporate right to fiscal self-management, undoubtedly gained much in return. Stability, calculability, and confidence replaced the more labile situation of the eighteenth century.

How, against this background of apparent quieta non movere, did the German universities (or rather, the leading ones) manage to revolutionize the concept of the university's role, firmly establish Wissenschaft as a principle, and raise both German research and German university teaching to a pinnacle of worldwide esteem? To what extent did political and social forces outside the universities influence this development? What changes took place within the university structure to encourage the permanent redefinition of the professors' roles, raise the standards expected of the students, and generally introduce a level of professionalism and scientific dedication hardly known in the eighteenth-century university?

How did the states support the rising role of Wissenschaft in the universities? How were students affected, and whence did they come? What new roles in society and politics did professors and students take upon themselves?

In order to answer these and other questions, this part of the study is thematically divided into two chapters. The first seeks to explain how and why the idea of Wissenschaft spread in the German university system. The second deals with the social, political, and financial sides of university history. In these chapters we leave the era when single universities reformed themselves and served as beacons for others. Although Berlin remained a challenging model for all, many other universities stepped into the competition for prestige and fame, shaking off the old habits of centuries of lethargy. Halle, Göttingen, and Berlin were joined by Leipzig, Bonn, and Heidelberg as great *universities by 1866, and even tiny and underfinanced univer-sities such as Giessen could make a mark in the world of Wissenschaft. The mobility of students and professors among institutions became accepted and lively. Rather than accentuat-ing their differences and achieving survival by protective legis-lation, the German universities tended to grow more alike. And the single most remarkable feature in common was the acceptance of the ideas of* Wissenschaft.

5

The professoriate and the research ethic, 1819–1866

In Parts I and II, we saw how change in the German university system was conditioned by social and political pressures. Visions of a different type of education among certain elite groups and the willingness of governments to innovate were major factors in the reform of higher education. The role of states and society in the evolution of the German universities between 1819 and 1866 differed substantially. The universities were discussed far less in public debates and were rarely attacked. Aside from complaints by a minority of educational reformers, such as those led by Adolf Diesterweg, and except for demands for reform during the 1848 revolutions, none of which led to any major changes, the German universities did not receive serious criticism. Conservative publicists did grumble about the generally liberal tone prevailing at many universities, but they did not offer radical plans for restructuring the universities. To what extent this relative lack of public criticism derived from the strict censorship and climate of repression in many German states it is impossible to say. The interventions of governments in university affairs were evidently limited. Aside from attempts to police the oppositional activities of students and professors, and aside from minor reforms and revisions that refined the general patterns of the beginning of the century, the role of governments in university affairs was relatively passive or indirect.

German governments were motivated by three major concerns in their dealings with universities during most of this period. First, they successfully discouraged an increase in the size of the universities. Among their reasons was a desire to restrict rises in government subsidies, the second of their major concerns; and they also wished to prevent the creation of an unemployed horde of university graduates who might form a troublesome academic proletariat. This latter motive also formed a part of the third general area of concern, preventing political radicalism at the universities. Low cost, a quantity of graduates just sufficient to provide recruits for the civil service and professions, and political quiescence summarize the demands of the states on the universities; these demands amounted to a program of stasis. There were also exceptions to this rule: The 1850s and early 1860s witnessed a period of heavier financing of the universities in general and less political repression than in the 1820s and 1830s. And some governments at different times favored certain innovations at the universities (such as more seminars) as long as they did not cost too much.

German society, while quiet in criticism of the universities, produced certain kinds of essential support for them. University enrollments rose after the Napoleonic wars until government intervention, rising costs, and other factors produced a reduction and stabilization in the 1830s. Few German universities then had to face crises because of insufficient enrollments. The generally poor prospects for promising careers in a sluggish German economy, the intensified competition for careers in the civil service and professions, and the opening of more underpaid but honorable positions on the teaching staffs of universities themselves all contributed to heightened prestige for university attendance in general and to heightened interest in the pursuit of *Wissenschaft* in particular. Distinguishing oneself at the university offered rewards of status and psychological benefit in an economically immobile society. Thus the external pressures and difficulties of German society during this period indirectly aided the rooting and expansion of *Wissenschaft* in the universities.

In the restricted climate of this period, it was natural for new canons of distinction to emerge. Within the universities, the ideal of original research and publication of new knowledge came to be established as the major criterion of distinction for professors and their best students. Small groups of professors and students gathered to explore the frontiers of knowledge together in the spirit of Humboldt. Despite the disappointment of neo-humanist hopes for injecting this spirit into the universities as a whole, the new scholarly spirit did live on in a slowly growing number of officially supported seminars and institutes. It became even more widespread as many professors converted their private lectures into seminar-style operations or met informally with small groups of interested students to explore new questions in their fields. Although the state did not rush to underwrite this mode of scholarly study, it did reward graduates and professors with outstanding scholarly credentials; and perhaps most importantly, it did not intervene in a negative way. Thus, although the states often attempted to gear production of university graduates to the available openings in the civil service and professions, they did not restrict the growth of the number of scholars and scientists.

The universities then reabsorbed some of these scholars into their own ranks, either as full professors or as a part of the growing ranks of the junior professors and lecturers. In both cases they reinforced the ethic of *Wissenschaft* in the universities with each passing generation.

The structure of academic staff

The most remarkable facet of the explosion of research and publication activity in the German universities in the mid-nineteenth century is that it occurred without a dramatic increase in the number of fully salaried employees on the teaching staff. One of the ways the German states stimulated the burst of

Wissenschaft was by holding the line on new chairs while extending hope to younger scholars that they might someday be eligible for professorships. Here the institution of the *Privatdozentur,* a university lectureship that carried prestige but no salary or corporate rights, was immensely beneficial.

From the end of the eighteenth century until the end of the period under discussion in this chapter, the number of *ordentliche Professuren* (regular, or full, professorships) is estimated to have increased from about 650 (in 1796) to about 725 (in 1864).[1] The average student enrollment at all German (non-Austrian) universities had just about doubled between the end of the eighteenth century and 1835, however, rising from around six to twelve thousand (where it remained, with minor variations, until the late 1860s).[2] One must keep in mind that many universities closed and thus eliminated professorships in the Napoleonic period; the contrast between the number of *Ordinarien* in, say, 1815 and 1866 would be sharper. Still, one could not describe the increase as dramatic, and it did not even keep up with overall increases in the size of the student body. Quantitatively speaking, the ratio of full professors to students in Germany was better in 1800 than in 1860. But this statistical observation does not tell the entire story.

The full professors, who constituted the closed circle of those entitled to exercise university self-government, and who absorbed the lion's share of the salary budget of all universities, were joined in the nineteenth century by a growing phalanx of *ausserordentliche* professors and, even more, *Privatdozenten.* Both of these university positions had existed in the eighteenth century, but they had not been so important. The "extraordinary" professorship had functioned then somewhat as the private lectureship began to do in the nineteenth century: as a holding position from which a teacher could be promoted to a higher rank when there was an opening.

In the period we are now investigating, the extraordinary professorship began to take on other functions. In some cases, its use supplemented the full professorships by allowing universities to appoint specialists in fields of narrower expertise than was traditional for a chair. The universities could thus expand and diversify their teaching programs without incurring the expense of new chairs, without diluting the power in intramural university affairs of the full professors (*Extraordinarien* had no voting rights in the corporation), and without committing themselves permanently to certain subdisciplines. The extraordinary professorship meanwhile maintained its traditional function as provider of a pool of middle-aged scholars from whom future full professors could be recruited. At the same time, the rank ceased to carry the implication of a *right* to such promotion, as it had in the eighteenth century.[3]

Extraordinary professors had constituted only a minority of teaching personnel as late as the end of the eighteenth century. According to one estimate, the ratio of full professors to all other teachers in Germany in 1796 was one hundred to thirty-seven, and among the thirty-seven only a few would have been *Privatdozenten*. By 1864, the ratio was about one hundred to ninety, and for every hundred full professors there were some forty *Extraordinarien*.[4]

The most significant development, however, lay in the area of the *Privatdozentur*. This was the fastest-growing part of the teaching staff in German universities in the nineteenth century. By 1864, there were fifty *Privatdozenten* for every hundred *Ordinarien* in German universities.[5] Anyone with a doctorate and sufficiently plausible promise of scholarly merit could apply to a university for a *venia legendi,* the license to give accredited lectures in connection with the university. At the beginning of the nineteenth century, the standards for granting the *venia* began to increase in some places – in Prussia, for example, by ministerial decree. By about 1820 the first signs of what later came to be standard procedure for obtaining the *venia* began to appear. After the doctoral dissertation and defense, the would-be *Privatdozent* had to present further scholarly evidence for his *Habilitation* or "becoming worthy" of being the peer of the university professors. This procedure,

increasingly formalized, had its parallels in the state bureaucracy, where the candidate (usually in law) had to pass a first
state examination (the equivalent stage to the doctoral work)
and, after some time as a junior clerk, a second examination to
qualify for further advancement. The would-be professor (who
also was aiming to become a senior civil servant) found it
increasingly difficult in this period to slip into an academic
career without rigorous proof of scholarly achievement.

In the Prussian educational system, for example, a certain
tug-of-war went on between the university faculties and the
ministry over the admission of *Privatdozenten,* the number of
professors at the university, and qualifications. Lenz reports
that under Altenstein's ministry, decisions about allowing
young men to become *Privatdozenten,* or *Privatdozenten* to
become extraordinary professors, were influenced by the minister's "benevolence, which he really had, and by his eagerness
and genuine respect for science, as well as ambition to raise up
the capital's university by any means."[6] The resultant swelling
of the faculty in the lower ranks (the Berlin professoriate increased from thirty-three professors to nearly double that
number between 1810 and 1828, with more extraordinary
than ordinary appointments, not counting *Privatdozenten*) was
effected chiefly under Altenstein, at a time when enrollments
were still high at Berlin.[7] Altenstein was still imbued with the
spirit of the reform period, at least insofar as a liberal policy of
accrediting young scholars at the university was concerned.
Once *habilitiert,* the *Privatdozent* in Prussia often hoped for a
promotion; once appointed to an extraordinary professorship,
he considered himself to be waiting for a chair.[8]

The faculty, on the other hand, tended to resist the creation
of large numbers of teaching posts. The state had to pay little
for the extraordinary teachers, sometimes nothing at all, and
paid no salary to *Privatdozenten.* Consequently, many of the
younger staff had to depend on the lecture fees paid them
directly by the students for much of their livelihood. In effect,
the younger faculty were competing with the *Ordinarien* for

students. But because Prussia cut back its expenditures for universities to a level far below that envisioned by Humboldt, and because prices tended to rise in the early nineteenth century without corresponding increases in professorial income, the professors began to grumble about superfluous teaching staff. Undoubtedly, the traditional corporate habit of restricting competition played a role in the petitions and requests of the Berlin faculty to overhaul and make stricter the liberal *Habilitation* rules, so as to give the faculty more power over the appointment of new professors.[9]

Compared to the typical traits of the eighteenth-century German universities, this situation was full of changes and ironies. Ministers had previously fulminated against the low standards and nepostistic abuses of the professoriate in appointing young professors and the rarer *Privatdozenten*. By the 1820s and 1830s, it was the government that favored liberal and numerous appointments of younger scholars and, in many cases, had taken the appointment of extraordinary professors into its own hands entirely. The full professors reacted by trying to cut down the supply at the starting point, namely at the *Habilitation,* by raising standards. It would seem that the professors were more successful in their aims in the early nineteenth century than the governments had been in the eighteenth: The relative stability of the number of full professorships cited earlier in effect meant a lessening of competition among the *Ordinarien* for students and lecture fees, which for them came to be more and more guaranteed anyway (as an indirect result of the increasingly demanding and rigid state examinations from the 1830s onward). The younger staff, while increasing in numbers throughout the century, found itself faced with higher and higher barriers to qualification for the *Privatdozentur* and *Extraordinariat*. One index of this rise in barriers is the increasing age of *Habilitation* and the widening gap between the year of entering the university as a student and that of entering the faculty as a *Dozent*.[10] Another index, and at the same time a product of rising standards of admission to the professorial antechamber, is an increase in the quality of scholarship done by the would-be future teacher.

Another result of the influx of young and hopeful scholars into many German universities during this period was the new competitive attitude toward older professors engendered by the higher standards of *Wissenschaft*. Whereas the eighteenth-century "corporate" university had often been so autonomous that the best way to make a career was to ingratiate oneself with the *Ordinarien,* the nineteenth century witnessed numerous conflict situations. The classic methods of making a career outlined in Salzmann's *Karl von Karlsberg* in the 1770s of course did not go away completely, as the persistence of familylike "schools" binding teacher and student, or even marriage by the student into professorial families, indicates. But the very dynamics of *Wissenschaft* by then implied that the best students would transcend the work of the teacher. Eighteenth-century "schools" tended to be much more static, with the students simply teaching the theories of the master. Quite often this dynamic and discovery-oriented vision of scholarship led the young scholar into conflicts with other authorities, and the resulting clash brought attention and fame to the young scholar. Furthermore, the drive toward specialization with each successive generation tended to favor the appointment of the most successful of these younger scholars to new positions as *Extraordinarien* or *Privatdozenten;* ultimately, new chairs would be created in their subdisciplines. In a few cases, young *Dozenten* frontally challenged the authority of senior professors within their own universities, a procedure that would probably have been fatal in the eighteenth century. Few, to be sure, went as far as young Arthur Schopenhauer, who purposely scheduled his philosophical lectures at the same hour as Hegel's when both were teaching in Berlin in the 1820s. But the very idea of dynamic scholarly development deriving from the new idea of *Wissenschaft* encouraged a certain breaking away from and progression beyond the canons of one's teachers, as well as the courage to dispute the theories of other, older scholars.

One interesting, if subtle, change in the academic world of Germany by the middle of the nineteenth century had taken place in the life-style of the professoriate. As a part of the increasing professionalization of academic life, professors tended to rise in social stature, to integrate themselves more closely into civic life, and to give up many of the habits that had set them off from civic society and, often, made them risible in the eyes of nonacademics. This process took placed over a considerable period of time and was not complete by 1860, and it was undoubtedly more pronounced in urban and large universities than in small, provincial ones.

Professors in the eighteenth century, as we have seen, usually functioned in a confusion of jobs and roles, holding positions outside and in addition to their professorships. Everything from their dress to their quarrelsomeness set them off from the rest of society. Contemporary chroniclers, even those defending the professoriate, conceded that many professors became peculiar as a result of being so cut off from civic society. Many forms of social deviancy existed, from very widespread pedantry and egoism to less frequent cases of misanthropy and alcoholism. Not even in his home was the eighteenth-century professor free to live a normal bourgeois existence. Typically, the professorial house united the functions of living and work, containing rooms for private lectures, collections, and books, not to mention rooms where students boarded. The professor's wife served not only as mistress of the home but as boardinghouse cook and hotel concierge. Professors tended to be provincial, traveling little and maintaining no extensive correspondence with others.

By contrast, the life-style of professors by the mid-nineteenth century had become markedly more urbane. A "new type, a model gentility [*Vornehmheit*]" had emerged among professors, many of whom were "lords in their appearance," equipped with "a wide perspective lent by classical–cosmopolitan education."[11] The improved economic existence provided by university reforms enabled professors to give up many of the outside jobs they had needed in the eighteenth century; and when they continued to hold outside jobs, these were likely to be closely related to their scholarly discipline. Although the caricature of the pedantic, graceless, unworldly *Stubengelehrter* (bookworm) persisted, the reality of professorial life-style was changing into a recognizable predecessor of today's. Following the general tendency of separation of workplace and living place common in modernizing societies, German universities began providing lecture halls, laboratories, and libraries as a normal part of their function (Berlin was the first to attempt to guarantee each professor down to the rank of *Privatdozent* a heated lecture hall). Travel, correspondence with other scholars, and interest in public affairs became decidedly more common. By about 1850 a man such as Schopenhauer, who had shut himself up in his apartment, bitterly maintaining that his dogs were his best friends, had already become an atavism from a previous age.

The professoriate and the research ethic

By the middle of the nineteenth cetury, the nature of motivation to pursue a productive scholarly career within the context of the professoriate had changed considerably from that of a century previously. By the mid-eighteenth century, some universities (notably Göttingen) had begun to place a premium on publication as such by professors. But the nature of knowledge then had encouraged publications of compendia, the end being the encyclopedic collection of all knowledge. As much as this encouragement had been a step forward toward the expansion of knowledge, discovery of new theoretical truths was not necessarily the central concern. Nor were all professors expected to participate in this activity, because many eighteenth-century writers believed that few professors had the requisite talent to write and publish. Publication was a sign of *Gelehrsamkeit* in the eighteenth-century mind, but not the only sign. By about 1850, however, various conditions had combined to make publication of research findings, and the ongoing process of research that led to new discoveries, a prerequisite for the successful professor. Standards of training and expectation had risen. The reasons for this change are partly environmental (the fears of some professors before a flood of would-be competitors, leading to stiffened standards for the *Privatdozentur,* for example). But there was also undeniably an idealistic element, a high valuation assigned to research as such.

The intervening intellectual movement that strongly conditioned this new research ethic was romanticism. Much more vigorously then in Western Europe, romanticism in Germany transcended the realm of the arts and literature to influence virtually every intellectual activity. In the guise of *Naturphilosophie* it even had a strong impact on German natural science. Historians of science have traditionally viewed *Naturphilosophie* as a harmful interruption in the development of fledgling natural science disciplines in early nineteenth-century Germany, although recently they are discovering more positive long-range effects. Romantic thought certainly bore fruit in many other disciplines, especially in combination with the ideas of the neo-humanists. The romantic conception of the *Volksseele,* to cite one example, furthered curiosity about language, history, and historical law.

Perhaps most important to the ethos of scholarly research in Germany, romanticism corroded the faith of eighteenth-century scholars in a relatively orderly, atomistic, and elegantly simple reality. The romantic outlook stressed individuality, the infinite and evolving essence of the universe, nature, organicism, and relativism. Probing into the secrets of the past, of language, or of the material universe depended on a belief that new and exciting discoveries could be made by the individual mind, if properly equipped. Among preromantic eighteenth-century scholars, there was a strong sense of the limited ability of man to discover more about the secrets of the universe than the general and extensive knowledge already achieved.

Nineteenth-century scholars in Germany, by contrast, were

convinced that the knowledge of their predecessors was superficial at best, and that bold acts of intelligence and will by the single scholar could uncover the profound secrets of the human world and the universe beyond. One is hard pressed to find any eighteenth-century professors who took research as seriously and passionately as many of the great discoverers and writers of the 1830s onwards. Ranke, for example, the founder of modern historical scholarship, approached the past as virtually a revelation of God. The documents that he was the first to consult critically were for him virtually divinely inspired clues, and to use them properly was to do more than write merely good history: It was, as Ranke himself remarked, a sort of *Gottesdienst*, an act of service to the creator. Justus von Liebig, the founder of modern laboratory-based experimental chemistry in Germany, was likewise driven by a passion to understand the true composition of organic matter and, in a philanthropic sense, to make his discoveries available for the material improvement of society. Alexander von Humboldt, an inspiration and patron for an entire generation of German scientists, did not subject himself to the incredible rigors of his famous voyage to the Orinoco because he was an adventurer, but because he wished to expand man's knowledge of the endless variety of flora – a passionate interest he had developed as a child (very probably as a distraction from the cold loneliness he felt while growing up on his family's estate in Tegel). One could list dozens of memorable scholars and scientists who were driven by this new passion to *discover* and, of course, to communicate their discoveries to others.

For along with the more dynamic approach to reality, implying new discoveries and revisions of previous theories every few years, came a growing need for written communication. From the early nineteenth century onward, the number and frequency of books, pamphlets, and papers from the pens of scholars increased. One by one, scholarly journals were established to speed up the flow of communication among specialists. And as new ideas and theories spilled out through the expanding communications network, they stimulated further critiques and ideas. Scholarly professors quickly became not merely leaders of discussions about recent discoveries before their individual classrooms, in the ideal of the neo-humanists, but leaders of scholarly discussion throughout Germany and abroad.

Interestingly, many of these voyagers into the unknown were as notoriously bad lecturers as they were famously strong inspirers of the young. Ranke was a disorganized mumbler before his audience, but he managed to communicate his zeal for the past and his methods for uncovering it to his close disciples in a seminar setting. Liebig was an indifferent lecturer, but he spent much of his available time supervising the dozen or so young men in his laboratory, initiating the questions for their research, pointing out where their experiments had gone wrong, and encouraging them to rethink and redo their experiments until they made a discovery. Alexander von Humboldt had great difficulties communicating his thoughts and discoveries in print, as did his contemporary, Niebuhr, the historian of Rome. Yet they personally inspired the next generation with their passion for research.

Official support for the research ethic also played a certain role in its spread throughout the German universities. The Prussian educational authorities, particularly Johannes Schulze, Altenstein's assistant, eagerly sought to give stipends to young professors to subsidize their research (as in the case of the young Ranke, for example) and to create prizes for original work by students. Although the monetary rewards of such prizes were not overly generous, the prestige of winning one and the psychological rewards were great. A prizewinning work was a good boost at the beginning of a career.

Characteristic of the institutionalization of the new spirit of *Wissenschaft* in the period between the 1820s and 1870s was the expansion of seminars and institutes at German universities.[12] Seminars had existed even before, but in small numbers, in the theological and philological disciplines, and with a more propaedeutic than research-oriented purpose. Institutes, which were the seminars in the medical and natural sciences, also existed in small numbers (chiefly in medicine) before 1820. After 1820, and particularly after 1850, they increased rapidly in number. At Berlin, for example, there were twelve formally constituted seminars and institutes by 1820 (seven in medicine, the rest in the theological and philosophical faculties). Six were constituted in the period 1820—49, half of them in the philosophical and theological faculties, half in medicine. Nine were added in the following two decades, six in medicine and three in philosophy.[13] The number of seminars and institutes more than doubled in fifty years (and doubled again from 1870 to 1909).[14] Heidelberg had eight seminars and three clinics in 1820; the number remained stable until the 1850s and grew slowly until the 1870s (there were thirteen in 1870, plus five clinics). By 1900, the number had doubled.[15] Tübingen had seven seminars and institutes, plus clinics, in 1820; thirteen by 1849; and eighteen by the 1870s.[16] In the first part of the nineteenth century, institutes and seminars were somewhat more personal than institutional. Many collections and laboratories were founded by individual professors and vaguely recognized by the state, only to lapse with the death or retirement of the professor. By the second half of the century, the seminars and institutes had become more official and permanent. Thus one cannot say with certainty how many seminars and institutes existed informally at a given time, until late in the century. But the pattern of growth and institutionalization of the seminar model is clearly delineated.

The formal recognition and funding of seminars and institutes by the state was not necessarily the beginning of the spread of the research ethic in the universities, but rather very often a culmination. At Berlin, for example, the historical seminar of the philosophical faculty was not formally set up until 1882; yet seminarlike courses had been offered by individual professors from the beginning of the university's existence, and under Ranke, from the 1820s on, they had most of the earmarks of advanced research seminars except the legal recognition and financial support of the state. In most cases, the professoriate took the lead in organizing such ongoing colloquia within the context of their freedom to offer whatever courses they wished. A selected number of students, usually no more than ten or a dozen per year, would meet regularly, not seldom in the professor's home (where there was likely to be a good library), to interpret difficult texts, undertake and report on independent research assignments, and receive the encouragement and criticism of the professor and the other students. Thus the early, informal seminars superficially resembled the institution of the same name in contemporary American universities. The later, state-supported seminars were more imposing organizations with their own directors, libraries or other collections, rooms or buildings, and budgets.

Whether informal or formally constituted, the seminars and institutes had a very selective and intellectually elitist character. Those that were formally constituted usually selected only the best applicants; successful candidates for the seminar were often given a scholarship, offered prizes for original work, and supported financially in the publication of their work. But even in the nonformal seminars, where direct rewards of this kind were not automatic, enough students were interested in pursuing the discipline that there was never any lack of highly qualified advanced students.

The attitude of the government educational bureaucracies toward seminars and institutes in this period was not particularly encouraging. Many professors (Liebig in Giessen is perhaps the most famous example) had at first to defray the expenses of research (in this case, laboratory equipment) out of their own pockets; and complaints about the niggardliness of the state were frequently heard. Sometimes the will to help existed in the education ministries (as under Altenstein in Prussia), but not the means. At other times, the narrow restriction of the universities' role to simple training of competent state servants blocked the path to an appreciation of the research ethic and its propagation through the seminar.

Eichhorn, the Prussian minister of the 1840s, for example, actually attempted to force the universities to inaugurate discussion sections for *all* courses. He clearly thought of turning such classes into a means of political control and indoctrination and undermining the prestige of seminars. The seminar idea had become so rooted, however, that the professors quietly refused to honor his orders.[17] The Berlin philosophical faculty in particular argued against Eichhorn's edict with a reasoned defense of the small-seminar method as the only fruitful type of small-classroom teaching, and one that necessarily involved only the more mature and pretrained students.[18]

Although crude political motives of such ministers as Eichhorn were rare, the state educational bureaucracies were still often led by a traditional utilitarian attitude toward seminar training. Throughout most of the eighteenth century, seminars had indeed been principally practical training grounds for future teachers, and they were associated with the theological faculties exclusively. They thus had a pedagogical rather than a scholarly character, aiming at preparing good teachers rather than good scholars. This had been the case with Francke's *Seminarium Praeceptorum* at Halle and its revival and continuation under Semler from 1757 on.

J. M. Gesner's seminar in Göttingen had taken a step toward modernization in that it was closely tied to the philosophical faculty as well as the theological.[19] C. G. Heyne, who directed the Göttingen seminar in the last half of the eighteenth century, introduced scholarly work more strongly, giving birth to the first real "philological" seminar that became a model for others. In Halle, F. A. Wolf pressed the scholarly and philosophical character of the Göttingen model to a new extreme, refusing even to allow theologians into it and insisting on the separation of *Schulstand* and *Predigerstand*.[20] Both August Boeckh, who later founded the influential philological seminar in Berlin (and directed it until 1867), and Johannes Schulze, the influential assistant of Altenstein, were enthusiastic graduates and admirers of Wolf's seminar.

Nevertheless, Schulze's vision was not shared by all educational officials even by 1850. Many adopted the utilitarian educational philosophy of the Enlightenment to conservative policies, continuing to regard seminars as the finishing schools more for loyal government servants (teachers and priests) than for independent researchers. And while the new, research-oriented seminars (whether official or informal) multiplied, the states continued to support the older, more practical pedagogical seminars, too.

The history of the new university seminars in this period is therefore not that of a simple linear fulfillment of a victorious idea inspired by the research ethic. On the one hand, seminar statutes (the "constitutions" of these small republics of learning) did increasingly stress scholarly training in the disciplines with encouragement of the students' own learned writings and research.[21] They mentioned preparation for teaching positions as the purpose less and less often. Even more firmly than in legal statutes, the Humboldtian vision of the university was anchored in the practice of the professoriate. The educational bureaucracies tended to tolerate these practices. On the other hand, the state was usually ungenerous and cautious in funding old and new seminars and institutes until after this period, and the threat of utilitarian pedagogical thinking in the ministries was never entirely absent. For the state, after all, the *primary* purpose of seminars was to train competent functionaries.

It is probably a reflection only on the utilitarian strain in the state bureaucracies that many research-oriented professors had doubts about the wisdom of institutionalizing their informal, personal seminars, or preferred to work within small, private "societies" uniting professors and students outside the normal curricular pattern. For example, the historical seminars of Breslau, Königsberg, Greifswald, Bonn, and Berlin began as "historical societies" led by prominent history professors.[22] The tension between "free" scholarship and the needs of the state, which Schleiermacher had discussed in his *Gelegentliche Gedanken,* was present in the minds of later professors, too.

The very depersonalization and regulation of scholarly work that state patronage brought with it was a disadvantage to be weighed seriously.

The social structure and group dynamics of these early and relatively small seminars deserve a study in their own right. The authority pattern was subtly shifted, particularly in the informal seminars and voluntary groups that preceded institutionalized, state-supported seminars and institutes. Alongside the traditional kind of professorial "authority," based on an initial differential between the knowledge of professor and student, the role of the professor as ultimate examiner of the students' knowledge in formal examination, and so on, there arose the habit of recourse to external "authority," in the scholarly sense. The professor in the seminar remained a guide, but more in method than in particulars, more in the technique of discovering than in the product of discovery. The successful seminar participant would end by surpassing the authority of the professor, at least in a limited sector of his expertise, rather than merely absorbing the authoritative information provided by the professor. Yet the student retained deference to the residual, traditional authority of the teacher, who remained a valued critic and, in a particular sense, a professional guide and patron. The tension between these types of professorial authority—the older, more static authority of fixed knowledge and institutional power and the newer, more dynamic authority of expanding research horizons and methodological concerns—provided a comfortable and very fruitful force field for facilitating the transformation of student into autonomous researcher. At the same time, it impeded the full-scale development of seminars and institutes into pure research organizations. This pedagogical handicap would not become fully apparent until the very late nineteenth century. For the period under consideration, however, it was anything but a handicap: Without the university seminars, even less organized research could have taken place, given the ambivalent attitude of the states toward such "pure" intellectual enterprises.

An almost inevitable side effect of the seminar method of teaching and fostering research was a progressive specialization of research itself. It may be argued that increasing specialization is built into any dynamic, developing scientific or scholarly discipline. Yet the seminar contributed its own particular inducements to specialization. Typically, the seminar leader (professor) would choose the general area to be investigated; the seminar members (students) would then divide the labors involved into discrete units. Very early in his scholarly career, the young researcher was thus introduced to habits of narrow thoroughness rather than the more universalistic drive characteristic of eighteenth-century writers. There is no question that this technique advanced knowledge on a broad front for several generations, as long as the successive generations of professors struggled to maintain an overview of their fields; but by the end of the nineteenth century, it resulted in both the growth and diversity of the university faculties, and the former condition (increased numbers of professors sharing less and less a common training background) was largely a result of the latter. Given the dynamics and success of the seminar method and the research ethic, what began as a means of circumventing the too universalistic approach of the general lecture and standard university curriculum in the name of deeper study ended in dominating the university curriculum and taking away much of the vaunted German sense of the "unity of science," a cardinal point of university ideology since Humboldt's day, but more and more honored in the breach as the nineteenth century wore on.

It is interesting to note certain morphological parallels between the development of the seminar method and the general developments in the German economy in this period. The universities, like the economy, were somewhat slow to grow before the 1870s. Yet many of them—Berlin and Munich, for example—were large enough to become, in effect, increasingly differentiated enterprises. For the majority of students, the task of acquiring sufficient training was discharged through a smooth machinery of lectures leading to state examinations.

What is striking about the minority that attended seminars and devoted themselves to *Wissenschaft* is the guildlike forms in which they worked. The seminar's stress on mastery of method placed the student in a position comparable to that of the apprentice working under the close supervision of the master. While the guilds were facing increasing competition in the world of the German economy, their training methods and spirit were being revivified in the academic sector. This revival was possible in an academic world characterized by relatively constant demand; yet, like the guilds, the seminars produced more trained apprentices and journeymen (those who went on to the *Habilitation*) than the academic market could absorb. As Max Weber would later argue, the German academic world was characterized by the fact that "many are called but few chosen." This could also be said of real guilds in the Germany of 1819–66, however. Ultimately the German guilds succumbed to the burgeoning economic forces of industrial capitalism. The academic world, with its relatively inelastic system of supply and demand, was able to maintain a guildlike system throughout the nineteenth century. The guildlike characteristics of voluntary subjection to a "master"; the quasi-familial relationships among "apprentices" and "masters," at least before the 1890s; and the frequent financial and moral support accorded to the "apprentices" in this system have never been noted by historians of German higher education. Although an expert observer such as Joseph Ben-David has seen the essential advantage of the German (seminar) training system over the French *université* in stress on method instead of subject matter, he and others have missed the difference between the guildlike structure of the German seminar and the relative atomism of the *université* experience.

The research ethic and the selection of staff

The rise of the research ethic and the qualifications of the university professoriate during the first half of the nineteenth century may have been connected to the rationalization of the personnel selection process. Something like a standard process emerged throughout most of Germany by the 1860s and has remained fundamentally unchanged since then. The outlines of personnel replacement procedures, so-called *Berufungsverfahren* or processes for "calling" new professors, were already apparent in the late eighteenth century; but there had been little uniformity and no guarantee that the suggestions of the faculties would be taken seriously by the responsible educational administrators. By turning their suggestions of names to fill vacant chairs into ostentatiously objective and "scientific" reviews of the state of the discipline and the value of the scholarship of the recommended professors, the various faculties could and did impose a certain compelling logic on the ministries. At the same time, of course, they imposed this same logic upon themselves and thereby built higher barriers against favoritism, nepotism, and other traditional professorial abuses. Their recommendations were not always followed, but the scholarly tenor of their arguments did not go unheeded in education ministries. Even with occasional *Oktroyierungen* (or cases of forcing unpalatable professorial replacements down the throats of an unwilling faculty), the ministries usually felt obliged to justify their choices when they deviated from the recommendations of the university professors. Thus in fact the process of *Berufung* developed in the early and mid-nineteenth century was quite different from the spirit of corporate personnel recommendations and choices of the preceding century.

The ideal type of the statutory personnel-replacement process in German universities by about 1850 appears to have been as follows. Upon the vacation of a chair (usually through the death or departure of the holder), the faculty to which the chair had been attached met. Prior to this meeting, however, individual professors quite commonly solicited advice from leading authorities in the field of expertise represented by the chair. Taking this advice into account, and often adding some recommendations of their own, these professors then attempted to persuade their colleagues of the merits of this or that individual. All these inquiries were, as a rule, carried out informally and discreetly, although sometimes the faculty minutes mention the solicitation of outside opinion. When the faculty met, and after an indeterminate amount of discussion, it would usually agree to recommend several names (often three) to the government. The faculty's *votum* or formal recommendation contained a detailed description of the scholarly works and academic standings of the candidates and an assessment of their teaching abilities (although the latter became less prominent as the century wore on), not to mention extraneous information that might enhance the case (e.g., native birth in the same state, religious affiliation, etc.) or explain away unfavorable aspects. The ministry, having received this document, would then usually begin to sound out the nominees, or direct one of its agents (e.g., another professor) to open negotiations. Sometimes these led nowhere, because the candidates were not interested or conditions could not be met; but in the majority of cases, as far as statistics are available, they were concluded in such a way that one of the names on the faculty's list finally became the faculty's new colleague. The new professor usually worked out terms (such as salary) directly with the ministry. Because the office of full professor was also a specially privileged rank in the state civil service, the appointment was good for life (or, in practice, until the professor resigned or requested emeritus status; mandatory retirement, in the absence of a pension system, was not in effect).[23] In the cases of filling a new chair for the first time or of adding a lower (extraordinary) professorship, the governments usually took a much stronger initiative, often not consulting the faculty in question formally.

This system differed from the more widely varying practices of the eighteenth century in some important respects, but it appears to have satisfied the faculties and the ministries when (as was normally the case) no conflicts arose about the nomination list. Although it trimmed the rights held by many eighteenth-century university faculties to name virtually whomever they pleased without much control from above (one extreme of previous practice), it gave a certain statutory guarantee to all faculties to be heard on personnel questions. And although it took away much of the autonomous decision-making powers enjoyed by many eighteenth-century governments (one need think only of Hanover), it guaranteed that the governments would not have to cope with passive resistance and unhappiness among the faculties. For both sides, it meant discouragement of subjective criteria in the selection of professors for the nascent research universities. Both the faculties and the ministries of education, in order to justify themselves, tended to seek learned advice outside the university and even from all over the German-speaking world in making their recommendations; thus a note of professional control sounded louder and louder in the choices.

This ideal type was not, of course, identical with historical reality, nor was a system exhibiting most of its characteristics most of the time obtained without a struggle. The case of Prussia is illustrative of the variations and historical evolutions through which the personnel-selection model traveled before it became classic. In the first place, some faculties did not possess the automatic right to make nominations (that depended on their particular statutes); others found that complaints about disrespect of their express nominations were counterproductive and brought them threats from the ministry.[24] As late as 1849, demands of Prussian professors at a ministerial conference show that the rights of the faculty in making suggestions were not yet fully secure, even if they were customarily observed most of the time: They asked that the ministry consult the faculties in all cases before making appointments, that the faculties have a veto right over appointees chosen by the ministry, and that they be allowed to make nominations at the extraordinary professor level, as well.[25] The Prussian ministry still clung formally to its personnel rights, but they were hard to enforce in practice.[26] During the Altenstein ministry (1817–

Table 4. *Prussian university appointments to full professor-*
ships in law (in percentages)

Nature of appointment	1817–40	1840–8, 1850–8	1862–95
Recommended by faculty	68	61	79
Made without consulting faculty	22	30.5	17
Made against faculty's wishes	10	8.5	4

40), for example, 50 full professorships in law were filled: 34 were chosen from faculty recommendations of the various universities in Prussia; 11 were named without consulting the faculties; and 5 were made over the protests of the faculties. The Eichhorn ministry (1840–8) made only 8 of 15 such appointments from faculty recommendations. But after the 1848 revolution, whether because of greater faculty circumspection or greater ministerial accommodation, the ratios improved to the satisfaction of the faculties. Under Raumer, 6 out of 8 appointments were those recommended by the faculty, and there were no *Oktroyierungen;* under subsequent Prussian education ministers, between 1862 and 1895, 112 out of 142 appointments were faculty recommendations, and only 6 of the appointments were forced on unwilling faculties. Expressed in percentages, these figures give the picture shown in Table 4.

The figures for all Prussian extraordinary-professor appointments (except in the philosophical faculty) are similar: Between 1817 and 1895, about two-thirds of the theological extraordinary professorships, nearly three-quarters of the juridical ones, and over three-quarters of the medical extraordinary professorships were filled on the recommendations of the faculty; the great bulk of these fell in the period starting with the 1860s.[27] In appointing extraordinary professors, the government officials thus found it difficult not to consult the faculties, even though they might not be bound to do so under university statutes. The reason for this tendency is probably that most extraordinary professors were promoted from the ranks of the *Dozenten;* these were often the professors' protegés, and their scholarly qualifications were much better known to the university professors than to the central ministerial officials.

The failures of the Prussian and other education ministries to respect the wishes of the faculties should not be construed in all cases as violations of academic freedom and professional standards, although in quite a few cases they did constitute just that. For the faculties themselves could be as unprofessional and biased as the educational bureaucracy at its worst. Consider the complaints of Germany's leading chemistry professor of the early nineteenth century, Liebig, in writing to his friend Baron von Dalwigk, the prime minister of Hesse-Darmstadt:

> At a university, scholarly and personal interests are always getting mixed up, and so one cannot turn over direction and decision making to the professors. It is doomed to extinction if the majority votes of the academic senate are made the guidelines of ministerial decisions, because every vote is more or less influenced by the personal or financial interests of those who are voting. This situation is to be found in no other collegial body. If one left the administration of the university's affairs to the members of an academic senate, the university would be nothing more than an institution for gain by means of the examination system or by exploitation of the students through the lecture system . . . Therefore their affairs must be led by an intelligence higher than theirs. Never has a university attained a dignified position out of its own resources; this has only happened because of individual outstanding persons in government, such as Reitzenstein in Baden, Münchhausen in Hanover, Altenstein in Prussia.[28]

One reads such complaints about greed, selfishness, and mediocrity of the professoriate more and more rarely after the 1840s, doubtless in part because the professional standards reflected in Liebig's scientific conscience became more generalized and tended to repress, if not eliminate, more sordid considerations among the professoriate. At the same time, the willingness of various education ministries both to listen to the expert advice of a Liebig and similar "outstanding persons" and occasionally to act on it even against the wishes of the faculties was another cause of appointments without consultation. Thus, although the appointive power of education ministries was often abused for political or other nonscholarly reasons, it also sometimes resulted in first-rate appointments that might not have been recommended by the faculties.

Still, as the Prussian statistics from Table 4 indicate, appointments against the faculties' wishes or made without their participation were the exception, not the rule. Except for the highly reactionary decades on either side of 1850, the faculties tended to select their own members. They had to do so with increasing attention to professional standards, however, in order to uphold their nomination rights against the educational bureaucracy. Similarly, government ministers were less and less able to make appointments for purely political reasons, like those of Professors Friedrich Julius Stahl and Viktor Aimée Huber at Berlin in the 1840s; even when political favorites were played after the 1850s, the government's choices had to have at least some qualifications for their posts.

In this way, the research ethic received an institutional value: Its product—notable scholarship—came to be the major national criterion for appointments in the ceaseless struggle between ministries and faculties. The rivalries among the German universities, in which Joseph Ben-David and others have seen a mainspring of research growth and vitality, did play a considerable role.[29] Yet these rivalries, or the potential for them, had always been present in the German university system. It required a high premium to be placed on scholarship in the first place before universities could compete with one another for the rare innovators among the professoriate. Why such standards came to be established at many German universities before 1870 requires an explanation other than merely competitiveness.

Although the German university system was indeed expanding in size for a time after 1819, its enrollment growth slowed after the 1830s and finally stabilized. The number of full professorships did not expand even as rapidly as the student body. Governments were reluctant to invest more money in chairs and tended to meet crying needs by appointing less expensive extraordinary professors. The professoriate helped hold down the expansion of its own ranks (and consequent dilution of authority and fee income) by colluding in the raising of standards for appointments over which it had control (full professorships) and for the achievement of *Habilitation*. In an era of limited economic opportunities in the stagnant German economy, the dual profession of teaching and research in universities must have been increasingly attractive, once the professorship had lost some of its old economic insecurity and social ambivalence. The expanding private and state-financed seminars produced larger and larger numbers of dedicated scholars imbued with the scientific values and methods of men who virtually founded their disciplines on a critical basis. Expansiveness and competition may have had more to do with scientific growth after 1870; but between about 1820 and 1870, the criteria of what was "scientific" were just being established in many fields. Perhaps the most prominent arena of "competition," or rather of struggle, lay between the newly assertive education ministries and the increasingly self-conscious faculties, particularly in the sensitive area of new appointments.

Having lost the last vestiges of their medieval corporate identity and privileges, the universities in the post-reform era found themselves confronting a state bureaucracy more determined (and entitled) than ever to interfere in their activities. Scholarship, *Wissenschaft,* was not only a product of the general European scientific culture of this era, but was, in Germany, stimulated by the nature of the university system. *Wissenschaft* could always be invoked by either faculties or ministries to gain an extra measure of control, particularly in the all-important area of professorial appointments. It could also be invoked to restrict competition for scarce funds to the more qualified.

Of course this success of the research ethic in German universities was not yet a triumphant one by 1870; some provincial universities (for example, Marburg or Rostock) were still running in their outworn grooves as late as the 1860s. But in the larger states, the process was virtually complete by the time of the founding of the German Empire.

German society also added impetus to the growth of the research ethic in universities. The German *Bildungsbürgertum* grew rapidly in the early nineteenth century, but opportunities for professional employment for its sons did not expand much. The life of science, *der Wissenschaft leben,* had become, more than at the time of Humboldt, a respectable, gentlemanly calling that attracted into professorships the intellectually active scions of the lower nobility and of the upper bourgeoisie. Increasing wealth and leisure (necessary for the long years of study and *Privatdozentur*), restricted opportunity in the general German economy, and the rising prestige of both *Wissenschaft* and the university professorship undoubtedly help explain the rapid rise in standards and quality among the ranks of the university faculties.

How these same social and political forces, as well as the new ideal of *Wissenschaft,* affected the German students, we shall see in the next chapter.

6

Students, finances, and politics, 1819–1866

As we saw in the preceding chapter, the changes in the German university system between 1819 and 1866 were largely the work of innovations by the professoriate. The students, for various reasons, did not agitate much for change, although their cooperation in the goals and practices of the emerging world of *Wissenschaft* was important. The states, too, played a mostly passive or repressive role, attempting to hold back "demagoguery" at the universities and to restrain the rising financial needs of the universities, all without completely stifling innovations in research and teaching.

Students and Wissenschaft

Student life and the free expression of student opinion were in many ways more fettered by government repression during the period under discussion than at any other time in modern history (excepting of course the Nazi period). Under the guidance of Prince Metternich, the Germanic Confederation set up, as one of the few all-German institutions transcending particularism, a system for spying upon and punishing political activism at the German universities. Even after the plenipotentiaries of the Conferation had been swept away with the 1848 revolution, they were often supplanted in spirit by suspicious educa-

tion and police officials of the reactionary individual governments of the 1850s. The campaigns of the Metternich era
against the *Burschenschaften* were at least superficially successful, for example. These "reformed" student fraternities,
which questioned the rough, clannish, beer-soaked, and pug-
nacious traditions of the old student *Landsmannschaften,*
threatened the ideological foundations of the restored world of
German petty states. The Confederation was able to tolerate
the "harmless" *Landsmannschaften* (or *Korps*), because they
stressed particularism and, in any case, attracted the more aristocratic and conservative element in the student body. The
Burschenschaften were, on the other hand, a more modern
type of student organization, despite their occasional postur-
ings as restorers of old Teutonic virtues. The serious, sober
nature of most of the *Burschen* and their devotion to real
discussion of political and university issues made them suspect
in the eyes of most German governments. Yet despite the
powers of the *Bund* to drive them out of the universities and
suspend or arrest the leaders, the *Burschenschaften* were only
driven underground, where they continued to exist in a shad-
owy way. Many of the German nationalist leaders of the
1848–66 period derived their ideas from discussions held in
the *Burschenschaften* and looked back to their prison sen-
tences or suspensions from the university with a certain pride.[1]

The suppression of the *Burschenschaften* is merely the most
glaring example of the type of control over intellectual and
student life for which the Metternich era was notorious. Professors, too, were investigated and harassed by the plenipotentiaries, by agents of their own governments, and by the university's own disciplinary courts. This will be discussed more fully
later in the chapter.

Insofar as German students of the period were still able to
express themselves in a critical manner, their concerns seemed
more narrowly focused on national political questions than on
the nature of university education. If the scanty historical records we have are any indication, student groups tended to

admire the professoriate; there is little sense of intergenerational conflict here. If students were disgruntled or dissatisfied with the kind of university education they were receiving, they were unwilling or unable to articulate their feelings. The period just before 1848 was the major exception.

This lack of massive student unrest about the nature of university education must not mislead us, however, into thinking that university education was necessarily a direct reflection of the satisfied wishes of the student body. Instead, it could be a measure of the general indifference of students to their education, to the difficulty of articulating protest sentiments during the era of repression, and to the massive romanticization of student life (particularly the nonscholarly part of it) by later authors and even some responsible historians. Occasionally a disgruntled student or former student during this period would offer a critical peek behind the scenes of university life, as Heinrich Heine did of Göttingen in the 1830s in his *Harzreise:*

Before the Weende Gate I met two native schoolboys, one of whom said to the other: "I don't want to have anything more to do with Theodore; he is a jerk – yesterday he didn't even know the genitive of *mensa!*" As insignificant as these words are, they should be written on the city gates as the town motto; the young ones peep what the old ones crow, and those words exactly characterize the narrow, dry footnote-pride of the learned Georgia Augusta.

In a university town like this there is a constant coming and going; every three years there is a new student generation; it's a true human river, where one semester's wave washes away the last one, and only the old professors remain, in this general movement, unshakably firm, like the pyramids of Egypt – except that there is no wisdom hidden in these university pyramids.[2]

Much as Heine or others might mock the style of academic life, however, they had few serious programs of reform. Students who found university life boring rejected it for aesthetic rather than scientific or pedagogical reasons. Some, like Heine or Marx, wandered off into nonacademic fields of pursuit when they no longer felt that they could take the university seriously; others (a much larger group of students) turned to the initiation rites and rituals of dueling fraternities; the majority, no doubt, spent most of their university time at *Pauken* – cramming, rather than reflective scholarly inquiry – in order to be prepared for the increasingly difficult examinations for entry into state service, the teaching profession, law, and medicine.

For the simple fact was that the German university, in this period as in all of the nineteenth century, remained for most students a necessary vestibule on the way to the main door of the professions and civil service positions. A university education continued expensive and presumably became an even greater drain on families as the number of children who lived to university age increased. Employment opportunities in the civil service, the ministry, and the teaching profession on the college level and most opportunities for increased employment of university graduates in the private sector remained comparatively inelastic during a period of rapid population growth, with the simple result that university graduates found their careers made more difficult for them.

The process described here, which led to even greater stress on *Brotstudium* by students worried over their ability to make the grade in the competition for employment, may be illustrated with reference to the civil service in North Germany, especially in Prussia. In the period under question, the Prussian civil service made only insignificant increases in the number of senior civil service positions. In order to raise the barriers to entry into the civil service, Prussia (and most other states) adopted increasingly narrow criteria for entry (including, in the Prussian case, three years of university study). A series of examinations was made mandatory. Prussia periodically raised the level of difficulty of examinations beginning in 1827, and the system took on its classic form in 1834. Candidates first took a qualification examination administered at the end of the university period, but given by the state, not the university. Its subject range tended over the decades to emphasize more and more a formal juridical training, to the detriment of the broader administrative training in *Kameralistik* so common in the late eighteenth century or in the more humanistic approach to administrative education favored by Humboldt and the earlier generation of Prussian reformers. The later examinations consisted of an intermediate one at the end of the first in-service training period and a final one, controlling access to the first real salaried position in the bureaucracy. Both tended to be based more on what the candidate had learned on the job than on university theoretical training, so that candidates quickly learned that a broad-based, humanistic, or theoretical education at the university was not essential to a successful administrative career. Not only professors of law, but higher civil servants themselves, complained about these conditions; but they were impossible to change as long as the Supreme Examination Commission of the civil service was dominated by conservative, pedantic practitioners of the very evils of *Schreiberei* decried by so many liberal "pre-March" legal theorists.

The effect of the examination system for the universities was considerable. In the first place, it formally instituted the requirement of university attendance, which had not been so clearly defined before. In the second, it made certain kinds of courses (principally those involving private law, e.g., contract law) seem more important to students than certain other kinds (e.g., constitutional law). Nor were courses in economics much stressed in the curriculum of the budding civil servant (much to the distress of the directors of Prussia's customs union policies and early industrialization), a defect that was not even partly rectified until after 1866. As a result, student demand for the various subjects now called *Staatswissenschaften* (in effect, political science) dwindled, and the promising start made by German scholars in developing this discipline could not be followed through.[3]

Thus, through the examination system and the institution of a certain required amount of university education for a civil service career, the state both encouraged the German students to flock into the juridical faculties and indirectly contributed to the withering of certain other disciplines in Germany, notably political science. In South Germany, especially in

Württemberg, *Staatswissenschaften* were still required for a nonjuridical civil service career throughout most of this period, and more weight was given to university training than to in-service training. There, however, in contrast to North Germany, the social prestige of courts and the legal profession was higher than that of the general civil service.

Most contempory and modern observers conclude that there was a surplus of educated men in Germany in the 1830s and 1840s, at least in theological and legal fields.[4]

Perhaps for this reason, there were many signs in this period of a more serious attitude toward learning among students. Increasingly, as noted above, German students relied upon seminars, laboratories, and similar "exercises" (*Übungen*). At Berlin, for example, there were thirty-two students for every *Übung* offered in 1820 and again in 1830; by 1840 there was a seminar-type course for every twenty-five students, and by 1850, one for every sixteen. In the philosophical and medical faculties of Berlin, the ratios dropped as low as eight or ten students for every *Übung*. For every *Übung* offered at Berlin, there were nearly 6 lecture courses in 1820; 4.5 in 1830; 3.8 in 1840; and 3.5 in 1850. These very favorable ratios were impossible to maintain once the university student population began to grow more dramatically than the number of teachers, from the 1870s onward; but they illustrate a clear trend toward the seminar–laboratory model and away from the massive, impersonal lecture.[5]

Another index of the increasing burden of *Wissenschaft* on students is the age average of those students who were awarded the doctorate. At Berlin, for example, the average age of a doctoral awardee between 1810 and 1910 was about 25. This average, however, saw significant deviations at the beginning and end of the period. About 1810, the average age of a doctor of philosophy recipient at Berlin was 21.6 years; by 1909, it had jumped to 26.7 years.[6] In the case of other faculties, too, the trend from the middle of the nineteenth century on was toward increased age of the doctoral

Table 5. Doctorates awarded at Berlin, 1820–60

Decade	1820–9	1830–9	1840–9	1850–9	1860–9
Absolute number of doctorates	851	1,260	1,347	1,504	1,727
Doctoral awards as a % of students	5	9	12	16	15

recipients. By the same token, the age of successful applicants for government posts and teaching positions in Germany increased. The general scarcity of employment possibilities in the period 1820–70 helps explain why students intensified their search for knowledge, or at least academic credentials, and their tendency to stay longer at the university.

Another indication of rising standards was that more students took the doctorate as time went on. At the University of Berlin, for example, the number of doctorates awarded per decade increased as shown in Table 5.

The overwhelming majority of the Berlin doctorates were awarded in the field of medicine – over 80 percent of them until the decade beginning with 1860. The second most prolific faculty was the philosophical, which produced a steadily rising percentage of doctors, increasing from just under 7 percent to just over 14 percent of the total between 1820 and 1870. Doctorates in law also increased from about 1 percent to 7 percent of all doctorates awarded between 1820–9 and 1860–9. Theological doctorates remained statistically insignificant, fluctuating in the range of 0.5–2 percent of the total. Within the philosophical faculty, doctorates in the natural sciences and mathematics increased slightly in absolute numbers over the entire period but held relatively steady as a percentage of all doctorates: Roughly one-third of the philosophical doctorates were in the natural scientific and mathematical fields until after 1870, when they increased significantly.

Admittedly, Berlin was somewhat anomalistic, because it had come to play the role of a second-echelon university: Whereas in 1820 the majority of its new students came to it directly from schools, by 1860 the majority came from other universities and evidently regarded Berlin as a suitable place to finish their studies on a scholarly plane higher than that maintained by many provincial universities.[7] But if one examines the doctoral awards of a relatively provincial and less imposing university, such as Breslau, one finds a similar pattern of growth. In the decade beginning with 1820, Breslau awarded 117 earned (as opposed to honorary) doctorates, 78 of them in medicine; in the 1830s, 193 (131 in medicine); in the 1840s, 258 (168 in medicine); and in the 1850s, 303 (191 in medicine). The most dramatic rates of growth took place in the legal and philosophical faculties; in the former, doctorates doubled in number every decade; in philosophy, they increased from 24 in the 1820s to 85 in the 1850s.[8] In the years 1811–19, Breslau had awarded a total of 10 doctoral degrees in all fields other than medicine; by the 1850s, the number had risen to 112.

It is not easy to explain this increase in doctorates by any single factor. Interestingly, the field of study most closely connected to a later career, theology, witnessed the smallest rate of increase in doctorates. Presumably the tiny percentage of theology students taking the doctorate were bent on a career in university teaching. For the clerical career itself, the doctorate was unnecessary and, considering the traditionally impoverished social backgrounds of theology students, prohibitively expensive. In medicine and law, the doctorate was increasingly a badge of expertise that could be translated into career advantages.

That the largest absolute increase in doctorates took place in the medical faculties reflects the rapid growth of scientific medicine in the universities and the establishment of the M.D. degree as a virtual precondition for the practice of medicine. The number of doctorates in law, though numerically still small, rose rapidly and far beyond the needs of the universities for degree-holding professors. We must conclude that the tendency of the juridical degree to become a badge of general distinction had already become established by the mid-nineteenth century. The degree was a useful credential in society, even for graduates who did not practice or teach law; it was not required for the bar or civil service.

The rise in the number of philosophical doctorates had more diverse motives. Aside from the advantages to a prospective *Gymnasium* teacher of having a doctorate, the gradual expansion of careers in the natural sciences stood behind the increase. The doctorate came to represent a sign of independent scientific and scholarly achievement, or at least of promise, as it was associated more and more widely with research and writing (and usually publication as well) of a doctoral dissertation. The disputation, the traditional standard exercise for achievement of the dignity of doctor, died out in this period. Though dissertations were still often written in Latin and rarely took on the dimensions of a full-length book, they did represent a major step forward in the incorporation of high scholarly standards into degrees, especially when compared to the sometimes corrupt and meaningless disputations of the preceding century. For the traditional *Bildungsbürgertum,* the expertise implicit in the doctorate made it appear as a means, quite apart from career requirements, of personal distinction, setting off degree holders from the rest of the students. The costs of obtaining the doctorate tended to make it socially exclusive, as well: The extra time at the university, the fees, and the high costs of having the dissertation printed must have made a doctorate a forbiddingly high sacrifice for the less well-to-do students. Just as members of the *Bildungsbürgertum* tended to look upon the juridical doctorate as a means of gaining ground on the nobles in the civil services of the late seventeenth century, by the mid-nineteenth century they were increasingly looking upon the doctorate in philosophy as a means of social distinction, this time vis-à-vis the increasingly prosperous commercial middle class as well.

In social recruitment, the German university students of this period presented a heterogenous picture. The majority of students came from upper-middle-class and noble families. Doctors, lawyers, officials, professors, businessmen, large landowners, and people of a similar social level were the fathers of 60 to 80 percent of the students at Berlin, for example. Not until after 1870 was there any major change in the ratios of social origins of Berlin students, although the commercial and landowning groups made modest gains at the expense, primarily, of the lower-middle-class group.[9] Because university attendance remained expensive and the *Abitur* requirement institutionalized in many universities by the 1830s practically excluded those who could not afford to attend an expensive *Gymnasium* or similar school, the student body became more socially exclusive in the period 1820–70. No complete figures are available to establish what proportion of the nobility sent its sons to the university in this era, but what evidence there is indicates that it remained high.

In a survey of five non-Prussian universities between 1800 and 1870, Konrad Jarausch found that about one-eighth of the students, on the average, were of noble birth. Of these five, scientifically prestigious Göttingen and Heidelberg attracted the highest percentages (14.4 and 12.5, respectively), and mediocre Kiel had the lowest (5.8). The proportion of noble students fluctuated with total enrollments, reaching high points (18 percent in 1797 and nearly 15 percent in 1847) during periods of low general enrollments and declining (to just under 10 percent) in times when universities were attracting more students. Even as late as 1867, however, nobles constituted between 5 and 10 percent of the student bodies of the universities sampled.[10] University attendance had become virtually de rigueur for any higher state office, which the nobility successfully competed for; and by mid-century even *Junker* farmers were beginning to apply the principles of scientific agriculture to their farms and looked upon the agricultural and forestry chairs at the universities as a font of guidance in their endeavors.

The number of students coming from the commercial middle class (*Besitzbürgertum*) before about 1870 was only slightly larger, on the average, than that coming from the nobility. According to the samples cited above, only one-seventh of the students came from the commercial middle class. About half the students at the five universities studied by Jarausch came from academic families, that is, had fathers who had attended a university.[11]

Finally, the sons of the lower middle class and of the poor constituted a small part of the university student body. One must note, however, that the temporary high level of enrollments in the late 1820s and early 1830s was due in large measure to an additional influx from the lower middle class.

Student subsociety is hard to describe exactly, given the absence of reliable accounts and statistics, but if contemporary literature is an accurate guide, students fell into one of three rough categories. These were scholars, cavaliers, and *Brotstudenten,* and their primary orientations toward university life were, respectively, scholarly, social, and careerist. These categories did not correspond directly to social class origins, but one can say that there was a tendency toward a rough correlation between social standing and category at least among the *Kavaliere* and *Brotstudenten*. The former, whether bourgeois or noble, came largely from families of impeccable social repute and, generally, adequate wealth to support an ostentatious life-style. They were more prominent in North German and Protestant universities, somewhat less so in South German or Catholic ones. The experiences of Count Bismarck as a student at Göttingen, as recorded in his *Reflections and Reminiscences,* may be taken as symptomatic of the cavalier lifestyle: much drinking and dueling interrupted by only superficial attention to studies, usually in law. Although not in the majority at most universities, the cavaliers tended to set the social tone and created the many romantic myths of nineteenth-century German student life in their fraternities.

The *Brotstudenten,* who probably constituted the majority of students in most universities (particularly the provincial ones), had to rely less on the contacts and friendships for which the cavaliers had, in some measure, come to the university and more on their ability to pass through the rigors of the state examining system into a secure haven in the public service. Though more sober and single-minded in the pursuit of knowledge than the cavaliers, they were even more loathed by the research-oriented professoriate than the lighthearted wealthy. Their haste to get through the expensive university years, their narrow focus on subjects useful to pass state examinations, and their unimaginative industriousness threatened the ideal of *Wissenschaft* that was becoming a standard feature of professorial rhetoric.

Instead, the professoriate cultivated the smallest category of students, the scholars, who in a sense were the academic children of the professors and a guarantee that the ideals of *Wissenschaft* would live on into the next generation. The characteristics of this group of students are perhaps the most elusive of all. It would be mistaken to equate their numbers with the number of doctoral candidates, as many *doctores* (particularly in medicine) were also *Brotstudenten*, and as some of the most scientifically promising minds in seminars and laboratories did not turn their energies toward doctoral work. The social origins of the scholar students were also widely heterogeneous, ranging from the poverty of Georg Gervinus, a tanner's son, to the genteel impecuniousness of Leopold von Ranke, to the affluence and prestige of Heinrich von Treitschke, an aristocratic general's son, to name only three scholars who later became prominent history professors. Because the seminar or laboratory, with its objective standards of merit, was the scene on which the scholars appeared, family origins and narrowly defined future career interests did not play a predominant role in their university orientations. Performing well in the scholarly world of the seminar of course furthered one's career; but performing poorly in it was no help at all, and the unserious student would do better to retain the anonymity of *Brotstudium*, taking as many lecture courses as possible and cramming for specific examination topics. Given the open-ended nature of seminar and laboratory work, it was no special guarantee of doing well on narrowly focused state examinations, which tested knowledge rather than technique.

Brotstudium thus persisted in an era when the professoriate and (often) the educational bureaucracy sought to extirpate it and make a broad, theoretical education the reality as well as the ideal of German universities. Its persistence exposes the practical difficulty of giving an essentially pedagogical institution a research orientation. Quite evidently, the absolute number of students using the universities as a training base for a career rather than as an experimental laboratory leading to the lifelong mastery of *Wissenschaft* was a majority.

In summary, the rise of *Wissenschaft* in the German universities, coupled with restrictions and higher standards for admission to the university and the professions, had a pronounced, if not yet spectacular, effect on students. Compared to their eighteenth-century counterparts, the students of the period 1819–66 had to study more diligently because of the increasing value placed on scholarship and increasingly rigorous professional examinations. In an era of generally restricted career opportunities, the route of self-education through work in seminars and laboratories – "living for scholarship" – achieved a certain attraction for a growing minority of well-qualified students. They could set themselves off from the mass of *Brotstudenten* and engage in an ethically and socially more satisfying activity at the university than the mindless self-indulgences of the saber-wielding fraternity students.

Limitations on certain types of student activity (e.g., politics); the large degree of student recruitment from the professional, bureaucratic, and intellectual elites; the relatively high percentage of students from families prosperous enough to support a leisurely university stay; and the attraction of a socially esteemed involvement in *Wissenschaft* at a time when opportunities for other types of careers were severely limited all help explain the inclination of many students to accept the new canons of *Wissenschaft*. The expansion of public schools and rising standards for their teachers undoubtedly made serious study in the philosophical faculties more alluring; and it was especially in these faculties that the ideals of *Wissenschaft* took strongest hold.

At the same time, student groups in this period were severely circumscribed in their activities and appear to have exerted little direct influence on university policies. Students were to a large degree the objects of developments in the universities. For the vast majority of students, university attendance remained primarily a route to careers in the civil service and professions – indeed, virtually the only route, as entrance requirements into bureaucracy and professions were tightened. Improved discipline, the higher average age of the student body, and more rigorous qualifications for careers undoubtedly encouraged studiousness more than eighteenth-century conditions had done. But large numbers of cavaliers continued to attend the universities for social or conventional reasons, at least in part.

In the absence of high external rewards for pursuing *Wissenschaft* in the form of secure career opportunities for scholars, and considering both the high cost of university study and the modest funding of seminars and institutes in this period, one might even be surprised that so many students embraced the definition of the university as a seat of *Wissenschaft*. Let us now turn to these economic matters.

The economics of university Wissenschaft

In order to become firmly entrenched in the universities, the spirit of scientific enquiry depended on the bread of financial sustenance. One of the ways in which universities benefited from political reorganization around 1810–20 was in the much heightened degree of economic security and calculability. As mentioned earlier, the support of the state became regular and dependable, and supervision of the state introduced at last the efficiency of bureaucratic fiscal administration to replace the inefficient, semifeudal, corporate management that had characterized universities earlier. Security and calculability are important elements in any economy, and they should not be overlooked as contributory factors in the rise of the research ethic in early nineteenth-century Germany. Even a small amount of income, if regular and calculable, can have more impact than larger but more erratically delivered financial support. The creative spirit does not leap into activity at the opening of a purse, but must be built up over long periods.

The heightened commitment of the various German governments to a new concept of the role of universities between 1820 and 1870 is furthermore reflected in the allocation of state funds to the universities. Though the investment levels of the last third of the nineteenth century somewhat eclipsed the more gradual growth in public investment before the 1870s, one must recall that there was also a dramatic rise in university attendance to justify much of the increased budgeting, and that price inflation played a role in the late nineteenth century as well. Between 1819 and 1866, there was a relatively constant number of students at German universities, yet expenditures increased. Increases were most dramatic in the research sector.

Consider the case of Berlin University. Its budget grew from 241,000 thaler in 1820 to 774,000 thaler in 1870, more than tripling in fifty years.[12] Academic salaries, which consumed 181,000 thaler in 1820, had grown to 322,000 thaler by 1870. This meant that the salary budget had not even doubled, although the number of professors (full and extraordinary) had roughly doubled, from 50 to 108.[13] If one counts only full professors (who took the lion's share of university salaries), the number had increased from 30 to 50 – again, not quite double. Where did the large increase in the budget go? Not for buildings and the physical plant, nor for prize money (which actually declined); administrative costs did increase, but remained relatively small. The most dramatic single item of budget increase was seminars and institutes. In 1820 they had together received 37,500 thaler; by 1870 the figure was

375,500 thaler, or a 1,000 percent increase.[14] Put another way, Berlin in 1820 had spent over six times as much on faculty salaries as on institutes and seminars; by 1870, the amount spent on the latter actually exceeded the total budget for professorial salaries.

The regular budget of Breslau University grew similarly. In 1821, the university spent a little over 67,000 thaler; by 1871, the figure had reached 121,000 plus considerable extraordinary subsidies totaling about 30,000 thaler per year, or roughly 150,000 thaler.[15] Although the overall budget increased by more than 100 percent, the professorial salaries did not keep pace, rising from 39,000 to 59,000 thaler or only about 50 percent. Costs of seminars and institutes, on the other hand, more than doubled, from 17,500 to 38,000 thaler.[16] The faculty (full and associate professors) had grown from forty-two to sixty over the same time period.[17] Although Breslau might be considered a university at the opposite extreme from prestigious Berlin, it also showed a pattern of considerable and disproportionate growth in expenditures for research institutions.

Such numbers do not, of course, indicate an equal distribution of funds to all areas of research: Much of the dramatic increase in outlay can be explained by the equally dramatic increase in costs involved in specific kinds of research and teaching, notably in medicine and the natural sciences. German medicine in 1820 was still dominated to a large degree by speculative *Naturphilosophie* and had little need of complicated facilities; by 1870, Berlin had become a world center of medicine and medical research. Nevertheless, the government also gave dramatically increased amounts of aid to many fields other than medicine and natural science.

Increased support to universities and especially to their research-oriented divisions, though dramatic, was still not lavish. This statement needs some elaboration. Compared to the late eighteenth century, support increased and continued to grow throughout this half century, even though student numbers did not grow much. Governments did respond to such trends as specialization and burgeoning research costs in science and medicine by increasing financial commitments. Most eighteenth-century scholars would have marveled at the levels of support and the economic security of their early nineteenth-century successors. Yet this financial support was not really *generous* and, in the view of many professors and even administrators of the early nineteenth century, was sometimes even inadequate. Certainly university funding between about 1820 and 1870 appears puny when compared to the rapid expansion of university budgets and state support after the unification of Germany.

At the beginning of this period, in the 1820s, the economic effects of a general slump, state financial difficulties, and perhaps a certain mistrust of the universities by conservative officials in the wake of liberal agitation there led to a steady but still minimal financial commitment to universities. Salaries were by then paid to professors more or less regularly, but they were still too low. Humboldt, for example, had envisioned a normal salary of 1,500 thaler for Berlin full professors; instead, just after 1820, the normal salary was about 800 thaler.[18] At the University of Tübingen, the highest salary for a professor was 1,400 gulden, or about 700 thaler, in 1829, and these rates remained in effect until 1858.[19] Some of the more backward universities still had not regulated salaries as late as the 1830s. At Marburg in 1818, salaries for *Ordinarii* ranged between 400 and 850 thaler. At Rostock, incomes were set completely arbitrarily until 1837. Thereafter, salaries for full professors were set at between 1,000 and 1,400 thaler. Even by 1870 the maximum salary had reached only 1,700 thaler, making Rostock professors some of the most poorly paid in Germany.[20] If the salaries of *Ordinarien* were insufficient, those of the growing number of *Nichtordinarien,* that is, extraordinary professors and *Privatdozenten,* were almost negligible. *Privatdozenten* received no salary, as a rule, and many extraordinary professors received little or none.

Funds for seminars, institutes, and collections were also not particularly generous in 1820. The most important seminars, scientifically speaking, were the philological ones. Although several of these were founded just before and after 1820, they did not require much investment, given the nature of philological research and teaching. The more expensive medical and natural science institutes that were founded between about 1820 and 1860 very often had to struggle against the penury of their budgets. Liebig, who founded his famous chemical laboratory at Giessen in 1825, had to complain constantly about lack of state support and purchased much of the equipment himself. In 1834, Prussia allotted 400 to 500 thaler to the physics collections of Bonn and Berlin, but only 60 thaler for Greifswald – not nearly enough to buy, for example, an air pump.[21]

Things had not improved much by the middle of the 1830s. A glance at some figures from the 1830s will give an idea of how modest the financial commitment of German governments to their universities then was. Tables 6 and 7 show that the largest item in the Prussian university budget was still professorial salaries, which averaged from a high of 1,200 thaler at Berlin University in 1834, down to a low average of about 850 thaler at Breslau. Those averages involved the *Ordinarii,* a few dozen professors at each university. Thus, for Berlin University, over 50,000 thaler or well over half the state's budget still went to salaries for full professors.

The proportions were roughly the same in other states: In Hesse-Kassel, for example, about half the budget for Marburg (totaling 22,000 thaler) went to professorial salaries.[22] Not only did the Prussian state spend more on the average full professor's salary than on most of the seminars and laboratories, but, at least in the case of Berlin in 1834, more than on the entire library. This is not to say that professors were overpaid; they had to depend on their income from lecture and other fees (dissertation fees, etc.) to augment their salaries. In the aggregate, to be sure, income from such sources probably rose somewhat in the early nineteenth century: Rising numbers of stu-

Table 6. *Prussian university economics in 1834*

Institution	Enrolled students	Professors: (parentheses: full professors)	Faculty–student ratio	Total univ. budget (thaler)	Budgeted cost per student (thaler)	Full profs.' avg. salaries (thaler) (parentheses: extraordinary profs.)	Profs.' lecture fees	Other fees (average)
Berlin	1,777	74 (46)	1:12	99,846	56	1,203 (368)	746	387
Bonn	828	57 (46)	1:12	89,684	108	1,040 (300)	374	n.a.
Breslau	951	58 (39)	1:13	72,298	76	846 (348)	n.a.	n.a.
Halle	844	57 (39)	1:11	70,737	83	985 (295)	n.a.	n.a.
Königsberg	431	37 (27)	1:7	60,912	141	934 (319)	117	n.a.
Greifswald	217	15 (9)	1:5	57,696	265	897 (567)	135	n.a.

Note: The Prussian thaler was worth about three marks; it equaled $0.71, or a bit less than 3s.

Source: Wilhelm Dieterici, *Geschichtliche und Statistische Nachrichten über die Universitäten im preussischen Staat* (Berlin, 1836), pp. 106, 56–7, 67–70, 82, 45, 26, 35.

Table 7. *Expenditures of Prussian universities for specific seminars, laboratories, and collections, 1834 (in thaler)*

	Berlin	Halle	Bonn	Königsberg
Library	500	2,820	4,572	3,390
Medical institute	1,500	3,040	3,200	2,300
Surgical institute	3,300	1,210	3,300	2,455
Polyclinic	2,000	—	—	—
Midwifery institute	5,400	1,000	1,500	—
Botanical garden	500	1,090	2,500	2,100
Herbarium	1,200	—	—	—
Anatomical institute	3,167	1,470	1,500	1,180
Observatory	600	240	—	1,570
Mineral collection/ natural history collection	1,520	280	900	700
Theological seminar	630	—	600[a]	440
Philological seminar	500	550	500	400
Pedagogical seminar	2,000	—	—	1,060
Physics/chemistry laboratory	400	520	350	—
Mathematics/physics apparatus	500	—	400	158
Widows' fund	1,000	1,000	500	1,000
Scholarships (total, including private funds)	less than 10,000	4,400	6,000	7,000

[a] Both Protestant and Catholic seminars.
Source: Dieterici, *Nachrichten*, pp. 45–7, 56–7, 67–70, 80–2.

dents in the 1820s may have provided more fee income; and the regularization of royalties from book publications, the suppression of literary piracy, and increased volume of book sales may have raised private royalty income for many professors.

The best bargain for the state was the *Extraordinarius*, a rank comprising a rising proportion of the teaching staff even in 1834 (about one-third at Berlin, Halle, Breslau, and Greifswald universities), but drawing rather small salaries (about 300 to 350 thaler on the average). These associate professors were not able to augment their income from fees to nearly the degree the full professors were. Even though they had become an indispensable part of the teaching staff, they received from the state little more than subsistence wages and the encouragement that someday they might move up to professorships. To give some idea of how little their salaries were, their average income of 300 thaler or slightly more corresponded almost exactly to the estimated costs for a student attending the university.[23] In other words, many associate professors, the library of Berlin University, the astronomical observatory at Halle, and the philological seminars at four Prussian universities each received from the state less than the amount needed by one or two wretched freshmen for a year of university study.

The annual student costs estimated by the statistician Dieterici can also be regarded in another way: Because 300 thaler was about the same amount as an associate professor's salary, it may have been a forbiddingly great sum for poorer students. Dieterici pointed out that few scholarships were available to Prussian university students in the 1830s. State scholarships were only a fraction of the total scholarship funds listed in Table 7, much of which came from private, church, or municipal sources. The largest scholarship at Berlin amounted to 100 thaler, but there were very few of this size; most were in the range of 10 to 50 thaler. So, although the Prussian budget indicated an indirect subsidy to higher education ranging from 56 to 165 thaler per student in 1834, the students still had to provide the lion's share of the costs of their education. Although Dieterici and other observers of the 1830s commented unfavorably on the insufficiency of scholarship funds, it is not surprising that the governments took few steps to augment them; this was precisely the time when access to higher education was being restricted in order to choke off the rising number of poorer students who had begun to flood the universities in the 1820s.

One more way of placing university budgets, salaries, and student costs in perspective is to compare them to the general cost of living. According to reliable estimates, annual living costs in the Hanseatic port cities in the 1820s were about 150 thaler for an artisan family and 450 for "a modest bourgeois household" of a master baker or cabinetmaker; 600 thaler was the level of spending where some comforts could be expected, and an educated bourgeois family would have to spend in the range of 600 to 1,000 thaler a year to maintain its station. "In the first half of the nineteenth century, a thrifty bourgeois life-style would have cost at least 700–800 thaler; since the 1850s, 800–1,000."[24] The same author confirms that university graduates, at least in the early years of their careers, were very badly paid and could not in most cases have survived without either financial support from their families or postponing marriage, or both.[25] When one realizes that the cost of a single year of university study was roughly twice as much as an artisan could earn, one can begin to understand why so few students came from the working classes.

When it did finally raise university budgets, the state did not channel funds into areas that would greatly relieve the underpaid staff or encourage poor students; instead, it poured larger amounts of funds into scientific and scholarly institutes, seminars, collections, and libraries.

It is noteworthy that even as early as the 1830s, a considerable proportion of the Prussian university research funds went to institutes involved in science and, above all, medicine. Even so, during the earlier period, it was the marginally funded "word sciences" that gave the German universities a growing prestige in the world, rather than the natural sciences or even medicine. The latter were still backward and required stimulus to catch up with France.

In the second part of this period, 1840–66, state spending on universities increased more dramatically, overshadowing the funding of 1819–40. The state's contribution to the university of Berlin, for example, rose little, from about 80,000 thaler in 1820 to about 100,000 in 1840, and the university's self-generated income added very little more. By 1850 the state's contribution had increased to over 170,000 thaler. Although it was actually a little less in 1860 (155,000 thaler), by

1870 it had risen to 248,000 thaler, with the university gener-
ating about 10,000 more.[26] The single most important cause
of the rise in expenditures was the doubling, in most cases, of
expenditures for institutes and seminars from decade to decade: from 15,000 thaler in 1830 to over 28,000 in 1840; to
60,000 in 1850; to 125,000 in 1870. By 1870, expenditures
for institutes and seminars had surpassed faculty members'
salaries as the largest budget item; they had constituted only
one-fifth as much as salaries in 1820.[27]

The stimulus for greater government aid to seminars and institutes came usually from individual professors in the respective fields, rather than from within the government bureaucracy
or outside government and university. The only possible source
of greater funding in this period was the government, because
university budgets were still largely allocated to salaries, and
members of the university staff considered the salaries insufficient. An outstanding professor would normally bombard the
education ministry with one request after another for increased
funding, bolstering his case with arguments of scientific, pedagogical, and even practical necessity. Government funding was
earmarked, when it came, for specific institutes and seminars,
so that the universities as corporations did not dispose of the
funds. In return for giving financial support, the governments
maintained the right to supervise the seminars directly: The
directors of seminars and institutes were responsible to the ministry. This complicated arrangement has lasted down to the
present.

This is an important point, because the quasi-independent
status of the major research organizations within the university
was a major peculiarity of German universities at the time.
Professors and students in seminars and institutes did not have
to answer nearly so much to the faculties as to the state, and
this semiautonomy undoubtedly encouraged the freedom of
research. The state bureaucracy was not nearly so suspicious
of scholarly and scientific innovation as some conservative
professors on the general faculties (notably theology); nor was

it as likely to indulge in petty jealousies and obstructionism, another academic vice. On the other hand, the state held a large amount of latent power over the institutes and seminars through its fundings and control authority. Yet it does not appear that states abused this power.

One should note parenthetically that the German states during this period were undertaking unprecedented expenses in other areas of education. The creation of the system of classical high schools (*Gymnasien*), begun in earnest after 1815, does not properly belong to this study. But it consumed much of the energy of the ministries of education and a considerable part of the educational budgets. Other types of higher education received gradually increasing support, as well – most notably, the forerunners of the later technical schools (*Technische Hochschulen*).

The history of the *Gymnasium* shows that it stood in a close relationship to the university. It took over in part the propaedeutic functions of eighteenth-century *Artistenfakultäten*, serving as a preparatory institute for the university. Its teachers were often difficult to distinguish in accomplishment from university professors, and many of the former actually taught at universities as *Privatdozenten* or extraordinary professors. The virtual monopoly of *Gymnasium* graduates on entrance rights to the university after the 1830s tightened the relationship between elite school and university. Because the *Gymnasium* taught classical languages and mathematics, its preparation of students reflected the Humboldtian ideal of general knowledge based on nonpractical studies. Given the high fees and social exclusiveness of the *Gymnasium,* this close relationship guaranteed a high proportion of sons of the *Bildungsbürgertum* and nobility in German universities before 1870.

But although the states nurtured both university and *Gymnasium* and virtually prevented any other type of students than graduates of *Gymnasien* to study at universities, they did not altogether neglect the more practical but socially despised training schools for technicians. Having been excluded from the university curriculum by tradition, with reinforcement from the thinking of the neo-humanists, technical training nevertheless gained a foothold in Germany and received assistance from the state.

Although the great age of growth in technical education began only after the unification of the German Empire, the middle decades of the nineteenth century witnessed the founding and success of many important schools. In the growth of these, one can perceive very direct links between increasingly industrialized economies and their demand for practical and skilled education.[28] Very often these schools were promoted by private entrepreneurs and government agencies outside the educational bureaucracy.

In addition to the handful of specialized schools existing before the beginning of this era, there were seven more forerunners of *Technische Hochschulen* founded between 1819 and 1870 – in Karlsruhe (1825), Darmstadt (1826), Munich (1827), Dresden (1828), Stuttgart (1829), Hanover (1831), and Aachen (1870). Before 1819, there had been only a few schools of this type in German states outside Austria, for example, the mining academies of Freiberg and Clausthal and the small technical schools of Braunschweig and Berlin, the latter founded only in 1799. Austria had in fact taken an early lead in establishing technical schools on the French model, founding three before 1819 (Prague, Vienna, and Graz) and additional ones later in the century.

Typically, the new foundings were called schools and did not give higher degrees. But as the utility of the type of practical scientific training they gave became evident, they grew in size and stature. The Berlin technical school, for example, grew out of the combined Royal Academy of Architecture and the later Royal Vocational Academy; both had been practical training schools for adolescents, operated under the supervision of the Ministry of Trade, and run with the same kind of discipline as any secondary school. The Vocational Academy appears to have been designed initially to produce managers for small industry; it grew from thirteen pupils in 1822 to about a hundred in 1845. By 1850, when a reform was carried out, the average student age was raised considerably to nearly that of university students; in 1855, lecture fees were introduced and scholarships reduced, indicating rising social origins of students. By the 1860s the style of the institution was no longer schoollike, but rather more like that of a university; academic freedoms, specialization (as indicated in the appearance of departments), and self-government by the faculty were other reforms indicative of rising status. By 1879 the two schools were fused and entitled *Technische Hochschule*.[29]

The growth of the other schools was similar in outline. Gradually the technical schools lost their merely "vocational" focus and pursued applied scientific education on a more theoretical level; at the same time, their faculties and students came to resemble more and more those of regular universities. The universities resisted this upgrading of status for the technical colleges and refused to accept technical education as the peer of academic training. This rivalry between universities and technical schools, which became a serious problem only after 1870, will occupy us in Part IV.

Technical colleges were founded and supported by most of the major German states because of recognition that they lagged behind other countries, notably France and Britain, in both technology and industrial development. It is significant that one of the first new-model schools was founded in Prague in 1803, partly as a result of pressures from the commercial bourgeoisie in that city, and partly because of the interest among Bohemian noblemen (who dominated the Diet) in industrial progress. Throughout their history, they were much closer to local economic realities and needs than the universities. It was in these colleges that the intellectual foundations for Germany's increasing excellence in engineering, machine building, and other areas of applied science were laid.

In summary, the German states on the whole did increase their financial support of education in general and universities in particular during the period 1819–66. The university support increased most rapidly in the second half of the period, and the major proportion of increases went into support for seminars and institutes. The latter were of course engaged not solely in research, but in teaching on a high level as well. Nevertheless, the concentration of seminar members on problems often resting on the frontiers of scholarship and science led to many significant contributions to knowledge by seminar directors and graduates of these organizations. Though it is impossible to fix a ratio between investment and scientific production in this case (as in most others), it seems safe to say that the German governments received handsome dividends in scholarly advance from their rather small investment. But even this investment would have been wasted without the dedication to science and scholarship shown by many of the directors of institutes and seminars. Inadequate as the funding usually was from the professors' viewpoint, it was enough to give some minimal encouragement to the research ethic at German universities. In gradually stepping up their contributions to the universities (and especially the seminars), the states were evincing a willingness to invest not in scientific research as such, but rather in scientific training that had more and more clear results for the expansion of knowledge. Still groping largely in the dark, without an overall plan for the growth and evolution of the universities, many German state educational bureaucracies nevertheless met the demands of the universities partway.

Considering the financially strapped condition of most states, the general hostility of royal governments to subversion by intellectuals and innovators of ideas, and the desire to hold down university enrollments, it is surprising that the German states accomplished as much as they did for the universities. They certainly did much more than they had in the eighteenth century, with few exceptions. One can only speculate how much more rapidly the German research university would have developed if the governments had been richer, less prone to spend money on armies, or more willing to embrace modern science and scholarship as values in themselves. As it was, the funding of German universities was enough to allow them to struggle onward and develop their own commitment to *Wissenschaft* on a financial shoestring.

Universities and politics

The period 1819–66 was the setting of more political engagement (especially oppositional engagement) by German academics than occurred in any period before or since. Reform and revolutions had redefined the status of academics. Instead of being privileged subjects of the prince in a hierarchical, semifeudal social order, they were now defined as citizens in a gradually industrializing society. Many professors and students took their rights and duties as citizens quite seriously, while most governments in this era attempted to curb and even eliminate the boundaries of citizen activity. The resultant conflict produced many notable cases of hostility between individual university members and state bureaucracies. Universities were embroiled in controversies over academic freedom much broader in scope than those of previous centuries: Whereas most previous abridgments of academic freedom had resulted from conflicts with orthodox church doctrines, now the additional factor of conflicts with orthodox state political tenets appeared. Professors and students who had previously been content to leave things alone or merely agitate for some changes within the academic world now took on the role of spokesmen for political and social change in the broader community. Many became politicized by the frustration of their attempts to reform the universities. Many others (particularly professors appointed chiefly for this purpose) entered the same struggle on the side of throne and altar.

The German students had begun to generate a certain enthusiasm for reform and the national cause during the Napoleonic period. At a time when most German states were undergoing external challenges and internal reforms of a sweeping nature, when the universities themselves were being shut down or re-formed, it was natural for German students to ask themselves if they should reexamine their role. Students fought in the final wars against Napoleon, and many of the veterans returned to the universities with a new seriousness of purpose. Such student organizations as the *Burschenschaften* introduced a here-tofore unheard of moral earnestness and political awareness into German student life. Emboldened by the encouragement of these students and feeling a responsibility for them, some professors began to place themselves at the head of the students. Professors Oken and Fries at Jena are two radical examples. But Schleiermacher played somewhat the same role at Berlin, in a more moderate way. Suddenly students and professors were asserting leadership of movements for national unity, civil rights, and constitutional government.

After the three years of economic and political unrest in the wake of the Peace of Vienna, the European great powers began to rally to a policy of outright repression of such movements everywhere. By 1818 a period of deep reaction was beginning in Europe, led by Prince Metternich. Characteristically, the first major blow to progressive movements in Germany was dealt to the universities. In the wake of the assassination of the poet and alleged Russian agent Kotzebue by a student, Metternich summoned the members of the Germanic Confederation to Carlsbad and persuaded them to issue a set of decrees designed to repress student agitation and, to a lesser degree, professorial independence and political leadership.

These decrees established a plenipotentiary for each German university, equipped with considerable powers to punish political dissidents. As the Prussian proclamation of 1819 put it: "The federated governments oblige themselves to remove from universities . . . those teachers who have obviously demonstrated their incapacity to fill their office by demonstrable deviation from their duty, or transgressing against the limits of their profession, or misusing their proper influence on the young, or spreading harmful theories inimical to the public order and peace or destructive to existing political institutions."[30]

The heightened interest of the states in the activities of universities and their members can be explained by other factors than a mere fear of revolution. The expansion of educational bureaucracies reflected both an increased commitment to education by the states and a desire to administer more closely what the state was funding more generously. The rise of public education, especially secondary education, in the German states accounted for much of the increased activity of educational civil services. But the universities were intimately linked with secondary education, both as suppliers of teachers and as takers of pupils. State intervention therefore took not only the form of censorship and policing of "subversion," but also that of stricter regulations concerning entrance, curriculum, examinations, and other matters previously left largely to the universities. Governments had of course attempted such interventions in the eighteenth century as well, but they had been generally ineffective. State policies concerning licensing and employment of professional people (civil servants, doctors, clergymen, and teachers, for example) were increasingly intertwined in this period with the fear of universities producing too many unemployed, and potentially disgruntled, revolutionary graduates. Therefore state policy tended to restrict growth of student population and even chairs, while the separate dynamics of scientific growth and the expansion of knowledge through specialization pulled in the opposite direction. For large states such as Prussia, conflicting political priorities also had some impact, even if indirect, on universities. The desire to make the state more powerful and prestigious could be met by military expenditures, commercial expansion, and scientific and educational prominence, but the three areas could not be serviced equally well, given the continued relative poverty of German states.

The most vivid and spectacular confrontation of the academic world and the state in this era lay in the field of public policy and political debate. Whereas students and professors had become somewhat vocal about national and local political issues in the Napoleonic era, radicalism (especially the variant supporting stronger German national unity) had been driven largely underground by the Carlsbad Decrees of 1819. Only in exceptional times, such as the years just after the 1830 revolutions and again in 1848, did students and professors surface to make dramatic gestures for liberalism and national unity. The Hambach Festival in 1832, the abortive student coup of the Frankfurt *Wachensturm* in 1833, student leadership of the initial surge of the Viennese revolution in 1848, and student attempts to influence both university and general reform in the subsequent months of the 1848 revolution were isolated incidents that terrified governments but, even more typically, failed in the face of repression.

Professors, on the other hand, tended to choose more established channels of political activity and skirted away from violent challenges to the state. They chose three main methods of influencing politics: literary activity, often under the guise of professional publications; organization of like-minded academics in national scholarly guilds; and direct participation (where possible) in the political process. Advocates of progressive change were more successful in the last two methods. Conservatives naturally tended to follow the wishes of their governments, and most governments discouraged national organizations as vaguely subversive to the principle of the sovereignty of the various German states. Governments also tended to look with some suspicion upon the participation of professors in political life: Professors were civil servants, and as such they should be above politics. Even so, some governments attempted to counter the trend of election of liberal professors to parliaments by sponsoring conservative professors, often by appointing them to nonelective bodies such as parliamentary upper houses. These bodies, incidentally, often contained representatives of the universities by constitutional right. Their numerical weight was insignificant, but they did act as spokesmen for the universities in these usually arch-conservative legislative upper houses.

South Germany was the natural home of direct political engagement by professors, because it was the region of Germany that had complied most fully with the requirement of the Final Act of Vienna that German states have parliamentary bodies. Baden, which throughout the nineteenth century had the reputation of being the most liberal German state, also had the most active legislature and the most vocal professorial leadership in politics. Here such professors as Rotteck and Welcker were able to assume the mantle of oppositional leadership, even as early as the 1820s.

As representative institutions and constitutions were developed in other states, university professors often had considerable influence on them. The historian and political scientist F. C. Dahlmann, for example, aided in drafting the constitution for Hanover adopted in 1833, having previously established his reputation as a constitutional expert in the struggle against the wishes of the king of Denmark to abrogate certain traditional rights of Schleswig and Holstein. Sylvester Jordan, a professor at Marburg, drafted the Hesse–Kassel constitution of 1831. To be sure, the activities of oppositional professors before 1848 were largely a story of frustration and occasional persecution. K. W. R. von Rotteck and K. T. Welcker both faced repeated signs of displeasure from the Baden government; Dahlmann was forced to flee Hanover, along with other Göttingen professors, when the constitution he had helped create was abrogated by the new king in 1837. Friedrich List, who had taught at Tübingen and won a seat in the Württemberg legislature in 1819, was prevented from taking his seat and exiled from the country, the ultimate reason for his fateful emigration to Pennsylvania. Dozens of other cases can be cited involving professorial attempts to influence political life directly. And despite governmental chicanery and harassment, many of them did not give up.

By the time of the 1848 revolution, professors had won enough respect among the people to constitute a natural political talent pool for the elections to state and national parliaments. Although they did not constitute the largest bloc of professional people in the Frankfurt Parliament, for example, their disproportionate representation in that body prompted the coining of the misleading name "parliament of professors." Many others were active in the state parliaments elected at the same time. Their election testified to the prestige that had come to be accorded to the professoriate in Germany as a result of the international reputation of German learning by 1848. But it also proved that professors had worked politically in their states and communities to a point where they had become "notables." No doubt the very paranoid persecution of liberal professors by the various German states under the Carlsbad Decrees and other measures had given them, as a group, a certain fame and allure.

The failure of the Frankfurt Parliament has been attributed by some historians to the long-winded and pedantic style introduced into its deliberations by timid professors. In fact, the constitution produced by the Frankfurt Parliament (and not merely by the professors) was a classic document of nineteenth-century political thought, enough so to become the forerunner of the Weimar and current West German constitutions. What the professors lacked was authority, troops, money, and, in a word, power—not sagacity.

German voters, in any case, did not appear disillusioned with professors as political spokesmen after the failure of the revolution. They continued to elect professors to public office, indeed, more so than ever, in the 1850s and 1860s. More than that of any other country in the world, Germany's liberal tradition came to be closely associated with the names of men who were professors in regular life. It may well be a severe indictment of German political immaturity that the country had to turn to professors for leadership in the middle decades of the nineteenth century; but few can doubt the fact of professorial willingness to take risks or a high sense of civic responsibility. Professors have not usually made very effective politicans anywhere, as politics is not the science of ideas. But it is nevertheless a proud page in the annals of the German professoriate that it did not behave in these critical years as so many similar groups in other countries did, and as many of their German successors also did, by renouncing civic engagement as "unscientific," or at least inappropriate.

In one other area, that of university policy itself, the professoriate seized the opportunity of the 1848 turmoil to seek an augmentation of its power. The teaching staff generally asked for more control over staffing, with government guarantees of the right of faculties to nominate professors, the recognition of the right to nominate *Extraordinarien* as well, and government promises to appoint only those nominated by the faculties.[31] Greater self-administration rights and token reforms in the treatment of lower-ranking teachers, the elimination of government plenipotentiaries and curators, and reforms in academic justice also counted among professorial demands. The *Extraordinarien* and *Privatdozenten* had more radical ideas about university reform, to be sure, including heightened economic security and a larger role in university governance. And students had more radical demands still.[32]

A meeting of students at the Wartburg in the spring of 1848 produced, *inter alia*, demands for the end of separate faculties and the restoration of the principle of unity of learning; for the abolition of university attendance as a prerequisite for certain civil service jobs; for a greater role of students in the election of academic officials and the appointment of professors; for student self-government and the abolition of separate academic courts; and for complete freedom of teaching and studying. The meeting turned into a self-appointed student parliament, further demanding the abolition of lecture fees, the institution of salaries for *Privatdozenten*, the elimination of Latin requirements, and open enrollment of students.

A second student congress in Eisenach in the fall reaffirmed many of these points in a "constitution" for the German universities; in addition, the abolition of state examinations for the professions was demanded, and a new governing structure consisting of student–faculty committees to replace the bureaucracy was envisioned. These demands represented the viewpoint of the most radical students, with some support from *Privatdozenten.*

At a meeting of professors in Jena, proposals for change were much more modest, reflecting the preponderance of *Ordinarien* there. Though yielding on many points in a direction of change, the professors refused to abolish lecture fees or academic justice, or to make more than token changes in university governance, examinations, entrance requirements, and so forth. The professors did favor the abolition of the curator system, improvement of their own pay scales, and rights in professorial appointments. Even these modest requests were withdrawn during another meeting of professors in the far more conservative environment of 1849. Some of the radical students of 1848 fought on hopelessly in 1849; but most, along with the professors, acquiesced in the restoration of the status quo.

The reform of German universities was, in sum, as much a failure as the general revolutionary movement in Germany, and for parallel reasons: The various revolutionary groups fell out over where to draw the line on changes. Generally the full professors (or at least a majority) were the most conservative group. The first response of the Berlin *Ordinarien* to the revolution (joined by full professors from other Prussian universities) was to urge moderation and form "academic corps" of teachers and students to "keep order." The senate of Berlin went on record in November 1848 against "anarchy" and its most immediate form, the national assembly deputies' attempt to resist reaction by fomenting taxpayers' strikes.[33] Thus the professoriate tended to proclaim its loyalty to the monarchy, its opposition to radical change, and its interest in reforms of a moderate or only token variety. Yet not even these reforms were granted, for students, nontenured faculty, and *Ordinarien* were too divided about their goals to form a common force against the governments.

Whereas the number of professors engaged in direct political activity constituted a small minority, a somewhat broader group engaged itself in literary activity of a political or civic nature. Many professors realized that they would not cut satisfactory figures in the halls of parliaments but also that they could contribute much to the political education of the German people by publishing works not directly connected with their scholarship. In a country afflicted with a lame press and a journalistic community that was only beginning to transcend the image of servile, underpaid scribblers, professors constituted a reservoir of writing and editorial talent attractive to publishers and readers. Just as the educated and propertied classes in Germany were willing to vote professors into office, when possible, they were willing to subscribe to journals and newspapers whose tone was academic.

Professors had been deeply involved in national reviews even at the end of the eighteenth century, and they continued to submit articles on every variety of subject to learned general publications; but in addition, they founded, edited, and contributed to specifically political works and periodicals. Rotteck and Welcker's *Staatslexikon,* for example, was the bible of two generations of liberal Germans. Dahlmann edited the *Kieler Blätter;* Gervinus helped found the *Deutsche Zeitung,* aided editorially by Ludwig Häusser; Friedrich von Raumer, a liberal Berlin professor, founded the *Historisches Taschenbuch* series. Johann Bluntschli, a Munich law professor, carried on the work of Rotteck and Welcker with his influential *Staatswörterbuch.* The *Preussische Jahrbücher,* founded in the 1850s, was likewise a project involving professors. Even conservative professors, such as Ranke, were not above attempts to found and edit journals of contemporary affairs.

Professors engaged in literary activity had, like every other writer publishing in a realm outside *Wissenschaft,* to confront the problems of censorship. German censorship was comparatively harsh in this period. Its differential enforcement in the various states, however, ameliorated or even undermined the intent of the Bundestag's decrees, at least in some places. Professors critical of the current regime also learned to write in a sort of code, so that reader and author often saw and meant something different from what the dull-minded bureaucrats in the censorship offices perceived. The very abstract and idealistic jargon employed by professors had a distinct advantage, in that no censor could point directly to a statement subversive to throne and altar, whereas many readers could leap from the general statement to the specific criticism. One could, for example, attack *Schreiberei,* or the tendency of German bureaucracy to put everything down on paper, as Robert von Mohl did, without arousing the suspicions of censors (who had to suffer as much from "scribbledom" as anybody); yet the readers undoubtedly interpreted such words correctly, as an attack on bureacratic tutelage.

Unable to prevent such subtle assaults on their mode of operation, some German governments adopted the tactic, at least between 1830 and 1848, of subsidizing conservative journals edited by progovernment professors. The German public did not buy them, however, whereas their support of liberal professorial sheets continued unabated. Even resort to the courts to prosecute "subversive" professors for their writings could not be relied upon for results. Georg Gervinus's celebrated treason trial in 1853, for example, proved a fiasco for the state prosecutor, not only because it proved difficult to show that Gervinus's historical allusions constituted sedition, but also because expert witnesses and public opinion were on his side. Only arbitrary, extralegal means could guarantee success, as in the expulsion of seven professors from Göttingen in 1837 and a second expulsion of professors from Leipzig in 1850. Yet such arbitrary acts, though effective, reaped such a whirlwind of unfavorable publicity and denunciation at home and abroad that they were notable for their rarity. Professors were after all royal officials, too, and such high-handed dismissals violated the German bureaucractic tradition of due process sufficiently to upset the bureaucrats themselves.

In the end, the kings and princes had to content themselves

with sporadic persecution of their liberal professors, niggling discrimination, and bitter frustration that their loyal professors did not appeal to the tastes of the reading public. If one is tempted to ascribe little grandeur to the efforts of German professors to enlighten their fellow educated citizens politically, one is even less tempted to admire the decisiveness and strength of the governments that tried to prevent their impact on public opinion. The oppositional professors felt, quite correctly, that they were persecuted, but they went on publishing; the kings, less logically, felt that they were being undermined, but they were unable to develop effective countermeasures. They were incapable of the measures of modern totalitarian states; and, besides, they needed the universities and their professors for their own purposes. Rather than destroy one of the main sources of their states' intellectual prestige, they grudgingly lived with the literary activities of the oppositional professoriate. In any case the professors wounded only the vanity of kings and ministers, not their power. With few exceptions, the professors active in politics were loyal monarchists, asking at most that the royal government yield the principle of taxation with real representation. Even the most radical of German professors admired republican institutions only in a Platonic manner.

One of the reasons why the German professoriate in this period was held in some regard by the public was the degree to which professors transcended the parochialism afflicting German life. The professoriate, partly as a result of increasing scholarly and scientific contacts, maintained ties with all parts of Germany. One indication of the increasingly national scope of *Wissenschaft* was the foundation and national congresses of German learned societies. The very existence of these fairly innocuous organizations appeared as a threat to some conservatives simply because they *were* national in scope. The national congresses of scholars of German language and history (*Germanisten*) beginning in 1846 were typical. By 1870, many academic disciplines had instituted such periodic national congresses. Though academic and not political by nature, they gave to German professors a further opportunity to expand communication across state borders. Nervous conservatives in the various German governments watched their activities with some concern. Even though they were avowedly nonpolitical, they did represent some of the few attempts to organize on a German, rather than local, basis.

One must remember that the oppositional activities of German university professors, though significant in an age of public apathy and timidity, did not characterize the attitudes of the professoriate as a whole. Most professors were undoubtedly loyal and apolitical or, in many cases, served the state with unswerving conservatism. This attitude held by the majority of professors, rather than the opposition and dissatisfaction of the minority, probably explains the relative absence of harsh government persecution of the universities as such and the continuing good relations between state and university. University and state archives are full of letters from professors of this period expressing undying loyalty and subservience to royal authority, couched in the romantically tinged pathos of the era. Even in times of great openness and confusion, such as during the 1848 revolutions, academics tended to ask only for moderate and reasonable changes in the universities. Whereas students stood on the barricades, Nichtordinarien merely demanded greater rights and incomes, and full professors asked only for modest changes, such as respect by the state bureaucracy for the right to nominate for vacant professorships. Even so, the interests of Ordinarien, lower teaching staff, and students were too dissimilar, and the impact of demands for university reform were dissipated by disagreement among these groups. The failure of university reform movements in 1848 proved once again that professors and students acting alone could not face down the state bureaucracy, but needed broader support from general social movements. It also proved there were many members of the universities who were utterly satisfied with conservative policies. The theological faculties, in particular, outdid themselves in demonstrations of loyalty to the orthodox positions of the states; for a time, between 1819 and 1848, they were able to make considerable headway against "liberal" theology and modern conceptions of state and society.[34]

Even in areas closest to the rights and liberties of the universities, the professors did not oppose vigorously the tendency of the states to interfere. The limitations on admission to the universities, in the form of the increasingly high admission criteria enunciated by the Prussian *Abiturzwang* in the 1830s, not to mention state-inspired tightening of licensing criteria for *Privatdozenten,* generally met with the approval of the professoriate. In addition to their natural loathing of admitting students and young teachers who might not seem sufficiently qualified, the professors were motivated by distaste for students who could not pay private lecture fees or for younger teachers who could compete with them. Hardly a murmur of protest greeted the decision of Prussia and other states to grant a special status to university students in face of the universal military draft laws. Quite a few university students, in their first year, were in fact *Einjährigfreiwilligen,* or "one-year volunteers" in the military forces. These student–soldiers were earmarked for the reserve officer corps and were thereby in effect exempted from the normal rigors of draft into the army. This status may have been comforting and even desirable for the German middle class, but it contrasted strongly with the general exemption of students from military service common in the eighteenth century. Rather than protest this incursion of military life into the universities, however, the German professoriate tolerated and even greeted it. The one-year reserve officer candidate remained under military discipline (though loosened) while he studied.

One final area of contact between the world of political affairs and the universities should be mentioned, although its importance was not yet great. The new constitutions granted in some states after 1815 and expanded to most German states by 1848 opened a new front through which academic matters could be influenced by politics, in this case the wishes of the various state legislatures. The impact of the Landtage on higher education was in practice rather slight before 1848, simply because these bodies not only did not hold preponderant power and rarely challenged the state bureaucracy's decisions even when they held the power of the purse through budgets. The Frankfurt National Assembly did not spend much time debating university matters, aside from proclaiming academic freedom and leaving educational matters to the states. Only gradually, after the dust of 1848 had settled and state parliaments (and later the Reichstag) gained relatively more authority through their manipulation of budgetary power, did the interest of legislatures in university affairs quicken. One recent work on the Prussian parliament noted that "the deputies needed two to three sittings of five or six hours each to approve the universities' budgets [in the decade before World War I], whereas these debates could mostly be measured in minutes before 1870."[35] The more exciting debates of a nonbudgetary nature had to do with the wishes of Catholic deputies for greater concessions in the area of concern to the church, individual personnel cases, and other matters of a one-time, nonprogrammatic type.[36] Before 1870, the tendency appears to have been strong to consult or listen to Landtag deputies who happened to be university professors, and the differences of opinion tended to be more personal than party-based. Only in the last period of this study, to be considered in Part IV, will we find parliaments becoming seriously involved in, and having measurable impact upon, university policy.

In summary, the period between 1819 and 1866 produced a significantly altered relationship between the university and politics. The leadership of professors and students in the drive for closer national unification, more secure political and civic rights, and other public issues helped bring the German universities closer to the realities of German society than they had been. Even professors who opposed the innovatory agitation of avant-garde colleagues were drawn more deeply into matters of public life. The walls of corporate immunities between the academic and political spheres were weakened and lowered by the reforms and political intervention of the states. Universities did not, to be sure, become political institutions in any formal way. But many members of universities acted as though they took seriously some part of Fichte's ideal that the members of universities should realize their role as a special leadership elite in society. And though state bureaucracies, usually dominated by conservative tendencies, mistrusted the activism in politics of professors and students, they were rarely willing or obliged to punish the universities for actions of individual members of them. These bureaucracies appear to have been largely satisfied that the universities were doing their job well – producing competent and loyal professional graduates and lending prestige to the state through scholarly and scientific discoveries.

As we have seen in Chapters 5 and 6, the nearly half century between the Carlsbad Decrees and the Austro-Prussian War of 1866 can best be characterized as a period of general stability for the German university system. Heightened state control over the universities expressed itself in political watchfulness and suppression of national and liberal movements in the universities. Though much more dependent upon the states for financial assistance, the universities did not generally obtain the kind of support envisioned by Humboldt and the reform movement before 1819. Partly as a result of state intervention, enrollments remained stagnant after the 1830s. The teaching staff increased, but the growth areas were in the poorly remunerated ranks below full professors. Governments thus contributed far less than they could have toward a university system that provided them with efficient professional graduates and a rising international recognition as seats of world scholarship.

That the university system nevertheless accepted the canons of *Wissenschaft* and made considerable advances in most areas of scholarship and science, that the universities nevertheless enjoyed enough academic freedom to permit open inquiry and even to tolerate persons and groups critical of the German governments, that seminars could proliferate even in the absence of government willingness to fund them generously, and that a rising minority of students and young teachers were willing to make personal sacrifices for their interest in scholarship all indicate that considerable reservoirs of support for the new type of university flowed forth from German society. As positions suitable for the nobility and the professional middle class did not expand proportionately with the population, competition for these positions became keener and increasingly dependent on university education. As professorships at the universities and even at the new *Gymnasien* became more secure, and became respectable positions in society, their desirability led to an upgrading both of *Wissenschaft* as a scholarly activity and of pedagogical demands placed on students. The virtual university monopoly over access to high professional and civil service careers, combined with the prestige of university scholarship, resulted in a high degree of social support for the German university system. With its rather exclusive student body, the university system clearly did not serve the direct interests of the majority of German peasants or the commercial bourgeoisie. But it served those of the bureaucratic and professional elites well enough that the drumfire of criticism common in the eighteenth century virtually ceased during this period.

Despite many shortcomings and deficiencies, the German university system had attained by the 1860s a scholarly and pedagogical status of which Germans could begin to be proud and foreigners envious. Much of its prestige resulted from the individual acts of scientific creativity of the professoriate. If the German governments had been less than lavish in their encouragement, they had at least intervened less harshly than they might have, thanks to the combination of prudence on the part of the universities and the high degree of tacit support they enjoyed in the leading social groups of the German lands. At best, the German states had sometimes encouraged the universities within their means, as during the era of Altenstein in Prussia down to 1840. At worst, their more destructive interventions had been episodic and had failed to halt the quiet evolution of *Wissenschaft* within the universities.

PART IV

Universities in
the German Empire

The wars of German unification and the First World War have more than symbolic meaning for the history of the German universities. The former sealed the triumph of Prussia in German affairs, laid the groundwork for an extraordinary period of economic and social development, and extended Prussia's control over more than half the German universities. The First World War disrupted normal university work and brought about a series of economic, political, and social conditions that placed a great strain on the universities. During the period of the Bismarckian Reich, German universities further developed the tendencies and lines of the mid-nineteenth century; this was the classical age of these institutions. At the same time, the rapid development of Germany into a powerful, industrialized, modern society placed demands on the universities that they could not always meet and illuminated the shortcomings of institutions designed for a preindustrial order. Although some professors and educational bureaucrats fretted about these shortcomings, and although some minor reforms were carried out, the major changes on the German university scene were quantitative, not qualitative. Professors, students, and the public all appeared to be basically satisfied with the university system, and praise and emulation from abroad gave further reinforcement to such contentment.

The most stunning alterations to the universities were caused by their massive expansion. Student enrollments, stagnant since the 1830s, began to rise precipitously in the 1870s and continued to burgeon down to 1914. The specialization of the teaching and research functions of the university caused further increases in the size of the professoriate, the number of institutions such as seminars and institutes, and the magnitude of budgets. The combination of sheer size and ongoing differentiation of the universities caused many observers to compare the universities by 1900 with large industrial enterprises. We shall be occupied with these problems in Chapter 7.

The Bismarckian Reich, in making concessions to the German middle class, removed the most glaring causes of conflict between university and government by the 1870s. In return, the universities took on a more positive relationship with the state. The oppositional tendencies of professors and students diminished almost to the vanishing point. The universities became increasingly attractive to sons of the propertied middle class, who constituted a large proportion of the new students flocking to the universities. At the same time, concessions by the state to the German masses found little echo in the universities. Sons of the toiling poor had little chance to qualify for higher education. Students and professors who advocated greater opportunity for the lower orders, either as a part of general social policy or merely as a part of educational policy, met with open hostility and occasional persecution. Another important social group hitherto excluded from university study, women, had slightly better fortune in gaining the right to study, under severe limitations, after 1900.

The universities reflected the pressures of German politics and society in other ways than their social recruitment. German industry sought to influence the universities in ways beneficial to itself. Campaigns to introduce more practical studies (e.g., industry-related research) into the universities were mounted from the late nineteenth century on, although they fell far short of success: The universities tended to resist such intrusions. The universities' independence from the power of the state was also diminished, not by high-handed breaches of academic freedom (though there were cases of this), but by the steady and subtle flow of decision-making power into the hands of central state educational bureaucracies. Historians of this period of German higher educational history regularly identify it as the "Althoff era," thereby attesting to the importance of the Prussian Kultusministerium and its director of university affairs, Friedrich Althoff. Though his personality and methods had much to do with his power, one should not forget that his office and the concentration of many important decisions in government ministries constituted the real key to his successes.

The fact that one state, Prussia, had clearly emerged by 1870 as the major beneficiary of the industrial revolution, the major political force in the German world, the major gainer in population, and the administrator of the majority of German universities also signaled important changes in the political and social factors influencing higher education. The industrial revolution brought Prussia not only a much larger tax base with which to raise revenues undreamed of in the past, but a rapidly growing commercial bourgeoisie that showed a heightened interest in higher education.

The most direct way in which Prussia extended its influence over higher education by 1870 was by conquest. When the Prussians fought in 1866 and 1870–1, they conquered not only new territory, but also the universities located there. In addition to the six universities it already controlled in the 1850s, Prussia added those of Kiel, Göttingen, and Marburg. It also had major influence over the new Reich university in Strasbourg, founded in 1872, even though the province was technically a "land of the Reich," not a Prussian territory. Thus, Prussia directly or indirectly controlled the policies of over half the German universities from the 1870s onward. Of those outside the Prussian orbit — Tübingen, Freiburg, Erlangen, Giessen, Rostock, Jena, Heidelberg, Leipzig, and

Munich—only the last three were universities of great import for science and scholarship, and only Leipzig and Munich were among the five largest universities in Germany. Practically speaking, only Saxony, Bavaria, Württemberg, and Baden had the resources to maintain first-rate universities. One ought to mention that the German-speaking universities of Austria and Switzerland had also been gaining in quality from the mid-nineteenth century on and offered a certain rivalry to Prussian domination. But even so, Prussia ruled nearly half the German-speaking universities. In addition to this direct control and the enormous prestige of many Prussian universities, Prussia exercised her influence over German higher education by example and by organizing ministerial and university "conferences" to coordinate university policy in Germany. Finally, Prussia controlled one-third of the technical colleges (Berlin, Aachen, and Hanover), although the South German states had been the first to develop such institutions.

The rise of the technical colleges (Technische Hochschulen) and their challenge to the traditional, theoretical universities is another major theme of the period between the unification of Germany and the First World War. Most of the nine technical colleges founded in the nineteenth century dated their existence from the first half of the century, but they had been for the most part rather small institutions. Typically, they had arisen in response to certain practical professional needs not well served by the traditional universities but in demand by existing governments (e.g., civil engineering). The close link between the bureaucracy's need for technically trained personnel and the setting up of technical colleges is symbolized by the fact that all but one of the institutions (Aachen) was established in the capital city of the respective German state. All the large states (Prussia, Hanover, Bavaria, Saxony, Württemberg, Baden) and several smaller ones (Hesse-Darmstadt, Brunswick) had technical colleges by the end of the century; Prussia was the only state to have three. Though the THs hardly posed a direct threat to the traditional universities, on account of their differing approach to science, many university professors feared and resented them. The result was a sharp debate that spotlighted the deficiencies of the traditional universities in the industrializing world of late-nineteenth-century Germany. In addition to the technical colleges (and other new types of training institutions), new challenges to the universities' leadership in scholarship and scientific research arose. Even in Germany, the classic country of the unity of scholarship and teaching, independent research organizations began to spring up outside the universities before World War I. The establishment of the Kaiser-Wilhelm-Gesellschaft in 1911 is a case in point.

Within the realm of "pure" teaching and research, the universities nevertheless shouldered quite a number of new tasks for the sake of German society. Such governmental programs as social legislation and the creation of a colonial empire, for example, heightened the need for university-trained experts in economics and statistics or in exotic languages and tropical diseases. Even informally, university professors were called upon to make contributions to causes sponsored by the governments, ranging from public speeches in favor of naval expansion and Germanization of Polish minorities to justifications for Germany's war effort in 1914. Such services to the nation were not widely perceived as breaches of academic independence or mockeries of the professed "unpolitical" stance of the German professoriate. Although the universities were able to resist requests by industry for more practical teaching and research as unwarranted interference by special interest groups, a request to aid the country appeared consistent with their role.

Not only the ministries, the traditional representatives of state power, but the parliaments took a sharper interest in the universities in this period. As noted in the last chapter, the budgetary rights of the state and national parliaments entitled them to scrutinize the institutions of higher education, and they used this right to an increasing degree. At the same time parliamentary scrutiny increased, the university professors tended to show less and less taste for overt political roles. In contrast to the national assembly of 1848, the state and national parliaments of 1900 contained few professors. Though their influence on the universities before 1918 remained minor, the parliaments nevertheless held the power to reduce university funding, embarrass the education ministries, and serve as a forum for discussing university matters.

Against this background of increasing state control over and pressures of society on the universities, the reaction of the professoriate was understandable. The professoriate subscribed more than ever to the ideology of Wissenschaft, *attempting to protect rhetorically its traditional (and by now highly esteemed) role as an almost immune priestly caste. Fritz Ringer has aptly described the outlook of the professoriate as that of "Mandarins."[1] Socially esteemed, well-remunerated, basically satisfied with the political and social order in which they lived, and fully able to carry out the assignments of* Wissenschaft *within their professional duties, German professors of this period achieved something approximating the role envisioned for them by the reformers of the era of Humboldt. Yet their prestige was not solely the product of their intellectual and scientific standing; it was also a result of their ever-closer social association with the prestigious bureaucracy and professions and their political acquiescence in the goals of the leadership of the German Empire.*

7

The expansion of
the universities

In 1905, Adolph von Harnack, a noted theologian at the University of Berlin, published a small essay with a significant title, "Vom Grossbetrieb der Universität," comparing the work of universities to that of large-scale enterprises (*Grossbetriebe*).[1] The title reflects the uneasy reaction of many German professors to the massive growth and diversification (not to mention the implied threat of "mass production") that had characterized the university scene in the preceding three decades. Although dwarfed by the even more massive growth of the 1920s and 1960s, this surge in German university population and attendant efforts to cope with it were then unprecedented in scale. The problem of rapid growth was as wrenching and difficult for the universities as similar problems were for German society as a whole, and it was the most important motif for the period of German university history under the Hohenzollern Empire.

Population trends of the university
in the German Reich

The student population at German universities, as we have seen, varied only a little from the mid-1830s until the mid-1860s, with total enrollments fluctuating in the range of about twelve to thirteen thousand. This population crossed the fourteen thousand mark in 1870 for the first time since the early 1830s and continued to grow dramatically through the rest of the century, interrupted only by a pause in the years 1890–6. By 1900 enrollments stood at thirty-four thousand. By 1914 they reached sixty-one thousand.

Although most universities more than doubled their enrollments in keeping with the general increase in students, several of them made even more dramatic proportional gains. The largest growth was in the universities of states other than Prussia. The second Baden university, Freiburg, increased its student enrollment about eightfold; at Erlangen, in Bavaria, and at Giessen, in Hesse, the growth was fourfold. Two Prussian universities also registered large gains (Bonn and Kiel). Because most of the traditionally large universities (Berlin, Leipzig, Munich, Halle, Göttingen, and Breslau) did not grow so rapidly, one might hypothesize that the larger institutions were saturated or were losing some of their attractiveness for the new generation of students, partly because of the upgrading of several of the provincial universities, and partly because some of them were less demanding.[2]

In the 1860s, and on until the mid-1880s, it was the philosophical faculties of German universities that grew the fastest. In the 1870s the juridical faculties began to grow; in the 1880s it was the medical faculties' turn. Theological enrollments were the last to increase dramatically, and then only for a few years in the early 1880s. After a rapid period of expansion, medical enrollments dropped off after 1890 (having achieved briefly in that year the largest total enrollment of all four faculties at German universities). In the late 1890s, much of the continued growth took place in philosophical and legal faculties, whereas medical and theological enrollments absolutely declined. By 1902, nearly 13,000 of Germany's 35,500 university students were enrolled in philosophical faculties; nearly 11,000 in law; a little over 7,000 in medicine; and less than 4,000 in theology – just a bit more than half as many as in 1830.[3]

These population trends and those in the competing technical colleges appear to have reciprocated. Growing from a few hundred in the 1830s and 1840s, the enrollments in THs (*Technische Hochschulen*) fluctuated between 1,000 and 2,000 in the 1850s. By the 1860s, enrollments (along with the number of newly established institutions) shot up rapidly, reaching a total of nearly 5,000 in the academic year 1871–2, and reaching a peak of over 6,600 in 1875–6. Thereafter, enrollments declined, to under 4,000 in the period 1881–7. At the beginning of the 1890s, however, TH enrollments again increased rapidly, jumping from about 4,700 in 1889–90 to about 13,500 in 1899–1900. Thus the period of growth in the TH enrollments overlapped with declines in regular university enrollments, and increases in the universities' student bodies coincided with declines in TH enrollments, at least until after about 1896. Thereafter, both regular and technical universities grew with enormous rapidity – from about 28,500 students in regular universities and 9,400 in THs in 1896 to 35,000 (regular) and nearly 17,000 (THs) in 1903.[4]

One explanation for this inverse enrollment correlation in universities and technical colleges may lie in the socioeconomic sector. The periods of depression in technical college enrollments tended to coincide with depressions in the general economy. "[The universities'] disproportionate increases in an era of depression can be explained by the fact that families which sent their sons to universities were less dependent on economic developments than the fathers of sons who attended technical colleges . . . Also academic professions appear to become more attractive in years of economic crisis, so that sometimes businessmen have their sons trained for a bureaucratic career."[5] Psychological influences also played some role. The parents of German students were certainly themselves readers of the prominent national journals emerging after the 1850s, and in these the fears of the professoriate and others about "academic proletarianization" broke into print in waves roughly coinciding with each unusual spurt in enrollments overall or in given fields of specialization.

What caused the massive expansion of the German university in the Hohenzollern Empire? The central factors were growth of the general population, greater wealth to support university study, expansion of career opportunities for university graduates, the ability of more and more young men to qualify for university study, the attractiveness of university study to sizable groups of foreigners and women, and the lengthening of prescribed courses of study.

The student population of German universities had not kept pace with the growth of the general population between the 1830s and 1870; the reverse had rather been true. By contrast, student population grew much faster than general population after 1870. There had been a gradual decline in the number of students per 100,000 inhabitants over the period 1830–70. The number fell from an average of 40:100,000 in the decade 1831–41 to merely 33.5:100,000 in the 1850s; it did not rise above an average in the range of 30–40:100,000 until well into the 1870s. By the period 1876–81, there was an average of 44.5 students per 100,000 population in Germany; the figure was 56 in 1881–6, and 60 in 1886–91. The ratios continued to grow, with minor setbacks, and by 1905–6 the number of students per 100,000 population rose to 70.5. Thus, even when one considers the rapid population growth of Germany in this period, one can see that the rate of growth in student population was about twice as fast between 1870 and 1906.[6]

To some extent one might regard this phenomenon as natural and explain it by a catching-up effect. But governments and professors had not complained in the period 1840–70 about insufficient numbers of students. Given the frequency of such complaints in the eighteenth century, coupled with complaints of overpopulation in classrooms at the end of the nineteenth century, one could even regard the number of students in the middle decades of the nineteenth century as being close to the number German society could employ and absorb. Thus other factors must be considered.

Greater wealth, especially as distributed to the groups of the middle class that had previously shown only a limited inclination to send their sons to the university, undoubtedly played some role. The German industrial revolution, the most rapid of those in the major European countries, transformed German society between 1870 and 1914.

On balance, the career opportunities for the traditional graduates of universities (bureaucracy, professions) grew faster than those of the other levels in German society.[7] In addition to creating many industrial fortunes, industrialization raised the standard of living for large sectors of the middle class. Even the tertiary sector of professional people and administrators grew richer as a result of the new prosperity. Many more minor officials and small businessmen could evidently afford the cost of sending a son to study in a university.

If one studies the social composition of the student body, one sees some remarkable changes in the period after about 1870. Bearing in mind that university education became more expensive during this time and that scholarship aid did not keep pace with the increase in costs or the number of students, one should not be surprised to see the financially better-off groups in German society increasing their share of membership in student bodies. Friedrich Paulsen noted in 1902:

> The socially aristocratic trait which has emerged so visibly in the moral physiognomy of the German people during the last generation is also reflected in the fact that interest in "class honor" has become so excessively lively and pressing among the learned professions. It works primarily in the direction of resisting acceptance of children from families of the lower classes. If the concern earlier was for furthering gifted boys from families without means, now the ideas are moving in the completely opposite direction.[8]

Available statistics do appear to bear out the thesis that middle-class wealth flowed into the universities after 1870.

At the University of Berlin, for example, 45 percent of the students in 1860 had sprung from the professional classes (including high-ranking bureaucrats, physicians, judges, officers, etc.) and only 32 percent from the mercantile and large-landowning class. The other 23 percent came from the lower range of the middle-class social scale (lower officials, elementary schoolteachers, artisans, small landowners). These proportions had held relatively steady throughout the preceding fifty years at Berlin. But after 1860, a rapid change set in along with the growth in student enrollments. Though the professional classes also increased their contingent of sons sent to Berlin, when expressed in absolute numbers, they contributed a smaller proportion of the entire student body. In 1870 they sent only 38 percent of the student body, and in 1880 only 31 percent, a figure around which their representation at the University of Berlin hovered until World War I. The sons of the moneyed class (*Besitzbürgertum*) of businessmen and landowners increased their share of the students from a relatively stable 30 to 32 percent in the decades 1820–70 to 42 percent in 1880. The remaining students of less exalted social class constituted a percentage of the student body fluctuating between about 22 and 30 between 1850 and 1900.

Other statistics covering the entire Prussian university system tend to affirm the Berlin figures cited here. At all Prussian universities taken together, between 1886 and 1903, students from academically trained (including professional) and military officers' families constituted about 21 to 22 percent of all students; sons of the propertied middle class, 46 to 49 percent; and all others, 30 to 32 percent. The percentages did not vary much over this entire period.[9]

A recent study by Konrad Jarausch suggests the same trend overall, but distinguishes between a "plutocratization" of the student body during the first half of the Hohenzollern Empire and a disproportional push into the lecture halls by sons of the petite bourgeoisie during the second half, particularly in the philosophical faculties.[10]

If one considers that the propertied classes had the greatest means as a group to alter the life-style of the student body, their growing share of places at the university undoubtedly had a disproportionate impact on the social tone of university life. Thus it is not surprising that this period between 1870 and 1914 was the heyday of exclusiveness in student social life, which centered upon the dueling fraternities and was characterized by repeated expressions of concern from student organizations about letting "inappropriate" students (e.g., those of working-class or Jewish backgrounds) into the university or student fraternities. The fraternities also had the increasing social function of setting up lines of demarcation between students from the "establishment" and the increasing numbers of students from lower-middle-class homes who came to the university in the last decades before the First World War. It is indicative of the discrimination against and dissatisfaction among the latter that a competitive "free" student league, the *Freistudentenschaft*, was formed to protect the interests of nonfraternity students; it had a decidedly progressive, reformist, and democratic outlook and attracted predominantly students of lesser social and economic standing.

Economic and social background also influenced the choice of faculty by the students pouring into the universities after 1870. It is safe to say that children of the "propertied" class swelled the ranks of the legal and, to a slightly lesser extent, medical faculties. They had never provided much support for the theological faculties, and though they had comprised a considerable proportion of the students in the philosophical faculty (at Berlin, for example, 30 to 45 percent from 1870 to 1909), the proportion did not grow. By 1880, the propertied classes came to provide the largest social contingent to the legal and medical faculties at Berlin (in the legal faculty, almost half the total).[11]

The entry of large numbers of students from the propertied middle class into the traditional preserve of the sons of bureaucrats and professional people was not solely the product of their being able to afford university education. Another reason was linked with career and social aspirations for which the university was a convenient or even necessary route. As Germany's population grew and as its industry diversified, more functionaries of the traditional type were needed, along with functionaries of a new type, such as managers or "private officials" (*Privatbeamte*), to use the peculiar terminology fashionable around 1900. Whereas the industrial revolution antedated the creation of a large civil service in Britain and the United States, in Germany the situation was reversed, so that the new sectors of the economy adapted traditional models of bureaucratic administration. By extension of the parallel of training for the civil service, university education (particularly in law) thus seemed more desirable even for persons planning a career in the administrative sector of the private economy. Educational qualifications for the state service and for the professions also continued to rise. Higher civil service positions, for example, required more university training than ever, and civil service examinations were tied more closely to academic, as opposed to on-the-job, training.

The availability of openings in professional and civil service careers increased in the aggregate, encouraging more young people to attend universities and compete for positions. Given the free-market nature of university attendance, however, the relationship between positions to be filled and the number of students preparing for them was usually an uneven one. There were periods of over- and undersupply. In medicine, for example, Germany had too few physicians in the middle decades of the nineteenth century. A growth pattern beginning in the 1860s and ending about 1890 reversed this situation, so that the number of medical students per million inhabitants rose from an average of 61 in the early 1860s to 182 at the end of the 1880s. Discouraged in part by such competition, students began to turn away from medical studies. By 1905 the number of medical students had dropped by one-third, to about 100 for every million persons. This proportion was just sufficient for the needs of German society, and so it is not surprising that the enrollments began to increase again.[12]

Figures for the legal faculties indicate a spurt in enrollments in the period just after 1871 (caused perhaps by the growth of government and the liberalization of admission to the bar).

From a low point of 75 law students per million inhabitants in the last five years of the 1860s, the enrollment jump brought the ratio up to 99 per million in the period 1871–6. By 1901–6 the number had increased to such an extent that there were nearly 200 law students per million persons. The number of offices requiring juridical training had not grown nearly as rapidly, so that there were too many lawyers for the available civil service positions by the turn of the century at the latest. The disproportionately strong growth of private attorneys (from 91 per million in 1880 to 124 per million in 1903) indicates that many law graduates were forced to seek their livings outside government service.[13]

The most phenomenal growth rate in German university enrollments took place in the philosophical faculties. After the period of relative stagnation from 1830 to 1860, enrollments began to rise moderately in the 1860s and then steeply from the early 1870s onwards. Whereas there were about 114 students of humanities and sciences per million inhabitants in the 1860s, there were nearly 200 by 1881–6. The next decade brought a decided slump in enrollments, but by the late 1890s the figure was back up over 200, and it reached nearly 400 by 1906. The number of public schoolteaching positions requiring university attendance had roughly doubled between 1884 and 1904; mathematicians found many outlets in insurance companies, and chemists in the new chemical industries. Nevertheless, temporary shortages of qualified candidates (as in schoolteaching at the very end of the nineteenth century) almost always produced an overreaction. By the last decade before the war, far too many students flowed into the philosophical faculties for the positions that had been open a few years before. Nevertheless, philosophical faculty enrollments continued to grow down to the First World War. Because those faculties contained a large proportion of the less wealthy students, university and government officials worried about the creation of a new academic proletariat.[14]

Only the theological faculties failed to keep pace with the

general growth of student population. The overproduction of theologians in the 1820s and 1830s had led to a tight employment market. Expressed in terms of general population, there were fewer and fewer theological candidates per million inhabitants during the period 1860–80 (down from about 100 in the early 1860s to about 70 in the last years of the 1870s). The proportion of pastors also sank progressively. The number of students increased in the 1880s but fell again in the 1890s, presumably as vacant positions were filled up. The end of the *Kulturkampf* and the bright prospects for filling vacant Catholic parishes may have contributed something to the growth of enrollments in the 1880s, but Protestant student enrollments increased, as well. By the last five years of the 1890s, enrollments slumped again, so that there were only 72 Protestant theologians per million persons; the trend continued downward in the early years of the twentieth century, to the point where too few theologians were being produced by the universities. This anomaly may be explained by the general secularization of German culture, the relative loss of attractiveness of a priestly career, and the shift of interest among students who would previously have studied theology toward the philosophical faculties.[15]

The responses of students to opening and closing career opportunities can of course not be charted precisely, as German statisticans who labored over the problem admitted. Quite evidently, large numbers of students who attended the universities of the German Empire did not end in careers in the professions and civil service. They may have hoped to do so and, having failed, went into other careers. Or they may have attended the university for less specific reasons having to do with social prestige. This must be discussed later on.

Another factor explaining the enrollment growth was the fact that the German school system produced more students qualified to attend the university. In Prussia, for example, the number of pupils attending *Gymnasien* increased from 57,000 in 1869 to 95,000 in 1905. Though this expansion rate did not differ drastically from the pace of general population growth, the number of pupils who took the *Abitur* and thus qualified for the university did increase in the same time span from 2,300 to 5,100, and from 97 per million persons to 140 per million. The proportion of *Abitur* holders who went on to the university fluctuated from a high of 86 percent to a low of 73 percent over this time, but in 1905 it was still 76 percent. The erosion of the monopoly of the *Gymnasien* over university entrance also produced a new source of students from the *Realgymnasien* and *Oberrealschulen*. The latter taught "practical" subjects rather than the traditional, predominant *Gymnasium* fare of classics, and the former compromised between classical curriculum and practicality, teaching modern languages and mathematics strongly. By the end of the nineteenth century, the agitation to introduce modern subjects into the *Gymnasium* curriculum had become so strong as to be almost irresistible. Rather than dilute the classical curriculum of the *Gymnasium* and thereby diminish its social exclusivity, however, the German governments opted to allow first *Realgymnasium* pupils and later *Oberrealschule* graduates to take the *Abitur* and attend the university, at first under severe restrictions. The same sort of compromise had been applied to the demands of the THs for integration or equality with the universities by 1900, as we have seen: Rather than sully the "impractical" curriculum of *Gymnasium* and university with "practical" reforms, the privileges of the *Realgymnasien, Oberrealschulen,* and technical colleges were increased to lower, but not erase, the boundary between them and the classical educational route.

The effects of these changes on the universities were what the opponents of practical education had feared: a growing stream of university students from the two less "noble" types of high school. *Realgymnasien* did not grow absolutely very much from 1869 to 1905, but the number of *Abitur* holders more than tripled, and the percentage of these *Abiturienten* going on to the university rose from a little over 1 in 1869 to

54 in 1905. The number of *Oberrealschule* pupils in Prussia rose from twenty-six hundred to over twenty thousand in the same time period. The number of pupils taking the *Abitur* rose from thirty-four in 1885 to nearly six hundred in 1905. And by the latter date, over 40 percent of these *Abitur* holders went on to the universities. By 1905, some 15 percent of all Prussian university students had arrived via the alternate route of non-*Gymnasium* schools, whereas the percentage in 1869 had been near 0.[16]

Finally, two other groups of students swelled the ranks at German universities during the empire's life. Foreign students, who had always been attracted to German universities in respectable numbers, were even more strongly attracted by the prestige of the imperial universities. By the first years of the twentieth century, foreigners constituted nearly 9 percent of the students in the German universities, nearly double the rate of a generation before. Already burdened with unprecedented subsidies to the universities, some governments toyed with the idea of raising fees for foreign students.[17] On the other hand, prestige reasons discouraged the Althoff-era ministries from stemming the tide of foreigners, and Althoff himself was greatly interested in expanding international exchanges between German and foreign universities, especially those of the United States.

The other group of students new to the university consisted of women. After a long and bitter struggle for equal educational opportunities in the German Empire, women obtained a foothold on the eve of the First World War with the permission, under severely restrictive conditions, to attend the German universities. By 1914, women constituted about 7 percent of the student body in Prussia, a dramatic increase in their numbers since 1900. Thus by 1914 graduates of nonclassical high schools, foreigners, and women made up a considerable part of the German student body.

A final factor accounting for the increased size of the university enrollments is the lengthening time of study itself. Thanks to rising requirements for the civil service and the professions, students, sustained perhaps by greater financial resources, stayed longer on the average and were older upon quitting the university. In the field of medicine, for example, the mandatory number of years of study was raised to five in 1902. Although Prussia officially required only three years of university study for the civil service and professions (except medicine) at the time, the actual number of semesters students spent at Prussian universities exceeded the minimum considerably by the 1880s: The averages were nearly 8 semesters for Protestant theologians, 11 for Catholics; 7.5 for law students; over 11 for philosophical faculty students; and over 12 for medical students.[18] The number of semesters spent by the average student by the early years of the twentieth century was even higher.[19] One estimate accounts for 10 percent of the student enrollment growth between 1871 and 1918 by the lengthening of the average time of study.[20]

Since 1870, much had changed in the German student body. A relatively stagnant, predominantly Protestant, all-male body of graduates of classical *Gymnasien* drawn mostly from the professional and civil service elite had been transformed into a heterogenous mass. The old core of the university students remained intact, but it was strongly augmented in number by non-Protestants, sons of the commercial classes and even the petite bourgeoisie, more foreigners, and a few women. The German governments, led by Prussia, had grudgingly dropped one restriction after another on university study. Population growth, the promise (not always kept) of new career opportunities through higher education, and the attraction of new social groups to the university had contributed to the superficial impression of an opening up (though hardly yet a democratization) of the universities.

This point raises a most interesting question about the increased enrollments beyond the documentable needs of German society and from social groups that had not previously shown such a keen interest in academic study. In a country like

Germany, where social status had been tied directly to university education throughout modern history, it is axiomatic to say that a large proportion of the students and their families viewed the university as a means of gaining or maintaining status. The sons of university graduates comprised a very large percentage of students during the early nineteenth century, and the "inheritance" of social function (e.g., a profession) was widespread. Whether in order to assume a father's career (a classic example comes from the Protestant clergy) or merely to avoid the stigma of not achieving the same university credentials as one's father, students had to attend the university or suffer some status loss. The continuation of this pattern, under circumstances of general population growth and the corresponding expansion of the professions and civil service, accounts for a considerable part of the growth of the university enrollments in imperial Germany.

At the same time, imperial Germany was no longer a traditional society lacking in movement. Authoritarian, pseudo-parliamentary, and class-ridden as it was, it still showed many signs of movement toward greater openness and fluidity. The new middle class created as a result of the industrial revolution began to seek university education, partly as a means of securing greater access to the civil service and professions, but also partly for symbolic legitimation. Government policy, which had discouraged university study in the period 1830–70, ceased to apply restraints and, by 1900, indirectly encouraged it by changing university admission standards. The old educated middle class continued to send its sons to the university to assure traditional family status and the inheritance of professional standing. The wealthier members of the new middle class (e.g., industrialists) sent their sons in order to legitimate their economic status born of the industrial revolution. And the economically less prosperous members of the middle class (e.g., artisans or innkeepers) sent their sons in order to upgrade their status and provide them with the qualifications to break into the security of the civil service and professions. The university thus served a status-related purpose for the old professional classes and the newly wealthy; but given the overcrowding of the professions and civil service after 1900, it did not serve the interests of the lower middle class nearly as well.

Given the keen competition for professional careers, even the sons of the old *Bildungsbürgertum* or educated middle class had to redouble their efforts to maintain their status. But in the late nineteenth century, higher education (as well as classical *Gymnasium* education) took on, in addition, a heightened value even for those members of the middle class who did not necessarily intend to exploit their university training directly in their careers. A recent study of the bourgeoisie in western Germany argues forcefully that economically independent bourgeois began to integrate themselves socially and even maritally into the higher civil service stratum in the western provinces after 1860. Academic education served as the fluid that made social integration of bureaucracy and entrepreneur easier. "If property or artisanal–technological capacities had determined social position among groups of the economically independent before the onset of high industrialization, then education appeared as a new, socially effective status symbol along with the integration of the bureaucracy into the middle class."[21] Evidently many members of the *Besitzbürgertum*, which had traditionally chosen other forms of education more attuned to the practical needs of economic production and distribution, were sending their younger sons to the university at the end of the nineteenth century in order to legitimate their family wealth and place themselves on the same level of academic accomplishment as the academically trained civil servants. This phenomenon, if widely generalized, would help explain why university enrollments increased even though there were not enough professional careers to support all graduates. Not *Bildung* for its own sake alone – a value for the traditional educated middle class – but also the attainment of university credentials for social status became a value for the commercial bourgeoisie. One should be cautious in separating this phenomenon from "upward social mobility," because the commercial middle class did not gain a direct economic benefit from sending its sons to the university; but one might regard the phenomenon rather as a form of lateral mobility, enabling the commercial middle class to reinforce its claims of equal status with the educated middle class (in particular the bureaucracy) and to break down the persisting walls between political and industrial elites in imperial Germany.

For the lower middle class, university education took on a similar, if more illusory, attraction. As Johannes Conrad wrote in 1906:

> Another cause of the disproportionate rush to the universities and civil service careers lies in the lamentable class conflicts, which are sharper in Germany than in any civilized country . . . They are traceable to the difference of forms in the upper and lower circles of society, which are obtained only by education and training, given the lack of natural chic and ease with social forms among the Germans . . . In no country is educational arrogance [*Bildungsdünkel*] so widespread and crass as among ourselves . . . Under these circumstances it is understandable that the lower classes, overestimating the advantages to be expected [from university education], strive to have their children rise into higher social strata – this is especially true of petty officials, primary schoolteachers, artisans, tradesmen, and small manufacturers.[22]

Conrad's solution was to expand and make more attractive the alternative path leading through technical and business education at nonuniversity institutions. Conrad's attitude reflected that of the German education ministries and governments generally: The lower middle class should stay in its social place, but that place should be made more attractive by providing education and incentives for members of this class to enter trades and manufacturing. Universities were training the "staff officers," but there were too many of these; Germany needed more "noncommissioned officers."[23] This military parallel betrays the widespread hostility of the German ruling classes and academics to the hope of the lower middle class for social mobility through university education, because the gulf between sergeant and lieutenant in the German armies traditionally reflected the different class origins of the members of each rank. Government policy might be "progressive" in pleading for less snobbism about the trades and commerce as compared to the professions; but it was ambivalent about letting the lower middle class have genuinely equal access to the professions.

For although the less wealthy members of the middle class could attend the university even without preparation in a *Gymnasium,* they faced considerable economic sacrifices on the long march through university to profession or civil service. In addition to the long period of university study, which poorer students had often to protract by taking on a variety of low-paying jobs, the graduate had to look forward to many years of apprenticeship in civil service or professional positions. During these years, he would be obliged to support himself in large measure from personal income: The *Referendar* (trainee) was virtually unpaid, as was the *Privatdozent.* Scholarship aid, which might have spared at least the more gifted among the poor, was ludicrously insufficient in sum and doled out in such minute amounts as to be nearly worthless. In Prussia, for example, scholarship aid was given to 33 percent of the Prussian students in 1895–6 in an average amount of 181 marks; by 1902–3, only 25 percent of Prussian students were receiving scholarship aid, and the average amount had fallen to 175 marks. Without help from the family, even a scholarship student found his life one of "dire need."[24]

Judging by the often-heard complaints of German professors, the students from the lower middle class had other handicaps to overcome, as well. Charges of inadequate preparation often met the students who came from the non-*Gymnasium* schools. Thus they had to struggle harder to gain the qualifications they sought from the university. One of the major advantages of the university in the German Empire also remained virtually closed to them—membership in the student fraternities (*Korps*), where useful friendships were made not only among the student members themselves, but between students and "old boys" (*alte Herren*), who could be most helpful to a student's subsequent career. *Korps* were socially exclusive and expensive.

Thus, by a combination of disadvantages, the chances of the student of lower-middle-class origin at the university were considerably less than those of members of the higher social strata. "There was no clear connection between expansion of professional groups and upward social mobility in Germany before 1914," as one study concludes. "The development of Germany between 1850 and 1914 rather shows that—despite very rapid economic growth, a forced armaments policy, a strongly expanding health sector and the buildup of an educational system with a high production of technicians and scientists—this country was not forced to recruit new members for the upper social strata primarily from the middle and lower strata."[25]

Another index to the career motivations of students who swelled the universities' enrollments after 1870 is the ratio of doctoral to nondoctoral degree candidates. At the University of Berlin, the trend pointed generally in the direction of fewer doctorates per student as enrollments increased.

In theology, the number of students per doctorate awarded had remained in the area of 150 to 220 in the period 1817–60 (with the exception of the 1830s, when enrollments reached a peak and there were on the average 550 students enrolled for every doctorate awarded). In the 1860s, the number of students per doctorate averaged 280; in the 1870s, 370; and in the 1880s, when theology enrollments reached their absolute peak for the century, nearly 2,000 students per doctorate. As enrollments sank drastically over the next twenty years, however, the ratio of students to doctorates returned to earlier levels (250:1 in the 1890s, 140:1 in the first decade of the twentieth century).

In law, where the ratio had been falling in the period 1850–70, the number of students per doctorate jumped from an average of 41:1 in the 1860s to 170:1 in the seventies, about 180:1 in the eighties and nineties, and over 300:1 in the first decade of the 1900s. The medical faculty showed a similar trend. Whereas 1 student in 2 took a medical doctorate in the

1850s, it was 1 in 5 during the 1870s, 1 in 9 in the 1880s, and 1 in 14 in the first decade of the 1900s. Only the philosophical faculty held relatively steady, granting a doctorate for every 20 to 30 students in the entire period 1830 to 1910 (except for 1870–80, when the ratio jumped to 59:1).

Except for the philosophical faculty, then, the number of doctorates awarded did not keep pace with the expanding enrollments, even at a university that had increasingly come to be regarded as a finishing school for professional studies. From a high average of 1 doctorate for every 9.6 students in the decade of the 1850s, Berlin's ratio of doctorates fell to 1:24 in the 1880s and 1:28.6 in the first decade of the twentieth century.[26] Berlin may not have been representative, to be sure, as it was far easier to obtain a doctorate at some other universities, some of which had the reputation of being degree mills. Comparable data are not easy to obtain, but by way of comparison, the University of Leipzig awarded proportionately more doctorates and awarded them at a fairly steady ratio to student population during the empire. The ratio dropped only slightly from 1 doctorate per 7.25 students in the period 1884–9 to just about 1:7 in 1899–1909.[27] Nevertheless, the evidence from Berlin and Leipzig would suggest that the number of doctorates, though rising in absolute numbers after 1870, did not increase proportionately with the student body.

Falling ratios at Berlin and constant ones at Leipzig reflect the much faster growth of the total student body at the former university. Doctorates were not necessary except for students planning to enter higher education or private medical practice. Although many students took doctorates anyway, their value to some extent lay in their setting the doctoral student off from the herd of other students. The amount of time and effort needed to obtain a doctorate had increased considerably since the mid-nineteenth century, as well.

The growth of the German universities' student enrollments under the empire, in conclusion, had numerous causes, many of which were the result of shifts in German society and gov-

ernment policy. The rapidly rising prosperity of large elements
of German society permitted new types of families to send
their children to universities. Government policies eliminated
some of the traditional barriers to university study, and more
lavish subsidies to the universities than at any time past permitted them to expand their facilities and faculties to help
absorb the flood of students. The traditional prestige of university attendance, heightened by the worldwide fame of the
German universities under the empire, attracted many students
who would have been better advised to spend their time elsewhere, at least in the opinion of many contemporary observers. But the very speed of German economic growth had
outrun proper reorientation of values. Universities had become
increasingly "Americanized," to use the (usually pejorative)
word common before 1914, whereas German attitudes toward
the new industrial economy had not been. Universities were
becoming large-scale enterprises, at least quantitatively, and
the value of university study in terms of social status began to
sink as a result.

The sheer increase in student numbers placed the universities
themselves before massive problems. Quantitative changes had
qualitative repercussions. One of the most serious of these was
the alteration of the relationship between student and teacher.

The growth of the professoriate
in imperial Germany

While the German universities were being filled (and, in the
opinion of many contemporaries, overfilled), the ranks of the
professoriate also grew. From a total of about twelve hundred
at the German universities in 1835, the number of teachers of
all three ranks (ordinary and extraordinary professors, plus
private docents) grew very little until 1860, when it was still
only a little over twelve hundred. By 1870 it had increased to
over fifteen hundred; by 1880, to over eighteen hundred; to
over twenty-three hundred in 1890; twenty-seven hundred in

1900; and over three thousand by 1905.[28] Put another way, the total university teaching staff had doubled between 1870 and 1905. But the student enrollments had tripled. In absolute terms, the staff was growing by leaps and bounds, but in relative terms, the student–teacher ratios at German universities were becoming more and more disadvantageous.

The teacher–student ratio had been, on the average, 1:11 in 1835, 1:9 in the period 1840–70, and slightly better in 1870 (1:8.9). But then it slipped to 1:11 by 1880, 1:12 in 1890, and roughly 1:14 by 1905.[29] This situation was made worse by the fact that much of the overall staff growth had taken place below the level of the full professorships. Whereas in 1870 there had been 17 students for every ordinary professor, by 1905 there were nearly 34; and whereas the full professors made up 52 percent of the staff in 1840 and 53 percent in 1870, by 1905 they constituted only 41 percent overall. This percentage would have been even lower had it not been for the fact that two faculties, theology and law, resisted admitting as many *Privatdozenten* as the other two, medicine and philosophy, where the growth in junior staff was phenomenal.

Some figures will illustrate this development more clearly. In 1840 there were 83 full professors in German Protestant theological faculties; by 1870 there were only 87; but by 1905 there were 117, a 35 percent increase over 1870. At the same time, there were 28 extraordinary professors (EOs) in 1840, 24 in 1870, and 41 in 1905 – a 70 percent increase. The situation with *Privatdozenten* (PDs) was comparable: 35 in 1840, 15 in 1870, 38 in 1905 – a 150 percent increase over 1870, but actually the same level as in 1840! Figures for the Catholic theological faculties are comparable, with *Privatdozenten* holding relatively constant and few in number over the century.

In law, as in theology, the full professors were always a majority of teaching staff, reaching two-thirds in the early 1890s. EOs made up a tiny fraction of the staff (between 14 and 16 percent) throughout the nineteenth century. Whereas full professors of law increased from 108 (1840) to 126 (1870) to 184 (1905), a 46 percent increase between 1870 and 1905, law EOs increased 60 percent from 1870 to 1905 (from 30 to 48), and PDs increased only 49 percent (from 41 to 61).

In the medical and philosophical faculties, however, the growth of EOs and PDs completely eclipsed the growth in new chairs for full professorships. German medical faculties counted 135 *Ordinarien* in 1840; 166 in 1870; and 246 in 1905, or a 48 percent increase between 1870 and 1905. Medical EOs increased from 66 (1840) to 100 (1870) to 275 (1905) – a 175 percent increase within thirty-five years. PDs went from 84 (1840) to 146 (1870) to 450 (1905) – 208 percent over 1870. In medicine, the full professors constituted only 25 percent of the teaching staff by 1905.

The philosophical faculties also grew most rapidly in the lower ranks. *Ordinarien* numbered 270 in 1840, 383 in 1870, and 636 in 1905; they had thus increased by 66 percent between 1870 and 1905. But EOs jumped from 124 (1840) to 175 (1870) to 388 (1905), a 122 percent increase. PDs numbered 142 in 1840, 169 in 1870, but 467 in 1905 – a 176 percent increase. *Ordinarien,* in philosophy, ceased to constitute the majority of university teachers after the 1870s and had sunk to only 43 percent of the staff by 1905.[30]

One must of course take note of the distinction between *Dozenten* and other members of the teaching staff. The *Ordinarien* and *Extraordinarien* were, with some exceptions, regular teaching staff and salaried bureaucrats of the state. The *Dozenten,* on the other hand, were unsalaried academic freelancers licensed to teach by the regular university staff. Their only university income derived from student fees, insufficient to live on, and they were theoretically freed of the bureaucratic responsibilities to the state characteristic of the regular professors. In fact, many of the *Dozenten* may have taught little or not at all. Even if lectures were announced, there is no way of knowing if they were given; the announcement was enough to retain PD status. The medical PDs in particular included in their ranks a large number of men whose main motive for private lecturing was to advance their private practice through the prestige lent by association with the glamorous university.[31]

Evidence from the University of Berlin, one of the most prestigious urban universities, however, indicates that *Dozenten* as a group worked harder and gave more courses as the century neared its end: A fairly constant average of two lecture courses (in law three) per semester plus a growing number of hours in seminars (from an average of one-third seminar per semester in 1870 to one-half in 1909) was the norm for each *Dozent*. Even in medicine the number of lectures per *Dozent* remained at two a semester.[32] The courses meeting from one to four hours a week increasingly became the mainstream teaching period, rising from 43 percent of all courses in 1815 to over 90 percent in 1860 and 1909. In 1815, PDs had given about 25 to 30 percent of these one- to four-hour courses, the EOs about the same proportion, and the full professors well over 40 percent. The dominance of the *Ordinarien* in the courses meeting more than four hours a week in 1815 had been extreme: 86 percent. These were mostly the foundation courses for the disciplines. By 1909 the situation had changed dramatically. The majority of all lecture courses were conducted by EOs and PDs. Full professors at Berlin gave 23 percent of the one- to two-hour courses; PDs, on the other hand, gave 51 percent alone. PDs and EOs together gave 57 percent of the three- to four-hour courses and even 52 percent of the five- to six-hour courses.[33] Thus at Berlin the irregular teaching staff was doing the majority of the teaching by 1900. Let us bear these statistics in mind when we approach the entire problematical subject of the professoriate.

Some striking questions suggest themselves from the statistics cited previously on the growth of student bodies and teaching staff at all German universities between the wars of unification and the First World War. Why did staff grow the way it did? Why did staff growth not keep pace with expansion of enrollment? Why, in particular, did the number of professorial chairs grow at an even slower rate than that of lower-ranking teachers? Because this was a period of rapid specialization and subdivision within many of the academic disciplines (especially in medicine and natural and social sciences), one would expect to encounter a considerable pressure on governments to expand greatly the number of full professorships, to attempt to retain a favorably low ratio of students to full professors, and to unburden professors from some of their heavy teaching schedule, in deference to their increasingly obligatory research efforts, by hiring more staff. The financial condition of the various German states, particularly such industrially advanced ones as Prussia and Saxony, had never been so good; even though the finances of the Reich were increasingly vexatious after about 1900, this situation did not effect the states' finances in any decisive way. Because Germany's universities were among the most admired institutions in the world and helped to offset the fears aroused by the Prussian–German army, they were a public relations asset that governments could not afford to abuse. Nor were the university professors and students after 1871 a political thorn in the sides of governments: Staunch loyalty to the Hohenzollern Empire and a generally conservative stance characterized the overwhelming majority of professors and students, just as opposition had characterized them in the first half of the nineteenth century.

Growth as such was not universally welcomed by the professoriate or the governments. Like all change, growth in size tended to disequilibrate the universities and undermine many vested interests. German governments had carried on crusades in the 1820s, 1830s, and 1840s to drive students away, fearing, among other things, the political unrest that they believed the overproduction of intellectuals might bring in its wake. These crusades were not repeated after 1870, and as we have seen, governments indirectly facilitated growing student numbers by various reforms concerning restrictions on university study. But they did not actively press for growth in university enrollments or take steps to maintain the teacher–student ratios common before 1880. Fears of an intellectual proletariat were still very much in evidence as late as the eve of World War I.

The professoriate had reasons of its own to eye growth mistrustfully. One of these was financial. Until the reforms of the free-market system of academic fees in the 1890s, the teaching staff was heavily dependent on widely fluctuating income from students' lecture and other fees, paid directly to the teacher. One might assume that more students would mean more fees and that professors would therefore welcome increased enrollments. Yet despite their similar training and background, students did not all have the same aspirations. They were theoretically free to take whatever courses they wished, although in practice their choices were guided by, among other things, the system of examinations for the professions and civil service. Students tended to take the courses of certain famous authorities in the hope and expectation that these courses would benefit them in their examinations. The pecuniary interests of these professors (whatever their stated position about the matter) naturally disposed them to prefer "serious," that is, professional students over dilettantes, who would be less likely to feel the need for the "standard courses" in a given discipline. For the senior professors, therefore, the advantage lay in stressing the large lecture populated (or at least enrolled in) by aspirants to the professions and civil service.

The extraordinary professors, on the other hand, often held their positions precisely because of the uncertain status of their specialty. Whereas the *Ordinarien* were responsible for assuring that the entirety of the discipline was laid out before the students, the *Extraordinarien* represented more narrowly circumscribed subdisciplines that the governments had not yet decided to elevate to chair rank, and therewith permanency. The *Privatdozenten* were of course temporary staff members with few corporate rights and duties. But they enjoyed youthfulness, a fresh outlook, and very often a high reputation for stimulating and specialized courses. In a student world where bigness had begun to cut a trench between student and professor, the PDs offered accessibility and a certain intimacy and, in some cases, lower fees. For both EOs and PDs, enlargement of the student body was economically advantageous, in two respects: It assured them an overflow of students who could not be accommodated by the *Ordinarien;* and it put pressure on the authorities to increase the permanent staff, thus heightening for the EOs and PDs the eventual chances of moving up the academic ladder.

It is almost impossible to generalize the attitudes of teaching staff toward expansion of enrollment and staff itself, because too many factors and ideologies played roles. But one can probably state that economic interests alone exerted pressure on the *Ordinarien* to restrict the growth of permanent staff (mostly their own group) while allowing a certain growth in the number of students. The fact that this was exactly the trend of the period under discussion tends to raise suspicions that the *Ordinarien* on the whole achieved their best interest. This is not to deny, however, that there were powerful counterpressures, including the honest desire to uphold standards, to provide careers for the younger, talented *Dozenten* and extraordinary professors, and so on. If the *Ordinarien* had been interested only in their financial well-being, they could have used their power over granting the *venia legendi* to *Privatdozenten* to throttle competition from that quarter. It is a credit to the sophistication of the late-nineteenth-century German professoriate that one rarely encounters in faculty-meeting minutes the kind of naked fear of competition from below and loss of fee income that crops up so often in eighteenth-century minutes. One of the reasons for their magnanimity, of course, is that they were relatively very secure and well rewarded. Another is that the professionalization of the disciplines, more or less complete by this period, made the younger *Dozenten* very much dependent on the patronage of the *Ordinarien,* with whom they were unable or unwilling to compete directly.

Another consideration against admitting students massively was that, quite apart from qualitative factors, which will be discussed below, many professors and even teachers on the lower ranks did not necessarily stand to benefit from an enlarged student body. Because of the specialized nature of much professorial teaching by the end of the century, many teachers did not find themselves benefiting from expanding enrollments. There were vast discrepancies in the numbers of students attracted to the various professors, and correspondingly vast gaps between the lecture-fee income of all levels of teaching staff. These discrepancies were by themselves the major motive for the reform of the fee system in the 1890s, which, however, merely set parameters, bureaucratized the payment of fees, and by no means eliminated discrepancies.

A second set of influences on professorial attitudes toward expansion lay in standards. By 1870, the German professoriate enjoyed a considerable international and national prestige and regarded itself as the vanguard of an aristocracy of the mind. It universally endorsed cultural elitism, if for no other reason than its virtual monopoly over access to membership in the cultural elite. Expressions of concern about exposing less qualified members of the given youth cohort to the benefits of *Wissenschaft* were all but absent among the professoriate in the period under discussion. Instead, one reads numerous complaints about the decline of the overall quality of the swelling student body. The tendency to cling to and defend the classical *Gymnasium* curriculum as the sole acceptable route into the university – an increasingly panicky battle after 1890 – betrayed a certain fear of the erosion of the cultural el te on the part of the professoriate. Their fears had less to do with their statutory duties as professors than with their concern about their status as a group (churlish and ignorant university graduates would reflect on this) and about their membership in a numerically diminishing and increasingly powerless class – the *Bildungsbürgertum.*

It was during the period after 1870 that the German professoriate began to succumb to the myth of a golden age in higher education and to invoke the spirit of Humboldt in defense of the smaller, more elite, "purer" university. They based their views on a functional interpretation of society, however, which was far closer in spirit to the views of the utilitarian reformers at the end of the eighteenth century. They tended to see the university as *the* seat of *Wissenschaft,* looking down on practical education and the nonleisured classes alike. But at the same time they tended to lose sight of the deeper humanitarian interests of the Humboldt generation and accepted the old utilitarian notion that the university existed for the purpose of training professional and bureaucratic elites. Because there could be only so many members of these elites, unlimited university expansion appeared wasteful and harmful. The decline, proportionately, of students from cultivated homes and demanding classical schools signaled an end to the privileged position of the *Bildungsbürgertum* in professions and civil service, not to mention the universities themselves.

To say this is not to deny that the professoriate had some solid reasons for concern about the decline in overall qualifications of German students. But such a decline, to the extent that it existed (and here one can rely only on highly questionable assertions), was relative at best. German students may not have advanced as much in maturity, prestige, and expertise as their professors in the late nineteenth century, but they were surely more serious and better educated than their predecessors.

Another, more limited, but not unimportant consideration in the minds of the German professoriate when confronting growth was the disequilibrium in authority. The clublike atmosphere of the traditional faculties was no longer possible when professors at a given institution numbered in the hundreds instead of the dozens. At Berlin University, for example, the average number of full professors between 1810 and 1819 had been 28; nearly a century later (1900–9), it was 115. The total number of teaching staff for the same two periods had grown from an annual average of 54 to 450. Such figures may seem small in contrast to the teaching staffs of a few American superuniversities today, but one must keep in mind that fully involved academic self-government has become very difficult in such universities (many universities do not even have indoor facilities to hold a full meeting of all teaching staff); to the German professoriate, academic self-government was a precious right not to be delegated if possible. Whereas academics of the 1840s who claimed to be in the "in group" of professorial decision makers could report swift, socially satisfactory meetings over wine or coffee of a half dozen influential professors, the style by the 1890s included elaborate and empty banquets, endless correspondence with other professors, and a hectic pace of consultation.

Added to these problems was the implied threat from below. Despite the docility of the teaching staff of nonprofessorial rank, the fact that the majority of teaching staff was of that rank constituted an implied challenge to the authority of the statutorily all-powerful *Ordinarien*. In the sense of faculty governance, the German university has remained until very recently an *Ordinarienuniversität*. But like the German princes themselves, the *Ordinarien* decided and decreed conditions to an increasingly large body of "subjects" who outnumbered them. Challenges to this regime before the Weimar Republic were extremely limited and sporadic. But the potential for such challenges was increasingly present in the minds of the full professors and the governments.

The infamous *Lex Arons* in Prussia in the 1890s attests to this discomfort. The occasion was the reputed social democratic leanings of a young *Dozent,* Leo Arons. Professoriate and government were sufficiently alarmed at the possibility that such disloyalty could creep into even the lowest level of teaching staff that the entire relationship of *Privatdozent* to university and government was altered, much to the disadvantage of the traditional ideas of academic freedom. Thenceforward the *Privatdozent* was no longer a free scholar but was obliged to accept certain loyalty propositions previously incumbent only on *Beamten* (in this case, full professors), without, however, an alteration in the university's minimal obligations to the *Dozent*.

Because the social background and scholarly credentials of all *Dozenten* were in any case carefully scrutinized, and because the possibility of a member of the lower social orders even attending the university, let alone becoming a *Dozent* or professor, was virtually nil, the reaction of the Prussian authorities and many professors in the Arons case implied not only a demagogic victory for the Prussian right but a sense of insecurity among *Ordinarien* vis-à-vis a growing body of *Dozenten*.

The measures taken by many professors to control entrance from below into their own ranks, although not new, appear to have been more widely made into a system during the empire. On the one hand, *Ordinarien* promoted and urged on their own students or protegés so much that the term *Protektion* emerged about 1890 to describe this widespread relationship. With so many qualified candidates for professorships, the existing *Ordinarien* had to struggle hard to further the careers of their favorites. On the other hand, conformity to ever more narrowly conceived criteria of nonacademic conduct became vital to the aspiring younger teachers. Max Weber, for example, publicly complained about the treatment of young Robert Michels, who took a teaching position in Italy in 1908 because he was so discouraged with seeking a chair in Germany. Not Michels's scholarly or teaching qualifications had come under fire, Weber reported, but quite extraneous things: his advocacy of socialism, for one thing, and his refusal to have his children baptized, for another.[34] It was symptomatic of the increasing tension between lower and upper ranks of teaching staff that the number of academic squabbles aired in the newspapers reached a new high after about 1895, some of them achieving ludicrous and grotesque proportions. For their part, the members of the lower teaching ranks expressed their dissatisfaction with university conditions by organizing a national *Nichtordinarienbewegung* (movement of non-*Ordinarien*) after the turn of the century.[35]

If the dilution of *Ordinarien* authority was only an implied threat of the multiplication of junior staff, the dilution by the

government was more real. In many ways, government supervision and interference in faculty self-government increased.
Multiplication of staff and changing functions placed more
and more emphasis on intermediary institutions (such as the
institutes) or direct relations between professor and government, and less on the traditional locus of professorial decision
making and power, the faculties. Nor were seniority and hierarchy as important within the faculties, thanks to the multiplication of chairs. Obviously this problem was more serious in
the larger universities; in the small ones, the multiplication of
professors still did not shatter the intimate atmosphere.

Under the Althoff "system" in Prussia, for example, Max
Weber perceived a tendency toward the intertwining of professorial appointments and quasi-political goals of the educational administration. Instead of the faculties "calling" professors to vacant chairs on the basis of scholarly and teaching
merit alone, Weber charged, all too often the decision-making
rights of the faculties were subverted by Althoff's reliance on
Vertrauenspersonen (Althoff's personal contacts in the universities) and the intrusion of political considerations in the selection process, most notably at the University of Berlin.

A partly successful and partly unsuccessful effort is being made in a
number of faculties of the University of Berlin to limit the number of professorships, while simultaneously the number of students is increasing; at the
same time, one faculty has enacted a rule to limit the habilitation of teachers
from other universities and has attempted to use this restriction of its own
making as a means of preventing an admittedly outstanding scholar from
becoming a *Privatdozent;* this has happened against the vote of the qualified
experts. It is a peculiar irony that the very university in which such things
have happened is now willing to allow its professorships to be used for
purposes of patronage, whenever a ministry thinks it needs to have some
politically desirable research undertaken by a competent young man.[36]

Weber went on to predict that faculties that accepted such
manipulation and allowed political "operators" to be appointed to university chairs would "be incapable of offering
any resistance to public opinion or to the government because
of the weakening of their moral authority."[37]

Despite the increasing opportunities implied by an absolute and rapid expansion of the number of teaching positions in German universities, university teaching as a career became, on the whole, more exacting and difficult in this period. University teaching, which had never been very well remunerated, appears to have come more in line with other professions in terms of income in this period. After the reform of university salaries and fees in Prussia in 1897, a full professor began with a salary of four thousand marks (higher in Berlin) with an average yearly increase of one hundred marks, plus a housing allowance (five hundred to nine hundred marks). Just before the reform, when nearly 200 professors earned less than a thousand marks additionally from fees, about 160 had additional incomes in the range of one to four thousand marks, another 60 earned up to six thousand marks, about 30 earned up to eight thousand marks, and so on; four professors earned over twenty thousand marks in fees.[38] The reform raised the bottom incomes of many professors and limited the amount of fee income of popular professors to half their fee income over three thousand marks.[39] Assuming a fee income of about three thousand marks to be median, and assuming a professor of about fifty-five years of age, one could reasonably project the median income for a middle-aged Prussian professor as close to ten thousand marks per year. Although this was no princely sum compared to the earnings of doctors, successful lawyers, and so on, it evidently allowed for a fairly comfortable existence free of most cares. Outside consultation continued and increased for many professors, and for the EOs and PDs the connection with a university was often very advantageous to a private practice. The career of university professor had thus come a long way from earlier in the nineteenth century, when governments often fell into arrears in paying the tiny salaries they did offer, the amount of student fees was often low, and professors had to seek desperately for other sources of income, such as writing for gain, boarding students in their homes, and bombarding education ministries and princes with requests for salary raises, doles, and allowances.

But an income corresponding to professional status was still not a universal reward for the professoriate. The *Privatdozenten* in particular were in a constant state of economic destitution—not a new state, to be sure, but one made more painful by the growing prosperity of the *Ordinarien* on the one hand and by the lengthening of waiting for a regular, paid appointment on the other. Prussia officially recognized the economic problems of the *Privatdozentur* in 1875 by setting up a small fellowship fund for poor but talented PDs.[40] By the end of the century, published complaints mounted that the *Privatdozenten* were being forced to teach for no fees from many students. The students wished to take courses from *Privatdozenten* but also believed that they had to enroll (and pay the fees) in courses given by the *Ordinarien* covering comparable scholarly terrain. The widespread belief (encouraged by many professors) that the *Ordinarien* courses were essential to successful passing of examinations not only undermined the theoretical *Lernfreiheit* of the student but diminished his ability to pay PDs for courses he actually wanted to take.[41] This problem was undoubtedly compounded by the closer integration of state examination commissions and the professoriate toward the end of the nineteenth century, after a long period of domination of these commissions by bureaucrats.

The fact that the *Privatdozenten* as a body grew faster than the rest of the teaching staff in the German universities during this period thus indicates no particular improvement in their economic position. Furthermore, the fact that chairs were not multiplying as rapidly as qualified aspirants to them (PDs and EOs) indicates that the academic career was becoming more and more professionalized and exclusive. Just when the professoriate was becoming an increasingly attractive career, primarily because of its prestige, but also because of its relative economic security, the period of waiting for an appointment became a kind of investment that the financially unfortunate could less and less afford. The relative decline of the *Bildungsbürgertum* and rise of the *Besitzbürgertum* as sources of university professors unquestionably had much to do with the rise of academia as a well-paid, highly respected career of difficult access and long waiting, in which the aspirants had to support themselves for several years. One of the most galling facts to anti-Semites of the era illustrates this problem: The percentage of Jews in the ranks of Prussian *Privatdozenten* in 1901 was so high that it transcended the ratio of Jews to other Germans in the general population by nearly 700:1.[42] The willingness of many German Jewish families to finance the academic careers of their sons shed light both on the financial needs of *Privatdozenten* and on the respect paid to the academic profession as a means of social mobility, even for families with money but little social acceptability. The same can be said of non-Jewish families who financed the academic aspirations of their sons. Money, especially when made as rapidly as in Germany during the takeoff years after 1860, needed to be legitimized by the traditional sources of social prestige, one of which was the world of academe.

To some extent, the increasingly onerous norms for joining the professoriate in Germany were a measure of the general professionalization of careers. Nevertheless, certain evidence indicates that other careers were not increasing their entrance demands as rapidly as was the professoriate. Whereas the number of doctors, lawyers, and ministers was declining in proportion to the German population, for example, the rate of decline was not as precipitous as the decline of *Ordinarien* to population. The number of qualified personnel available for these three nonprofessorial careers was high, but not always inordinately so. The number of qualified personnel for the professoriate was, on the other hand, extremely high, and out of proportion to the demand. Contemporary observers ranging from Max Weber to Friedrich Paulsen agreed that the nature of the academic profession was full of risks and gambles, that is, that many would not achieve the place for which they set out or qualified.

These same observers of course had internalized the ideology of the academic profession and rarely questioned the policies of universities and education ministers, which contributed to the problem. By the end of the nineteenth century, the German academic world invoked the principles of Humboldt and Fichte like a litany, but the practice of the governments and even the evolution of the ideology of *Wissenschaft* had combined to make the utilitarian needs of the state, rather than the intellectual needs of the society, paramount. To be sure, Fichte and Humboldt had never envisioned the democratizing effects of their own proposals nor the mammoth swelling of Germany's population in the nineteenth century; thus their words could still be invoked against their spirit.

The actual outlines of the professorial career by the end of the nineteenth century had developed far away from the Humboldtian ideal so often invoked. In his function as teacher, the professor confronted problems much more difficult than those of his forerunners at the beginning of the nineteenth century. He was overwhelmed with the sheer size of the student body and had been forced (by his other responsibilities, to some extent, also) to retreat into the seminar or institute to devote his time to "serious," that is, specializing, students. But the ranks of specialists did not grow as fast as those of other students; the fraternity boys and *Brotstudenten,* antithetical types except for their common rejection of intellectual curiosity, seem to have become even more of a problem in the burgeoning German universities at the end of the century than at the beginning.

As one noted German professor described the fraternity members before the First World War: "We saw the *Kommilitonen* [brothers] at the formal occasions of the university, where they stood along the walls in full costume, often splendid figures, with their banners and swords; we saw them when we were invited to their fraternity houses for an evening's drinking; we saw them on picnics and in swimming pools in the summer, almost always with pleasure – but we saw them seldom or not at all in our lectures."[43] The *Brotstudenten,* on the other hand, were visible in lecture halls, but not much more:

> *Brotstudenten* . . . were mostly sons of the muses from families of small means who sought only to get into an office and an income as soon as possible on the shortest path, after barely passing their examinations. They, and their defensive slogan – "You don't need that for exams!" – could be found in all faculties. But they were especially numerous in the philosophical faculty. For the study of philosophical disciplines, with the goal of a teacher's career in the middle schools, was the shortest and cheapest, and thus it attracted for external reasons precisely the members of the poorer circles of the population whose study had to cost the least. But they also brought – brilliant exceptions notwithstanding – a relatively small intellectual-social culture with them.[44]

The same professor concluded sadly, "The German university accomplished excellent things in the training of scholars, but it failed in its task of intellectual education of the nation."[45]

Another reason for the erosion of contact between teacher and student was the professional definition of the teacher's research obligations. Even by the beginning of this period, by 1870, it had become customary to expect research productivity as a measure of professional excellence and a condition of a satisfactory career. During the last half of the nineteenth century, the definition of *Wissenschaft* had taken on some of the contours of a positivist ideology: If the extension of science and knowledge depended on hard, disciplined work rather than genius-inspired intuition, as the positivists believed, then every teacher could be a scholar. One need only read through one of the many late-nineteenth-century methods handbooks for evidence of the penetration of the concept of *Wissenschaft* as an edifice built of small blocks of research discoveries.

The same minute specialization and lack of a general intellectual framework of communication even erected barriers between the professors themselves in an unprecedentedly painful way. To cite Curtius again:

With the members of the medical faculties there were occasional contacts, such as through musical or artistic interests, through which overworked surgeons or internists liked to seek recreation, ... but no intellectual contacts. The natural scientists and mathematicians of our own faculty went their own ways; the legal professors were seldom inclined to regard the philosophy of law as anything more than an empty mental game ... The majority of professors were so taken up with the demands of their individual disciplines that few felt a need to glance across their boundaries ... With the growth of ever more special disciplines and the creation of ever more chairs for them, as was demanded by the development of modern science, it was natural that at even middle-sized universities such as Freiburg and Heidelberg even the full professors, to some extent, no longer knew each other personally. They came together only a couple of times a year to elect a rector and attend formal events.[46]

In order to meet ever higher standards of professional competence, a professor had to maintain a high standard of research activity for himself. He also had to keep up with the literature in his field, and this task demanded more and more time as professional journals multiplied.

Finally, the professor had to compete, *qua* researcher, with other researchers outside the university system. The near monopoly of university professors over scholarly research was crumbling rapidly by the end of the nineteenth century. Not only were the technical universities providing many discoveries of a theoretical nature, but nonteaching research organizations were becoming more and more common. Some of these were inaugurated, expanded, and supported by the states; others, by private industry. The Kaiser-Wilhelm-Gesellschaft, founded in 1911, was heavily supported by German industrialists to aid research projects on their own merits. Both industry and government had begun to realize in the 1870s and afterward that science was useful. But the utilitarian attitudes of government and industry were not always in line with the more theoretical orientations of university professors; hence the branching off of nonteaching research institutions from the universities. In the disciplines with little social utility, such as the classics or history, such extra-university research institutions did not spring up. As the continued vigorous growth and diversification of such nonutilitarian disciplines showed, the university was still fulfilling its research function quite well; but in certain areas, social demands simply outstripped the abilities of the German universities to meet them.

The prevailing attitude of the professoriate toward its teaching function was evidently one of concern, but its response to the new challenges of the expanded student body was insufficient. By the end of the nineteenth century, a certain note of resignation about students had crept into much of the debate about the teaching and learning functions of the university. Paulsen, for example, reported at considerable length on the sharp debates concerning the students' learning habits, but in the end nothing changed very much. Complaints abounded from the 1880s onward about students cutting classes; some professors even claimed that the majority of students never attended classes. Various remedies were proposed: obligatory attendance; roll taking with reports to parents about excessive cutting; the reduction of large lecture courses; and the substitution of small, seminar-style courses in which students would be both more readily induced to come to class and easier to watch. Paulsen, on the whole a defender of the late-nineteenth-century academic scene, argued that student irresponsibility was not as bad as suggested, that anyway abuses could not be wiped out, and that academic freedom was more important than regular class attendance. Paulsen also countered Professor Ernst Bernheim's proposal to reduce large lecture courses and substitute small group teaching with the argument that the seminar method was suited only to a minority of students. Bernheim's proposal went, however, to the heart of the problem of the teacher in the new, enlarged German universities; with constantly worsening teacher–student ratios, the Humboldtian ideal of combining *Wissenschaft* and *Lehre* was more and more chimerical.[47]

Despite the resistance and doubts of many academicians about these problems and their impact on academic freedom, the formal liberty of the students remained outwardly little affected. The states did tighten the screws on students around the turn of the century by raising the mandatory number of semesters or courses in a given preprofessional discipline (e.g., medicine, law). Furthermore, important changes in the composition of the state examination commissions reduced the power of the professional bureaucracy and increased that of university professors: Around the turn of the century, half the personnel of the legal examination commissions in Prussia consisted of university professors, and medical examination boards were usually predominantly composed of university teachers.[48]

The reintegration of university professors into the state examination bureaucracy, after several decades from mid-century on when the trend had been for the professional bureaucracy to set standards of admission examinations to its own ranks, meant several things to the position of the university professor as a professional. (Of course, only *Ordinarien,* and usually those with most prestige in their discipline, would normally be selected for the state examination commissions.) One effect was to bind the professor more closely to the state and its needs, and this process of binding necessarily diminished the academic freedom of professor and university. The same role altered the professors' stance in the eyes of students, as well: No longer merely an expert but fallible *Wissenschaftler* groping for the truth and hoping for correction and cooperation from his students, the professor–examiner was a state-sanctioned authority who could be challenged only at the peril of the student's career. No doubt the inclusion of professors and their domination in writing examinations on the government boards meant a theoretical upgrading and intellectualization of the examinations; but their reintegration also tended to undermine the distinction between "free" scholarship and "bound" state service that had been so important to the Humbolt era reformers. The professor–examiner could of course console himself with the notion that the state examinations tested only the well-known and generally accepted information in a given field, which it was the duty of the professor to "lay out systematically" in the large lecture courses. Yet this very fact tended to induce lazier students to restrict themselves solely to the well-known and accepted, and as little of that as was necessary to pass the examinations. The reintegration of some professors on civil service boards – for medical, legal, church, government, and school offices, among others – in effect altered subtly the function of the professional university teacher, changed the meaning of academic freedom without formally undoing it, and qualified the relationship of professor–examiners to their junior colleagues and to their students.

No doubt the growing helplessness of the state bureaucracy to write and administer fair examinations without the massive help of the professoriate was an understandable reason for calling in university staff. The very speed of scientific growth at the end of the nineteenth century made the senior bureaucracy more and more incapable of keeping up with recent developments, of which the state was of course willing to take advantage. Yet the choice of renowned *Ordinarien* to fill the task of writing more technically modern examinations did not fully meet the need, because many of the most imaginative new discoveries were being made and taught by the younger university staff. In an era of such scholarly and scientific dynamism, the reliance on *Ordinarien* to set the tone for examinations was a step toward recognition of the need for new types of expertise in the professions to which state examinations were an entree. But it was only one step; the *Ordinarien,* too, were apt to fall behind in their conceptions of the total overview of their disciplines and were themselves increasingly specialized. Thus the state examinations tended to become more and more dependent on "old" knowledge and set no premium on a student's originality or intellectual curiosity. This fact alone may help explain why so many of the new students who flooded the German universities seemed lacking in depth and spiritual power in the eyes of the professoriate. Whatever value there was for the state in the decision to include professors in the examination system, the effects on the independence of professors and students were ambiguous at the least.

The final, and perhaps most important, area of professional duties of the professoriate, as a group of teachers, was in the research institutes within the universities. Institutes and seminars had, as we have seen, been developing strongly before 1870, although they had often been developed on the initiative of a minority of the professors and received rather limited state support only after they had proved their utility. After 1870, the state took much of the initiative in generalizing the system of seminars and institutes. They tended to become *Staatsanstalten* in themselves, legally and financially responsible to the state, usually directly so, with the traditional corporate structure of the faculties and other university organs being bypassed. The seminars and institutes had many advantages for professors and students alike, and it was these institutions, a sort of university within the university, that gave the German higher education system much of its world renown in the late nineteenth century. Yet their structure, method of operation, and degree of autonomy within the universities were not completely unproblematical.

Most obviously, the rise of the institutes and seminars to a central position in advanced discipline-oriented training and research catered to the rapid specialization of many university functions. Though the advantages to the progress of science and advanced training were clear, the disadvantages to the unity of the university as a community and as the seat par excellence of an integrated scholarly view of man and nature suffered. The system of seminars and institutes helped overcome the threat of social and intellectual isolation of students in a burgeoning university, but only for the few. It turned away, equally, the threat of intellectual isolation of the faculty from one another and from students, but at a certain price. The walls of the institute and seminar buildings that began to go up in these years were mute representatives of the walls between disciplines, even within the same faculty.

Institutes and seminars

Parallel with the development of large size in student bodies and teaching staff in the period between 1866 and 1914, important structural changes were taking place in the German universities. Seminars and institutes, previously few in number and, as we have seen, more the offspring of individual faculty members than of state planning, multiplied and became the main concern, financially speaking, of governments.

At the University of Berlin, faculty salaries had comprised the largest single item in the annual budget in 1860 (nearly 250,000 marks). All seminars and institutes together had cost only 170,000 marks. Already by 1870, however, institutes cost more than salaries; they remained the largest item in the budget thereafter. Whereas salaries of professors increased from decade to decade by factors on the order of 20 to 70 percent, seminar costs virtually doubled every decade until 1890 and rose at a rate of more than 50 percent per decade thereafter.[49] By 1890 the costs of operating institutes and seminars were double those of staff salaries; by 1910 they were over three times as much. In addition, the costs of buildings and administration connected with the institutes grew rapidly. Berlin's building costs were in 1870 6,000 marks and by 1910 180,000 marks. The total cost of administration in the "self-administering" university had been only 35,000 marks in 1870, but it had reached nearly 190,000 marks in 1910. Every seminar had to be equipped with its own building, staff, and library; every scientific institute needed laboratory space, apparatus for experiments, and other things in addition to what seminars needed. By 1910, over half the university budget went for seminars directly, and a good deal more went to them indirectly.

Another example can be drawn from the medical faculties of all German universities: Between 1860 and 1914, no less than 173 institutes were founded. These were often for "new" disciplines (e.g., ear, nose, and throat; hygiene). In addition, governments lavished money on older institutes (e.g., anatomy, surgery) to create new buildings and adequate working conditions.[50] Medicine, to be sure, was a favored field in this period. But many institutes were founded in the other fields, particularly in the philosophical faculties. Seminar work was less suited to the teaching of law, and the theological faculties, with their falling enrollments, did not experience quite the same dynamic expansion in this area. Furthermore, because theology had led the way with seminars, many had been established before 1860.

The state of Prussia developed a feverish pace in establishing seminars and institutes, particularly under the guidance of Friedrich Althoff, chief of the Higher Education Section of the Prussian Culture Ministry between 1882 and 1907. At the nine Prussian universities (Berlin, Bonn, Breslau, Göttingen, Greifswald, Halle, Kiel, Königsberg, and Marburg), Althoff helped establish no less than nine seminars in law; four theological seminars; eighty-six medical institutes, laboratories, and clinics; and seventy-seven institutes and seminars in the philosophical faculties.[51]

In addition, Prussia established a new university at Münster just after the turn of the twentieth century, and many older institutes were rebuilt, expanded, and reequipped with more up-to-date instruments and collections. The non-Prussian states, although generally poorer in resources, also established and expanded the majority of their permanent seminars, institutes, clinics, and polyclinics during this period; naturally the universities of the bigger and richer states (Leipzig, Munich) and a few of those in smaller states favored by a liberal university policy (e.g., Heidelberg in Baden) kept up well with the Prussians' hectic activity.

The motives for founding institutes and seminars were of course directly linked with the rapid development of specialization in science and scholarship. It is no accident that the majority of new institutes and seminars devoted their activity to medical and natural science research and teaching, as these were the fields that were developing most rapidly. After the medical–scientific fields came the humanistic and social science disciplines. Theology and law, which were developing subdisciplines at a far slower rate, and which as disciplines were more concerned with application of knowledge than with discovery of new knowledge, came off worst in the founding of seminars.

The growing willingness of governments to initiate new seminars and institutes in the face of specialization was reciprocated by the professoriate, which sought to take advantage of it. As Althoff's biographer noted about "calls" to vacant chairs, "hardly one of those called came to Berlin without demanding an institute – or without receiving it, immediately or shortly thereafter."[52] As with most new specialties, the number of really outstanding candidates for new *Lehrstühle* was small at the birth of the discipline, and consequently the candidates were in a strong bargaining position.[53] An educational bureaucrat like Althoff, who fundamentally sympathized with the creation of institutes and seminars, could then turn to the state financial authorities with the argument that to refuse funds for an institute would lead to filling the vacancies with second-rate talent.

The German governments were increasingly motivated by a desire to put German higher education to work for the furtherance of certain social, political, and economic goals. The abandonment of laissez-faire economic policies and of alliance with German liberalism by Bismarck in 1879 signaled a heightened involvement of government in the life of the nation. Social legislation, concern for public health and hygiene, the establishment of a German colonial empire and later a fleet, and interest in aiding Germany industry to expand its international competitiveness all had repercussions for the German universities from the 1880s onward.

One way in which these concerns found expression in higher education was in the financial and status privileges lavished upon technical schools by the governments. Althoff, for example, though trained in the traditional discipline of law, shared the view of Felix Klein and others that the arrogant rejection of technical training by the universities was a serious mistake. The demand of German society and government for better technical education thus led to the deepening involvement of German education ministries in building up technical schools.[54]

It was with the same eye to the practical effects of science that Althoff looked upon university institutes. Medical and scientific institutes, in particular, were his favorites, even though there was nothing in his background to explain this favoritism by personal sympathy. Rather, he saw the task of improving public health, particularly in the mushrooming cities, both as a duty of the patriarchal Prussian state and as a means of attenuating the social misery that was widely believed at the end of the nineteenth century to be a motive force behind revolutionary propaganda.

The clinics and polyclinics opened in the Prussian universities not only served science by giving medical professors and students a constant flow of patients to observe and learn from; they also had a direct effect on the quality of health care and hygiene in the cities and towns in which they were located. (Althoff pointed this out to the Prussian cities in which universities were located, in an attempt to persuade them to bear part of the costs of such institutes, as was then done in France.[55]) Quite a few of the institutes and seminars were set up as a result of problems flowing from the rapid urbanization of Germany during this period. Such institutes as those of public hygiene, communicable diseases, skin and sexual diseases, lung diseases, neurological disorders, and forensics in the medical faculties or criminology and insurance seminars in the law faculties grew out of the mounting recognition by the states that modern social problems must be dealt with by science, encouraged and supported by the state. Even the theological faculties were drawn into the net of meeting the needs of an expansive Germany, as such seminars as that for "missionology" at Halle (1897) show.

The philosophical faculties also had much to contribute to Germany's social and political needs. The academic study of administrative science, economics, geography, and the language and literature not only of competing European peoples but of the colonial world owed much to Germany's new position as a dynamic political, economic, and colonial power. The need to train Germany's new "overseas" bureaucracy in their future roles led, for example, to the employment of lecturers in African and Asian languages, facilities for the training of colonial health officials, an institute for oceanography, a seminar for East European studies, and in general a much more vital interest in the affairs of European and non-European affairs and problems than had been conceivable before 1870.

Nor were the needs of German industry and business completely forgotten in the universities, even though there was considerable resistance from the professoriate toward serving the fires of a "materialistic" industry that they tended to reject. Institutes for applied science sprang up at many universities, even though applied science was the raison d'etre of the technical colleges. Tacitly, at least, the creation of institutes for applied electrotechnics, mathematics, chemistry, and physics were an admission by the universities of the competitive pressures of the technical universities as well as an attempt to reconcile engineering and pure science. New institutes for agronomy showed the vital link between science and agriculture and maintained the traditional link (often an uncomfortable one for the more "theoretical" professors) between the universities and the oldest of the technical disciplines (they were not, oddly enough, relegated to the technical universities). Finally, the attempt by German businessmen to stimulate and subsidize the creation of university seminars more in keeping with their free-enterprise views of economic "science" bore fruit in Leipzig.

The establishment and support of seminars and institutes by the German states had a considerable impact on the mode of life of the universities, particularly that of the faculty members.

The sociological fact of a central locus of work forced certain rearrangements. Instead of working mostly in his library at home, the professor could now go to his office at the institute, where an extravagant *Handapparat* or laboratory setup aided him in his research. Although he still gave lectures in various university rooms, as had his predecessors, his seminars and exercises normally took place in the institute. The institute became his second home.

At the same time, the institute became a second home for advanced students. Here the specialized library or equipment was available, and here the professors could be sighted and drawn into conversation in a way impossible in the lecture hall. Against the threat of anomie arising from the rapid growth of the universities, the institute offered some shelter, at least for the select group of students who wished to use it. Most students would rarely, if ever, be seen there. But for the candidates for doctorates (and it was during this time that it became socially respectable to add "cand. phil." or "cand. juris" to one's calling card), the institutes were of major importance.

The institutes were not, as later American university departments were, responsible for the administration of education. In some ways they were comparable to American departments, but in theory they were merely facilities for the furtherance of the older obligations of the university, which remained unchanged. The faculties as self-governing bodies and the professors as individuals remained responsible for the fulfillment of the governments' assignment, that is, seeing to the teaching of all subjects in a proper manner. Technically, the institutes served much the same function as libraries and collections, as a sort of aid to education. In practice, however, they constituted the center point of a new orientation in the German universities. The director of an institute was often the leading professor in a given field; he had an authority and power that was heightened by the entitlement as director. Unlike other university offices (such as that of dean or chancellor), the institutes' directorships did not have to change annually. The institute director was selected for his expertise rather than his seniority or collegial qualities. Furthermore, the director of an institute or seminar had a direct connection with the government, because the latter had the power of choice and control over institutes. Although institute members still enjoyed academic freedom *qua* professors, the institute was really a major breach of the traditional corporate relationship between university and government. Governments did not often intervene in the running of institute affairs, but they did not often feel the need. They appointed the directors and established the statutes of new institutes, they dictated the general lines of research and teaching, and the men they appointed to fulfill the institutes' tasks generally were selected carefully enough to avoid conflicts.

The rapid development of seminars and institutes in German universities after the founding of the German Empire clearly reflected the diversification of research and teaching functions inherent in the growth of *Wissenschaft* itself. To a very large extent, the reputation of German universities as centers of scholarship and discovery rested on the inclusion of these dynamic institutions in the ancient body of the universities. It is a lasting tribute to the scholarly drive of the professoriate and some part of the student body, as well as to the flexibility of the German universities, that the new could be so easily grafted onto the old. Yet other factors were also necessary to this expansion of scholarship and science within the framework of seminars and institutes. Without the massive growth of the student body and the ability and willingness of the states to raise significantly their financial support, the expansion would have been far less dramatic. On one level, the institute network by 1914 appeared to be a wonderful fulfillment of Wilhelm von Humboldt's vision, allowing thousands of students and professors "to live for *Wissenschaft*." Yet on another level, governments and society expected them to produce trained officials and benefits for the country in the same way the utilitarian reformers of 1800 had.

It is also important to remember that the institute system encountered two types of demands that it could not easily meet. On the one hand, most students at universities in the empire were less interested in living for *Wissenschaft* than in passing through the traditional set of lecture courses leading to a career: Though the research ethic had permeated the professoriate, it had infected only a minority of the students. Many students clearly did fit into the category of an "aristocracy of the mind," but the majority aspired simply to maintaining or creating membership in elites of a more mundane type. The dichotomy between the new institutes and seminars, with their dozens of dedicated students, and the old massive lectures for their hundreds of careerists, with their half-empty benches on the many days of *Korps* festivals, pointed to the ultimate frustration of the very Humboldtian ideals that professors liked to claim had been realized in the German university.

On the other hand, institutes and seminars could not easily accommodate themselves to the mushrooming needs of an industrial society. Types of research and teaching vital to such a society were rejected as nontheoretical and tainted with crass materialistic aims. In the long run this refusal probably did not damage German industrial progress, because government and industry turned to other institutions to fulfill such needs. But it may have damaged the vitality of German universities in various ways, undercutting their monopoly on science and scholarship and encouraging within the universities (and among their students) a vague hostility to the modern world.

Concomitant with this restlessness about serving the needs of German society, the German universities showed less and less restlessness about serving the needs of the state. It is to this relationship between state and university in the Hohenzollern Empire that we may now turn.

8

The universities, state, and society, 1866–1914

The relationship of German universities to the state altered considerably in fact, if not formally, during the age of the Hohenzollern Empire. The state bureaucracy, particularly the educational bureaucracy, achieved a degree of control and initiative in university affairs that was unprecedented in its scope. The rapidly expanding scale of universities, combined with much higher demands on the financial strength of the state, helped bring this situation about. The concentration of administrative and fiscal power over so many German universities in one state, Prussia, directly or (by emulation) indirectly set standards and limits for all universities to an unprecedented degree.

Although the universities were benefiting from the new prosperity begotten by the German industrial revolution, they were largely unable or unwilling to cement an alliance with the industrial middle class that would have acted as a counterweight to state control. By posing itself between the burgeoning German economy and the universities, the state was able to heighten its control.

To a large degree, the state also found itself interposed between the university and the political life of the nation. Universities gave up much of their previous role as centers of political discussion, leadership, and opposition. By 1914, the German professoriate had indeed become, in DuBois-Reymond's words, the intellectual bodyguard of the Hohenzollern realm, at least to an extent sufficient to make this statement merely an exaggeration, not an untruth. In return for generous support and protection from the state, the universities of the German Empire had offered up the sacrifice of the spirit, if not all the forms, of corporate independence from the state.

Bureaucracies and universities

The clear trend in relationships between state and university in the German Empire ran toward greater control and initiative of the former at the expense of the latter. This trend was of course the continuation of earlier ones, but it differed in several important ways. The attempt by late eighteenth-century governments to gain greater control over universities had often been frustrated by the distraction or disorganization of the state administration; the lack of state funds, which would have heightened the power of the bureaucracy to gain its ends; and the corporate resistance of the entrenched professoriate. Only in cases when the will to supervise had been strong, the ability to finance had been constant, and the faculties had been divested of many of their medieval privileges, as with early Göttingen, had government control and initiative been strong. The years of reaction after 1819 had witnessed active attempts by government to control the universities, at least in terms of political loyalty, but initiative had been difficult in the conditions of stagnation and relative paucity of funds. Even as late as the "Falk era" in Prussia in the 1870s, as in the preceding decades, ministries were often distracted by other pedagogical matters (school issues, religious strife) and frequently left the universities to their own devices.

Beginning by about 1880, however, the same combination of ministerial willfulness, the lure of rising state funding, and the weakening of corporate resistance brought on a new era of state initiative and control in Prussia and, by emulation, in the other German states as well. For the presence of all three of these factors, the expanding size of the German state, economy, and university bears much responsibility.

Ministries of education had become a standard feature of virtually all German states in the wake of governmental reorganizations during and after the Napoleonic period. To be quite precise, however, most of these ministries were not exclusively involved with education alone, and certainly not with higher education alone. They had usually evolved out of eighteenth-century commissions or other bodies primarily assigned to overseeing the churches and the educational tasks traditionally assigned to these. The Prussian ministry was the largest, but even it bore testimony to the multiplicity of its functions in its official title, Ministry of Clerical, Educational, and Medical Affairs. Some other large states separated the medical affairs sections and placed them under the ministries of the interior (e.g., Bavaria, Saxony), leaving education ministries in charge of religion and all levels of education. A small state such as Baden subordinated all educational matters to the ministry of the interior until 1880, then set up a ministry of justice and education, and established an independent education ministry only in 1911. Before the 1870s *Schulsachen* (school matters) dominated the activity of these ministries, and the degree of ministerial assertiveness over universities generally seems to have depended upon the personality of the minister himself. In Prussia, these ministers sometimes took a strong and benign interest (as with Altenstein down to 1840) or an irritable and distracted one (as with Eichhorn in the 1840s). From about 1860 onward, judging by the ministerial archives, university matters were not high on the list of priorities for Mühler and Falk; these were the years of the wars of unification and of the *Kulturkampf.*

In 1882, however, a young law professor from the new University of Strasbourg was called to Berlin to take over the university desk in the Prussian Education Ministry. As a former professor, he understood the workings of universities quite well; as a trained administrator, he manipulated the workings of ministerial bureaucracy smoothly; and as an intelligent and hardheaded man, he placed his stamp on the university policies of Prussia and eventually the whole Reich. This man was Friedrich Althoff. His skills made him virtually indispensable to the ministry, so that he managed to remain in his office and build its power until his retirement in 1907. Ministers of education came and went while Althoff stayed. The former were increasingly caught up in cabinet work; Althoff became a sort of modest czar over the many Prussian universities and technical colleges. Althoff, like Münchhausen, had a clear vision for the universities; unlike Humboldt, he also had the opportunity to oversee university affairs for a protracted period and could usually count on the support of his ministers. Like Altenstein and his assistant Johannes Schulze, Althoff cared deeply about education. But whereas the former had eaten up much of their energy building up the classical *Gymnasium* and stealing crumbs from the meager Prussian budget to do so, Althoff devoted himself to building up the universities with the much richer resources of an industrialized and powerful state.

Financially speaking, all the German states were in a better position to aid higher education after 1870. Universities and technical colleges together received about ten times as much money from Prussia, Bavaria, and Saxony in 1910 as in 1866.[1] When Althoff came to the Prussian Education Ministry in 1882, he watched over the allocation of 9.6 million marks to universities and technical colleges; when he left in 1907, the sum had risen to nearly 26 million marks. With this kind of funding came increased power for the state bureaucracy.

The third factor that tended to heighten state control over universities lay in the weakening of corporate solidarity among the university professors themselves. The sheer size of the professoriate militated against the formation of a common front against the government. The dissatisfaction of the junior teaching staff, as exemplified in the *Nichtordinarienbewegung* after 1900, further weakened the sense of corporate solidarity among the university teachers. Althoff's practice of maintaining separate (and often secret) contacts with influential professors at various universities both augmented the information at his disposal and gave the opportunity of exploiting these allies to implement his wishes. Finally, rivalries and disputes among the professors themselves appear to have reached a new height under the empire, with rancor and recriminations spilling even into the public press.[2]

Let us examine these three factors in the rising control of the bureaucracy over the universities in somewhat greater detail.

The Prussian Education Ministry during Althoff's quarter century of office set a new tone in relations between the state and the universities. Althoff himself knew the academic world firsthand from his days as a university professor. This knowledge of and general sympathy for the universities lent him weapons in dealing with the university professoriate, but it also inclined him to make decisions in what he viewed as the best interests of the universities. Though often accused of high-handedness, Althoff was never accused of stupidity or complete dishonesty. But on one point there can be no doubt: Althoff perceived himself as the agent of the state and universities as state institutions. He had no wish to destroy the freedom of teaching and learning peculiar to the German university system; but he had only a limited respect for the notion of complete autonomy entertained by many university professors. He might disagree with Bismarck's expressions of exasperation and threats concerning the "republic of letters" and do what he could to protect a reasonable amount of freedom for the scholars. But, as he wrote to a professor friend a few years after joining the ministry, "You are wrong if you hold me to be as patient and yielding as I was in Strasbourg. Here we live closer to Bismarck and learn from him."[3] And like Bismarck, in a more circumscribed way, Althoff often confused the interests of the state with his own judgments.

Under Althoff, the most important decisions about Prussian universities were made in Berlin, not the university towns. Curators were reduced even further in importance; Althoff ignored them and dealt directly with faculties and individual professors. In the most crucial area of university decision making, that of professorial appointments, Althoff was particularly active. Even his apologetic biographer admits the turnabout that took place under him: "In the last decades before his entering the ministry, the Prussian educational administration – departing from the proven tradition of Altenstein and Schulze and against the conception of Bismarck – had followed the [appointment] suggestions of the faculties ever more uncritically. Under the liberal 'Falk–Goeppert' era, the appetite for autonomy among the faculties had emerged strongly. Althoff tried to control this appetite."[4] Althoff did encourage the faculties to nominate candidates for vacancies in full and associate professorships; but he also reserved the final decision for himself, including the decision to ignore the faculties' wishes altogether. By calling upon expert opinions from outside the faculties, he attempted to set up his office as one more open to wisdom and full information than the faculties themselves. By foreknowledge of what tendencies and opinions might prevail in the faculties at recommendation time, and by exerting influence on the faculties through his *Vertrauensleute* (men of trust), Althoff was often able to appoint the person he wanted without coming into direct conflict with the faculties.

The influence of cultural policy on universities developed far beyond the traditional interference of educational bureaucracies into matters of individual professorial appointments, however. In a state such as Prussia, the multiplicity of universities, especially after 1866, posed problems of duplication and waste. Such duplication had for centuries been a notable feature of the German university system; many have argued that the competitiveness engendered by duplicate functions at many universities drove on the development of German scholarship. Such competition tended, however, to reflect the traditional rivalries of the German states, large and small. No sooner had Prussia conquered more universities than discussions arose in the government about the desirability of reducing còmpetition and overlap. The Prussian education minister Mühler wrote to Bismarck in 1866 suggesting ways to suppress competition among the old and new universities. Mühler lamented the "unfortunate German custom of overbidding to retain or obtain popular teachers."[5] Mühler's essentially fiscal concern was transformed by Althoff into a broader concept of *Schwerpunktpolitik,* a policy of concentrating on the heavy development of certain disciplines at certain universities. Specialization, the relative ease of travel for students, and spiraling costs all played a role in the decision to concentrate excellence in various disciplines at one or two Prussian universities. Examples of this policy were the concentrations of Protestant theology at Halle, mathematics at Göttingen, and classics and history at Berlin.[6] Such concentrations were of course beneficial to advances in research and exposed capable students to better learning opportunities than had been possible before. At the same time, they discouraged the creation of more chairs at the universities unfortunate enough not to be designated discipline centers and thus led to disadvantages for those students who could not afford to study far from home, if their regional university did not happen to excell in their chosen field. And no matter how advantageous to the furtherance of scholarship, central planning of this type clearly indicated yet another breach in the traditional autonomy and self-government of the individual universities.

Broader political considerations also entered into the policy making of Althoff. Personnel matters were always settled under clouds of partisanship. Professors suspected of sympathies with the lower classes always faced difficulties in obtaining appointments, even when they had the support of university and ministry alike. Minister J. R. Bosse stated one of the axioms of Prussian policy when he declared in 1898 that professors have not only to teach but "to fill youth with respect for the monarchy and the constitution and . . . our state institutions" and to be themselves "exemplary models in this area."[7] Most professors at German universities appear to have agreed with this vision of loyalty to God, king, and country, which for them was above politics. An open-minded or critical attitude on these subjects was possibly even more of a barrier to a professorial career than had been the case before German unification.

The *Kulturpolitik* of Prussia, as well as other states, did not however, steer away from partisan political issues. The government did not even attempt to claim that its appointment policies were based entirely on merit. Minister Bosse, Althoff's superior, defended himself against attacks in the Prussian Landtag in the 1890s by rejecting the charge that too many liberal or left-wing professors were being named to chairs. Characteristically, he chose to defend his ministry not by claiming that it ignored partisan considerations, but rather by maintaining that it followed a policy of balancing out political tendencies in making individual appointments.[8] Althoff's attempts to implement this policy often led to clashes with the otherwise loyal professoriate, particularly when a policy of appeasing various political groupings led to what Protestant scholars viewed as favoring Catholics. Althoff's idea of establishing a chair in history for Catholics at Strasbourg University, for example, brought the Protestant historical establishment to its feet and provoked a number of public discussions. Prussian Catholics themselves discussed much more radical ideas and from 1889 onward attempted to interest the government in setting up a "purely Catholic" university. This would have presumably meant an all-Catholic teaching staff, student body, and curriculum.[9] Some Protestant professors went so far as to argue that believing Catholics simply were unqualified for professorships because they lacked the freedom to think without prejudice, which Protestantism allegedly guaranteed to its adherents.[10] Althoff also protected such controversial figures as the *Kathedersozialist* Schmoller. Clearly, Althoff was attempting to make small concessions to the two largest groups of dissidents in the empire, Catholics and workers, in order to strengthen their loyalty to the Hohenzollern state.

Althoff's intervention in personnel matters reached down even to the level of the petty. He was famous for calling professors in for consultation or encouraging them to speak to him personally, but his treatment of these august representatives of German scholarship was often calculated to make them feel small and powerless. Friedrich Meinecke, for example, was made to wait endlessly in a dark room with nothing to distract him but a sign that read, *"In diesem Zimmer dacht' ich oft, Man wird alt, indem man hofft* [In this room I've often thought one gets old while one hopes]," a mocking pun on the *Ministerialdirektor's* name.[11] Althoff was also known to press some professors into making secret agreements as a condition for their appointments. The so-called *Reverse* were attacked by Max Weber and others as an infringement upon academic freedom. The Prussian Education Ministry tried to bury the controversy over *Reverse* by claiming that they were innocent and reasonable agreements, for example, a promise by a candidate for a professorship not to accept an outside offer for a stated period of years.[12] But other evidence indicates that Althoff was quite willing to use the weapon of appointments and promotions to extract all sorts of promises from professors. In the case of Hans Delbrück, the famous military historian at Berlin, Althoff attempted to force him to alter the editorial policy of the *Preussische Jahrbücher,* which Delbrück also directed, as the price for a promotion to full professor.[13]

Althoff's imperious style and his humiliations of professors were in themselves not new, to be sure. Many similarly positioned government officials in Prussia and elsewhere had struck similar postures vis-à-vis the professoriate in the past. Nor was intimidation the only weapon used; Althoff went out of his way to honor professors, appealing to their vanity or thirst for recognition by interceding for the award of higher ranks and titles (e.g., *Excellenz*) than a university professorship usually carried with it. Indeed, Althoff was personally fairly popular with the professors. At most they grumbled that the high-flying power of the Education Ministry in Althoff's day was tolerable, but that it might become something quite different in the hands of less competent successors – a charge that Althoff himself, along with many professors, raised after his retirement. Yet this concentration of bureaucratic power was not solely the result of a strong personality. As the Education Ministry under the Weimar Republic later discovered, certain other weapons were needed to make the concentration complete. One of these was financial power; the other, the feebleness of a corporate consciousness in the universities that could arouse opposition to the will of the bureaucracy. The same educational bureaucracy with the same powers, and often the same personnel, lacked money and faced an ideologically hostile professoriate and student body in the 1920s, thereby dooming much of its policy to failure.

The finances of the universities will be treated in detail in a separate section of this chapter. Suffice it to say here that bureaucracy was naturally strengthened in the German states by the increased amount of funding that poured through it into the universities. In the eighteenth century, as we saw, the erratic and meager funding of universities by most German states went hand in hand with the universities' ability to evade the wishes of the governments and retain their independence at the unpleasantly high price of starvation budgets. By the late nineteenth century, however, the elaborate universities had become used to stable and almost adequate state funding, and there was no realistic way back to the poverty-stricken independence of previous generations. The very fact that the German governments could dangle new laboratories, seminars, collections, and chairs before the professoriate had a natural tendency to drive the latter into a more dependent role. At the same time, the rising power and curiosity of legislative bodies allowed the education ministries to deflect some of the natural resentment of the professoriate about political interference. One of Althoff's standard tactics was to pose as the protector of the universities' financial needs vis-à-vis the budget-slashing habits of the Finance Ministry or the Parliament. Althoff was once reported to have said, "When I go to [Finance] Minister Miquel, I will in future always carry a pistol with me; otherwise I won't be able to get any money from him to meet the needs of the universities."[14] The universities and individual professors never found an effective way to deal with such bodies directly, and so they found themselves obliged to cooperate with the education ministries.

The third element allowing the "Althoff system" and its imitations in other states to develop the degree of control they did was the weakening of corporate solidarity among the professors themselves. Some of the reasons for this phenomenon have been discussed in the previousOhapter. The sheer size of the professoriate even at small universities, the walls of specialization, the national and even international scope of recruitment with its consequent breakdown of provincial loyalties — all these had made the faculties less cohesive and more unwieldy as centers of initiative and resistance. Formally, to be sure, the rights of self-government were much the same as they had been in the early nineteenth century. But the very fact that statutes governing the operation of university self-government were rarely changed indicates a certain hollowness in those formulas to begin with. Both in the early nineteenth century and at the beginning of the twentieth, the few professors who broke the unspoken rule of never discussing university politics *extra muros* in print unanimously wrote about other things than faculty meetings and formal votes. What happened in the formal process of self-government was, it would appear, largely predetermined by negotiations and discussions among professors and civil servants.

The diminution of corporate solidarity, then, was not so much a process of formal loss of power as an erosion of the ground of common goals and attitudes. Just as the traditional German university was organized as a guildlike corporation largely responsible to itself, the university of the Wilhelmine era increasingly reflected the industrial society around it in some ways. Traits similar to those of business entrepreneurs were increasingly discovered by critics of the contemporary academic scene. Empire building, careerism, and cliquishness were alleged to be more and more common, replacing the corporate solidarity and noble ethos of the academic community. Contemporary observers who decried the moral and intellectual weakness implicit in academic entrepreneurship undoubtedly exaggerated the purity of past generations of professors, to be sure, but they undoubtedly also placed their fingers squarely on a phenomenon that reflected greater temptations. Earlier generations of scholars simply had not been faced with such a large number of opportunities for advancing their careers by cooperating with the state or working in cliques to advance their own ends rather than the goals of the university as a whole. Entrepreneurial behavior, whether in business or in academia, can flourish only when markets offer rewards for such behavior. Fichte's vision of the university being held together by the undisputed role of the philosophers had never been realized in the nineteenth century, and the corporate solidarity of the university had been highest in times when the universities faced hostility from outside forces, including the state. Under the changed circumstances of the Hohenzollern Empire, however, hostility had been replaced with a wary and conditional benevolence toward the universities. Under these conditions it is not surprising that many professors thought first of their own welfare or the welfare of their specialities, their institutes, or their friends, rather than of the increasingly mythical or abstract concept of the "corporation." Yet, however understandable and perhaps inevitable this decline in a common corporate ideal anchored in the notion of the autonomy of free and critical thought, its consequences were dangerous for the universities. The shameful collapse of the German universities before the Hitler regime in 1933 made this perfectly clear.

The universities and the economy

The industrial revolution had profound consequences for the German universities. Education and research, including that carried out at universities, came to interest German industrialists more than ever, and they began to bring pressure to bear in order to reshape these activities in a sense favoring their interests. As a benefit of industrialization, the German states also found themselves increasingly able to finance higher education more generously through steadily rising tax receipts. This financial power aided the German states in their continuing and increasing control over universities. Despite the rise of private fortunes and the willingness of many entrepreneurs to devote some of their money to higher education, the states held onto their virtual monopoly over higher education. At the same time, enough concessions were made to keep German industrialists reasonably satisfied with existing higher education. The mediating role of the states thus eliminated the possibility of a development similar to that of the United States at the same time, in which private industrial fortunes contributed heavily to the buildup of the national university system.

One of the many ways in which German society and government impinged upon the traditional immunities and concerns of universities after the founding of the Bismarckian Reich lay in the mounting concern of businessmen and government about research. Perceiving in advanced technology the competitive edge that could boost German industry, more and more entrepreneurs sought from the universities not just trained men, but also applied and basic research in a host of scientific problem areas. Cooperation between technical colleges and industry had naturally gone quite far by the 1870s, but such ties between industry and universities were rare. Prevailing attitudes in the universities reflected the Humboldtian ideal of the "unpurposeful" nature of research: Though science was bound to benefit society, the benefits were indirect. The solving of specific scientific problems for the immediate benefit of industry was still an alien idea at the universities. Nevertheless, increasingly between 1870 and 1914, private enterprise took an interest in the expansion of certain kinds of research at universities, offered to pay part of the costs of such research, and lobbied in ministerial chambers and state and national parliaments for applied science at the universities. Having not always succeeded in this quest, industrialists also sought to further and support nonuniversity research organizations. Either way, by successful penetration of the universities or by bringing about the creation of research organizations competitive with the universities, German businessmen and industrialists had a marked impact on the function of the university by the Wilhelmine era.

An early example of such pressures by German industry involved the creation of the Physikalisch-Technische Reichsanstalt (PTR). As early as the time of the Franco-Prussian War, German industrialists were bemoaning the backwardness of their country in precision mechanics (e.g., optical precision instruments). After many years of agitation, during which such conservative scientific bodies as the Prussian Academy opposed the idea, the Reichstag finally approved a national institution for both mechanical–technical and basic physical research in 1887. Not only the Prussian–German army but such industrialists as Werner Siemens, Carl Zeiss, and Otto Schott had given the PTR vocal support and (in Siemens's case) had offered large private gifts to get the PTR started. The PTR, as a result of this creation, was the first major publicly funded research laboratory not connected with an academy (most of which had very modest facilities anyway by this time), a university, or a technical college, and certainly the first in Germany to be given the assignment of basic and applied scientific research meant to benefit German industry.[15]

An even more significant extra-university development in the field of scientific research took shape in the final years before the First World War – the Kaiser-Wilhelm-Gesellschaft. This organization was envisioned on a much larger scale and with greater differentiation into subsidiary research institutes than anything that preceded it. Furthermore, unlike the PTR, it was not financed primarily by the state, but rather by contributions from private means, chief among them the pockets of German industrialists. At the same time, the state (especially the Prussian state) lent its support in various ways, so that one can perceive in the Kaiser-Wilhelm-Gesellschaft the realization of a high degree of cooperation between industry and government in the common interest of strengthening the scientific basis of German production.

The notion of private participation in research sponsored by the state had come up in the 1890s at the latest, to a large degree inspired by the activities of American businessmen. The Prussian Education Ministry favored such private support, although the idea of completely private research or educational institutions for Germany (except for industrial laboratories, etc.) never met with its favor. One result of the interest among industrialists in more industry-related research was the foundation in 1898 of the Göttingen Union for Applied Mathematics and Physics, described as "an alliance of industrialists . . . for the acquisition of means required by the Physics Institute of the University [of Göttingen] to expand teaching and research in the field of applied physics."[16] The Kaiser-Wilhelm-Gesellschaft carried this principle much further and cut the ties between research and established university or technical college units. The operating budget of the society in its first year (1911–12) was half that of the average budget of an individual Prussian university.[17] The Prussian Finance Ministry had resisted such a large state commitment. Private enterprise therefore had to shoulder most of the operating costs, despite the support given the society by the Prussian Education Ministry and the emperor himself.

The reasons for the willingness of German industry to support such scientific research establishments are not far to seek. In particular industries based heavily on new technology, such as chemicals and electrical products, basic research was perceived as vitally necessary. Yet the scale and cost of such research presented problems. Most individual university institutes were simply not equipped to undertake the kinds of projects envisioned by the industries. Nor were the professors universally willing to give up their research independence in order to serve the interests of applied research. In fact, the Göttingen Union was rather an exception, given the opposition of the German professoriate to smuggling vulgar applied research into university institutes. The bitter fight toward the end of the century to raise the status of technical college education against the widespread opposition of university professors reflects this mistrust of a technical, applied role for university research. And although German industry did maintain its own research facilities, they were expensive. Small enterprises were often unable, and large enterprises unwilling, to establish their own laboratories if they could persuade the state to take on some of the responsibility and also to pool their contributions in an organization such as the Kaiser-Wilhelm-Gesellschaft. Another strike against the universities, articulated from the 1890s on, was that their growing enrollments and specialization placed too heavy a pedagogical burden on them; as they trained more and more students, they were allegedly less able to carry on research of a type and on a scale satisfactory for the needs of industry.[18]

What did the rise of research institutions outside the universities by the beginning of the twentieth century mean for the universities? On the one hand, it weakened the monopoly of the universities over scientific research. This university *Wissenschaftsmonopol* stretched back to the Middle Ages; the secularization of *Wissenschaft,* reflected in the decline of the theological faculties and the rise of the philosophical ones by the early nineteenth century, had not broken the monopoly, but merely altered its terms. But the industrial revolution had placed a severe strain on the universities' ability (and willingness) to serve social needs while also maintaining the "unity of science" and the nonpurposeful essence of scholarship and research derived from the gentlemanly ideal of the neo-humanist reformers. For many decades in the nineteenth century, the product of university-based research had indeed "poured out blessings" on Germany and the world; but these blessings had not been achieved on demand, and many of them were of a nonpractical type. The breach of the universities' research monopoly necessarily reduced their importance in German life to some degree and opened them later to charges of irrelevance or class arrogance.

On the other hand, the success of the professoriate in virtually excluding applied research (and necessary structural changes that it implied) did constitute a victory for the principle of unfettered research and the independence of mind from society and its pressures. In practice, of course, this threat of impingement came principally in the realm of the philosophical faculties, because it was here that the natural scientists were located in most universities. To a much lesser degree, the social sciences (such as economics) interested German industrialists. Theology, law, and medicine remained disciplines in which the universities retained their traditional monopoly, and the monopoly of the philological–historical wing of the philosophical faculties was only slightly eroded by the rising privileges of technical schools and research organizations such as the Kaiser-Wilhelm-Gesellschaft.

While the universities were increasingly losing their dominant position in research before 1914, they were also losing ground in the monopoly over higher education. The various technical schools had, since the era of German unification, claimed and gradually received more and more of the attributes of universities. By 1900, after a bitter dispute with the universities, they received the right to award doctorates – an important sign of their being placed on parity with the traditional universities. This breakthrough by the technical schools was a blow to the pride of many university professors, but it was largely their own fault that technical education had been excluded from the universities in the first place. Furthermore, given the division of labor between the university and the technical school, the university's loss of the *Bildungsmonopol* was less a threat to the university than its champions made out.

We saw in Part III how the various polytechnical schools, loosely modeled on the Prague and Vienna models, later on the Karlsruhe model, had sprung up in several German states by mid-century. Few of these were large or differentiated enough to claim status higher than that of a technical school. But after the 1850s, German *Polytechniken* could study and envy the success of the Swiss Federal Polytechnic School in Zurich, which from its inception (1855) had possessed equal rights with the university and indeed shared professors with the latter. By the 1860s the Verein Deutscher Ingenieure (German Engineers' Association) lobbied for the extension of university-style privileges to the technical schools. For example, in a resolution dated 1875, the association asked all German governments to (1) unify all their technical schools into a single comprehensive *Technische Hochschule* or technical university; (2) require completion of a *Gymnasium* or *Realgymnasium* for admission to all higher studies; (3) grant the technical universities the same organization, self-administration, "collegial" structure, and academic freedom as traditional universities; and (4) recognize technical studies as equal to traditional university curricula.[19]

As a result of the industrial boom of the 1870s, the voices of engineers, industrialists, and professors at technical colleges received more and more auditors. In 1897, as we have seen, the Prussian Parliament approved the amalgamation of the Prussian Academy of Architecture with the Academy of Trades, creating the Technical College of Berlin-Charlottenburg. The various departments were made equal in the manner of university faculties, and the right to nominate professors, to elect a rector, and to govern themselves was granted to the teachers of the new institution. Other THs received university-type constitutions during the 1860s (Hanover, Karlsruhe, Munich) and 1870s (Aachen, Dresden, Stuttgart, Darmstadt, Braunschweig). Between 1879 and 1890, they were also granted the new title of

Technische Hochschule. Only in about 1880 did the Prussian THs receive a sort of elevation to higher pedagogical status by being switched from the control of the Ministry of Trade to that of the Ministry of Education.

The 1890s brought further favors for the technical colleges, particularly under the patronage of William II, who perceived the advantages of technology for Germany's world position. Wilhelm decreed in 1892 that professors at THs should have the same rank as university professors and be allowed to wear similar academic garb.[20] In 1898, he called the rectors of Prussia's three THs to sit in the House of Lords, previously a privilege only of universities. And finally, in 1900, after a protracted public discussion about the status of the THs, these institutions were granted the right to award doctorates in engineering. Where Wilhelm II led the way in Prussia, most other federal states followed. It must be noted, however, that the granting of equal degree-granting rights in 1900 was in itself a sort of compromise. Many spokesmen for the THs (though certainly not all) had been agitating for the fusion of the THs and universities in cities or areas where this was practical.[21]

Thus, German technical colleges went their separate way and achieved a sort of monopoly over applied science education in imperial Germany, a monopoly gladly granted them by most professors of regular universities. The THs, for their part, often introduced humanistic studies to supplement purely technological training. They thereby recognized more clearly than their alienated sisters, the universities, the dangers of sundering "pure" and "practical" education. The continued growth of THs after the slump of the 1880s had to come at least in some degree at the expense of university enrollments.

The resistance of the German universities to both upgrading and possible integration of the technical colleges with the universities is in itself worthy of some further comment. In justifying their condescension toward the THs, university professors invoked the Humboldtian insistence that "pure" and nondirected research is the only type that has a place at universities.

They made their resistance to the THs into an ideological test. Because integration of technical with theoretical studies did not cause the ruin of universities elsewhere (notably in the United States, which had a strong influence on German reformers in the 1890s), one can only conclude that the majority of university professors were motivated by a fear of status loss and a stubborn conservatism that tended to affirm their identity of interests with the German upper classes.

The financial history of the universities tends to bear out the impression that the universities were gradually losing their favored position relative to other research and educational institutions, although in absolute terms they did very well. Germany's largest state, Prussia, with about 60 percent of the population and national income, increased its annual budget from 455 million marks in 1866 to 4,812 million in 1914. In the same period, the Prussian budget for universities rose from 2 million marks to nearly 27 million (over 36 million including THs). Comparatively, the general budget had grown over ten times as large, while the university budget had grown over thirteen times as large, as in 1866. Bavaria's budget had grown from 78 million to 232 million marks between 1868 and 1914, and the university budget had increased from .5 million to over 5 million marks (all types of higher education) in the same period. In Saxony, the budget had increased from 55 million to 114 million marks between 1866 and 1914, but the university and technical college budget had risen from 400,000 marks to over 5 million. Württemberg's budget went from 30 to 111 million marks in the same period; its higher educational establishment received 300,000 marks in 1866 and over 1 million in 1914. Baden, the smallest of the larger states, spent 28 million marks in 1866 and 105 million in 1914; universities received 700,000 and 4 million marks, respectively. In other words, Prussia, Bavaria, and Saxony all increased their university budgets tenfold or more, even though Prussia's was the only state budget to multiply by anything like that figure. Baden's university budget increased almost six times, for example, whereas its total budget increased not quite four times.[22]

These figures indicate that the universities more than held their own in obtaining a share of state funds. On the other hand, that share was relatively low by comparison to university subventions by states in industrial countries in our own time. In Prussia, for example, the universities' share of the budget fluctuated between .4 and .7 percent. In the smaller states, it was proportionately higher: between .8 and 1.6 percent in Bavaria; between .7 and 4.6 percent in Saxony. The smaller states also exceeded Prussia in the per capita expenditures on universities.[23]

Two other indicators show that the universities were not keeping step with budget outlays for cultural, educational, and scientific purposes, however. In all the larger German states, the universities' share of the total budgets of educational and cultural ministries slipped somewhat over this period, indicating a relatively stronger growth pattern in nonuniversity areas. The Prussian universities, for example, consumed 15 percent of the "cultural" budget in 1866, but only 6.4 percent in 1910. In Saxony the universities and technical schools together used 25 percent of the educational budget in 1866 but only 13 percent in 1910. Bavarian universities, too, received a lesser portion of the cultural budget in 1910 than in 1866, though the decline was small. Likewise, the proportion of funds earmarked for universities compared to those allocated for scientific research in general declined over the years. This fact would indicate that the universities were well financed, but that other needs in the area of nonuniversity education and research were being funded even more heavily by the states. Similarly, the government of the Reich (which was constitutionally not authorized to subsidize universities, except for Strasbourg) increased its expenditures for general scientific work from about one million to nearly twenty million marks between 1871 and 1914.[24]

The expenditures of the Reich government on scientific and

scholarly pursuits tended to go increasingly to institutions that promised to bring immediate benefit to the German economy, in such fields as agronomy, technology, and applied science, for example. The federal states, on the other hand, spent most of their money on "general" scientific and educational purposes – for example, on universities. Nevertheless, when one looks at the expenditures of all governments (central and state) over the period 1866–1914, one sees a clear tendency of gain for the "economically" oriented forms of research and teaching, at the expense of "general" forms.[25] This fiscal information tends to bear out the impression that the universities were gradually losing their monopoly over scientific education and research, because they were not able (or willing) to adapt to the perceived needs of German society in an industrial age.

The budgets of the German states did not reflect the entire financial picture of the universities, to be sure. They still drew a considerable portion of their revenues from other sources, particularly income from student fees. The University of Berlin, for example, drew nearly a quarter of its 1910 budget from sources other than state subsidies, not including student fees. Not quite a quarter of the 4.6-million-mark budget went for academic salaries, which were still heavily augmented by student fees.[26] But the state had stepped in to regulate the income of professors even from such fees.

Professorial incomes had always varied widely in Germany, as we have seen repeatedly. By the end of the nineteenth century, however, these variations had become more awesome than ever. Paulsen reports that in the year 1894–5, before the reform, there were 4 Prussian professors who cleared over twenty thousand marks a year in lecture fees; 119 professors earned between four thousand and twenty thousand marks annually, and 191 made less than one thousand marks from lecture fees. These extraordinarily variable incomes are not explicable solely in terms of age or seniority, as Paulsen mentioned only the *Ordinarien*.[27]

Austria had already undertaken a reform of similar abuses,

and Prussia followed. In 1897, Althoff obtained a set of royal decrees regulating the professorial incomes of the Prussian universities.

A standard system of salaries was introduced under which a beginning associate professor would receive 2,000 marks basic salary and a full professor 4,000, and both would have raises in quadrennial steps amounting to 100 marks per year. Professors at Berlin started out higher, given the greater cost of living. In addition the government paid a housing allowance of 540 to 900 marks per year.[28] The crucial change involved a partial state absorption of student fees to a given professor above and beyond a fixed amount. Each professor was allowed to keep lecture fees up to 3,000 marks (4,500 at Berlin) per annum; amounts above these cutoff levels were to be divided between the professor and the state, with the state's portion returned to other needs of the universities. Althoff's plan was hardly a radical one, and he maintained that it affected only about one-fourth of the Prussian full and associate professors. Furthermore, the system was optional for professors already holding chairs, so that the full effect would not become obligatory for a generation. Even so, there was much protest and controversy about Prussia's interference in the traditional autonomy of professors to name and collect their price. The philosophical faculties, where professors tended to receive modest fees, were generally least unhappy, but medical and legal professors especially cried out. Althoff justified his move on the grounds of equity and pointed out that many of the high-income professors enjoyed their wealth because they sat on government examining commissions (and were therefore much sought out by students) or controlled institutes and seminars that the state supported. Althoff's salary reform was nevertheless widely resented by important professors and drove yet another wedge of envy and suspicion between junior and senior professors. It was not copied by the other German states before World War I.[29]

Thus the total effect of efforts to regulate and align the incomes of German professors was a half reform, and one applying only to the Prussian universities at that. The professors with large or (in practice) semimandatory lecture courses continued to earn high incomes, although a sort of tax had been placed on these in Prussia. The material condition of associate professors with small classes was little affected, and *Privatdozenten* continued to labor under serious financial handicaps, alleviated in practice only by outside income from private wealth or private practice. Althoff's only major achievement for the *Privatdozenten* in Prussia was to raise the maximum amount of state fellowships for them to six thousand marks (before his administration it had been an unrealistic fifteen hundred), without, however, increasing significantly the total amount of money available for such fellowships.[30]

The improvement of the financial condition of the younger university teachers was a matter of much discussion in Germany during the "Althoff era," but as long as the old system continued to produce enough qualified candidates for higher professorships, little was done. Despite the fact that the German universities would have been physically unable to meet their teaching obligations without the hosts of unsalaried *Dozenten,* and despite the tendency to load them down with official obligations unknown in previous generations, the lower ranks of teachers received little support for their wish for a more secure economic existence. Even such an outspoken critic of the university scene as Max Weber, in comparing the impecuniousness of German *Dozenten* with the relatively well-paid positions of American junior professors, would not grant any superiority to the American system. The latter, he thought, contained an element of insecurity and high demands on teaching hours that diminished the young teacher's ability to do research.

The decision not to renew or extend the appointment of a younger [American] university teacher is not made as frequently as it could be made; nonetheless it is made very often. Furthermore, in return for their salaries, the younger generation of American university teachers are required to carry a teaching burden of a magnitude which is unknown in Germany.

I occasionally ask myself but always to no purpose: how can a young American assistant make progress in his research under conditions in which the full professor teaches three hours weekly while he himself teaches many times that?[31]

Given the unwillingness of German governments to increase the number of university chairs in accordance with growing university enrollments, however, the greater freedom of the *Dozenten* to undertake research and make themselves "worthy" of chairs became less and less functional for careers. Almost all the economic improvements for the universities benefited the senior professors—assured incomes, adequate lecture fees, and satisfactory research apparatus, assistance, and space paid for by the state. The notion of the self-reliance and self-generation of scholarship, which had been very strong in the universities of the early nineteenth century, had by 1900 given way to a dual system. The *Ordinarien* no longer had to provide their own research apparatus and scramble to supplement their meager university incomes with outside work. The lower-ranking teachers, on the other hand, were still thrown on their own resources to a significant extent. Humboldt's ideal of "living for *Wissenschaft*" (with its implicit assumption of outside means being available to the scholar) was realized, ironically, to a higher degree by the *Dozenten* than by the senior professoriate. For the latter, the state had made it possible to "live off *Wissenschaft*."

Despite the questionable aspects of the form of state financial patronage, it did enable the German universities to retain their freedom vis-à-vis the leaders of the burgeoning German economy, unlike professors at many American universities. Thanks to the patronage of the American business community, academic doctrines considered heretical by the barons of industry were frequently suppressed by personnel policy interventions. The dismissal of Scott Nearing from the University of Pennsylvania (which led directly to the founding of the American Association of University Professors) and the hounding of Thorsten Veblen from one post to another are good examples. Even entire professional organizations, such as the American Economic Association, have found it advisable to trim sail toward the prevailing winds of big business ideology.[32]

In Germany, by contrast, the state watched carefully over its direct control of universities, and they were forced to make far fewer concessions to the industrial world in order to maintain adequate funding. On the other hand, the states were increasingly strapped for funds and by no means discouraged private gifts to further *Wissenschaft* inside and outside the universities, as long as some degree of state control was left. The Kaiser-Wilhelm-Gesellschaft was one such answer. The founding of the new University of Frankfurt/Main, initially based on private donations, was another.[33]

Yet in spite of the best efforts of Althoff and others, the riches of the German business community were never as fully exploited for the support of universities and technical colleges as they could have been before 1914. Clearly the German business community had shed much of its traditional indifference to higher education, and in the case of industrialists whose enterprises could directly benefit from better training and more advanced research, a certain willingness to give generously was becoming more apparent. But no Carnegie or Rockefeller foundations appeared in Germany before the First World War, and most university professors would have eyed them with considerable suspicion if they had. Control and interference by the state in return for funding was something they could live with, given the prevailing ideology of the day: The state was presumed to be above parties and interests and so could be construed as not threatening academic freedom. Business, on the other hand, represented interests unworthy of "free" academia. It would take only the experience of the coming war and the period of the Weimar Republic to show how illusory this freedom was – and how temporary was the financial security gained by the universities in the Hohenzollern Empire.

Universities and politics

The tendencies toward the greater integration of the universities with the administrative and economic structures of imperial Germany were, as we have seen, strong and yet limited. The fame and prestige of the German university system owed something to its being administered strongly from above; the fiscal basis for its achievements, furthermore, owed much to the state and, indirectly, to the industrializing German economy. The professoriate often grumbled privately about the high-handed ways of educational bureaucrats, although in public they usually had more positive things to say. The suspicion of "interests," particularly business interests, was also considerable among the professoriate. But given a choice between interference by the state and demands by society, the university professors of the Hohenzollern Empire would generally have chosen interference by the state. The state, in the view of most professors, had come to assume a role of protector from the manifold and confusing pressures of society, including those expressed in the word "politics." For the characteristic feature of the Bismarckian and Wilhelmine periods of German university history, as far as political attitudes are concerned, was a progressive shift of professors (and to a large extent of students) from a stance of independent-minded public leadership to one of acquiescence in the initiatives of the Reich leadership. "The German academic community as a whole had fallen into the role of a vaguely conservative and decidedly official establishment," to quote a recent study.[34] To be sure, many professors and students had been quiescent supporters of the status quo in state and society before the Bismarckian unification of Germany. But at the same time, the universities had produced countless critics and reformers. By 1900, the group of critics and oppositional leaders within the universities had dwindled to a marginal, if frequently outspoken and brilliant, band of outsiders.

The relationship of the German universities to the broader

political life of Germany was determined by a number of situations. One of these was the general satisfaction of professors
and students with the accomplishment of German national
unity, a cause that university members had led par excellence
before 1866 and one that had often arrayed them against the
German governments. Although some dissatisfactions with
Bismarck's work remained, professors and students often saw
themselves as posed before acceptance and defense of it or
before adherence to the "enemies of the Reich," variously defined as Ultramontanes, socialists, Jews, national minorities, or
progressives. To many, this choice seemed simple. As Gustav
von Schmoller, the Berlin economic historian and frequent
critic of German social policy, wrote, "In an empire that is not
called 'German' for nothing, it is for a German not a matter of
politics but a matter of course to think as a German nationalist."[35] This kind of circular patriotic logic permeated the
thinking even of those professors who at times maintained a
critical stance toward individual government policies.

A second factor in the rapprochement of the professoriate
and the political status quo was the pursuit by both university
bodies and education ministries of a professorial appointment
policy that helped assure the exclusion of *Reichsfeinde* from
teaching posts. As Max Weber commented flatly in 1908 (emphasis his): *"The 'freedom of science' exists in Germany
within the limits of ecclesiastical and political acceptability.
Outside these limits there is none."*[36] A more moderate observer, Friedrich Paulsen, maintained that academic freedom
was "generally . . . a recognized and undisputed right at German universities." But he went on to qualify this remark:

Only at some points attempts are now and then made to set limits, if not
in theory, certainly in practice. These are where scientific research, because
of its subject, touches upon the powers of public life, the state, and the
church, i.e., where its subject is religious, political or social matters . . . All
sciences that are occupied with the foundations of historical forms of life will
necessarily encounter the resistance of the establishment. The latter expects
and demands from the sciences that they recognize and prove its reasonable-
ness and necessity. If they do not wish to do this, their work appears as a

dangerous subversion of the existing order. Measures against them seem even more possible and justified, because the institutions for scientific research are not only created and maintained by the public powers but are also designated for the instruction of the future officials of state and church. How should they be allowed to work on the loosening of the foundations of precisely the existing order whose preservation is their office and calling?[37]

Paulsen's answer to this question was simply an appeal for tolerance and understanding. Yet Paulsen's nervousness about such "conflicts," though justified by a number of publicly debated cases, was not shared by most professors, it would seem. Thanks to the Althoff system in Prussia and its counterparts in other states, conflicts were more often avoided than not by the process of consultation, cooptation, and exercise of influence on the professoriate. These conflicts were prevented in most cases by an investigation of the *Gesinnung* (ideology) of candidates for professorships before appointments. And although some states, such as Baden, continued to be havens for professors who were too controversial for other states, the ability of such professors to play upon the diversity and heterogeneity of the German university system had shrunk considerably since the founding of the German Reich.

A third factor in the creation of a new relationship between the university and political life derived from the contemporary definition of *Wissenschaft* itself. Specialization made it increasingly necessary to concentrate on a narrow band of expertise and yield many a claim to universal knowledge and activity, including political activity. In addition, the broad turn from speculative to empirical and even positivistic modes of thought in the universities led to a sundering of *Wissenschaft* from "opinion" in the minds of most professors. As the generation of scholars such as Treitschke and Mommsen died out, few of their younger successors were willing to mix so freely the scholarly and the political element in their work. Many, indeed, solved the problem simply by invoking the principle of objectivity and shying away from political engagement, except for that which was allegedly above party. This became apparent in the field of history, for example, which had always been close to the political struggles within Germany: there were attempts to mount a "Ranke renaissance" from the 1890s on.[38] On the other hand, the period of the German Empire was notable for the demise of the field of political science, where the empirical and strict methods of the late nineteenth century might have led to a systematic critique of power and policy.

A fourth factor in the alteration of the relationship between university and political life was a transformation in the nature of political engagement, especially among professors, brought about by cooptation for approved work for the "national cause." This might be termed the active version of the first factor mentioned above; that is, many prominent scholars, often at the urging of government offices, began to address themselves publicly to issues such as the building of the German fleet. Because such issues were considered above party, professors could embrace them without much danger and still maintain their self-esteem as leaders of the nation.[39]

A fifth factor in the changing relationship between professoriate and political life lay in changes in the latter. In the early and mid-nineteenth century, before Germany was organized along partisan lines, the professoriate had indeed been able to offer leadership to the nation without seeming to compromise its integrity. That system, with its virtually powerless parliaments, politically immature electorate, and clumsy, vulnerable bureaucracy, lent itself well to the rhetorical and writing talents of the professors. With the founding of the Reich, however, a new type of politics had begun to emerge. Democratic franchises made standing for elective office a matter of "demagoguery" in the eyes of the professoriate, and few of them ran for public office. Another cause for distaste was the widespread belief that political life had become corrupt or at least ethically indefensible. The partisan groupings in the Reichstag and the local parliamentary bodies appeared to be little more than interest groups trying to cloak their selfish aims in the garb of principle. Insofar as professors continued to play a role in political life, they tended to do so either in appointive office (e.g., in a house of lords) or through the propagandistic activities previously mentioned. But even here, they appeared increasingly as "experts" rather than as political leaders who just happened to be professors. Students emulated the professors and also began to decry involvement in "partisan" politics. The political attitudes of the German student bodies under the Hohenzollern Empire were largely conservative, nationalistic, and uncritical.

The political world the universities confronted was, furthermore, a much larger and more complicated one than the professoriate of the *Vormärz* had known. The administrative bureaucracy more than doubled in size between 1870 and 1914. The Reichstag provided a noisy forum for national political debate for the first time, replacing to some extent the role of professorial discussions in national journals. State legislatures, too, became more complex and demanding. As mentioned in an earlier chapter, the amount of energy expended by German Landtage on higher education matters alone increased exponentially between the 1870s and the period before World War I.

There were, to be sure, exceptions to the general trend of professorial withdrawal from active political life. A few professors stood for Landtag and Reichstag elections. Several of the major journals of political and social commentary in Wilhelmine Germany were edited by professors, for example the *Preussische Jahrbücher* by Hans Delbrück and the *Jahrbuch für Gesetzgebung, Verwaltung und Volkswirtschaft* by Gustav Schmoller. Although both men had to pay a high price in suspicion and hostility from the authorities and even their own colleagues, they managed to exercise a considerable influence on the thinking of Germany's elites. Significantly, both came close to losing professorships in Prussia because of their publicly advocated political views.[40] Although both were staunchly loyal to the Hohenzollern monarchy, the Bismarckian Reich, and such "national" projects as fleet building and colonialism, they still managed to offend certain interest groups and bureaucrats with their relatively frank discussions in the pages of their journals. For many people in German political life, "loyal opposition" was still a contradiction in terms.

Far more common than loyal opposition was loyal support of the reigning political notions and ideologies of the Prussian–German state and its domestically conservative, internationally aggressive policies. To defend that state against enemies, real or imagined, appeared as the highest duty to a vast majority of those university professors who remained politically active. This is not the place to catalog the political debates of the Hohenzollern Empire, particularly because a number of recent works deal with the subject in great detail. A few examples should, however, suffice. Some of the noisiest "political" debates from the 1870s on concerned religion. Some professors, led by Treitschke (and opposed by Mommsen), undertook to show in the 1880s that Jews were the "misfortune" of the German Reich. During the same decade, no doubt taking a cue from their teachers, German student groups began voicing anti-Semitic feelings, as well The *Kulturkampf* against the church of Rome also drew many professors into print, but even as late as the first decade of the twentieth century, scholars could still enter into heated debate (mostly one-sided) about whether believing Catholics actually possessed the qualification of *wissenschaftliche Voraussetzungslosigkeit,* that is, whether they were capable of teaching and doing research "objectively."[41] Many Protestant scholars (who themselves revived the old Hegelian argument that Luther's revolt was the beginning of intellectual freedom) denied this qualification to their Catholic colleagues. Socialists were likewise regarded as *Reichsfeinde,* and professors sometimes tilted at this danger from below and stood by with little protest as their own rights to nominate professors were restricted so as to exclude all suspected of leftist sympathies.

Extremism in favor of hypernationalist causes, on the other hand, was not strongly discouraged either before or during the

First World War. Propaganda for a German fleet had already been mentioned as a sluice through which professors could enter both public debate and the good will of the government. Overseas colonialism was another issue that found the backing of large numbers of professors, if only because it justified a fleet. Even internal colonialization in the form of Germanization of minorities in the Reich (and, during the war, annexation of eastern territories) found the active support of some professors. After 1900, many of them found themselves allied with the conservative interests of the Agrarian League in a campaign to prevent the "horrors of a preponderantly industrial state," that is, the gradual demise of agriculture, uncontrolled urbanization, dependence on world trade, and the swelling of a dangerous proletariat.[42] It is important to remember that most of these issues generated *debate* among professors and that not all fell into the camp of defenders of conservative, nationalist policies; yet the critics were generally by far the smaller of the two minorities among the professoriate who engaged in such debates.

Explanations for the political position (or, more commonly, inactivity) among the German university community are not difficult to find. The satisfaction of the most prominent demand of a large segment of the pre-March professoriate and student body – the creation of a nationally unified state ruled under law – was one such explanation. But social accommodation, in which the professoriate became more prosperous and found its role in the state regarded as an asset, also helps explain the demise of critical political thought and action at the universities. Owing much of their prosperity and prestige to the state that made their work financially possible, the professors often confused thankfulness with a duty to approve blindly the general policies of their governments. And if they forgot this lesson, educational bureaucrats or members of the parliaments were always ready to remind them.

In the field of political leadership, then, the German universities tended to move in the same direction as in their relationship to society at large—into a vaguely defensive and conservative posture. Just as they were unable and unwilling to accommodate themselves to the needs of certain rising sectors of society, notably the economic sector, they were unable to continue giving Germany the type of critical political advice that had characterized the professoriate of the decades before and after 1848. Secure in the unshakable objectivity of their *Wissenschaft* and the security of their state-supported chairs and institutes, the professoriate was content to let the universities drift into a position of tension with the general society that was to have serious consequences after the First World War.

9

Conclusion

The German university system in 1914

Looking back at the German university system before the First World War, Abraham Flexner could understandably call it "a jewel in the imperial crown."[1] Despite criticisms from reformers of all stripes, ranging from liberal students to the Social Democrats and from industrialists to German Catholics, "the universities were more highly developed, more nearly autonomous, far more highly respected, and exerted a wider influence" than their American and English counterparts, Flexner believed.[2]

Although not disputing the development and influence of the prewar university system, a recent East German study described it in terms of subjection to the prevailing interests of an imperialistic state and society dominated by Junkers and great capitalists:

> The integration of the universities and of the teaching bodies of the places of academic education into the total system of Wilhelmine Germany succeeded for the ruling classes to the disadvantage of the nation. A tight network of scientific specialty organizations tied the scholars by their disciplines to the system, in which the political–ideological content of the reactionary ideas of the Pan-German League was formed. Monopolistic industry chained the researcher economically via contract research, absorption as a participant, and the grant system. In the field of social policy the ties were no less strong. The oaths and statutes of the universities and technical schools, activities in state commissions and offices, and a feudal–monarchical code of honor – outwardly recognizable by titles and decorations – completed the integration and subordination of higher education and its representatives.[3]

Such a statement undoubtedly underestimates the degree of autonomy enjoyed by the universities in 1914, just as Flexner minimized the problems besetting them. The degree of integration of the German universities into German society and under the rule of the German states was undoubtedly greater by 1914 than at any time before. But German universities were far from being appendages of German industry, and spirited resistance to government interference, coupled with shrewd cooperation with government to the benefit of the universities, continued. The professoriate in 1914 was undoubtedly patriotic and monarchistic in sentiment, but it was far from being homogeneous in its political outlook, let alone being a mere sounding board for the Pan-German League. German science and scholarship, although serving the nation, still functioned largely under the dictates of their own disciplinary canons and imperatives, rather than those of industry and government. The organized student groups such as the *Korps* and *Burschenschaften* had succumbed in some measure to imperialistic hurrah-patriotism, anti-Semitism, class superciliousness, and uncritical acceptance of the status quo. But the less organized students, it must be remembered, were being recruited in ever expanding numbers from social strata that had been represented weakly or not at all in the student body of previous generations. The universities were slow to cope with the pressures introduced by such growth, and no major structural reforms were being contemplated. But the university system had proved by its record that it was capable of change and reform of a piecemeal type.

There were thus numerous signs of strain and discontent with the university system in 1914, but there were no signs of crisis. The universities were financially sound, filled with students, endowed with superior research and teaching facilities, graced by world-renowned professors, favored and furthered by the emperor, and productive of competent professional graduates and significant achievements of science and scholarship. With some justification, most professors and students looked upon their universities with satisfaction.

Yet the satisfaction of the majority was tempered by the complaints of the minority. Some professors, like Max Weber, continued to complain that the state educational administrations, especially that of Prussia, intervened too often in university affairs, especially in questions of professorial selection. The dominance of Prussia in higher education was a cause for worry to many, even though the educational authorities of some German states, such as Baden and Saxony, still put up resistance to Prussia's attempts to coordinate higher education in the Reich. The demand of some sectors of German industry that the system of higher education respond more willingly to their needs also continued to encounter resistance, especially in the universities. The loss of the universities' research monopoly by 1914, added to their more long-standing loss of an educational monopoly, had diminished their importance somewhat, but the price of relative freedom in choosing research topics appeared worth paying to most professors.

The most serious problems of the universities lay in their pedagogical mission. The rapidly growing student body, which reached over sixty thousand by 1914, brought with it certain strains and dislocations. Careers for all the university students were not available. For reasons of social policy, the educational authorities were willing to allow the restrictions on university study itself to remain lowered. Inadequate scholarship aid and the high cost of university education did not stem the tide of students flocking in from the less affluent stratum of the middle class, and official warnings about the lack of career prospects for students had little effect. Attempts to raise entrance requirements would have alienated further such powerful political groups as the Social Democrats and the Catholics. Government policy relied on maintainence of high entrance requirements into the professions, which was easier to justify. Despite concern among professors about the dilution of educational standards by less discriminate admissions policies, many professors benefited financially from increased masses of lecture fees. The loud resistance of German professors to curtailment of the lecture-fee system frustrated thorough reform of income structures and indirectly undermined equally loud calls for the imposition of higher entrance standards.

The plight of the students in the crowded universities was compounded by the failure of German governments to deal with the worsening ratios of teachers to students. Motivated by the concept of creating new teaching positions in response to the continuing specialization of disciplines, German educational authorities did not perceive the problems of worsening ratios as a major pedagogical problem. Furthermore, they did not solve the dilemma of the younger teachers, the *Nichtordinarien,* who provided much of the instruction but received a totally inadequate reward in remuneration, status, or power. Trading on the prestige of university titles, the willingness of German families to support their sons through the arduous years of underpaid teaching, or the ability of *Dozenten* to sustain themselves through outside work or practices, the *Ordinarien* and government authorities clung to an increasingly unrealistic system that exploited the skills and patience of the *Nichtordinarien.* Here indeed imperial Germany extracted tangible benefits from the "code of honor" of the German bourgeoisie among the aspirants for professorships.

The generally conservative stance of professors and students alike in the face of major questions of national policy has elicited more critical comment since 1914 than it did at the time. Yet one can legitimately ask how wide the boundaries of academic freedom were in a university system where an uncritical and even enthusiastic acceptance of the leadership and goals of William II was the norm. The system efficiently fostered a high degree of consensus on values in the universities by careful professorial selection, by the tendency of professors and even students to place themselves above politics and to avoid conflicts with the state, and by encouraging university members to identify themselves as a part of the imperial establishment. We may smile today at the naiveté of professors in the Wilhelmine period proclaiming both their scientific objectivity and their loyalty to the aggressive, nationalistic, and elitist policies of their government. But we must remember that this sort of behavior was not a sign of cowardice or capitulation to force on the part of the professoriate; it was rather an index of the very high degree of integration among university, state, and society in Germany before 1914. Far from feeling intimidated into following the lead of government or of the dominant social forces in imperial Germany, the universities and their members confidently joined in with a feeling of belonging.

German universities in the twentieth century

These feelings did not change during or after the First World War; only the political system and social forces changed. The German universities were largely denuded of students as the war ground on, and large numbers of the teaching staff involved themselves in some way with the war effort – either through war research, or writing to justify Germany's claims, or in uniform. The collapse of the Wilhelmine Reich in 1918 was a severe blow for most professors and students. They carried their nostalgia for the empire with them into the Weimar Republic. The professoriate, with few exceptions, showed no sympathy for the new republic, and many professors published vituperative attacks on everything the German revolution and the republic stood for. Many German universities became bastions of conservative, monarchist, and later Nazi sentiment. The German National Student Association was taken over by National Socialist elements as early as 1931.[4]

That many professors would remain loyal to the ideas of the prewar period is perhaps understandable. That academic youth could be seduced by National Socialism is not so self-explanatory. One of the main reasons for the inroads made by the Nazis was the sense of insecurity felt by students in the Weimar Republic. The same growth curve in enrollments apparent before the war took a sharp upward turn after it: Veterans returning to their studies and many new students hoping to shelter themselves from the storms of societal maladjustment in years of inflation, depression, and unemployment swelled the German universities from their prewar level of over sixty thousand to around one hundred thousand by 1931.[5] This staggering increase in enrollments put a greater strain on the universities than ever, and at a time when they had barely the resources to function well with half that many students. Financially, the universities had less at their disposal, in real terms, than before the war. The growth of teaching positions also lagged even further behind the growth in the student body. Whereas the former increased by nearly 50 percent, the total teaching staff rose by only 32 percent between 1910 and 1931. The number of *Ordinarien* was appreciably raised during the Weimar Republic, however, increasing about 41 percent in the same time period.[6]

Under such conditions, the quality of university education inevitably sank to disturbing levels. The reaction of the students—to blame their problems on the Weimar "system"—was echoed by the professors. Nazi student organizations gave vent to student grievances and resentments in the most vocal and violent way, thereby outbidding the more moderate student groups.

Relationships between the German states and their universities were often tense during the Weimar period. Despite the failure of the revolutionary German republic to institute any sweeping reforms in higher education, many German professors looked upon the governments, particularly those dominated by the "Weimar coalition," with suspicion. If the republican governments attempted to appoint professors who were in sympathy with the new order, the university faculties would frequently roar out against "political interference." In fact, the education ministers of the Weimar Republic were generally men of the old school, torn between the Humboldtian rhetoric of the past and the urgent need to carry out reforms in the present. As well as lacking the necessary decisiveness and constant parliamentary backing, would-be reformers in the education ministries faced the problem of having insufficient funds to carry on adequately, let alone introduce costly innovations and experiments. In the end, very little came of reform ideas of the 1920s as far as the German universities were concerned. They remained an intact foreign body in the lifeblood of the Weimar Republic, bolstered by their world prestige and united by a common distaste for the new order in Germany.

The universities suffered to some extent in their research functions as well as their pedagogical ones. The disastrous inflation of the early 1920s and the great depression beginning in 1929 undermined the ability of scholars and scientists to carry on their work in the same way as before the war. In response to needs so dire that at times scholars could not afford to buy paper on which to write their books, emergency relief, such as that provided by the Emergency Community for German Science, could act only as a palliative, no matter how welcome.

If the condition of the German universities during the Weimar Republic was serious in some ways, it became catastrophic after the advent of Hitler to power in 1933. The Nazi "revolution" drove hundreds of professors—some of the great names of twentieth-century science and scholarship among them—into exile and drastically reduced the overpopulated ranks of the student bodies from the 104,000 of 1931 to 43,000 by 1938.[7] The reduction of faculty and student numbers naturally followed National Socialist racial and political criteria, rather than constituting any restoration of intellectually elitist standards—indeed, the situation was quite the contrary of elitism.

By a combination of *Gleichschaltung,* cooptation, and intimidation, the Nazis attempted to turn the German universities into docile instruments of their primitive educational and research policies. Yet sporadic attempts to inaugurate "Aryan" science and scholarship in the universities were, on the whole, failures, if only because of the brief time available to build up such programs before the outbreak of the Second World War.

And despite all the opportunism, cowardice, and apathy of the German university community, the irreducible problem remained that the Nazi view of the world was irreconcilable with the methods of modern science and scholarship: The former could destroy or undermine the latter, but it could not infuse it with more than propaganda phrases toward a "German science." Given the contempt of the Nazis for the life of the mind, it is even remarkable that the universities were not abolished outright. But the Nazi movement also needed, at first, the support of whatever German public institutions that they could penetrate and coopt. Thus the universities were subjected instead to the process of hollowing out so typical in those institutions the Nazis retained for their own use. The Second World War, with its draft of all able-bodied students, bombing of university cities, and general confusion, reduced the universities to a point where their closing became virtually a moot point.

The victorious Allies, agreeing that the reeducation of the German people must have a high priority, reopened the universities shortly after the war. The problems for the universities were formidable: student bodies swollen by veterans trying to pick up the threads of their lives; faculties decimated by the purges of the Nazis and then by the Allies; lack of facilities, libraries, money, and even heat and light in the lecture halls.

Even as rebuilding went on, the student population of the universities tended to outpace the resources made available by the states. West German universities and technical schools had a combined enrollment of about 150,000 in 1950, 265,000 in 1960, and 440,000 in 1969; East Germany's enrollments rose from 28,000 in 1950 to 126,000 in 1969.[8] In neither case could significant general population increases have affected enrollments. Yet there were fewer full professors per student in 1953 than there had been in 1931. Younger teaching staff, the *Nichtordinarien,* took on an even heavier burden of teaching, although now they were generally remunerated, if not given much voice in the governance of the universities.

The latter part of the 1960s witnessed considerable agitation for reform in West German universities. University government was restructured to give representation to students and younger teachers, scholarship aid was regulated in a manner enabling most students to study without having private means, new universities shot up to accommodate the overflowing enrollments, and higher education has generally been well funded, except for the lean decade or so after the war. A species of planning has come about through such commissions as the Science Council and through the formulation of a "framework law" for all universities in the Federal Republic, although both have been heavily criticized. Certain disciplines have been restricted by a *numerus clausus* system intended to discourage the overproduction of graduates. The old utilitarian view of university education has taken a firm place in the councils of government, and the Humboldtian ideal of the university has become more chimerical than ever, despite rhetorical invocations. In the German Democratic Republic, where all aspects of university education are much more rigidly controlled, admissions, curriculum, teaching, and research have been thoroughly subordinated to the need of the state for efficient and uncritical functionaries.

Despite all the difficulties, struggles, and conflicts since 1945, however, the universities have unquestionably returned to an important place in German life. They offer higher education to a much larger proportion of the population than at any time in their history. The quality of instruction may be somewhat impaired by overcrowding and, in the case of the German Democratic Republic, by ideological limitations, but it is technically solid. In most fields of scholarship, much of the ground lost during the Nazi period and in the misery of the immediate postwar years has by now been recovered. Although some critics would disagree, it is fair to say that the universities have integrated themselves into German society rather well. In West Germany at least, universities have been responsive to the needs of the larger society, and the relationship between them and such governmental bodies as education ministries and parliaments has generally been good.

State, society, and university in retrospect

The history of the German university system since 1914 very dramatically illustrates the perpetual dilemma of cooperation with or resistance to the much more powerful forces of state and society. The tension and hostility between the university community and the Weimar Republic, which were largely political in nature, damaged both the republic and the universities but were acted out in the name of academic freedom. The immense damage done to the universities in the Nazi era demonstrated how tenuous this freedom is and how pernicious total capitulation to the demands of a totalitarian state and regimented society can be. Compared to these dramatic, even violent episodes, the history of the German university system in the eighteenth and nineteenth centuries appears almost tranquil – enough so that the universities have appeared to some as having existed in a golden age of immunity and freedom.

As I have argued throughout this work, however, the German university system has never been immune to the pressures of state and society. Nor has it consistently resisted these pressures. When the universities did resist, the results were not uniformly advantageous to themselves. The self-protective resistance of moribund universities to reform in the eighteenth century, as we have seen, consisted more of defending well-entrenched practices of corruption, incompetence, and tradition than of true academic freedom.

On the other hand, resistance to pressures from state and society have sometimes been salutary for the universities. The unwillingness of professors in the early nineteenth century to yield to a totally utilitarian view of higher education led to the establishment of the system of seminars and institutes that became one of the most distinctive features of the universities. By their insistence on the right to speak and publish freely, the universities of the nineteenth century helped enrich and broaden German life in the face of widespread public apathy and an official penchant for stifling unorthodox ideas.

The dialectic of university and society of course requires that the universities have privileges and the respect necessary to defend them. Their own sense of identity and tradition has prevented them, many times over, from blindly following fads and whims popular for a few years in the minds of social reformers or government officials. Their resistance has thus always been a necessary condition of their existence. Yet totally successful resistance in all cases would unquestionably have led to the universities becoming irrelevant atavisms, as they very nearly did in the eighteenth century, and to their being demolished as so many old structures empty of meaning.

The question at the outset of this study was how universities changed, through interaction with social and political forces, from the nadir of 1700 to their classic high point in 1914. It would now be useful to summarize the major turning points in this process of evolution and in particular to relate them to the general dialectic of the university, on one side, and the larger society and governments, on the other.

The first and second reform movements in eighteenth-century Germany had to attack virtually every aspect of university life: structure, rights and immunities, curriculum, finances, standards for the professoriate, the relative position of the traditional faculties to one another, the status of scholarship, the number and quality of students, and the relationship of the entire university to those social functions demanding educated men. In most cases, however, dissatisfaction with the universities by governments and interested social groups tended to focus upon only some of these aspects of higher education at any given time. Many parents in those groups of society that might have sent children to universities educated them in other ways. Governments frequently issued decrees to regulate curriculum, improve the preparation of professionals, curb student abuses, and hold professors to their duties. But they much less frequently came forward with the kind of financial support that would enable universities to carry out many of these demands. As long as the professoriate remained largely dependent on student fees, the professors were not likely to enforce regulations about student conduct strictly, for fear of driving the students away to more lax institutions. Nor were the professional standards of professors likely to rise when dependence on jobs outside the university remained a necessity of existence for much of the teaching body. Furthermore, governments were not likely to succeed in enforcing reform by altering university privileges and immunities when these in themselves still constituted a major attraction, for both teachers and students, of association with the universities.

It is thus hardly surprising that the most successful path to reshaping university education in keeping with the demands of enlightened bureaucracies and their allies in the nobility and middle class should have been that of founding entirely new universities. The major examples in the eighteenth and early nineteenth centuries were Halle, Göttingen, Erlangen, and Berlin. The new university at Bonn was also launched on a promising footing, only to be extinguished during the wars of the French Revolution and to be revived in 1818. In all these cases, governments and interested social groups, whether through tax subsidies or by sending their children, took a strong initiative, and corporate resistance by entrenched professors was entirely absent. Those professors who chafed under the somnolent conditions of older universities went quite willingly to form the often brilliant teaching bodies of the new universities. Such allies were important, as the case of the flawed reform of Jena demonstrated, but they could not usually carry the day against stubborn resistance by the traditional professoriate in established schools. In the case of the reforms attempted at many universities in the second reform period of the late eighteenth century, one of the major factors enabling even partial success was the removal of the Jesuits from the teaching bodies of existing universities. Even so, no existing university was reformed in all necessary areas during the eighteenth century; the path of new foundings was by far more successful.

Despite considerable competitive incentive to follow the successful model of the new universities, the traditional ones in Germany could not be reformed easily until the intrusion of extraneous political events undermined all but the last remnants of their positions. The closing of many marginal universities by French occupation troops, the closing of others in the reorganization of Germany, and the new energy breathed into reform efforts of the German states all contributed to a strengthening of the university system. This peculiar conjunction of forces enabled governments, under strong compulsion to reform and strengthen themselves, to push through many changes in cooperation with professors imbued with a new attitude toward learning and scholarship. The structure of the universities was largely retained, despite some short-lived experiments with new French models. But the rights of the universities underwent redefinition. The curriculum, under the double impact of closer government supervision and an expanding corps of professors attentive to new developments in science and scholarship, was modernized. Financial inadequacies and bad fiscal administration were alleviated, thanks in part to the consolidation of larger tax bases. Higher standards for the professoriate resulted from the erosion of protected enclaves for poor professors with the collapse of less viable schools, from the greater attractiveness of a professorial career, and from the long-term penetration of the professoriate by new ideas about *Wissenschaft*. The high value placed on the philosophical faculties, now largely freed of their traditional inferior status, eased the entrée of modern science and of a richer cultural and scholarly context into the professionalizing routines of the universities.

Although the consolidation of the available pool of students into fewer universities undoubtedly helped overcome the long-standing enrollment crisis of the eighteenth century, the absolute increase in German students reflected a new confidence in the value of higher education beyond the carrying group of noble and bourgeois state servants and professional people.

University attendance had become increasingly important for the traditional old professions and several new ones, and the habit of attending the university simply for general acculturation had also deepened. Despite the failure of either the utilitarian reformers or the "neo-humanists" to carry the day in the struggle for university reform, their combined efforts had succeeded in defeating traditionalism and introducing both better professional training and the possibility of using the university as a resource for the cultivation of the personality through *Wissenschaft*.

After the passage of the Carlsbad Decrees, German governments were generally content with the universities, excepting their activity as harbors for political opposition and free questioning of the status quo. It was not necessary for them constantly to intervene in order to assure the proper education of state servants and members of the professions. Despite several stunning interventions and breaches of academic freedom, they were normally willing to let the universities govern their own affairs under their reformed statutes. The major areas of intervention otherwise were those of student enrollments (discouraged in part by raising admissions standards) and finances (governments, by then providing a large part of university income, were not very generous toward them for several decades after 1820).

The professoriate, partly as a rationalization for curbing the temptation of the state to intervene in personnel selection, progressively accepted the standard of scholarly achievement as the chief touchstone for calling a new professor to a chair. Scholarly prestige thus gradually replaced both the older collegial values of the eighteenth century and the primary concern for good teaching credentials as the chief criterion for professorial recruitment. Within certain limits, the professoriate gained tenuous rights for itself far beyond those stated in the university statutes. The major change in teaching method, the increasing adoption of seminars and institutes, often on a voluntary and private basis at first, symbolized the new willingness of the professoriate to take the initiative in the few university innovations of the period. The relative stability of student enrollments from the mid-1830s until the end of the 1860s in many ways assured that changes in the universities would be qualitative—as in the case of the institution of seminars—rather than quantitative in nature. The heightened standards of admission, though motivated by a restrictive social policy of German governments, combined with the enforced calm of a long period of political reaction, helped raise the quality of students and turn their energies, at least in some cases, toward serious scholarly inquiry.

Thus, during a period when university reform was hardly desired by the German states, certain important changes did come about in the universities, largely through the initiative of the professoriate. Sometimes, as during Altenstein's tenure as education minister in Prussia, these changes received quiet encouragement; at other time, as under Eichhorn's ministry in the 1840s, they had to be protected. The leadership role of many academics in the public political life of the period, important in itself for German history, occasionally provoked persecution from the authorities. But a much more important fact was the growing self-confidence, sense of mission, and prestige of the university professoriate derived from *Wissenschaft*. The universities were in the process of building up a legally unrecognized but psychologically vital form of immunity based on their scholarly expertise and the prestige and solid pedagogical achievements it brought as dividends to German states and society.

By 1870, the German university system had developed structures and functions that it would retain down to 1914. The *Ordinarien* consisted of major scholarly authorities in rapidly specializing fields; exercised the functions of university self-government; recommended, generally with respect from governments, their own replacement personnel; conducted the major courses leading to entry into civil service and professions; and directed ongoing research and training in a large number of seminars and institutes. They were aided by a large number of *Extraordinarien* and *Privatdozenten,* who, however, had relatively few rights and a low income. The curriculum was set by the professors and altered in keeping with the evolution of science and scholarship. The purely theoretical nature of university education had been upheld with the relegation of technical higher learning to the growing *Technische Hochschulen.* The right to pursue pure learning for its own sake was theoretically guaranteed to both teachers and students. For the latter, however, the system of state examinations and educational qualifications for careers placed practical limits on the course of study. Despite increasing state subsidies to the universities (most of which went into seminars and institutes), students tended to come from the more affluent classes, indicating a high threshold for the freedom to study. The German universities had already established their position of world leadership in teaching and research, judging by the lively curiosity and tendency toward emulation shown by foreign academic observers in the 1860s.

The unification of Germany under Bismarck and the rapid economic and social evolution of the country brought about new realities in the relationship between the university system and state and society. Prussia's Education Ministry now controlled half the German universities directly and exercised an unprecedented influence on the remainder. The universities were called upon to serve the interests of the state in extensive ways in return for much more generous financing. State involvement in the life of the universities grew considerably in the "Althoff era," even though formally the relationship between educational bureaucracy and universities remained little changed. State educational ministries took their right of reviewing candidates for vacant chairs proposed by universities more seriously, and they possessed considerably more room for initiative through the opening of many new institutes and seminars, whose directors were responsible to the state as well as to the university. Formal autonomy of the faculties in making personnel appointments was further undercut by the informal practice of maintaining a network of individual professors who enjoyed the confidence of the ministries. Finally, the rapid expansion in the size of the faculties and the increasing specialization and impersonality of professorial life tended to weaken the corporate solidarity of the universities vis-à-vis governments.

The rapid industrialization and urbanization of Germany under the empire produced conditions in German society that induced a swift rise in university enrollments and raised a host of new needs for teaching and research for the universities to confront. Student enrollment grew much more rapidly than the general population, fed by a complex set of factors including greater prosperity, a growing belief among the industrial and lower middle classes in the value of university education, the expansion of career opportunities, and gradually relaxed standards of admission to the universities. Teaching bodies were not expanded as rapidly as enrollments, and the major expansion that did take place introduced more underpaid and underprivileged *Nichtordinarien* into teaching roles. Recognition of the social importance of science and increased demand for academically trained schoolteachers, among other things, fueled a dramatic and disproportionate increase in the size of the philosophical faculties. Hopes of German industrialists that the universities' pedagogical and research activities could be better geared to industry's needs went largely unfulfilled, however; and the technical schools, raised to a position of virtual equality with the universities by the turn of the century, carried most of the burden of technical higher education. The monopoly of the universities over higher research in many fields was further eroded by the rise of such extra-university research foundations as the Kaiser-Wilhelm-Gesellschaft.

Despite the universities' resistance to shouldering all the demands made upon them by the rapidly changing society around them, they did adapt in many ways. The widespread consent to the "work of Bismarck" among the professoriate brought about an ideological and working alliance between the state and the social establishment. In addition to training competent and loyal functionaries and professional people, the universities lent their prestige to the defense of imperial German domestic and foreign policies. German professors proved willing and able advisors to government as they gradually gave up their previous leadership of criticism and opposition. Yielding reluctantly to the thirst for higher education among non-*Gymnasium* school leavers, sons of the lower middle class, and even women, the universities in the last decades before the war took a few steps toward accepting a wider pedagogical role in German society. Yet the distaste exhibited by many professors for these "ill-prepared" students, for the "materialism" of an industrial society, for "dirty" parliamentary politics, for the *staatsfeindlich* industrial proletariat, and for many other aspects of modern Germany merely reflected the high degree of dependence on the old elites and authoritarian governments that had come to characterize the university's position.

The evolution of the German university system from 1700 to 1914 took place, as we have seen, within a clear context of social and political forces. The university system of 1914 was far more broadly integrated into German society than that of 1700, and it was far more dependent on the patronage of the state. That patronage and, less directly, the support forthcoming from German society enabled the German university system to weather the crisis of the eighteenth century, build gradually on the sound if modest foundations of the Humboldt era, consolidate the German model of uniting higher education with scholarly research, and expand to meet at least part way the needs of a burgeoning modern society under the empire. At the same time, patronage and support were not the only faces of interaction between the universities and their environment. The universities' traditions, immunities, internal ethos, and apartness from everyday life were also vital to their existence.

The complexity of the dialectic among university, state, and society can be expressed in one example, the wedding of pedagogical and research functions in the university. The research ethic of some German professors at the beginning of the nine-teenth century received some moral support from the thin stra-tum of the educated middle class and sympathizers in state governments. But the decision by the states to foster scholarly and scientific inquiry in the universities, rather than in acade-mies or other specialized bodies, derived in large measure from the inability of the states to support such scholarly activity alone. Out of this peculiar conjunction came a set of expecta-tions that is almost universal in the universities of today.

Other university systems have made comparable adjustments in comparable dialectic processes. Woodrow Wilson could proclaim "Princeton in the Nation's service," a claim that would have been incomprehensible to the students and profes-sors of America's colonial colleges. Gibbon, who fled Oxford as a pit of idleness and intellectual torpor, would only barely have recognized the Oxford of 1914. To some degree, foreign universities had changed by 1914 through emulation of the German ones (though less than is generally supposed). Yet whatever changes they adopted, through emulation and home-grown reform, took place in a process of confrontation with their own societies.

The evolution of the German university system, in broad outlines, was thus not unique. In its particulars, however, its evolution can be understood only with reference to its espe-cially close relationship to the German states and to influential sectors of German society.

Notes

CHAPTER 1. INTRODUCTION

1 Talcott Parsons and Gerald M. Platt, *The American University* (Cambridge, Mass., 1973), p. 3.
2 Abraham Flexner, *Universities: American, English, German* (New York, 1930), p. 13.
3 Lawrence Stone (ed.), *The University in Society,* 2 vols. (Princeton, 1974), I, v.
4 Friedrich Paulsen, *Die deutschen Universitäten und das Universitätsstudium* (Berlin, 1902), p. ix.
5 See Fritz K. Ringer, *Education and Society in Modern Europe* (Bloomington, Ind., 1979), and Detlef K. Müller, *Sozialstruktur und Schulsystem: Aspekte zum Strukturwandel des Schulwesens im 19. Jahrhundert* (Göttingen, 1977), two recent, excellent studies of schools and society.

PART I. THE EIGHTEENTH CENTURY

1 Franz Eulenburg, "Die Frequenz der deutschen Universitäten von ihrer Gründung bis zur Gegenwart," *Abhandlungen der philologisch-historischen Klasse der königlich sächsischen Gesellschaft der Wissenschaften* 24 (Leipzig, 1906), treatise 2, pp. 164–5, 102–3.
2 Ibid., pp. 164–5.
3 Ibid.
4 J. G. von Meiern, quoted in Götz von Selle, *Die Georg-August Universität zu Göttingen, 1737–1937* (Göttingen, 1937), p. 27.
5 Mack Walker, *German Home Towns: Community, State and General Estate, 1648–1871* (Ithaca, N.Y., 1972), p. 119.

CHAPTER 2. THE FIRST EIGHTEENTH-CENTURY REFORM MOVEMENT

1 Benjamin Beischärff, "Wie eine Academie Electorale . . . anzurichten," memorandum dated Stolberg, October 16, 1710, in *Hist. lit.* 83,

Niedersächsische Staats- und Universitätsbibliothek, Göttingen, F.R.G., Papers of the University of Göttingen.

2 The university was one of the two important new creations of the Hanoverian state in the eighteenth century; the other was the High Court of Appeals in Celle. Both, significantly, were financed by the estates *(Stände),* in which the nobles predominated. The estates paid three quarters of the university's annual operating expenses, with the remnant coming from the *Klosterfonds,* a special fund deriving from secularized ecclesiastical properties. The elector's exchequer thus made no contribution, at least at the outset, to the current budget of the university.

3 Selle, *Göttingen,* p. 14.

4 R. Steven Turner, "The Prussian Universities and the Research Imperative, 1806–1848" (Ph.D. dissertation, Princeton University, 1973), p. 70.

5 Selle, *Göttingen,* p. 27.

6 Selle somewhat dramatically, but not incorrectly, saw in this provision "the pivot for the great turning in German life, which moved its center of gravity from religion to the state" (Selle, *Göttingen,* p. 41).

7 Reinhold Wittram, "Die Universität und die Fakultäten," *Göttinger Universitätsreden* 39 (Göttingen, 1962), p. 7.

8 See undated estimate, probably from 1734, leaves 131–3, *Hist. lit.* 83, Niedersächsische Staats- und Universitätsbibliothek, Göttingen. Salaries for full professors ranged up to nine hundred thaler plus pensions, and the professors could expect very high income from fees from the many noble students' *privatissime* tutoring sessions. Professor Pütter, the famous cameralist, demanded a fee of one hundred thaler per course from noble students. See Wilhelm Ebel, "Zur Geschichte der juristischen Fakultät und des Rechtsstudiums an der Georgia Augusta," *Göttinger Universitätsreden* 29 (Göttingen, 1960), p. 22.

9 The Göttingen library is still one of the best university libraries in the world, with impressive eighteenth-century holdings. Not only were professors encouraged to treat it as their own; even students were given borrowing privileges. Professor Pütter identified such privileges as "an advantage that hardly any other library in Germany, and perhaps in other areas, can challenge" (Johann Stephan Pütter, *Versuch einer akademischen Gelehrtengeschichte von der Georg-Augustus-Universität zu Göttingen,* 2 vols. [Göttingen, 1765–88], I, 219).

10 See the excellent discussion of the "research imperative," with an emphasis on the difference between eighteenth-century "fame" and "publication" on the one hand and nineteenth-century "prestige" and "research" on the other, in Turner, "Prussian Universities." Turner argues forcefully that there was a fundamental difference between the public-oriented writings of eighteenth-century *scholars* and the discipline-oriented writings of nineteenth-century *scientists.* The primary orientation toward research in professorial recruitment, he correctly points out, was lacking in most of the eighteenth-century definitions of professorial roles, even in those of

Göttingen professors themselves. In many other universities, it was lacking completely. Doubtless scientific reference groups, with their internal prestige structures, were much stronger and more influential in the nineteenth century. Yet the shift in values from teaching to research excellence was perhaps not as sudden as Turner argues. Fame and prestige undoubtedly rested on different bases, that of the first being more the educated public and that of the latter, the specialized scientific community. Yet both had in common the function of drawing attention to the scholar and his teaching institution, enabling both to compete more readily with others. Göttingen appears to have been the first university to do this in a systematic way. Given the lack of specialized scientific communities and the comparative breadth of education in the eighteenth century, fame and publication, it may be argued, served the same social (recruiting) function as prestige and scientific research in the nineteenth, even though the results for the furtherance of science were quite different.

11 Selle, *Göttingen,* p. 27.

12 See Wittram, "Universität," p. 8. Wittram perhaps goes too far in denigrating the "appearances" Göttingen tried to keep up as he attempts to reduce its many claims to being first and best to the modest scale of the eighteenth century. Academic freedom, for example, may have been far from perfect when compared to a later time, but it was still considerable to Münchhausen's contemporaries.

13 Gerlach Adolf von Münchhausen, "Nachträgliches Votum" for the Geheimes Ratskollegium, April 16, 1733, in Emil F. Roessler, *Die Gründung der Universität Göttingen: Entwürfe, Berichte, und Briefe der Zeitgenossen* (Göttingen, 1855), p. 36.

14 See the university cost estimates in leaves 131–3, *Hist. lit.* 83, Niedersächsische Staats- und Universitätsbibliothek, Göttingen.

15 Johann David Michaelis, *Raisonnement über die protestantischen Universitäten in Deutschland,* 4 vols. (Frankfurt/Main, 1768–76), I, 193–234. It is rather remarkable that Michaelis, a theologian, considered the wellbeing of the philosophical faculty more vital than that of his own to the health of the university.

16 Turner, "Prussian Universities," p. 30.

17 As cited in Pütter, *Versuch,* I, 296–308.

18 Münchhausen, "Nachträgliches Votum," in Roessler, *Gründung,* p. 34.

19 Münchhausen, to Professor Gebauer, dated Hanover, April 8, 1737, in Roessler, *Gründung,* p. 140.

20 Georg D. Strube to Münchhausen, dated Hildesheim, November 1, 1734, in Roessler, *Gründung,* p. 248. Strube was a Hanoverian official and friend of Münchhausen.

21 See the course listings for public lectures as of 1765 in Pütter, *Versuch,* I, 281–9.

22 Ernst Landsberg, *Geschichte der deutschen Rechtswissenschaft,* 3 vols. (Munich and Leipzig, 1880–1910), III, pt. 1, p. 322.

23 Christoph Meiners, *Ueber die Verfassung und Verwaltung deutscher Universitäten*, 2 vols. (Göttingen, 1801), II, 147.
24 Münchhausen's and Michaelis's opinions on this point contrast strongly with those of Meiners, writing three decades later. Meiners ridiculed the effort of Göttingen to train "courtiers" and pleaded for a shift away from purely utilitarian subjects (*Verfassung und Verwaltung*, II, 36). At the same time, his conception of the purpose of education was more idealistic, moralistic, and limited than Münchhausen's or Michaelis's.
25 Götz von Selle (ed.), *Die Matrikel der Georg-August-Universtät zu Göttingen, 1734–1837*, 2 vols. (Hildesheim and Leipzig, 1937), II, 1.
26 Johannes E. Conrad, "Die Statistik der Universität Halle wahrend der 200 Jahre ihres Bestehens," *Festschrift der vier Fakultäten zum zweihundertjährigen Jubiläum der vereinigten Friedrichs-Universität Halle-Wittenberg* (Halle, 1894), pt. 4, pp. 18–20.
27 The curial constitution of Hanover degenerated as the townsmen and prelates either gave up sitting separately, did not attend sessions at all, or were outmaneuvered when they did sit separately, depending on which province one observes. See Ernst von Meier, *Hannoverische Verfassungsgeschichte*, 2 vols. (Leipzig, 1898–9), I, 225 ff. "The same estate [nobles] that dominated in the diets also became the ruling element in the civil service" (ibid, p. 462).
28 Ibid., p. 517.
29 For the financial crisis of the Prussian nobles, see Fritz Martiny, *Die Adelsfrage in Preussen vor 1806 als politisches und soziales Problem* (Stuttgart and Berlin, 1938).
30 C. F. Pauli, *Einleitung in die Kenntnis des deutschen hohen und niederen Adels* (Halle, 1753), pp. 30–1. Pauli furthermore implied that much of the jockeying for positions of honor among the nobles derived from massive confusion about their rank owing to the convoluted development of titles since the late Middle Ages. For an elaborate description of the contemporary hierarchy, as Pauli saw it, see pp. 36–8.
31 The High Court of Appeals in Celle, founded in 1711, was an "aristocratic" creation in the sense that the noble *Stände* provided the funds for it. It provided a dualistic legal review system, with one "learned bench" to represent the Roman law tradition of the *doctores* and a "noble bench" to represent the German (common) law interests of the nobility. The first pushed, the second braked, the centralizing, despotic tendencies of the electoral house. Significantly, this court was the first Hanoverian governmental body to require an examination in law. An electoral rescript of 1711 laid down the rule that "noble persons [on the bench] should not be less well provided with sufficient erudition for the administration of their office than the learned [i.e., non-noble] persons" (Meier, *Hannoverische Verfassungsgeschichte*, I, 480). Yet nobles were not expected necessarily to have doctorates. Furthermore, in the course of the eighteenth century, educational qualifications requisite for more stringent

examinations were strengthened, but primarily for the lower, local offices. A typical lower office, that of second officer in an *Amt* or local agency of the government, was held by a bourgeois or new noble who had to pass university-based legal examinations. The place of first officer was often held by a young noble of old family, who was exempted from the examination, even though he might have attended a university (ibid., pp. 549 ff.). In fact, many higher offices required university training by custom as time went on, so that the exemption of the old nobility from examinations for the lowest offices appears to have guaranteed a minimum of sinecure without express qualification, but not a maximum of power and income.

32 Meier, *Hannoverische Verfassungsgeschichte,* I, 462.
33 Ibid.
34 For a brief description of the creation of Erlangen University in 1743 (on the foundations of a *Ritterakademie*), see Theodor Kolde, *Die Universität Erlangen unter dem Hause Wittelsbach 1810–1910* (Erlangen and Leipzig, 1910), pp. 5–12.

CHAPTER 3. THE SECOND EIGHTEENTH-CENTURY REFORM MOVEMENT

1 W. H. Bruford, *Germany in the Eighteenth Century* (Cambridge, 1965), p. 244.
2 Eulenburg, "Frequenz," p. 165.
3 The most recent of such writers is Turner, in "Prussian Universities," passim. According to the estimates of one prominent statistician, however, the number of students per hundred thousand inhabitants declined from thirty-five in the 1790s to only twenty-eight in the early 1820s and late 1840s. In other words, the real fluctuations in numbers of students adjusted to population seem less dramatic than raw figures and should soften the image of a sharp or sudden enrollment crisis. See Conrad, "Die Statistik der Universität Halle," p. 17.
4 Eulenburg, "Frequenz," p. 165.
5 Ibid.
6 Henri Brunschwig, *Enlightenment and Romanticism in Eighteenth-Century Prussia* (Chicago, 1974), chaps. 8 and 9.
7 Wilhelm Bleek, "Die preussische Reform: Verwaltungsqualifikation und Juristenbildung (1806–1817)," *Die Verwaltung* 7 (1974), 187. See also Clemens von Delbrück, *Die Ausbildung für den höheren Verwaltungsdienst in Preussen* (Jena, 1917), pp. 1–7.
8 Eulenburg, "Frequenz," p. 310.
9 For an interesting picture of the incomes and outlook of the professional men about this time, see Brunschwig, *Enlightenment and Romanticism,* chap. 8.
10 Martin Hasselhorn, *Der altwürttembergische Pfarrstand im 18. Jahrhun-*

dert (Stuttgart, 1958), p. 53, citing Balthasar Haug, *Versuch einer Berechnung des wissenschaftlichen Zustandes von Württemberg im Verhältnis gegen Deutschland* (1774, 1790).

11 Ibid., p. 4.

12 Konrad Jarausch, "Die gesellschaftlichen Auswirkungen der Humboldtschen Universität, 1800–1870" (unpublished manuscript, University of Missouri, Columbia, February 1975, diagram V. Jarausch's calculations, based on matriculation registers of Tübingen, Erlangen, Göttingen, Heidelberg, and Kiel, show a tendency of decline in the proportion of students from academic and lower-middle-class families after 1786, whereas those from the nobility and the propertied middle class rose proportionately. Nobles, who constituted nearly 20 percent of the student body in the peak year of 1797, declined as a proportion to just under 10 percent in 1837, when lower-middle-class students had returned to swell the ranks of the student body after the Napoleonic wars.

13 Ebel, "Zur Geschichte der juristischen Fakultät," p. 22.

14 "Vorschläge der Professoren wegen Verbesserung der Zustände der Universität," *Büschel* 2593, *Urkunden* 50, *Repositur* A 202, Württembergisches Hauptstaatsarchiv, Stuttgart, F.R.G., Privy Council Papers; "Abstellung der Missbräuche auf der Universitat," *Nummer* 7836, *Bestand 5*, Hessisches Staatsarchiv, Marburg, F.R.G., Papers on the University of Marburg.

15 Michaelis, *Raisonnement*, I, 272 ff.

16 Christoph Martin Wieland, "Denkschrift" (1778), in Wilhelm Stieda, "Erfurter Universitätsreformpläne im 18. Jahrhundert," in *Sonderschriften der Akademie gemeinnütziger Wissenschaften zu Erfurt 5* (Erfurt, 1934), pp. 128–243.

17 Fritz Hartung, *Das Grossherzogtum Sachsen unter der Regierung Carl Augusts, 1775–1828* (Weimar, 1923), pp. 142–8.

18 R. Kink, *Geschichte der Kaiserlichen Universität zu Wien*, 2 vols. in 3 (Vienna, 1854), I, pt. 1, 448–51.

19 Ibid., p. 486.

20 See Christoph Thienen-Adlerflycht, "Wandlungen des österreichischen Studiensystems im Übergang vom 18. zum 19. Jahrhundert," in Christian Helfer and Mohammed Rassem (eds.), *Student und Hochschule im 19. Jahrhundert* (Göttingen, 1975), pp. 27–46.

21 See Robert Haass, *Die geistige Haltung der katholischen Universitäten Deutschlands im 18. Jahrhundert* (Freiburg/Breisgau, 1952), pp. 41–3.

22 Ibid., pp. 46–53.

23 Ibid., pp. 75–80.

24 Ibid., pp. 59–60.

25 Ibid., pp. 32–4.

26 See Max Braubach, *Die erste Bonner Hochschule: Maxische Akademie und kurfürstliche Universität, 1774/77 bis 1798* (Bonn, 1966), pp. 36–51.

27 Ibid., p. 239.

28 Adolf Stölzel, "Die Berliner Mittwochgesellschaft über Aufhebung oder Reform der Universitäten (1795)," *Forschungen zur brandenburgischen und preussischen Geschichte* 2 (1889), 202.

29 Ibid., p. 206.

30 Ibid., p. 204.

31 Johann Heinrich Campe, "Ueber Universitäten," in J. H. Campe (ed.), *Allgemeine Revision des gesammten Schul- und Erziehungswesens*, 16 vols. (Hamburg, 1785–92), XVI, 145, 154, 169, 177, 215–16.

32 See Michaelis, *Raisonnement;* Christian G. Heyne's *Judiciorum de Universitatibus recognitio* (Göttingen, 1792), a counterattack on those who favored dissolution of universities; the prolific writings of Christoph Meiners, particularly *Geschichte der Entstehung und Entwicklung der Hohen Schulen*, 4 vols. (Göttingen, 1802–8); and Ernst Brandes, *Ueber den gegenwärtigen Zustand der Universität Göttingen* (Göttingen, 1802).

33 Eulenburg, "Frequenz," p. 319.

34 Brunschwig, *Enlightenment and Romanticism*, p. 136.

35 Franz Eulenburg, *Der akademische Nachwuchs* (Leipzig and Berlin, 1908), pp. 9–11.

36 *Büschel* 2552–3, *Urk. 50, Rep.* A202, Württembergisches Hauptstaatsarchiv, Stuttgart, Privy Council Papers.

37 For these and other examples see *Blätter* 15, 97–100, 174–80, *Nr.* 53, *Abteilung* II, *Rep.* 76 alt, Deutsches Zentralarchiv II, Merseburg, G.D.R.

38 Ibid., *Bll.* 109–11, 115, 186–9, *Nr.* 54; Wilhelm Schrader, *Geschichte der Friedrichs-Universität zu Halle*, 2 vols. (Berlin, 1894), II, 35.

39 Ibid., *Bl.* 78, *Nr.* 248.

40 Ibid., *Nr.* 320–2.

41 R. Steven Turner, "University Reformers and Professorial Scholarship in Germany, 1760–1806," in Stone (ed.), *The University in Society*, II, 524.

42 Ibid., p. 520.

43 Ibid., p. 524.

44 Ibid.

45 For a discussion of the *Spruchkollegien*, see Gerhard Pätzold, *Die Marburger Juristenfakultät als Spruchkollegium* (Marburg, 1966), pp. 30–8.

46 Brunschwig, *Enlightenment and Romanticism*, p. 34.

47 Hartung, *Grossherzogtum Sachsen*, p. 158.

48 Brunschwig, *Enlightenment and Romanticism*, pp. 38–40.

49 Alexander Busch, *Die Geschichte des Privatdozenten* (Stuttgart, 1959), p. 7.

50 Rostock University, *750 Jahre Rostock* (Rostock, 1968), pp. 71–2.

51 Turner, "Reformers and Scholarship," p. 500; Conrad Varrentrapp, *Johannes Schulze und das höhere preussische Unterrichtswesen in seiner Zeit* (Leipzig, 1889), p. 509; Schrader, *Friedrichs-Universität zu Halle*, I, 566–73.

52 *Nr.* 31, A 2/23, *Bd.* I., University Archive, Leipzig.

53 *Nr.* 1, A/23, *Bd.* II, ibid.

54 *Bll.* 131–3, *Hist. lit.* 83, Niedersächische Staats- und Universitätsbibliothek, Göttingen. The actual budget proposed by the government for the first year of operation was 16,600 thaler plus an additional 10,000 for one-time opening costs. See Roessler, *Gründung,* pp. 54–6.

55 Friedrich Paulsen, *Geschichte des gelehrten Unterrichts auf den deutschen Schulen und Universitäten vom Ausgang des Mittelalters bis zur Gegenwart,* 2 vols. (Berlin, 1919–21), I, 550.

56 Ebel, "Zur Geschichte der juristischen Fakultät," p. 15.

57 Klemens Pleyer, *Die Vermögens- und Personalverwaltung der deutschen Universitäten* (Marburg, 1955), p. 43.

58 Michaelis, *Raisonnement,* I, 3.

59 Ibid., II, 168.

60 Wilhelm Roessler, *Die Entstehung des modernen Erziehungswesens in Deutschland* (Stuttgart, 1961), pp. 95, 129.

61 Ibid., p. 153.

62 Meiners, *Verfassung und Verwaltung,* II, 20. Pütter, in his writings of the 1790s, emphasized the relatively small social distance between the lower nobility and the *Bürger* and thereby encouraged marriage between these two estates. See his *Ueber den Unterschied der Stände* (Göttingen, 1795) and *Ueber Missheiraten deutscher Fürsten und Grafen* (Gottingen, 1796).

CHAPTER 4. REVOLUTIONARY UPHEAVALS AND THE RISE OF BERLIN

1 Klaus Epstein, *The Genesis of German Conservatism* (Princeton, 1966), pp. 8 ff.

2 A classic sampling of these may be found in Ernst Anrich (ed.), *Die Idee der deutschen Universität: Die fünf Grundschriften aus der Zeit ihrer Neubegründung durch klassischen Idealismus und romantischen Realismus* (Darmstadt, 1960). References to the thought of Humboldt, Fichte, and Schleiermacher in this chapter refer to these writings.

3 For Reitzenstein's role in the reform of Heidelberg, see Richard August Keller, *Geschichte der Universität Heidelberg, 1803–1813* (Heidelberg, 1913), esp. pp. 126–38; also 1170, Papers of the Baden Ministry of Culture (GLA 235), *Badisches Generallandesarchiv,* Karlsruhe, F.R.G. On Montgelas, see Eberhard Weis, *Montgelas, 1759–1799: Zwischen Revolution und Reform* (Munich, 1971); Karl Prantl, *Geschichte der Ludwig-Maximilians-Universität in Ingolstadt, Landshut, München,* 2 vols. (Munich, 1872), I, 700–8; and Laetetia Boehm and Johannes Spörl, *Ludwig-Maximilians-Universität, Ingolstadt, Landshut, München. 1472–1972* (Munich, 1972), pp. 75 ff.

4 Prantl, *Geschichte der Ludwig-Maximilians-Universität,* I, 648.

5 Ibid., pp. 608, 616; Hermann Weisert, *Die Verfassung der Universität Heidelberg* (Heidelberg, 1974), p. 152.

6 A good account of Beyme's thinking may be found in Max Lenz, *Ge-*

schichte der Königlichen Friedrich-Wilhelms-Universität zu Berlin, 4 vols. (Halle, 1910–18), I, 35–70. The reforms for Königsberg are discussed briefly in Götz von Selle, *Geschichte der Albertus-Universität zu Königsberg in Preussen*, 2nd edn (Würzburg, 1956).

7 Bleek, "Die preussische Reform," p. 186.

8 E. M. Butler, *The Tyranny of Greece over Germany* (Boston, 1958), pp. x–xi.

9 See Martiny, *Die Adelsfrage in Preussen*, p. 110.

10 The classic statement in defense of the philosophical faculties at about the same time is Immanuel Kant, *Der Streit der Fakultäten* (1798), in *Kants gesammelte Schriften*, Prussian Academy edn., 24 vols. in 26 (Berlin, 1910–66), VII, 1–116.

11 Eulenburg, "Frequenz," p. 313.

12 Helmut Schelsky, *Einsamkeit und Freiheit: Idee und Gestalt der deutschen Universität und ihrer Reformen* (Reinbek/Hamburg, 1963), pt. I.

13 Ibid., p. 99.

14 Lenz, *Geschichte der . . . Universität zu Berlin*, III, 493.

15 Ibid., p. 521.

16 Schelsky, *Einsamkeit und Freiheit*, p. 44.

17 Printed matriculation lists do not exist; my request to use the originals in the archive of the Humboldt-Universität (East Berlin) has been denied.

18 Bleek, "Die preussische Reform," pp. 185–6.

19 Adolf von Harnack, *Geschichte der königlichen preussischen Akademie der Wissenschaften*, 3 vols. in 4 (Berlin, 1900), I, pt. 2, 961–2.

20 Barthold Georg Niebuhr, "Vorrede" to Ludwig von Vincke, *Darstellung der inneren Verwaltung Grossbrittaniens*, in *Nachgelassene Schriften* (Hamburg, 1942), p. 462.

21 Eulenburg, "Frequenz," pp. 165, 303.

22 Ibid., p. 225.

23 Ibid., pp. 302–7.

PART III. THE REVOLUTION IN WISSENSCHAFT, 1819–1866

1 For student life during much of this period, see the chapter by Konrad H. Jarausch, "The Sources of German Student Unrest, 1815–1848," in Stone (ed.), *The University in Society*, II, 533–69.

2 The estimated population of the territories comprising the later Bismarckian Reich rose from about twenty-five million in 1819 to about forty million in 1866.

3 The decline of enrollments in theology undoubtedly had much to do with the static state of clerical positions. Prussia, for example, had about the same number of clergymen (forty-eight thousand) in 1848 as in 1815. Meanwhile, the Prussian population had increased from ten to sixteen million—a 60 percent gain. See Robert M. Bigler, *The Politics of German Protestantism: The Rise of the Protestant Church Elite in Prussia, 1815–*

1848 (Berkeley, 1972), p. 55. Prussia deliberately kept the size of its civil service stable and tried to discourage students from contemplating civil service careers. See John R. Gillis, *The Prussian Bureaucracy in Crisis, 1840–1860: Origins of an Administrative Ethos* (Stanford, 1971), pp. 40–1.

CHAPTER 5. THE PROFESSORIATE AND THE RESEARCH ETHIC

1 Eulenburg, "Frequenz," p. 319; Christian von Ferber, *Die Entwicklung des Lehrkörpers der deutschen Universitäten und Hochschulen, 1864–1954*, in Helmuth Plessner (ed.), *Untersuchungen zur Lage der deutschen Hochschullehrer,* 3 vols. (Göttingen, 1956), III, 195, 210.

2 Eulenburg, "Frequenz," pp. 165, 255, 260.

3 Busch, *Geschichte des Privatdozenten,* p. 108.

4 Ibid., pp. 75–6.

5 Ibid., p. 76.

6 Lenz, *Geschichte der . . . Universität zu Berlin,* II, pt. 1, 408.

7 Ibid., p. 407.

8 Ibid.

9 Ibid., pp. 411–13.

10 The average age of *Habilitation* for most of the eighteenth century had been just under 27; by the period 1850–69, the average age was as high as 28.5; no eighteenth-century statistics are available for the period of time spent on the preparation of *Habilitation* work (e.g., a second thesis after the doctorate), but it lay between 2.7 and 4.3 years in 1850–69. A reasonable guess for the eighteenth century would be 1 to 3 years. See Busch, *Geschichte des Privatdozenten,* p. 107; and Ferber, *Entwicklung des Lehrkörpers,* tables 16 and 23.

11 Busch, *Geschichte des Privatdozenten,* p. 39.

12 See Wilhelm Erben, "Entstehung der Universitätsseminare," *Internationale Monatsschrift für Wissenschaft, Kunst und Technik* (1913), pp. 1247–64, 1335–47.

13 Lenz, *Geschichte der . . . Universität zu Berlin,* III, app. following p. 446.

14 Ibid.

15 Weisert, *Verfassung der Universität Heidelberg,* p. 151.

16 Württemberg, Statistisches Landesamt, *Statistik der Universität Tübingen* (Stuttgart, 1877), pp. 61–7.

17 Lenz, *Geschichte der . . . Universität zu Berlin,* II, pt. 2, 88–9.

18 Ibid., p. 89.

19 Erben, "Entstehung der Universitätsseminare," p. 1250.

20 Ibid., p. 1255.

21 Ibid., p. 1258.

22 Ibid., p. 1262.

23 Full professors ranked automatically as *Rat vierter Klasse* in Prussia after 1817, and extraordinary professors held the rank of *Rat fünfter Klasse.*

These ranks corresponded to *Regierungsrat* and *Regierungsassessor* ranks, respectively. In addition, the bureaucratic rank of a professor could be raised by royal decree, so that many illustrious scholars bore even higher titles, including that of *Geheimrat* or privy counselor. See Conrad Bornhak, *Die Rechtsverhältnisse der Hochschullehrer in Preussen* (Berlin, 1901), p. 50.

24 Ibid., p. 30.

25 Ibid., p. 31.

26 The formal rights of faculties and governments received a classic formulation in the 1838 statutes for Berlin and Bonn, which are relatively vague about the right of nomination. See Johann F. W. Koch, *Die preussischen Universitäten: Eine Sammlung von Verordnungen, welche die Verfassung und Verwaltung dieser Anstalten betreffen*, 3 vols. (Berlin, 1839–40), I, 62–168 (Berlin), 219–91 (Bonn).

27 All these figures are from Bornhak, *Rechtsverhältnisse*, pp. 31–3.

28 Cited in Adolph Kohut, *Justus von Liebig, sein Leben und Wirken* (Giessen, 1904), pp. 242–3, from *Aus dem Briefwechsel Justus von Liebigs mit dem Minister Freiherr von Dalwyck* [sic] (Darmstadt, 1905), pp. 5–6.

29 Joseph Ben-David, "Scientific Growth: A Sociological View," *Minerva* 2 (1964), 473.

CHAPTER 6. STUDENTS, FINANCES, AND POLITICS

1 For an excellent recent study on the German student movement in this period, see Jarausch, "Sources of German Student Unrest."

2 Heinrich Heine, *Die Harzreise* (Stuttgart, 1960), pp. 8, 9.

3 For an interesting discussion of this development, see Wilhelm Bleek, *Von der Kameralausbildung zum Juristenprivileg* (Berlin, 1972), chap. 3.

4 See Lenore O'Boyle, "The Problem of an Excess of Educated Men in Western Europe, 1800–1850," *Journal of Modern History* 42 (1970), 471–95, esp. pp. 473–8.

5 Lenz, *Geschichte der . . . Universität zu Berlin*, III, 512–13.

6 Ibid., p. 527.

7 Ibid., pp. 525–6.

8 Georg Kaufmann, *Geschichte der Universität Breslau, 1811–1911*, in G. Kaufmann (ed.), *Festschrift zur Feier des hundertjährigen Bestehens der Universität Breslau*, 2 vols. in 1 (Breslau, 1911), I, 57–8.

9 Lenz, *Geschichte der . . . Universität zu Berlin*, III, 521.

10 Jarausch, "Die gesellschaftlichen Auswirkungen der Humboldtschen Universität," pp. 18–22, tables 6 and 7, and diagram V.

11 Ibid., p. 19.

12 Lenz, *Geschichte der . . . Universität zu Berlin*, III, 529.

13 Ibid., pp. 490–1.

14 Ibid.

15 Kaufmann, *Geschichte . . . Breslau*, p. 68.

16 Ibid.

17 Ibid., pp. 59–60.

18 Busch, *Geschichte des Privatdozenten*, p. 34.

19 Württemberg, Statistisches Landesamt, *Statistik der Universität Tübingen*, p. 38.

20 *Universitätsakten, Rep.* 22b, *Nr.* 58, Hessisches Staatsarchiv, Marburg; Rostock University, *750 Jahre Rostock*, p. 95.

21 Busch, *Geschichte des Privatdozenten*, p. 74; Wilhelm Dieterici, *Geschichtliche und statistische Nachrichten über die Universitäten im preussischen Staate* (Berlin, 1836), pp. 25, 68, 81.

22 *Universitätsakten, Rep.* 22b, *Nr.* 58, Hessiches Staatsarchiv, Marburg.

23 Dieterici, *Geschichtliche und statistische Nachrichten*, p. 71.

24 Rolf Engelsing, *Zur Sozialgeschichte deutscher Mittel- und Unterschichten* (Göttingen, 1973), p. 35.

25 Ibid., p. 41.

26 Lenz, *Geschichte der . . . Universität zu Berlin*, III, 529.

27 Ibid.

28 This does not mean that technical training can be proved to have had a decisive impact on industrial or economic growth, but merely that German policy makers believed that it would. For a pessimistic appraisal of the effect of education on economic growth in Germany, see Peter Lundgreen, *Bildung und Wirtschaftswachstum im Industrialisierungsprozess des 19. Jahrhunderts* (Berlin, 1973).

29 Berlin, Technische Hochschule, *Die Technische Hochschule zu Berlin, 1799–1924: Festschrift* (Berlin, 1925), pp. 39–50.

30 Prussia, "Allerhöchste Bekanntmachung, die Bundestagsbeschlüsse vom 20. September 1819 betreffend. Vom 18. Oktober 1819," in Koch, *Die preussischen Universitäten*, I, 15.

31 These requests were made of the Prussian education ministry during a conference with professors in 1849; see Bornhak, *Rechtsverhältnisse*, p. 31.

32 See *Officielle Protokolle über die Verhandlungen deutscher Universitätslehrer zur Reform der deutschen Hochschulen* (Jena, 1848); Jarausch, "Sources of German Student Unrest," pp. 558–64; and Karl Griewank, *Deutsche Studenten und Universitäten in der Revolution von 1848* (Weimar, 1949).

33 Kultusministerium, *Rep. 76-Va., Sek.* I, *Abt.* I, *Nr.* 13, *Bd.* 1, Deutsches Zentralarchiv II, Merseburg.

34 For a thorough discussion of the struggle of conservative theologians to extend control over university theological faculties, see Bigler, *The Politics of German Protestantism*.

35 Norbert Andernach, *Der Einfluss der Parteien auf das Hochschulwesen in Preussen, 1848–1918* (Göttingen, 1972), p. 1.

36 Ibid., pp. 8–54.

PART IV. UNIVERSITIES IN THE GERMAN EMPIRE

1 Fritz K. Ringer, *The Decline of the German Mandarins: The German Academic Community, 1890–1933* (Cambridge, Mass., 1969) p. 5.

CHAPTER 7. THE EXPANSION OF THE UNIVERSITIES

1 Adolph von Harnack, "Vom Grossbetrieb der Universität" (1905), in *Aus Wissenschaft und Leben,* 2 vols. (Giessen, 1911), I, 10–20.

2 The German university system did not, however, seek to solve its problems by creating new universities. Aside from the University of Strasbourg inherited from France in 1871, the only new university before 1914 was essentially an expanded theological faculty in Münster. Frankfurt-am-Main was founded in 1914, but its history, along with Hamburg's (1919), belongs to the postwar period.

3 Eulenburg, "Frequenz," p. 255.

4 Karl-Heinz Manegold, *Universität, Technische Hochschule und Industrie,* (Berlin, 1970), pp. 320–1.

5 Frank R. Pfetsch, *Die Entwicklung der Wissenschaftspolitik in Deutschland, 1870–1914* (Berlin, 1974), p. 177.

6 Johannes Conrad, "Einige Ergebnisse der deutschen Universitätsstatistik," *Jahrbücher für Nationalökonomie und Statistik* 3, No. 32 (1906), p. 436.

7 Linking professional careers to the upper class in German society between 1850 and 1914, one recent study concludes that "The growth of the upper social strata was on the whole greater than that of the population" (Hartmut Kaelble, "Sozialer Aufstieg in Deutschland 1850–1914," *Vierteljahrschrift für Sozial- und Wirtschaftsgeschichte* 60 [1973], 49). Whereas large landowners and pastors were the largest groups in these upper strata of German society in 1849, physicians and civil servants were the largest groups in 1907 (ibid., p. 50).

8 Paulsen, *Die deutschen Universitäten,* p. 160.

9 Conrad, "Einige Ergebnisse," pp. 448–9.

10 Konrad Jarausch, "Frequenz und Struktur: Zur Sozialgeschichte der Studenten im Kaiserreich," unpublished manuscript, November 1976, p. 19, forthcoming in M. Schlenke (ed.), *Staat und Bildung in Preussen und im Deutschen Reich* (Stuttgart).

11 Lenz, *Geschichte der . . . Universität zu Berlin,* III, 522. Lenz divides students into three social groups: those whose fathers were civil servants or professional people; those whose fathers were businessmen, industrialists, or large-scale farmers; and those whose fathers were middle and lower officials, schoolteachers, artisans, or small farmers. The first group had had university education as a necessity of career and was financially well-off, but not necessarily rich; many social historians refer to this group as *Bildungsbürgertum.* The second grouping had in common chiefly wealth, but not necessarily university education; this is the

Besitzbürgertum. The fathers of the third category presumably had neither much money nor much higher education; this is what I have called the petite bourgeoisie. Unfortunately, German statistics of the period do not allow much correlative study.

12 Conrad, "Einige Ergebnisse," pp. 465–7.

13 Ibid., pp. 459–65. The number of attorneys more than doubled between 1880 and 1911: for every attorney in 1880, there were nearly eleven thousand Germans; but by 1911 there was one for every six thousand (Busch, *Geschichte des Privatdozenten,* p. 86).

14 Conrad, "Einige Ergebnisse," pp. 467–74.

15 Ibid., pp. 452–9.

16 Ibid., p. 442.

17 Ibid., pp. 439, 488.

18 Paulsen, *Die deutschen Universitäten,* p. 381.

19 Conrad, "Einige Ergebnisse," pp. 455, 464, 467.

20 Jarausch, "Frequenz und Struktur," p. 5.

21 Hansjoachim Henning, *Das westdeutsche Bürgertum in der Epoche der Hochindustrialisierung, 1860–1914: Soziales Verhalten und soziale Strukturen,* pt. I, *Das Bildungsbürgertum in den preussischen Westprovinzen* (Wiesbaden, 1972), p. 484.

22 Conrad, "Einige Ergebnisse," pp. 484–5.

23 Ibid., p. 486.

24 Ibid., p. 489.

25 Kaelble, "Sozialer Aufstieg," p. 70.

26 Lenz, *Geschichte der . . . Universität zu Berlin,* III, 526.

27 Franz Eulenburg, *Die Entwicklung der Universität Leipzig in den letzten hundert Jahren: statistische Untersuchungen* (Leipzig, 1909), p. 207.

28 Conrad, "Einige Ergebnisse," pp. 474–5.

29 Ibid., p. 476.

30 Ibid., pp. 474–5.

31 Ibid., p. 477; Hans Heinz Eulner, *Die Entwicklung der medizinischen Spezialfächer an den Universitäten des deutschen Sprachgebiets* (Stuttgart, 1970), p. 13.

32 Lenz, *Geschichte der . . . Universität zu Berlin,* III, 509–13.

33 Ibid., p. 511.

34 Max Weber, "The Alleged 'Academic Freedom' of the German Universities," in "The Power of the State and the Dignity of the Academic Calling in Imperial Germany," ed. and trans. by Edward Shils, *Minerva* 11, No. 4 (1973), 17. The article originally appeared in the *Frankfurter Zeitung,* September 20, 1908.

35 Busch, *Geschichte des Privatdozenten,* pp. 109–17.

36 Max Weber, "The Bernhard Affair," in "The Power of the State," p. 5. The original article appeared in the *Frankfurter Zeitung,* June 18, 1908.

37 Ibid., p. 6.

38 Paulsen, *Die deutschen Universitäten,* p. 106.

39 Ibid., p. 114.
40 Ibid., p. 136.
41 Ibid., p. 112.
42 Ibid., p. 199.
43 Ludwig Curtius, *Deutsche und Antike Welt* (Stuttgart, 1950), p. 330.
44 Ibid., p. 331.
45 Ibid., p. 332.
46 Ibid., pp. 324 ff.
47 Paulsen, *Die deutschen Universitäten*, pp. 250 ff., 366 ff.
48 Ibid., pp. 432 ff.
49 Lenz, *Geschichte der . . . Universität zu Berlin*, III, 529.
50 Eulner, *Die Entwicklung der medizinischen Spezialfächer*, pp. 495–511.
51 Arnold Sachse, *Friedrich Althoff und sein Werk* (Berlin, 1928), pp. 237–44.
52 Ibid., p. 234.
53 Joseph Ben-David and Awraham Zloczower, "The Idea of the University in the Academic Market-Place," *Archive Européenne de Sociologie* 2 (1961), 311.
54 Sachse, *Friedrich Althoff*, p. 304 and passim.
55 Ibid., p. 245.

CHAPTER 8. THE UNIVERSITIES, STATE, AND SOCIETY

1 Pfetsch, *Entwicklung der Wissenschaftspolitik*, pp. 70–8.
2 Ringer, *Decline of the German Mandarins*, p. 57.
3 Sachse, *Friedrich Althoff*, p. 177. The letter was to Althoff's lifelong friend Professor Studemund, dated March 20, 1885.
4 Ibid.
5 Mühler to Bismarck, dated August 27, 1866, *Rep.* 76 I, *Sek.* I, *Nr.* 81, Deutsches Zentralarchiv II, Merseburg.
6 Pfetsch, *Entwicklung der Wissenschaftspolitik*, p. 178.
7 *Rep. 76-Va, Sek.* I, *Abt.* IV, *Nr.* 42, *Bd.* II, Deutsches Zentralarchiv II, Merseburg.
8 *Nr.* 44, *Bd.* I, ibid.
9 *Rep. 76-Va, Sek.* I, *Abt.* I, *Nr.* 21, ibid.
10 See, for example, Max Lenz, *Römischer Glaube und freie Wissenschaft* (Berlin, 1902).
11 Friedrich Meinecke, *Werke*, ed. by E. Kassel, vol. 8, *Autobiographische Schriften* (Stuttgart, 1969), p. 132.
12 Max Weber, "American and German Universities," in "The Power of the State," pp. 27–9. The original article appeared in *Verhandlungen des IV. Deutschen Hochschullehrertages* (Leipzig, 1912), pp. 66–77.
13 See Charles E. McClelland, "Berlin Historians and German Politics around 1900," *Journal of Contemporary History* 8 (1973), 3–33.
14 Weber, "American and German Universities," p. 27.

15 For an account of the founding of the PTR see Pfetsch, *Entwicklung der Wissenschaftspolitik,* pp. 109–23.
16 Quoted by Manegold, *Universität, Technische Hochschule und Industrie,* p. 171.
17 Lothar Burchardt, *Wissenschaftspolitik im wilhelminischen Deutschland: Vorgeschichte, Gründung und Aufbau der Kaiser-Wilhelm-Gesellschaft zur Förderung der Wissenschaften* (Göttingen, 1975), p. 133.
18 Ibid., pp. 14–15.
19 Manegold, *Universität, Technische Hochschule und Industrie,* pp. 68–9.
20 Ibid., p. 83.
21 For a thorough discussion of the idea of fusion, especially as represented by the Göttingen mathematician Felix Klein, see ibid., chap. 3.
22 Pfetsch, *Entwicklung der Wissenschaftspolitik,* pp. 72–9.
23 Ibid.
24 Ibid.
25 Ibid., pp. 63–4.
26 Lenz, *Geschichte der . . . Universität zu Berlin,* III, 529.
27 Paulsen, *Die deutschen Universitäten,* p. 106.
28 Ibid.
29 Sachse, *Friedrich Althoff,* pp. 206–11.
30 Ibid., pp. 212–13.
31 Weber, "American and German Universities," p. 30.
32 See Robert L. Church, "Economists as Experts: The Rise of an Academic Profession in America 1870–1917," in Stone (ed.), *The University in Society,* II, 571–609.
33 Paul Kluke, *Die Stiftungsuniversität Frankfurt am Main, 1914–1932* (Frankfurt, 1972), explores the interconnections between West German businessmen and the state that ultimately led to the founding of the new university.
34 Ringer, *Decline of the German Mandarins,* p. 127.
35 Gustav von Schmoller, "Nachwort zu Hans Crüger," *Jahrbuch für Gesetzgebung, Verwaltung und Volkswirtschaft im Deutschen Reich* 36 (1913), 825.
36 Weber, "The Alleged 'Academic Freedom' of the German Universities," p. 17.
37 Paulsen, *Die deutschen Universitäten,* pp. 291–3.
38 Hans-Heinz Krill, *Die Rankerenaissance, Max Lenz und Erich Marcks* (Berlin, 1962).
39 For a further discussion of this kind of activity, see Charles E. McClelland, "Berlin Historians"; Wolfgang Marienfeld, *Wissenschaft und Schlachtflottenbau in Deutschland, 1897–1906,* Suppl. 2, *Marine-Rundschau,* 1957; and Klaus Schwabe, *Wissenschaft und Kriegsmoral: Die deutschen Hochschullehrer und die politischen Grundfragen des Ersten Weltkrieges* (Göttingen, 1969).
40 See McClelland, "Berlin Historians," pp. 7–8.

41 See Lenz, *Römischer Glaube,* passim.

42 See Kenneth D. Barkin, *The Controversy over German Industrialization, 1890–1902* (Chicago, 1970).

CHAPTER 9. CONCLUSION

1 Flexner, *Universities,* p. 345.

2 Ibid.

3 Max Steinmetz (ed.), "Geschichte der deutschen Universitäten und Hochschulen: Ein Ueberblick," *Studien zur Hochschulentwicklung* 25 (1971), 60.

4 Anselm Faust, *Der Nationalsozialistische Deutsche Studentenbund; Studenten und Nationalsozialismus in der Weimarer Republik,* 2 vols. (Düsseldorf, 1973), II, 17.

5 Germany, Hochschulverwaltung, *Deutsche Hochschulstatistik* 12 (1933–4), *20.

6 Ferber, *Entwicklung des Lehrkörpers,* pp. 195, 210.

7 Estimates of the number of exiled professors vary, but most authorities now appear to agree that about one-third of the professoriate was driven out of the universities. See Ferber, *Entwicklung des Lehrkörpers,* pp. 145–6.

8 UNESCO, *Statistical Yearbook, 1963,* pp. 220–1, and *Statistical Yearbook, 1971,* pp. 362–3.

Bibliography

UNPUBLISHED SOURCES

State archives

Badisches Generallandesarchiv, Karlsruhe, F.R.G. Papers of the Baden Ministry of Culture (GLA 235).

Deutsche Staatsbibliothek, East Berlin, G.D.R. Personal papers *(Nachlässe)* of Friedrich Althoff and Hans Delbrück.

Deutsches Zentralarchiv II, Merseburg, G.D.R. Papers of the Prussian Ministry of Churches, Education, and Medical Affairs (*Repertorium 76 alt,* 76; personal papers [*Nachlässe*], *Rep.* 92).

Hessisches Staatsarchiv, Marburg, F.R.G. Papers on the University of Marburg (5, 9A, 22b, 305–7).

Niedersächsische Staats- und Universitätsbibliothek, Göttingen, F.R.G. Papers of the University of Göttingen (*Hist. lit.* 77–116).

Württembergisches Hauptstaatsarchiv, Stuttgart, F.R.G. Papers of the Württemberg Ministry of Culture (E 202) and of the Ministry of Interior (E 146); Cabinet Papers (E 11, 14); Privy Council Papers (E 31, 33; A 202); and papers on the University of Tübingen (A 274).

University archives

University Archives of Bonn, Freiburg im Breisgau, Giessen, Halle, Heidelberg, Jena, Leipzig, Munich, and Tübingen.

PRINTED SOURCE MATERIALS

Statistics

Baden. Statistisches Landesamt. *Statistisches Jahrbuch für das Grossherzogtum Baden.* 44 vols. Karlsruhe, 1869–1938.

Bavaria. Statistisches Landesamt. *Statistisches Jahrbuch für Bayern.* 29 vols. Munich, 1894–1972.

Conrad, J. *Das Universitätsstudium in Deutschland während der letzten 50 Jahre*. Jena, 1884.

"Die Statistik der Universität Halle während der 200 Jahre ihres Bestehens." *Festschrift der vier Fakultäten zum zweihundertjährigen Jubiläum der vereinigten Friedrichs-Universität Halle-Wittenberg*. Halle, 1894. Pt. 4, pp. 5–78.

"Einige Ergebnisse der deutschen Universitätsstatistik." *Jahrbücher für Nationalökonomie und Statistik* 3, No. 32 (1906), 433–92.

Dieterici, W. *Geschichtliche und statistische Nachrichten über die Universitäten im preussischen Staate*. Berlin, 1836.

Eulenburg, F. "Die Frequenz der deutschen Universitäten von ihrer Gründung bis zur Gegenwart." *Abhandlungen der philologisch-historischen Klasse der königlich sächsischen Gesellschaft der Wissenschaften* 24 (Leipzig, 1906), treatise 2.

Germany. Statistisches Reichsamt. *Statistisches Jahrbuch für das Deutsche Reich*. 59 vols. Berlin, 1880–1942.

Leutenberger, H. "Untersuchungen über die Besucherzahl der Universität Jena von den Anfängen bis zur Gegenwart." *Wissenschaftliche Zeitschrift der Universität Jena* 3 (1953–4), 361–90.

Prussia. Königliches Statistisches Bureau. *Preussische Statistik*. 138 vols. Berlin, 1861–96.

Saxony. Statistisches Landesamt. *Statistisches Jahrbuch für das Königreich Sachsen*. 45 vols. Dresden, 1871–1939.

Schubert, F. W. "Zur Geschichte der Statistik der akademischen Studien und gelehrten Berufe in Preussen seit 1840." *Archiv für Landeskunde der preussischen Monarchie* 2 (1857), 188–204.

Württemberg. *Württembergsche Jahrbücher für Statistik und Landeskunde*. 111 vols. Stuttgart, 1818–1938.

Statistisches Landesamt. *Statistik der Universität Tübingen*. Stuttgart, 1877.

Matriculation sources

Birt, T. (ed.). *Catologus studiosorum Marpurgensis* [1653–1830]. Marburg, 1903.

Erlangen. University. *Matrikel der Universität Erlangen, 1743–1843*. Erlangen, 1843.

Erler, G. *Die jüngeren Matrikel der Universität Leipzig, 1559–1809*. 3 vols. Leipzig, 1909.

Die Matrikel und die Promotionsverzeichnisse der Albertus-Universität zu Königsberg in Preussen, 1554–1829. 3 vols. Leipzig, 1910–17.

Freninger, F. X. *Das Matrikelbuch der Universität Ingolstadt-Landshut-München* [1772–1872]. Munich, 1872.

Friedländer, E. *Aeltere Universitätsmatrikeln, Universität Frankfurt/Oder* [to 1811]. 3 vols. Leipzig, 1887–91.

Gundlach, F. *Das Album der Christian-Albrechts-Universität zu Kiel, 1665–1865.* Kiel, 1915.

Hermelink, H., A. Bürk, and W. Wille. *Die Matrikel der Universität Tübingen* [to 1817]. 5 vols. Tübingen, 1906–54.

Hess, W. *Matrikel der Universität Bamberg.* 2 vols. Bamberg, 1923–4.

Hofmeister, A. and E. Schäfer. *Die Matrikel der Universität Rostock* [to 1831]. 7 vols. Rostock, 1895.

Jena. University. *Die Matrikel der Universität Jena* [to 1737]. 3 vols. Jena and Weimar, 1944–61.

Knod, G. *Die alten Matrikel der Universität Strassburg* [to 1793]. 3 vols. Strasbourg, 1897–1902.

Merkle, S. *Die Matrikel der Universität Würzburg.* Munich, 1922.

Praetorius, O. and F. Knöpp. *Die Matrikel der Universität Giessen.* Pt. 2 [1708–1807]. Neustadt/Aisch, 1957.

Richter, G. *Die Studentenmatrikel der Universität Fulda, 1734–1805.* Fulda, 1936.

Schmalhaus, B. *Bibliographie der Hochschulmatrikeln.* Göttingen, 1937.

Selle, G. von. *Die Matrikel der Georg-August-Universität zu Göttingen, 1734–1837.* 2 vols. Hildesheim and Leipzig, 1937.

Steinmeyer, E. von. *Matrikel der Universität Altdorf, 1575–1809.* Würzburg, 1912.

Töpke, G. *Die Matrikel der Universität Heidelberg von 1386 bis 1870.* 7 vols. Heidelberg, 1903–16.

Other source materials

Anrich, E. (ed.). *Die Idee der deutschen Universität: Die fünf Grundschriften aus der Zeit ihrer Neubegründung durch klassischen Idealismus und romantischen Realismus.* Darmstadt, 1960.

Arnim, M. *Corpus Academicum Gottingense, 1737–1928.* Göttingen, 1930.

Asen, J. (ed.). *Gesamtverzeichnis des Lehrkörpers der Universität Berlin, 1810–1945.* Leipzig, 1955.

Campe, J. H. (ed.). *Allgemeine Revision des gesammten Schul- und Erziehungswesens.* 16 vols. Hamburg, 1785–92.

Conrad, E. "Die Lehrstühle der Universität Tübingen und ihre Inhaber, 1477–1927." Ph.D. dissertation, Tübingen, 1960.

Ebel, W. *Catalogus Professorum Gottingensium, 1734–1962.* Göttingen, 1962.

(ed.). *Die Privilegien und ältesten Statuten der Georg-August-Universität zu Göttingen.* Göttingen, 1961.

Fichte, J. G. *Einige Vorlesungen über die Bestimmung des Gelehrten.* Jena, 1794.

Germany. Reichsschulkonferenz. *Die Reichsschulkonferenz von 1890: Verhandlungen über Fragen des Höheren Unterrichts.* Reprint. Frankfurt, 1969.

Die Reichsschulkonferenz von 1900: Verhandlungen über Fragen des Höheren Unterrichts. Reprint. Frankfurt, 1969.

Günther, J. *Lebensskizzen der Professoren der Universität Jena seit 1558 bis 1858.* Jena, 1858.

Gundlach, F. *Catalogus professorum academiae Marburgensis . . . 1527 bis 1910.* Marburg, 1927.

Jeismann, K. E. (ed.). *Staat und Erziehung in der preussischen Reform, 1807–1819.* Göttingen, 1967.

Jellinek, G. *Gesetze und Verordnungen für die Universität Heidelberg.* Heidelberg, 1908.

Jena. University. *Statute der Universität Jena.* Jena, 1829–1907.

Koch, J. F. W. *Die preussischen Universitäten: Eine Sammlung von Verordnungen, welche die Verfassung und Verwaltung dieser Anstalten betreffen.* 3 vols. Berlin, 1839–40.

Lehnert, G. and H. Haupt (eds.). "Dozentenverzeichnis der Universität Giessen, 1607–1907," in *Die Universität Giessen, 1607–1907.* 2 vols. Giessen, 1907. I, 411–67.

Schelling, F. W. J. *Vorlesungen über die Methoden des akademischen Studiums.* Tübingen, 1803.

Weber, M. "The Power of the State and the Dignity of the Academic Calling in Imperial Germany: The Writings of Max Weber on University Problems." Ed. and trans. by E. Shils, *Minerva* 11, No. 4 (1973), 1–62.

Weischedel, W. (ed.). *Idee und Wirklichkeit einer Universität: Dokumente zur Geschichte der Friedrich-Wilhelms-Universität zu Berlin.* Berlin, 1960.

GENERAL WORKS ON HIGHER EDUCATION

Alexander, T. and B. Parker. *The New Education in the German Republic.* New York, 1929.

Aulard, F. V. A. *Napoléon I. et la monopole universitaire.* Paris, 1911.

Baumann, J. *Für freie Universitäten neben den Staatsuniversitäten.* Langensalza, 1907.

Becker, C. H. *Gedanken zur Hochschulreform.* Leipzig, 1919.

Ben-David, J. "Akademische Berufe und die Professionalisierung." *Kölner Zeitschrift für Soziologie und Sozialpsychologie, Sonderheft* 5 (1961), 104–21.

"Professions in the Class Systems of Present-Day Societies." *Current Sociology* 12, No. 3 (1963–4), 247–330.

"Scientific Growth: A Sociological View." *Minerva* 2 (1964), 455–76.

"A Comparative Study of Academic Freedom and Student Politics," in R. Bendix (ed.), *State and Society.* Boston, 1968. Pp. 402–22.

The Scientist's Role in Society: A Comparative Study. Englewood Cliffs, N.J., 1971.

and Awraham Zloczower. "The Idea of the University in the Academic Market-Place." *Archive Européenne de Sociologie* 2 (1961), 303–15.

"Universities and Academic Systems in Modern Societies." *Archive Européenne de Sociologie* 3 (1962), 45–84.

Berlin. Free University. *Universitätstage 1966: Nationalsozialismus und die deutsche Universität.* Berlin, 1966.

Bischoff, C. H. E. *Einiges, was den deutschen Universitäten Noth tut.* 2 vols. Bonn, 1842–8.

Blondel, G. *De l'enseignement de droit dans les universités allemandes.* Paris, 1885.

Bock, K. D. *Strukturgeschichte der Assistentur: Personalgefüge, Wert- und Zielvorstellungen in der deutschen Universität des 19. und 20. Jahrhunderts.* Düsseldorf, 1972.

Bohrmann, H. *Strukturwandel der deutschen Studentenpresse: Studentenpolitik und Studentenzeitschriften, 1848–1974.* Munich, 1974.

Bornhak, C. *Geschichte der preussichen Universitätsverwaltung bis 1810.* Berlin, 1900.

Die Rechtsverhältnisse der Hochschullehrer in Preussen. Berlin, 1901.

Die Korporationsverfassung der Universitäten. Berlin, 1910.

Bourdieu, P. and J. C. Passeron. *Les héritiers: Les étudiants et la culture.* Paris, 1964.

Braubach, M. "Die katholischen Universitäten Deutschlands und die französische Revolution." *Historisches Jahrbuch* 49 (1929), 263–303.

Brinkmann, C. "Der Nationalismus und die deutschen Universitäten im Zeitalter der deutschen Erhebung." *Sitzungsberichte der Heidelberger Akademie der Wissenschaften* 22 (1931–2), treatise 3.

Bruford, W. H. *The German Tradition of Self-Cultivation: "Bildung" from Humboldt to Thomas Mann.* Cambridge, 1975.

Busch, A. *Die Geschichte des Privatdozenten.* Stuttgart, 1959.

Delbrück, C. von. *Die Ausbildung für den höheren Verwaltungsdienst in Preussen.* Jena, 1917.

Dolch, O. *Geschichte des deutschen Studententums von der Gründung der deutschen Universitäten bis zu den Freiheitskriegen.* Leipzig, 1858.

Erben, W. "Entstehung der Universitätsseminare." *Internationale Monatsschrift für Wissenschaft, Kunst und Technik* (1913), 1247–64 and 1335–47.

Erman, W. and E. Horn. *Bibliographie der deutschen Universitäten.* 3 vols. Leipzig and Berlin, 1904–5.

Eulenburg, F. *Der akademische Nachwuchs.* Leipzig and Berlin, 1908.

Eulner, H. H. *Die Entwicklung der medizinischen Spezialfächer an den Universitäten des deutschen Sprachgebiets.* Stuttgart, 1970.

Faust, A. *Der Nationalsozialistische Deutsche Studentenbund; Studenten und Nationalsozialismus in der Weimarer Republik.* 2 vols. Düsseldorf, 1973.

Flexner, A. *Universities: American, English, German.* New York, 1930.

Gall, F. "Die Archive der deutschen Universitäten in Deutschland, Oesterreich und der Schweiz." *Archivalische Zeitschrift* 50/51 (1955), 141–51.

Gerbod, P. *La condition universitaire en France au XIXe. siècle.* Paris, 1965.

Goldmann, K. *Verzeichnis der Hochschulen.* Neustadt/Aisch, 1967.

Griewank, K. *Deutsche Studenten und Universitäten in der Revolution von 1848.* Weimar, 1949.

Haass, R. *Die geistige Haltung der katholischen Universitäten Deutschlands im 18. Jahrhundert.* Freiburg/Breisgau, 1952.

Harnack, A. "Vom Grossbetrieb der Universität" (1905), in *Aus Wissenschaft und Leben.* 2 vols. Giessen, 1911. I, 10–20.

Hartshorne, E. *The German Universities and National Socialism.* London, 1937.

Haupt, H. and Paul Wentzke. *Quellen und Darstellungen zur Geschichte der deutschen Burschenschaften und der deutschen Einheitsbewegung.* 17 vols. Heidelberg, 1910–40.

Helfer, C. and M. Rassem (eds.). *Student und Hochschule im 19. Jahrhundert.* Göttingen, 1975.

Herrlitz, H. G. and H. Tietze. "Ueberfüllung als bildungspolitische Strategie: Zur administrativen Steuerung der Lehrerarbeitslosigkeit in Preussen, 1870–1914." *Die deutsche Schule* 68 (1976), 348–70.

Heubaum, A. *Geschichte des deutschen Bildungswesens seit der Mitte des 17. Jahrhunderts.* Berlin, 1905.

Heydorn, H. J. and G. Koneffke. "Zur Bilungsgeschichte des deutschen Imperialismus: Die Schulkonferenzen von 1890, 1900 und 1920." *Studien zur Sozialgeschichte und Philosophie der Bildung.* 2 vols. Munich, 1973. II, 179–280.

Hoffbauer, J. *Ueber die Perioden der Erziehung.* Leipzig, 1800.

Horn, E. *Kolleg und Honorar: Ein Beitrag zur Verfassungsgeschichte der deutschen Universität.* Munich, 1897.

Hufen, F. "Ueber das Verhältnis der deutschen Territorialstaaten zu ihren Landesuniversitäten im alten Reich." Ph.D. dissertation, Munich, 1955.

Jacob, L. H. *Ueber die Universitäten in Deutschland, besonders in den königlich preussischen Staaten.* Berlin, 1798.

Jarausch, K. H. "The Sources of German Student Unrest, 1815–1848," in L. Stone (ed.), *The University in Society.* 2 vols. Princeton, 1974. II, 533–69.

"Frequenz und Struktur: Zur Sozialgeschichte der Studenten im Kaiserreich," unpublished manuscript (November 1976), forthcoming in M. Schlenke (ed.), *Staat und Bildung in Preussen und im Deutschen Reich.* Stuttgart.

"Neuhumanistische Universität und bürgerliche Gesellschaft: Zur Sozialgeschichte der Studenten, 1800–1870." *Vierteljahrschrift für Sozial- und Wirtschaftsgeschichte.* Forthcoming.

Jaspers, K. *Die Idee der Universität.* Berlin, 1946.

Kaelble, H. "Chancengleichheit und akademische Ausbildung in Deutschland, 1910–1960." *Geschichte und Gesellschaft* 1 (1975), 121–49.

Kaufmann, G. *Die Geschichte der deutschen Universitäten.* 2 vols. Stuttgart, 1888–96.

Kelley, R. "Professors in the Third Reich: National Socialism and German University Teachers." Ph.D. dissertation, University of Washington, 1973.

Kerr, C. *The Uses of the University.* Cambridge, Mass., 1963.

Kilian, H. F. *Die Universitäten Deutschlands in medizinisch-naturwissenschaftlicher Hinsicht.* Heidelberg and Leipzig, 1828.

Klein, E. *Von der Reform zur Reaktion: Finanzpolitik und Reformgesetzgebung des preussischen Staatskanzlers Karl August von Hardenberg.* Berlin, 1965.

Kluge, A. *Die Universitäts-Selbstverwaltung: Ihre Geschichte und gegenwärtige Rechtsform.* Frankfurt, 1958.

König, R. *Vom Wesen der deutschen Universitäten.* Berlin, 1935.

Kreutzberger, W. *Studenten und Politik, 1918–1933: Der Fall Freiburg im Breisgau.* Göttingen, 1972.

Laqueur, W. and G. Mosse (eds.). *Education and Social Structure in the Twentieth Century.* New York, 1967.

Leipzig. University. *Bedeutende Gelehrte in Leipzig.* 2 vols. Leipzig, 1965.

Lexis, W. *Die deutschen Universitäten.* 2 vols. Berlin, 1893.

(ed.). *Das Unterrichtswesen im Deutschen Reich.* 4 vols. Berlin, 1904.

Lilge, F. *The Abuse of Learning.* New York, 1948.

Lundgreen, P. *Bildung und Wirtschaftswachstum im Industrialisierungsprozess des 19. Jahrhunderts.* Berlin, 1973.

Techniker in Preussen während der frühen Industrialisierung: Ausbildung und Berufsfeld einer entstehenden sozialen Gruppe. Berlin, 1975.

Manegold, K. H. "Das 'Ministerium des Geistes'; zur Organisation des ehemaligen preussischen Kultusministeriums." *Die deutsche Berufs- und Fachschule* 63 (1967), 512–24.

Universität, Technische Hochschule und Industrie. Berlin, 1970.

Meiners, C. *Ueber die Verfassung und Verwaltung deutscher Universitäten.* 2 vols. Göttingen, 1801.

Geschichte der Entstehung und Entwicklung der Hohen Schulen. 4 vols. Göttingen, 1802–8.

Kurze Darstellung der Entwicklung der hohen Schulen des protestantischen Deutschlands. Göttingen, 1808.

Michaelis, J. D. *Raisonnement über die protestantischen Universitäten in Deutschland.* 4 vols. Frankfurt/Main, 1768–76.

Müsebeck, E. *Das preussische Kultusministerium vor 100 Jahren.* Berlin, 1918.

Munich. University. *Die deutsche Universität im Dritten Reich.* Munich, 1966.

Newman, J. H. *The Idea of the University.* New York, 1896.

Nitsch, W., U. Gerhardt, C. Offe, and U. K. Preuss (eds.). *Hochschule in der Demokratie: Kritische Beiträge zur Erbschaft und Reform der deutschen Universität.* Berlin, 1965.

Parsons, T. and G. M. Platt. *The American University*. Cambridge, Mass., 1973.

Paulsen, F. *Die deutschen Universitäten und das Universitätsstudium*. Berlin, 1902.

Geschichte des gelehrten Unterrichts auf den deutschen Schulen und Universitäten vom Ausgang des Mittelalters bis zur Gegenwart. 2 vols. Berlin, 1919–21.

Petersilie, A. *Das öffentliche Unterrichtswesen im deutschen Reich und in den übrigen europäischen Kulturländern*. 2 vols. Leipzig, 1897.

Petry, L. "Deutsche Forschungen nach dem zweiten Weltkrieg zur Geschichte der Universität." *Vierteljahrschrift für Sozial- und Wirtschaftsgeschichte* 46 (1959), 145–203.

Plessner, H. (ed.). *Untersuchungen zur Lage der deutschen Hochschullehrer*. 3 vols. Göttingen, 1956.

Pleyer, K. *Die Vermögens- und Personalverwaltung der deutschen Universitäten*. Marburg, 1955.

Poten, B. von. *Geschichte des Militär-Erziehungs- und Bildungswesens in den Landen deutscher Zunge*. 5 vols. Berlin, 1889–1900.

Prost, A. *Histoire de l'enseignement en France, 1800–1967*. Paris, 1968.

Rassem, M. "Die problematische Stellung der Studenten im Humboldtschen System." *Studien und Berichte der Katholischen Akademie in Bayern* 44 (1968), 15–36.

Reinhardt, A. *Das Universitätsstudium der Württemberger seit der Reichsgründung*. Tübingen, 1918.

Richarz, M. *Der Eintritt der Juden in die akademischen Berufe*. Tübingen, 1974.

Riedler, A. *Unsere Hochschulen und die Anforderungen des 20. Jahrhunderts*. Berlin, 1898.

Riese, R. *Die Hochschule auf dem Wege zum wissenschaftlichen Grossbetrieb: Die Universität Heidelberg und das badische Hochschulwesen, 1860–1914*. Stuttgart, 1977.

Ringer, F. K. *The Decline of the German Mandarins: The German Academic Community, 1890–1933*. Cambridge, Mass., 1969.

Education and Society in Modern Europe. Bloomington, Ind., 1979.

Robertson, P. "Students on the Barricades: Germany and Austria, 1848." *Political Science Quarterly* 84 (1969), 367–79.

Rönne, L. von. *Das Unterrichtswesen des preussischen Staates*. 2 vols. Berlin, 1854–5.

Rössler, H. and G. Franz (eds.). *Universität und Gelehrtenstand, 1400–1800*. Limburg/Lahn, 1970.

Roessler, W. *Die Entstehung des modernen Erziehungswesens in Deutschland*. Stuttgart, 1961.

Rothblatt, S. *Revolution of the Dons: Cambridge and Society in Victorian England*. New York, 1968.

Samuel, R. and R. H. Thomas. *Education and Society in Modern Germany*. London, 1949.

Savigny, F. C. von. "Wesen und Werth der deutschen Universitäten," in *Vermischte Schriften*. 5 vols. Berlin, 1850. IV.

Schelsky, H. *Einsamkeit und Freiheit: Idee und Gestalt der deutschen Universität und ihrer Reformen*. Reinbek/Hamburg, 1963.

Schlenke, M. (ed.). *Staat und Bildung in Preussen und im Deutschen Kaiserreich*. Stuttgart, forthcoming.

Schulze, F. and P. Ssymank. *Das deutsche Studententum von den ältesten Zeiten bis zur Gegenwart*. Munich, 1932.

Schwarz, J. *Studenten in der Weimarer Republik: Die deutsche Studentenschaft in der Zeit von 1918 bis 1923 und ihre Stellung zur Politik.* Berlin, 1971.

Seier, H. "Der Rektor als Führer." *Vierteljahreshefte für Zeitgeschichte* 12 (1964), 105–46.

Spranger, E. *Wilhelm von Humboldt und die Reform des Bildungswesens.* Tübingen, 1960.

Steffens, H. *Ueber Deutschlands protestantischen Universitäten*. Breslau, 1820.

Steiger, G. and M. Straube. "Forschungen und Publikationen seit 1945 zur Geschichte der deutschen Universitäten und Hochschulen auf dem Territorium der DDR." *Zeitschrift für Geschichtswissenschaft* 8 (1960), 563–99.

Steinberg, M. S. *Sabers and Brown Shirts: The German Students' Path to National Socialism.* Chicago, 1977.

Steinhausen, G. "Die Idealerziehung im Zeitalter der Perücke." *Mitteilungen der Gesellschaft für deutsche Erziehungs- und Schulgeschichte* 4 (1894), 209–46.

Stölzel, A. "Die Berliner Mittwochgesellschaft über Aufhebung oder Reform der Universitäten (1795)." *Forschungen zur brandenburgischen und preussischen Geschichte* 2 (1889), 201–22.

Stone, L. "Literacy and Education in England, 1640–1900." *Past and Present* 42 (1969), 69–139.

(ed.). *The University in Society*. 2 vols. Princeton, 1974.

(ed.). *Schooling and Society*. Baltimore, 1976.

Thieme, W. *Deutsches Hochschulrecht*. Berlin, 1956.

Thiersch, F. W. von. *Ueber die neuesten Angriffe auf die deutschen Universitäten*. Stuttgart, 1837.

Thwing, C. F. *The American and the German University*. New York, 1928.

Turner, R. S. "The Growth of Professorial Research in Prussia, 1818 to 1848 – Causes and Context," in R. S. McCormmach (ed.), *Historical Studies in the Physical Sciences* 3 (1971), 137–82.

"The Prussian Universities and the Research Imperative, 1806–1848." Ph.D. dissertation, Princeton University, 1973.

Van de Graaff, J. H. "The Politics of German University Reform, 1810–1970." Ph.D. dissertation, Columbia University, 1973.

Varrentrapp, C. *Johannes Schulze und das höhere preussische Unterrichtswesen in seiner Zeit*. Leipzig, 1889.

Vaughan, M. and M. S. Archer. *Social Conflict and Educational Change in England and France, 1789–1848.* Cambridge, 1971.

Vierhaus, R. "Bildung," in *Geschichtliche Grundbegriffe.* Stuttgart, 1972. I, 508–51.

Weil, H. *Die Entstehung des deutschen Bildungsprinzips.* Bonn, 1930.

Wieruszowski, H. *The Medieval University.* Princeton, 1966.

Wiese, L. *Deutsche Briefe über englische Erziehung.* Berlin, 1850.

Wittram, R. "Die Universität und die Fakultäten." *Göttinger Universitätsreden* 39 (Göttingen, 1962).

Wolf, F. A. *Ueber Erziehung, Schule, Universität.* Quedlinburg, 1835.

Zorn, W. "Hochschule und höhere Schule in der deutschen Sozialgeschichte der Neuzeit," in *Spiegel der Geschichte: Festgabe für Max Braubach.* Münster, 1964. Pp. 321–39.

"Student Politics in the Weimar Republic." *Journal of Contemporary History* 5 (1970), 128–43.

MEMOIRS, AUTOBIOGRAPHIES, BIOGRAPHIES

Curtius, L. *Deutsche und Antike Welt.* Stuttgart, 1950.

Eilers, G. *Zur Beurteilung des Ministeriums Eichhorn von einem Mitglied desselben.* Berlin, 1849.

Fichte, I. H. *Johann Gottlieb Fichtes Leben und literarischer Briefwechsel.* 2 vols. Leipzig, 1862.

Hoffmann, M. *August Böckh, Lebensbeschreibung und Auswahl aus seinem wissenschaftlichen Briefwechsel.* Leipzig, 1901.

Kaehler, S. A. *Wilhelm von Humboldt und der Staat.* Göttingen, 1927.

Kohut, A. *Justus von Liebig, Sein Leben und Wirken.* Giessen, 1904.

Menze, C. *Die Bildungsreform Wilhelm von Humboldts.* Hanover, 1975.

Müller-Dietz, H. *Das Leben des Rechtslehrers und Politikers Karl Theodor Welcker.* Freiburg, 1968.

Sachse, A. *Friedrich Althoff und sein Werk.* Berlin, 1928.

Schenkel, D. *Friedrich Schleiermacher: Ein Lebens- und Charakterbild.* Eberfeld, 1868.

Steffens, H. *Was ich erlebte; aus der Erinnerung niedergeschrieben.* 10 vols. Breslau, 1840–4.

Weis, E. *Montgelas, 1759–1799: Zwischen Revolution und Reform.* Munich, 1971.

INDIVIDUAL UNIVERSITIES

Berlin. Technische Hochschule. *Die Technische Hochschule zu Berlin, 1799–1924: Festschrift.* Berlin, 1925.

Bezold, F. von. *Geschichte der Rheinischen Freidrich-Wilhelms-Universität von der Gründung bis zum Jahr 1870.* Bonn, 1920.

Boehm, L. and J. Spörl (eds.). *Die Ludwig-Maximilians-Universität in ihren Fakultäten.* Berlin, 1972.

Ludwig-Maximilians-Universität, Ingolstadt, Landshut, München, 1472–1972. Berlin, 1972.

Bonn. Universität. *Statuten der Königlich Preussischen Rheinischen Friedrich-Wilhelms-Universität.* Bonn, 1828–60.

Bonner Gelehrte–Beiträge zur Geschichte der Wissenschaften in Bonn. 10 vols. Bonn, 1968–.

150 Jahre Rheinische Friedrich-Wilhelms-Universität zu Bonn (1818–1968). Bonn, 1968–.

Brandes, E. *Ueber den gegenwärtigen Zustand der Universität Göttingen.* Göttingen, 1802.

Braubach, M. *Die erste Bonner Hochschule: Maxische Akademie und kurfürstliche Universität, 1774/77 bis 1798.* Bonn, 1966.

Bonner Professoren und Studenten in den Revolutionsjahren 1848/49. Cologne, 1967.

Craig, J. "A Mission for German Learning: The University of Strasbourg and Alsatian Society, 1870–1918." Ph.D. dissertation, Stanford University, 1973.

Deuerlein, E. *Geschichte der Universität Erlangen in zeitlicher Uebersicht.* Erlangen, 1927.

Dresden. Technische Hochschule. *125 Jahre Technische Hochschule Dresden.* Dresden, 1953.

Ebel, W. "Zur Geschichte der juristischen Fakultät und des Rechtsstudiums an der Georgia Augusta." *Göttinger Universitätsreden 29.* Göttingen, 1960.

Memorabilia Gottingensia: Elf Studien zur Sozialgeschichte der Universität. Göttingen, 1969.

Engelberg, E. (ed.). *Karl Marx Universität, Leipzig, 1409–1959: Beiträge zur Universitätsgeschichte.* 2 vols. Leipzig, 1959.

Engelhardt, J. G. V. *Die Universität Erlangen von 1743 bis 1843.* Erlangen, 1843.

Eulenburg, F. *Die Entwicklung der Universität Leipzig in den letzten hundert Jahren: Statistische Untersuchungen.* Leipzig, 1909.

Franze, M. *Die Erlanger Studentenschaft, 1918–1945.* Würzburg, 1972.

Freiburg. Universität. *Beiträge zur Freiburger Wissenschafts- und Universitätsgeschichte.* 38 vols. Freiburg, 1954–76.

Friedrich, K. (ed.). *Heidelberger Professoren aus dem 19. Jahrhundert.* Heidelberg, 1903.

Gerber, H. *Der Wandel der Rechtsgestalt der Albert-Ludwigs-Universität zu Freiburg im Breisgau seit dem Ende der vorderösterreichischen Zeit.* 2 vols. Freiburg, 1957.

Giessen. Universität. *Ludwigs-Universität: Justus-Liebig-Hochschule, 1607–1957.* Giessen, 1957.

Hautz, J. F. *Geschichte der Universität Heidelberg.* 2 vols. Mannheim, 1862.

Hegel, E. *Geschichte der katholisch-theologischen Fakultät Münster, 1773–1964.* 2 vols. Münster, 1966–71.

Hermelinck, H. and S. A. Kaehler. *Die Philipps-Universität zu Marburg, 1527–1927.* Marburg, 1927.

Hoffbauer, J. C. *Geschichte der Universität zu Halle bis zum Jahre 1805.* Halle, 1805.

Iwand, F. G. *Die juristische Fakultät der Universität Strassburg von 1538–1870.* Strasbourg, 1917.

Jolly, L. von. *Zur Geschichte der staatswissenschaftlichen Fakultät der Universität Tübingen.* Tübingen, 1909.

Jordan, K. von (ed.). *Geschichte der Christian-Albrecht-Universität Kiel, 1665–1965.* Kiel, 1965–9.

Just, L. and H. Mathy. *Die Universität Mainz: Grundzüge ihrer Geschichte.* Mainz, 1965.

Kaufmann, G. (ed.). *Festschrift zur Feier des hundertjährigen Bestehens der Universität Breslau.* 2 vols. in 1. Breslau, 1911.

Keller, R. A. *Geschichte der Universität Heidelberg, 1803–1813.* Heidelberg, 1913.

Kink, R. *Geschichte der kaiserlichen Universität zu Wien.* 2 vols. in 3. Vienna, 1854.

Klingelhöfer, J. G. *Die Marburger Juristenfakultät im 19. Jahrhundert.* Marburg, 1972.

Klüpfel, K. *Geschichte und Beschreibung der Stadt und Universität Tübingen.* Tübingen, 1849.

Die Universität Tübingen in ihrer Vergangenheit und Gegenwart. Leipzig, 1877.

Kluke, P. *Die Stiftungsuniversität Frankfurt am Main, 1914–1932.* Frankfurt, 1972.

Kosegarten, J. G. L. *Geschichte der Universität Greifswald mit urkundlichen Beilagen.* 2 vols. Greifswald, 1856–7.

Lenz, M. *Geschichte der Königlichen Friedrich-Wilhelms-Universität zu Berlin.* 4 vols. Halle, 1910–18.

Leussink, H., E. Neumann, and G. Kotowski (eds.). *Studium Berolinse: Aufsätze und Beiträge zu Problemen der Wissenschaft und zur Geschichte der Friedrich-Wilhelms-Universität zu Berlin.* Berlin, 1960.

Moeller, F. (ed.). *Die Technische Hochschule Carolo-Wilhelmina zu Braunschweig: Aus ihrer Geschichte und ihrem Wirken bis 1951.* Braunschweig, 1952.

Pätzold, G. *Die Marburger Juristenfakultät als Spruchkollegium.* Marburg, 1966.

Pfister, E. *Die finanziellen Verhältnisse der Universität Freiburg von der Zeit ihrer Gründung bis zur Mitte des 19. Jahrhunderts.* Freiburg, 1889.

Prantl, C. *Geschichte der Ludwig-Maximilians-Universität in Ingolstadt, Landshut, München.* 2 vols. Munich, 1872.

Prutz, H. *Die königliche Albertus-Universität zu Königsberg in Preussen im 19. Jahrhundert.* Königsberg, 1894.

Pütter, J. S. *Versuch einer akademischen Gelehrtengeschichte von der Georg-Augustus-Universität zu Göttingen.* 2 vols. Göttingen, 1765–88.

Roessler, E. F. *Die Gründung der Universität Göttingen: Entwürfe, Berichte, und Briefe der Zeitgenossen.* Göttingen, 1855.

Rostock. University. *750 Jahre Rostock.* Rostock, 1968.

Schäfer, K. T. *Verfassungsgeschichte der Universität Bonn 1818 bis 1960.* Bonn, 1968.

Schneider, F. *Geschichte der Universität Heidelberg.* Heidelberg, 1913.

Schrader, W. *Geschichte der Friedrichs-Universität zu Halle.* 2 vols. Berlin, 1894.

Schreiber, H. *Geschichte der Albert-Ludwigs-Universität zu Freiburg im Breisgau.* Freiburg, 1857–60.

Schulze, A. *Die örtliche und soziale Herkunft der Strassburger Studenten, 1621–1793.* Heidelberg, 1926.

Selle, G. von. *Die Georg-August Universität zu Göttingen, 1737–1937.* Gottingen, 1937.

  Geschichte der Albertus-Universität zu Königsberg in Preussen (2nd edn). Würzburg, 1956.

Specht, T. *Geschichte der ehemaligen Universität Dillingen.* Freiburg, 1902.

Steiger, G. (ed.). *Vom Collegium Jenense zur Volksuniversität.* Jena, 1960.

Steinmetz, M. (ed.). *Geschichte der Universität Jena 1548/58–1958: Festgabe zum 400-jährigen Universitätsjubiläum.* 2 vols. Jena, 1958–62.

Stieda, W. "Erfurter Universitätsreformpläne im 18. Jahrhundert," in *Sonderschriften der Akademie gemeinnütziger Wissenschaften zu Erfurt* 5 (Erfurt, 1934), 128–243.

Vienna. University. *Studien zur Geschichte der Universität Wien.* 8 vols. Graz, 1965–73.

Volbehr, F. L. C. and R. Weyl. *Professoren und Dozenten der Christian-Albrechts-Universität zu Kiel, 1665–1915.* Kiel, 1956.

Vollert, M. *Geschichte der Kuratel der Universität Jena.* Jena, 1921.

Wachsmuth, R. *Die Gründung der Universität Frankfurt.* Frankfurt, 1929.

Wegele, F. X. *Geschichte der Universität Wirzburg.* 2 vols. Würzburg, 1882.

Weisert, H. *Die Verfassung der Universität Heidelberg: Ueberblick, 1386–1952.* Heidelberg, 1974.

Wentzke, P. "Die alte Universität Strassburg, 1621–1793." *Elsass-lothringisches Jahrbuch* 17 (1938), 37–112.

MISCELLANEOUS

Ackerknecht, E. H. "Beiträge zur Geschichte der Medizinalreform von 1848." *Sudhoffs Archiv* 25 (1932), 61–183.

Andernach, N. *Der Einfluss der Parteien auf das Hochschulwesen in Preussen, 1848–1918.* Göttingen, 1972.

Biedermann, K. *Deutschland im 18. Jahrhundert.* 3 vols. Leipzig, 1880.

Bigler, R. M. *The Politics of German Protestantism: The Rise of the Protestant Church Elite in Prussia, 1815–1848.* Berkeley, 1972.

Bleek, W. *Von der Kameralausbildung zum Juristenprivileg.* Berlin, 1972. "Die preussische Reform: Verwaltungsqualifikation und Juristenbildung (1806–1817)." *Die Verwaltung* 7 (1974), 179–97.

Borscheid, P. *Naturwissenschaft, Staat und Industrie in Baden (1848–1914).* Stuttgart, 1976.

Brauer, L., A. Mendelssohn-Bartholdy, A. Meyer, and J. Lemcke (eds.). *Forschungsinstitute: Ihre Geschichte, Organisation und Ziele.* 2 vols. Hamburg, 1930.

Brunschwig, H. *Enlightenment and Romanticism in Eighteenth-Century Prussia.* Chicago, 1974.

Burchardt, L. *Wissenschaftspolitik im wilhelminischen Deutschland: Vorgeschichte, Gründung und Aufbau der Kaiser-Wilhelm-Gesellschaft zur Förderung der Wissenschaften.* Göttingen, 1975.

Busshoff, H. "Die preussische Volksschule als soziales Gebilde und politischer Bildungsfaktor in der ersten Hälfte des 19. Jahrhunderts." *Geschichte in Wissenschaft und Unterricht* 22 (1971), 385–96.

Carsten, F. L. *Princes and Parliaments in Germany from the Fifteenth to the Eighteenth Century.* Oxford, 1959.

Deppermann, K. *Der hallische Pietismus und der preussische Staat unter Friedrich III. (I).* Göttingen, 1961.

Engelsing, R. *Zur Sozialgeschichte deutscher Mittel- und Unterschichten.* Göttingen, 1973.

Eyck, F. G. "The Political Theories and Activities of the German Academic Youth between 1815 and 1819." *Journal of Modern History* 27 (1955), 27–38.

Franz, G. (ed.). *Beamtentum und Pfarrerstand, 1400–1800.* Limburg/Lahn, 1972.

Gerhard, D. (ed.). *Ständische Vertretungen in Europa im 17. und 18. Jahrhundert.* Göttingen, 1969.

Gerth, H. *Die sozialgeschichtliche Lage der bürgerlichen Intelligenz um die Wende des 19. Jahrhunderts.* Frankfurt, 1935.

Gillis, J. R. *The Prussian Bureaucracy in Crisis, 1840–1860: Origins of an Administrative Ethos.* Stanford, 1971.
Youth and History: Tradition and Change in European Age Relations, 1770–Present. New York, 1974.

Goodwin, A. (ed.). *European Nobility in the Eighteenth Century.* London, 1967.

Hagstrom, W. *The Scientific Community.* New York, 1965.

Harnack, A. von. *Geschichte der königlichen preussischen Akademie der Wissenschaften.* 3 vols. in 4. Berlin, 1900.

Hartung, F. *Das Grossherzogtum Sachsen unter der Regierung Carl Augusts, 1775–1828.* Weimar, 1923.

Hasselhorn, M. *Der altwürttembergische Pfarrstand im 18. Jahrhundert.* Stuttgart, 1958.

Heinzen, K. P. *Die preussische Bureaukratie.* Darmstadt, 1845.

Henning, H. J. *Das westdeutsche Bürgertum in der Epoche der Hochindustrialisierung, 1860–1914: Soziales Verhalten und soziale Strukturen.* Wiesbaden, 1972.

Hintze, O. *Der Beamtenstand.* Leipzig, 1911.

Gesammelte Abhandlungen. 3 vols. Göttingen, 1962–7.

Historische Kommission, Munich. *Geschichte der Wissenschaften in Deutschland.* 24 vols. Munich, 1864–1913.

Hufbauer, K. G. "The Formation of the German Chemical Community (1700–1795)." Ph.D. dissertation, Berkeley, 1970.

Jeismann, K. E. *Das preussische Gymnasium in Staat und Gesellschaft.* Stuttgart, 1975.

Kaelble, H. "Sozialer Aufstieg in Deutschland, 1850–1914." *Vierteljahrschrift für Sozial- und Wirtschaftsgeschichte* 60 (1973), 41–71.

Kant, I. *Kants gesammelte Schriften* (Prussian Academy edn). 24 vols. in 26. Berlin, 1910–66.

Lampe, J. *Aristokratie, Hofadel und Staatspatriziat in Kurhannover, 1714–1760.* 2 vols. Göttingen, 1963.

Lenz, M. *Römischer Glaube und freie Wissenschaft.* Berlin, 1902.

Liebel, H. P. "Enlightened Bureaucracy versus Enlightened Despotism in Baden, 1750–1792." *Transactions of the American Philosophical Society,* N.S. 55, (1965), pt. 5.

Lotz, A. F. K. *Geschichte des deutschen Beamtentums.* Berlin, 1909.

Martin, A. von. "Der Humanismus als soziologisches Problem: Ein Beitrag zum Problem des Verhältnisses zwischen Besitzschicht und Bildungsschicht." *Archiv für Sozialwissenschaft und Sozialpolitik* 65 (1931), 441–74.

Martiny, F. *Die Adelsfrage in Preussen vor 1806 als politisches und soziales Problem.* Stuttgart and Berlin, 1938.

Meier, E. von. *Hannoverische Verfassungsgeschichte.* 2 vols. Leipzig, 1898–9.

Meusel, J. *Das gelehrte Teutschland oder Lexikon der vom Jahr 1750 bis 1800 verstorbenen teutschen Schriftsteller.* 23 vols. Lemgo, 1796–1834.

Meyer, R. "Das Berechtigungswesen in seiner Bedeutung für Schule und Gesellschaft im 19. Jahrhundert." *Zeitschrift für die Gesamte Staatswissenschaft* 124 (1968), 763–76.

Müller, Detlef K. *Sozialstruktur und Schulsystem: Aspekte zum Strukturwandel des Schulwesens im 19. Jahrhundert.* Göttingen, 1977.

Müller, J. *Die wissenschaftlichen Vereine und Gesellschaften Deutschlands im 19. Jahrhundert.* Reprint. Hildesheim, 1965.

Neumann, S. *Die Stufen des preussischen Konservatismus.* Berlin, 1930.

O'Boyle, L. "Klassische Bildung und soziale Struktur in Deutschland zwischen 1800 und 1848." *Historische Zeitschrift* 207 (1969), 584–608.

"The Problem of an Excess of Educated Men in Western Europe, 1800–1850." *Journal of Modern History* 42 (1970), 471–95.

Pauli, C. F. *Einleitung in die Kenntnis des deutschen hohen und niederen Adels*. Halle, 1753.

Pfetsch, F. R. *Zur Entwicklung der Wissenschaftspolitik in Deutschland, 1870–1914*. Berlin, 1974.

Plessner, H. "Zur Soziologie der modernen Forschung und ihrer Organisation in der deutschen Universität," in *Diesseits der Utopie*. Düsseldorf, 1966. Pp. 121–42.

Preradovich, N. von. *Die Führungsschichten in Oesterreich und Preussen (1804–1918)*. Wiesbaden, 1955.

Rössler, H. (ed.). *Deutscher Adel: Büdinger Vorträge*. 2 vols. Darmstadt, 1963–5.

Ruppel, W. "Ueber Berufswahl der Abiturienten Preussens in den Jahren 1875–1899." Ph.D. dissertation, Göttingen, 1904.

Schwabe, K. *Wissenschaft und Kriegsmoral: Die deutschen Hochschullehrer und die politischen Grundfragen des Ersten Weltkrieges*. Göttingen, 1969.

Stekl, H. *Oesterreichs Aristokratie im Vormärz*. Vienna, 1973.

Stephan, G. *Die häusliche Erziehung in Deutschland während des 18. Jahrhunderts*. Wiesbaden, 1891.

Stichweh, R. "Ausdifferenzierung der Wissenschaft – Eine Analyse am deutschen Beispiel." Report 8. *Science Studies* [University of Bielefeld]. Bielefeld, 1977.

Thomas, R. H. *Liberalism, Nationalism, and the German Intellectuals, 1822–47*. Cambridge, 1952.

Treue, W. "Zerfall und Einheit: Zum Wandel der europäischen Führungsschicht seit dem 17. Jahrhundert." *Die Sammlung* 6 (1951), 19–29, 111–19.

Vondung, K. *Das wilhelminische Bildungsbürgertum*. Göttingen, 1976.

Walker, M. *German Home Towns: Community, State and General Estate, 1648–1871*. Ithaca, N.Y., 1972.

Wiese, L. A. *Das höhere Schulwesen in Preussen: Historisch-statistische Darstellung*. 4 vols. Berlin, 1864–1902.

Wunder, B. "Die Sozialstruktur der Geheimratskollegien in den süddeutschen protestantischen Fürstentümern (1660–1720): Zum Verhältnis von sozialer Mobilität und Briefadel im Absolutismus." *Vierteljahrschrift für Sozial- und Wirtschaftsgeschichte* 58 (1971), 145–220.

Zierold, K. *Forschungsförderung in drei Epochen: Deutsche Forschungsgemeinschaft*. Wiesbaden, 1969.

Index

Most place-name entries refer to German universities or other institutions of higher learning.